sg · nov · 02

/11.50

Ⓑ

European
Socialists
Respond
to Fascism

European Socialists Respond to Fascism

Ideology, Activism and Contingency in the 1930s

GERD-RAINER HORN

New York   Oxford
Oxford University Press
1996

Oxford University Press

Oxford   New York
Athens   Auckland   Bangkok   Bogota   Bombay   Buenos Aires
Calcutta   Cape Town   Dar es Salaam   Dehli   Florence   Hong Kong
Istanbul   Karachi   Kuala Lumpur   Madras   Madrid   Melbourne
Mexico City   Nairobi   Paris   Singapore   Taipei   Tokyo   Toronto

and associated companies in
Berlin   Ibadan

Published by Oxford University Press, Inc.
198 Madison Avenue, New York, New York 10016

Oxford is a registered trademark of Oxford University Press

I want to thank the Fondation Jules Humbert-Droz for giving me copyright permission for an article
I wrote some years ago, which was an early version of Chapter 3. The article appeared as "Efforts at United Fronts:
The Relations Between the Communist International and the Labour and Socialist International, 1932–1935,"
in *Centenaire Jules Humbert-Droz, Colloque sur l'Internationale communiste* (La Chaux-de-Fonds: Fondation Jules
Humbert-Droz, 1992).

Library of Congress Cataloging-in-Publication Data
Horn, Gerd-Rainer.
European socialists respond to fascism : ideology, activism,
and contingency in the 1930s / Gerd-Rainer Horn.
    p.   cm.
Includes index.
ISBN 0-19-509374-7
1. Socialism—Europe—History—20th century.   2. National socialism.
3. Europe—Politics and government—1918–1945.
I. Title.
HX23B.H67   1996
335'.0094—dc20   95-46426

9 8 7 6 5 4 3 2 1

Printed in the United States of America
on acid-free paper

Preface

This study concerns a crucial transnational "moment of opportunity and crisis" in the 1930s. It presents an analysis and description of one of those rare incidents in modern European history when seemingly utopian visions suddenly appeared realizable. By sheer coincidence, the archival research for this study paralleled the life span of yet another transnational event in twentieth-century history. I landed in Düsseldorf roughly two weeks after the Hungarian government opened its Austrian border to would-be emigrants from Eastern Europe to the West. I left Amsterdam for my return trip to Detroit two weeks after the 3 October 1990 elections that sealed the unification of former East and West Germany.

In those turbulent thirteen months between September 1989 and October 1990 I visited nineteen archives in six countries (seven if one takes into account that in April 1990 the German Democratic Republic was nominally still an independent state). Rather than listing each archive separately, I would like to express my gratitude collectively for permission to examine their holdings. A significant proportion of my research year was indeed spent in these archives. My memories of 1989–90 will forever include the majestic view of Amsterdam's old harbor from the reading room of the IISG; the meandering walks through the old center of Salamanca while waiting for new dossiers to arrive in the AHNS; the wintry morning walks from the Leopoldstadt through the Kärntnerstrasse to the VGA in the old SPÖ party headquarters on the Rechte Wienzeile; and much else.

Archives merely furnish raw materials; it takes people to examine their holdings and extract meaning from them. Countless individuals have helped me make sense of this project; I can mention only some of them here. This work is based upon my dissertation (University of Michigan, 1992) and I want to thank the members of my dissertation committee—Kathleen Canning, Geoff Eley, Janet Hart, Ronald Suny—for putting up with the demands of this transnational study and for their continuing encouragement and help. In addition, Denise De Weerdt, Andrew Durgan, Santos Juliá Diaz, Fritz Keller, A. H. van Peski, Michael Schneider, Adrian Shubert, Carl Strikwerda and Reiner Tosstorff have given me substantive feedback on one or several draft chapters or have aided me in other crucial ways. Two unorthodox Belgians—

Jan de Man and Léo Moulin—were particularly enthusiastic in supporting my undertaking by providing extensive personal recollections. Eric Weitz was one of the select few who not only managed to work his way through an early draft of the entire work but also found the time to give me valuable feedback. Early on I linked up with Gilles Vergnon, who was then working on a closely related topic. Although we never met, his expert advice and interest in my topic served as a constant inspiration. Few people know the world of interwar European social democracy as intimately as the polyglot Helmut Gruber. I am very fortunate to have met him. Our initial evening-long discussion in a Chicago hotel in March 1992 marked the beginning of a fruitful relationship. Without his assistance, this study would have turned out quite differently. Very few historians would have agreed to oversee so vast a project as this one. Only someone with a breadth of vision and the theoretical perspicacity to weigh the advantages and limitations of my work could have guided such an undertaking. Geoff Eley is one of only a handful of scholars in the English-speaking world who possesses such a Continental outlook. I thank him for his ongoing support. The ideas contained in this book are the product of almost two decades of involvement in political activism and historical analysis. During most of this period, Mary McGuire discussed and shared many of my ideas. Although we have gone our separate ways, this book reflects our long-standing intellectual rapport.

Financial aid has played as important a role in the publication of this book as has intellectual support. I therefore want to thank the Friedrich Ebert Stiftung, the Mellon Foundation, the University of Michigan's Rackham Graduate School and the Department of History for granting me sufficient resources to complete the archival leg of this journey and to mold these materials into my dissertation. Since I never stayed in one location for more than ten weeks, the logistics of housing turned out to be a continual and pivotal (financial) concern during my year abroad. I want to express my gratitude to my parents, Christel and Erwin Horn, Paul van Kuijeren, Claudia Lego, Juan Felix Larrea and Marie-Dominique Cavaillé. Without their generous offer of living space and friendship, I could never have succeeded in carrying out my tasks. Last but not least, the office of the dean of Liberal Arts at Western Oregon State College provided me with a summer fellowship and release time to complete my final manuscript.

Finally, a note on the larger meaning of this book. Its origin dates back to my keen interest and involvement in the politics of the Left in the 1970s, when the crises and the questions surrounding the interwar period often served as inspiration for the hoped-for answers in this much later critical moment. That the answers provided in the 1930s could not serve as guidelines in the final quarter of the twentieth century soon became clear to most participant observers. But what this author refuses to discard is the belief in the possibility of a qualitatively different world. Perhaps this is the real reason for my emphasis on the notion of contingency with which this study concludes. At the very beginning of the 1930s, few individuals would have predicted the stunning developments affecting the politics of the Left between 1933 and 1936. Writing these lines at another inauspicious moment for progressive culture and politics, who is to say that another set of innovations may not be waiting in the wings?

Contents

List of Abbreviations

Organizations

ALÖS	Auslandsbüro österreichischer Sozialisten (Foreign Office of Austrian Socialists)
BES	Bureau d'Études Sociales (Office of Social Studies)
BOC	Bloc Obrer i Camperol (Workers' and Peasants' Bloc)
BWP	Belgische Werklieden Partij (Belgian Workers' Party)
CEDA	Confederación Española de Derechas Autónomas (Spanish Confederation of Autonomous Rightist Groups)
CNT	Confederación Nacional del Trabajo (National Confederation of Labor)
EKKI	Exekutivkomitee der Kommunistischen Internationale (Executive Committee of the Communist International)
FAI	Federación Anarquista Ibérica (Iberian Anarchist Federation)
FNTT	Federación Nacional de Trabajadores de la Tierra (National Federation of Agricultural Laborers)
FSL	Federación Sindicalista Libertaria (Libertarian Syndicalist Federation)
ICE	Izquierda Comunista de España (Communist Left of Spain)
IR	Izquierda Republicana (Republican Left)
ISAOL	Internationale Socialistische Anti-Oorlogsliga (International Socialist Antiwar League)
JGS	Jeunes Gardes Socialistes (Socialist Young Guards)
JJSS	Juventudes Socialistas (Socialist Youth)
KPD	Kommunistische Partei Deutschlands (Communist Party of Germany)
KPÖ	Kommunistische Partei Österreichs (Communist Party of Austria)
LSI	Labor and Socialist International
NB	Neu Beginnen (To Begin Afresh)
PCC	Partit Comunista de Catalunya (Communist Party of Catalonia)
PCE	Partido Comunista de España (Communist Party of Spain)
PCF	Parti Communiste Français (French Communist Party)
PNR	Partido Nacional Republicano (National Republican Party)

POB	Parti Ouvrier Belge (Belgian Workers' Party)
PSOE	Partido Socialista Obrero Español (Spanish Socialist Workers' Party)
RSD	Revolutionäre Sozialisten Deutschlands (Revolutionary Socialists of Germany)
RSÖ	Revolutionäre Sozialisten Österreichs (Revolutionary Socialists of Austria)
SAI	Sozialistische Arbeiter-Internationale (Labor and Socialist International)
SFIO	Section Française de l'Internationale Ouvrière (French Section of the Labor and Socialist International)
SPD	Sozialdemokratische Partei Deutschlands (Social Democratic Party of Germany)
SPÖ	Sozialistische Partei Österreichs (Socialist Party of Austria)
SYI	Socialist Youth International
UGT	Unión General de los Trabajadores (General Workers' Union)
UR	Unión Republicana (Republican Union)
USC	Unió Socialista de Catalunya (Socialist Union of Catalonia)

Newspapers/Journals

AZ	*Arbeiter-Zeitung*
DD	*Documents and Discussions*
II	*International Information*
NZ	*Die Neue Zeit*
ZfS	*Zeitschrift für Sozialismus*

Archives

AdsD	Archiv der sozialen Demokratie
AHNS	Archivo Histórico Nacional de Salamanca
AHPCE	Archivo Histórico del Partido Comunista de España
AMVC	Archief en Museum van het Vlaamse Cultuurleven
CRHMSS	Centre de Recherches sur l'Histoire des Mouvements Sociaux et du Syndicalisme
FPI	Fundación Pablo Iglesias
IfZ	Institut für Zeitgeschichte
IGA	Institut für Geschichte der Arbeiterbewegung
IISG	Internationaal Instituut voor Sociale Geschiedenis
OURS	Office Universitaire de Recherche Socialiste
VGA	Verein für Geschichte der Arbeiterbewegung
ZPA	Zentrales Partei-Archiv

European
Socialists
Respond
to Fascism

ONE

Introduction

On 30 January 1933 an official government announcement made public President Hindenburg's decision to appoint Adolf Hitler chancellor of the German Reich. In the last hours and days preceding this move, the forces favoring democracy attempted to block the slide into dictatorship by any means at their disposal. For the German labor movement, this entailed a recourse to its traditional means of public demonstrations and parades. The most notable protest action occurred in the capital city of Berlin.

One day prior to Hitler's rise to power, on 29 January 1933, the "Iron Front," an antifascist coalition of the German Social Democratic Party (SPD), the German General Trade Union Federation and the SPD's paramilitary group, the Reichsbanner, organized mass demonstrations in the streets of Berlin. The plan was to arrange for a series of feeder marches in various locations throughout that city which were, in turn, to converge on the central Lustgarten for a closing rally. The outpouring of support was truly overwhelming. Even before the feeder marches got off to a start in the working-class suburbs of Berlin, it became obvious that the response surpassed all expectations. Each assembly point turned into the scene of massive demonstrations comprising tens of thousands of protesters. A sea of banners, red flags and other symbols of opposition to the course of the German government added its own distinctive note of determinacy to this last-ditch effort to avert catastrophe. Around noon, the protests began to move toward the city center. Songs and music accompanied the endless columns streaming through the busy streets. Long before the speeches began, the central Lustgarten was filled to the brim, and the continuously advancing marchers were directed toward neighboring open spaces and streets.

In his keynote address the SPD's Berlin party chairman, Franz Künstler, implored his audience to heed the writing on the wall. "It is a matter of life and death! The constitutionally guaranteed rights of citizenship of the entire people are at stake! The social legislation, the manifold rights which the working population has obtained, are at stake! We must oppose the arbitrary actions and the forced domination by a decadent class of exploiters." Künstler castigated the lack of unity on the part of the German working-class Left, and he emphasized the imperative necessity to forge

3

closer ties. "The united front of the proletariat will be born in struggle, and only in struggle." "The day may come — perhaps it is not all that far away — when Berlin will decide for all of Germany. Woe to the working class if this day does not find it united!"[1]

When the first columns of marchers left the Lustgarten to return to their homes on this Sunday afternoon, they found their way blocked by fresh contingents of men and women hoping to block the slide into dictatorship. By late afternoon the major thoroughfares of Berlin witnessed hundreds of thousands of demonstrators moving in both directions, to and from the city's core. Sympathetic onlookers on the sidewalks and in the windows of homes adjoining the route further enhanced the militant and festive character of the popular, semispontaneous event by expressions of support. Their hopes were in vain. Within twenty-four hours Hitler was nominated as the next German chancellor. And within months some of the key bastions of the European Left,[2] including the SPD, the Communist Party of Germany (KPD) and the major trade union organization were destroyed. Their leading activists and many more adherents were forced into illegal activities, exile, prison sentences or fruitless attempts to win over the new masters of their destiny. The German tragedy brought to a sudden end an era of hope.

Social Gains in Interwar Europe

When World War I had finally come to a close, and the postwar central European disturbances had run their course, it seemed as if some form of parliamentary democratic system of government would become the rule across the entire Continent. The demise of the Hohenzollern and Habsburg monarchies opened up the chances for an extension of democracy in Germany and Austria and the possibility for national self-determination in the non-German-speaking areas of the former Habsburg empire. Perhaps the most notable improvements in the areas of democratic rights could be registered in the qualitative extension of the electorate throughout western Europe. Largely, but not exclusively, due to the inclusion of women in the category of citizens with the right to vote, the numbers of the electorate more than doubled in the space of a very few years, with the notable exceptions of France, Belgium, Italy and Switzerland.[3]

In the area of social legislation, too, the postwar years were generally a time of steady advances. While in most countries some form of social insurance legislation had been instituted in the decades prior to World War I, the fifteen years between the end of World War I and the consolidation of the Nazi regime saw the qualitative enhancement of the social safety net beyond already existing limits. In western Europe, notable improvements in the provision of pension, unemployment and health insurance were enacted in almost every single state. Table 1 presents an overview of social legislation in western European states between 1918 and 1933.

The European Left, and others, had long fought for the enlargement of social and political democracy. The postwar gains had largely been obtained either as a result of direct pressure from below or as a consequence of "pre-emptive reforms."[4] In either case, they were regarded as a vital part of the enhanced quality of life in interwar Europe. These and other improvements in social legislation and the extension of political citizenship were increasingly threatened by the economic and political

TABLE I   Significant Social Legislation Enacted in 1918–33

Country	Unemployment	Pension	Health
Austria	1920	1927	—
Belgium	1920*	1924	—
Denmark	—	1921/22	1933
France	—	—	1930
Germany	1927	—	—
Italy	1919	1919	1928
Netherlands	—	—	1929
Spain	—	1921	—
Switzerland	1924*	—	—
UK	—	1925	—

Source: Peter Flora, *State, Economy, and Society in Western Europe, 1815–1975*, 2 vols. (Frankfurt: Campus, 1983), 1:454. except for Spain, where the data are culled from Raymond Carr, *Spain, 1808–1975* (Oxford: Clarendon Press, 1982), p. 462.

Dashes almost always denote previously existing arrangements. Dates marked with an asterisk refer to the introduction of voluntary insurance schemes. All other schemes were compulsory insurance programs. Some compulsory programs introduced in 1918–33 expanded on previously existing voluntary arrangements. The fourth major category of social insurance schemes, occupational injury insurance, was already firmly in place in all listed countries prior to 1918.

instability engendered by the Great Depression and the rise of the radical Right. When SPD Berlin party chairman Franz Künstler exclaimed on the morrow of Hitler's victory: "The constitutionally guaranteed rights of citizenship of the entire people are at stake! The social legislation, the manifold rights which the working population has obtained are at stake!"[5] his audience was fully aware of the implications of this threat. By 1933, however, the process of the gradual fascization of Europe had already been under way for some years.

The Tilt Toward Dictatorships

The first country to abandon the democratic path had witnessed the most significant revolutionary disturbances in the immediate postwar era, with the exception of the czarist empire: Italy. In a gradual process of dismantlement of democratic conquests starting in late 1922, Benito Mussolini set about to create a fascist state. While most pillars of the corporate state were not in place until 1926, the elimination of the socialist opposition in parliament in the late spring of 1924 may serve as a useful signpost indicating the destruction of meaningful democracy in Italy. Other countries followed suit. Particularly in the newly created states of eastern Europe, the fragile conquests of democracy disintegrated under the twin blows of ethnic rivalries and social conflicts. Albania (1925), Poland (1926), Lithuania (1926) and Yugoslavia (1929) instituted some version of an authoritarian regime even prior to the outbreak of the Great Depression. In southern Europe, apart from Italy, the dictatorship of Primo de Rivera in Spain (1923–30) gave a preview of subsequent Spanish experiments in authoritarian governments, although Primo de Rivera's regime was the sole case of an interwar dictatorship whose fortune was eventually reversed, if only for several years. Portugal, instead, suffered from an autocratic regime for decades after 1926.

The economic malaise of the 1930s only worsened the chances for the survival of democracy. Hungary, under the semidictatorial regime of Admiral Miklas Horthy ever since the suppression of the Hungarian Soviet Socialist Republic in early 1919, definitely adopted the antidemocratic route in 1932 with the appointment of Gyula Gömbös as prime minister. Then came the Nazi takeover of Germany in January 1933. The year 1934 was notable not only for the definitive crushing of Austrian democracy, but the Baltic States of Latvia and Estonia likewise opted for what Stanley Payne terms "preventive authoritarianism." A military coup paved the way for the abandonment of democracy in Bulgaria in January 1935. And in early August 1936, roughly two weeks after the coup d'état of Generalissimo Francisco Franco in Spain, General Metaxas opted for dictatorship in Greece.[6]

This, then, was the political backdrop to the process of rethinking on the European Left. An unprecedented wave of dictatorial regimes appeared destined to alter the course of European society, which had only recently witnessed the long-desired introduction of significant political and social gains for its subaltern population groups. Not all of the dictatorial regimes were openly fascist ventures. Indeed, most were military or civilian dictatorships with little or limited mass support. Some were in open conflict with more militant fascist movements on their right. Yet, whether "moderate" dictatorships or fascist regimes, the suppression of democracy shattered the dreams of many European socialists who had come to believe in the vision of an increasingly "democratic" Continent, which would create the preconditions for the gradual evolution toward socialism. Combined with the sudden growth of fascist movements in the remaining Continental democracies, the future of European politics suddenly turned dark.

The growing threat of fascism, most visible in the rapid spread of dictatorial regimes and the gain in social power of fascist movements elsewhere, was compounded by the increasingly realistic threat of military expansionism of fascist regimes. This became particularly ominous in the case of the German Nazi state. At the latest after the reintroduction of a military draft in Germany in March 1935, all signs pointed in the direction of a coming war. The October 1935 Italian invasion of Ethiopia only served to underscore this trend. The combined threat of fascism and war greatly contributed to a sobering of expectations by European socialists and helped prepare the ideological terrain for the experimentation with novel strategies.

Unemployment in Comparative Perspective

One of the factors, though by no means the decisive one, behind the onslaught of the radical Right was the devastating impact of the Great Depression, which could be felt throughout the European Continent but to varying degrees. Table 2 shows the extent of unemployment in the five countries under review, as well as the Netherlands. What becomes immediately apparent are the remarkable differences in the extent of unemployment even within the five countries targeted in my study. Table 3 concentrates on unemployment in industry alone and thus leaves out the important

TABLE 2 Unemployment Rates in Select Western European
Countries, 1933–36

Country	1933	1934	1935	1936
Austria	26.0	25.5	24.1	24.1
Belgium	20.4	23.4	22.9	16.8
France	14.1	13.8	14.5	10.4
Germany	26.3	14.9	11.6	8.3
Netherlands	26.9	28.0	31.7	32.7
Spain	12.8 (619)	12.9 (667)	— (674)	— (801)

Source: The 1933 and 1934 unemployment rate in Spain is taken from Albert
Balcells, *Crisis económica y agitación social en Cataluña de 1930 a 1936* (Esplugues
de Llobregat: Ariel, 1971), p. 54. All other data are from Ekkart Zimmermann and
Thomas Saalfeld, "Economic and Political Reactions to the World Economic Crisis of the 1930s in Six Countries," *International Studies Quarterly* 32 (1988): 321.

While percentage figures for 1935 and 1936 are unavailable, I include the total figure of unemployed (in thousands) for all four years (see Balcells, p. 53) to show that
for most of this period the Spanish unemployment rate was rather low compared to
most other surveyed states.

fluctuations affecting the agricultural labor force, at that time still an important factor in the respective overall labor force of most industrialized states. Yet the broader
range of comparison in table 3 underscores one important insight regarding the interplay of politics and economics in the 1930s: the absence of any positive connection between the extent of unemployment and the rise of the radical Right. For among
the countries with the highest unemployment rates stood Norway, Denmark and the
Netherlands, all three being countries where fascist movements made little headway
throughout that decade. By contrast, some of the countries with the highest degree
of class polarization throughout that decade had rather low unemployment figures,
particularly when compared with some northern European states.[7] The lack of a
positive correlation between the rates of national unemployment and the respective
national policy evolution renders simplistic versions of materialist explanations for
the history of interwar Europe irrelevant and strongly suggests other causal factors.
Anticipating one of my conclusions, I merely want to briefly draw attention to the
mediating role of ideology in policy choice during the Great Depression. For, as will
become apparent in the body of my work, the ability to put forward a coherent answer to the economic, social and political malaise affecting European states weighed
rather heavily in the reconfiguration of political allegiances. It is for this reason that
I propose to concentrate on the genesis and articulation of novel socialist strategies.
For the ability to capture the popular imagination was perhaps the most important
factor behind all successful political initiatives.

The Impact of the German Tragedy

The systematic destruction of the German labor movement not only affected the
discussions within the German Left but profoundly altered the terms of debate in
other European countries. Whereas the successes of Mussolini, Salazar, Piłsudski

TABLE 3　Unemployment Rates in Industry

Country	1933	1934	1935	1936
Belgium	16.9	18.9	17.8	13.5
Denmark	28.8	22.2	19.7	19
France	14.1	13.8	14.5	10.4
Germany	36.2	20.5	16.2	12.0
Netherlands	26.9	28.0	31.7	32.7
Norway	33.4	30.7	25.3	18.8
Sweden	23.2	18.0	15.0	12.7
UK	19.9	16.7	15.5	13.1

Source: Barry Eichengreen and T. J. Hatton, "Interwar Unemployment in International Perspective: An Overview," in *Interwar Unemployment in International Perspective*, ed. Barry Eichengreen and T. J. Hatton (Dordrecht: Kluwer, 1988), pp. 6–7.

and other dictators of pre-1933 interwar Europe had certainly contributed to the clouding of the political horizon, these failings of "democracy" did not fundamentally alter the hopes, wishes and predictions of the major Left groups. The unexpected removal of Germany from the list of countries with a vibrant political culture shook up much of what was vital within the European labor movement. Time-honored strategies and tactics were cast aside. An unprecedented degree of openness to new ideas and conceptions could be felt in remote corners of that continent. And the ensuing forty months witnessed a flowering of new proposals, guides to action and a reconceptualization of the tasks at hand.

The responsiveness of the European Left to the tragedy of German labor had, of course, much to do with the similarity of circumstances confronting the respective national organizations. Against the backdrop of the Great Depression, the forces of the radical Right appeared to be on the upswing throughout much of Europe. In this context the combined defeat of the model political organization of the socialist Left, the SPD, and the most influential communist party outside the Soviet Union, the KPD, created a political vacuum which remained unfilled for several years. A free space emerged in which new strategic conceptions could be articulated, defended and applied. The years between January 1933 and the spring of 1936 must be seen as one of the most important periods in relation to the genesis, articulation and practical application of significant strategy proposals by the working-class Left since its formation in the early decades of the nineteenth century. In respect to the formulation and practical testing of novel strategies for the Left, these years may perhaps only be compared to the turbulent events of 1917–19. While it may not have been as explosive a time as the crisis at the end of and immediately after World War I, it was certainly as portentous as the only other transnational European social upheaval since the midthirties, the moment of liberation in the southern tier of Europe in 1943–45. In the latter instance, however, with few exceptions, from the outset a self-limiting and defensive strategy for social change helped predetermine the ultimate defeats. From 1933 to 1936, by contrast, strategies were more plainly up for grabs.

Years of Social and Political Crisis

The years 1933–36 were therefore an extremely crucial time span not only for the history of Europe's beleaguered Left but for all other social groups and classes. The threat to interwar democracy, dramatically demonstrated and symbolized by Adolf Hitler's smooth and legal rise to power, increasingly determined the parameters of politics in Europe. Authoritarian alternatives to democracy emerged as powerful contenders in the struggle over the political future of existing states, including countries with long-standing traditions of democratic rule, such as Belgium and France.

The political parties claiming to represent the working class were not the only political bodies undergoing a process of reconfiguration, a wrenching debate on strategies and, wherever possible, the testing of novel solutions. Bourgeois parties, in some cases only recently attuned to the demands of the post–World War I extension of democracy, were faced with unprecedented choices. The polarization of European politics between a radical Left and a radical Right began to take its toll. Moderately conservative or liberal parties saw diminishing electoral returns and began to search for new political partners. This marginalization of the political middle was, of course, a process which had characterized the waning years of the Weimar Republic. In Germany it had been precisely the need to find a solution to this crisis of confidence by the electorate which, in the end, pushed bourgeois and landed elites to accept Adolf Hitler as an ally. Caught between a threatening bloc of socialist and communist votes to their left and a dynamically expanding radical Right, the political class of Weimar Germany opted for cooperation with the latter, in the hopes of keeping it under control. Of course, what was meant as a temporary arrangement for the benefit of traditional elites quickly emerged as the ticket to undisputed dominance by Hitler and his entourage.[8]

Little is known about the direct impact of the demise of German democracy on bourgeois politics in other European states. It would be wholly surprising if the sudden end of democracy in Germany would not have called forth a flurry of debates on a scale perhaps not too dissimilar from the heated exchanges of opinion among the European Left. But the exact extent of the reverberations remains unfortunately unclear. What can be reconstructed, however, are the rapid switches in policy orientation by a number of representative political parties in the course of very few years. The Spanish Radical Party, for instance, briefly joined the alliance of Republicans and social democrats which governed Spain at the beginning of the second republic but left the cabinet in December 1931. Yet, from 1931 to 1933, Radical members of parliament supported most major pieces of legislation introduced by the ruling coalition. In the course of 1933, however, Radical politicians began to embark on an opposition course which partially accounted for the demise of the Republican-Socialist coalition in the summer of that year. In the wake of elections favorable to the Right in November 1933, Alejandro Lerroux, the head of the Radical Party, then governed Spain for ten months with the tacit support of the corporatist, protofascist Catholic Right. Finally, in the fall of 1934, the Radical Party formed a coalition with the Catholic Right, thus triggering in response a military uprising by social democrats and anarchists, who considered the participation of the Catholic Right in any coalition government the equivalent of Hitler's rise to power on the coattails of traditional conservatives in Germany. Within very few years, then, the Spanish Radical Party transformed itself from a fairly reliable bloc of supporters of a Republican-Socialist government to a party in power seeking the support of an organization openly proclaiming corporatist goals.[9] The Spanish Radical Party's political itinerary in the 1930s may exemplify the state of indecision and the search for new political formulas characteristic of bourgeois politics in the crucial decade leading to World War II, at least in those parts of continental Europe still under the rule of parliamentary democracies. Thus far, however, there exists no study attempting to summarize and analyze in a comparative framework the specific trajectory of traditional (bourgeois and/or landed) elite politics at this crucial conjuncture.

The Contemporary Relevance of the European Left

The same situation of relative neglect characterizes the state of historical scholarship for the political organizations of the working-class Left. As I explain later in greater detail, the wealth of secondary works on national, regional or even local working-class politics stands in stark contrast to the absence of comparative works of major value. It is this lacuna I propose to address. Why is it important to study the broad outlines, let alone the finer points, of the political evolution and trajectory of the working-class Left? After all, by the end of the 1930s, most hopes and aspirations of the European Left had vanished in the losing battles of the Spanish Republican army, whose last detachments surrendered to Franco's forces exactly five months to the day prior to the outbreak of World War II.

Throughout the 1930s, the European Marxist Left played a pivotal role in national and international politics quite distinct from its direct or indirect impact on national and world affairs in later decades. Social democrats, communists and others were, for most of the 1930s, key players in the determination of the political future of the Continent, though generally unpredictable ones. As I will demonstrate, continental European social democracy underwent a serious identity crisis, and several sections of the Labor and Socialist International (LSI) embarked on insurrectionary roads or otherwise interrupted the process of political moderation characteristic of social democracy since its inception. Communism, generally under strict hierarchical control by Moscow, repeatedly switched its strategies and constituted another volatile component of the European Left. Most significantly, a process of rapprochement between the various organizations of the European Left occurred for several years within most Continental states, opening up an inherent dynamic toward socialism then and there. From the summer of 1934 until late 1935, it even appeared possible for the two largest rival factions of the European Left—social democracy and communism—to join forces in an international united front, which could have definitively changed the face of European politics.

Apart from the enhanced political volatility of communism and social democracy throughout the 1930s, what was their numerical significance at the time? Throughout its existence, the Communist International (Comintern) was always significantly weaker than the social democratic LSI. A comparison of membership figures for six key countries in 1928—the Soviet Union, Germany, Czechoslovakia, France, the United States and England—shows 6,637,622 members for the LSI and 1,707,769 for the Comintern.[10] In subsequent years, membership figures for the LSI remained stable, whereas communist membership declined up to the midthirties only to experience a rebound during the era of popular fronts. In terms of electoral returns, the sole communist party in the five countries under review in my study—Austria, Belgium, France, Germany and Spain—which had significant support at the polls prior to the late thirties was the German Communist Party, receiving 16.9 percent of the popular vote at its high point in 1932.[11] But by 1936 the French Communist Party also received 15.3 percent of all votes, although the Belgian and Spanish Communist Parties still remained rather insignificant at the polls and the Austrian Communist Party was by then outlawed.[12]

Social democracy's parliamentary returns were more impressive. In the last general elections prior to the end of Austrian democracy, the Austrian Socialist Party won 41.1 percent of the popular vote; the Belgian Workers' Party garnered 37.1 percent in 1932 (32 percent in 1936); the French Socialist Party 20.5 percent in 1932 (19.9 percent in 1936); Germany's social democrats received 20.4 percent in the last free elections in 1932 (down from 29.8 percent four years earlier); and Spanish socialists held 24.2 percent of all seats in 1931, 12.8 percent in 1933 and 18.8 percent in 1936.[13]

These numbers, then, may serve to underscore the significance of Europe's Marxist Left in terms of its popularity at the polls. They were serious contenders for political power in a number of these states, and, in the course of the time period under review, social democrats formed part of ruling coalitions in Belgium, France and Spain. Given the volatility of continental Europe's political climate and the fluid nature of social democratic and communist politics at that time, an overall assessment of the changing contours of Europe's Left is therefore long overdue. What social democrats and communists said and did in the remaining democracies of Europe immediately affected national politics and helped influence the outlook of more conservative forces too. Yet, as I have repeatedly emphasized, it is important to recognize that the political contours of the European Left underwent several crucial mutations in the course of very few years. Social democracy in 1933 by and large pursued different goals from social democracy in 1934. By the end of the time period under review, roughly June 1936, political strategies had once again changed in a fundamental manner. In assessing the political itinerary of the European Left between 1933 and 1936, it is therefore of key importance to pay close attention to the rapidly changing strategies and the corresponding changes in political practice.

Moments of Opportunity

Peter Gourevitch, in his study of comparative responses to international economic crises, underscores that "moments of greatest freedom are crisis points,"[14] a shrewd observation which can also be read to mean that crisis points are moments of maximum choice. In his analysis of three major crises of the recent past, Gourevitch draws attention to the profound impact of the Great Depression on class alliances and policy assumptions by all major actors in the affected states:

In its ability to disrupt existing political alignments, the Depression rivaled war. Coalitions formed in the first international trade crisis [1873–96] were strongly shaken by World War I and then "recast," as Charles Maier aptly labels the post-war readjustment. The Great Crash of 1929 shook the members loose from these coalitions. Rather quickly Europe and North America came to resemble a building site without an architectural plan—chunks of material lay around, available to be assembled in any number of ways. New patterns and formulas were tried, and some succeeded.[15]

What I propose to do, then, is to illuminate the role of working-class organizations in this moment of opportunity as it unfolded before their very eyes. I intend to reconstruct the major lines of development as they affected the most vital debates within this Left and the societies in which it operated. As can be concluded from the course of European history in the 1930s, this will not be a story of glowing successes. Instead, it is more a description and analysis of a series of false starts and bloody defeats. Nevertheless, apart from the inherent importance of the politics of Europe's Left in the 1930s I discussed earlier, these strategic reorientations demand the utmost attention for one additional important reason.

Given the highly volatile nature of societies in motion, it is incumbent to reflect on another observation by Gourevitch. He rightfully insists that "stable times" leave little room for choices. "In moments of flux, on the other hand, choices widen, but analysis becomes more complicated because relationships change."[16] What this implies is not just a sense of the difficulties of my project but also a promise of the unforeseen and unexpected. Whereas opportunities for radical societal change, in any direction, are narrowly circumscribed in the vast majority of historical moments, such rare instances do occur. When they do appear, predictions of the immediate future are outdated soon after they are made. To quote Gourevitch once again: "In the search for generalizations the contingent can never be ignored, and in the thirties, it loomed large."[17] In the concrete context of 1933–36, this meant that no inherent necessity or inbuilt determination predestined the ultimate sequence of events within the societies at large and, more specifically, the politics of the Left. These years were some of those exceptional moments in the interplay of agency and structure when the former reached maximum potential. It was a period when voluntarist notions, viewpoints that stressed the subjective factor in historical change, were widely disseminated and accepted within all segments of the European Left. For once, the impossible appeared to be within reach. Contingency was seemingly reigning supreme. In this sense, also, this reconstruction of a forgotten moment of the past should be seen as an implicit contribution to the sadly neglected debate on the suppression of historical alternatives.[18]

The Comparative Dimension

This book developed as a comparative study early on in my research, when I decided to pursue some leads hinting at the unique conjuncture of the year 1934, in particular, as one of those rare moments when confusion reigned supreme and no single policy orientation seemed simultaneously to structure and constrain the actions of the powerful European Left.[19] Within each national context a number of insightful works served as a solid point of departure. Many of them implicitly clarified some of my points of contention with the dominant view in the historiography of the European Left. Some authors showed quite ably in their empirical research that there was no *direct* transition from the period of fratricidal infighting up to early 1934 to the subsequent era of popular fronts, and others likewise underscored that the degree of radical potential, rocking the foundations of the capitalist social and economic order, was actually greatest precisely in the period around 1934 and not in the more famous, later era of popular fronts.[20] But the overriding deficiency of these national or regional studies, apart from their lack of explicit reperiodization, remains their geographically narrow scope and appeal. Conclusions are, understandably, held to apply only to each given, narrowly circumscribed, geographic area, and larger generalizations often go astray. Thus Paul Preston, in a most revealing passage, exemplifies this tunnel vision when he writes that the radicalization of the Spanish Socialist Workers' Party (PSOE) was "unique in Europe at a time when most socialist movements were evolving towards ever more moderate positions."[21]

From recognition of the restrictive geographic and conceptual limits of historical research, it was only one step to the formulation of my research project as a comparative, transnational study. Marc Bloch's stress on the paramount importance of comparative approaches to European history became an imperative demand. As long ago as 1928, Bloch asserted that "it is high time to set about breaking down the outmoded topographical compartments within which we seek to confine social realities, for they are not large enough to hold the material we try to cram into them." He went on to forcefully support comparative methods, "for where has it ever happened that social phenomena, in any period, have obligingly and with one accord stopped their development at the same boundaries, these being precisely the same as those of political rule or nationality."[22]

My own work is by no means the first such attempt to analyze the broader contours of this era for the Left. Some of the best comparative works on this period were actually written by activists of the 1930s.[23] But, whether participants' accounts or analyses from afar, they all suffer from one or several serious limitations. Some studies are country-by-country overviews of this period with little attempt to draw overall conclusions.[24] Others concentrate on one particular aspect of those struggles.[25] None of them are based on archival research. A fair number of social scientists, none of them historians, have attempted to demonstrate underlying patterns and overall determinants of the historic process in those years.[26] I have relied on their conclusions for some of my hypotheses and general explanations. Yet these analysts, too, even more so than their historian colleagues, have failed to base their projects on a systematic search for documentary evidence, leading to easily detectable oversimplifications and the tendency to rigid schematizations.[27] My research proposes to bridge the gap between the contributions of comparative scholars and the groundwork developed by numerous historians in local, regional and national archives. In this study I attempt to integrate the research findings of the existing secondary literature by historians, sociologists and political scientists with my own collection of archival data emanating from nineteen archives in the six countries I visited during the course of my research. In the process I hope to have avoided at least some of the pitfalls of concentrating on "a maze of little local facts"[28] without succumbing to the temptations of overgeneralizations when faced with daunting big structures, large processes and huge comparisons.[29]

My intention to base my comparative study on primary data required that I limit the focus to five countries: Austria, Belgium, France, Germany and Spain. While I intend to stray occasionally beyond the borders of these states, they form the core area of my research. Germany could hardly be excluded, as the prima facie catalyst for this period of radical changes, Hitler's ascension to power, was felt most directly in this state and because Germany's working-class Left had played an exemplary guiding role in the political life of the European Left in previous decades. Austria saw the first-ever armed uprising of a social democratic force, the Schutzbund uprising; Spain repeated the Schutzbund action on an even grander scale. Spain and France were the only countries in western Europe with, at least momentarily, successful popular fronts. Belgium, on the other hand, was the sole country where another creative socialist response, radical planism, gained the upper hand. Additional reasons for choosing these states could easily be defended, but the most compelling rationale for concentrating on these five disparate countries lies precisely in their social and political heterogeneity. For in the face of a common enemy, despite widely dissimilar political cultures and governments ranging from liberal democracies to fascist dictatorships, the Left was able to develop a unifying language across national frontiers. It will thus become apparent that what have hitherto been regarded as ever so many peculiarities were part of more general transnational patterns.

Overview of This Book

Concretely, I propose to look first at the overall evolution of social democracy in the targeted forty months. The most important debates and the largest room for maneuver in these years could be found within the ranks of the LSI. To be sure, the Comintern underwent a similarly momentous policy evolution at that time, and the path traversed by communist parties between early 1934 and early 1936 was a far more radical strategic turn than the LSI could ever have hoped to institute. As a matter of fact, *official* LSI policy really never changed at all. To their discredit, LSI viewpoints were one of the very few stable points of reference throughout this entire period. Yet, in contrast to the structure of the Comintern, the LSI leadership bodies were important but not all-powerful oversight committees. Contrary to LSI statutes, life revolved essentially around the lower levels in the hierarchy of the Second International. Indeed, within the LSI during the thirties, formal international ties came to be increasingly meaningless bonds. The national, regional and local instances of the LSI shaped the contours of the debates. And, in examining the political evolution of LSI sections, it will, hopefully, become apparent that significant elements of European social democracy underwent a process of radicalization on a quasi-Continental scale far surpassing the judgments of historians to date.

In the second part of chapter 2, I analyze the trajectory of Comintern policy between 1933 and 1936. This is the only chapter that relies heavily on secondary literature, given the well-known difficulties of gaining access to the pertinent archives. At the time I carried out my research, the French and Austrian parties still exercised tight control over their holdings. In Belgium the Communist Party's archive welcomed independent researchers but had virtually no unpublished primary sources for the period under concern. The Berlin Institut für Geschichte der Arbeiterbewegung, formerly the Institut für Marxismus-Leninismus, opened its vast holdings too late for me to carry out more than superficial research. Therefore, the only Communist Party document center with relevant holdings accessible to me was the Madrid Archivo Histórico del PCE. Unfortunately, during my residence in Madrid, technical difficulties forced me to rely almost exclusively on the limited number of hardcopy documents at their disposal, a serious drawback given that most items of interest are on microfilms transferred from the Soviet Union. Nevertheless, these and other documents, in conjunction with the steadily growing store of secondary literature, permitted me to reconceptualize the periodization of Comintern policy evolution in these years. I question the view of current historiography of a linear move away from "united fronts from below" toward popular fronts, once the Kremlin heights gave the green light for change. Instead, I propose that this evolution passed through several distinct stages, none of them necessitating each succeeding step. Chapter 3 takes a close look at attempts to foster unity in action between leading elements in the LSI and the Comintern.

Chapters 4 through 6 will concentrate on the analysis of the three socialist strategies emerging from the fight against fascism in the context of the Great Depression in western, central and southern Europe. First I analyze and describe the rise and demise of united front politics within national borders. The genesis and implosion of radical planism will be the focus of chapter 5. Chapter 6 dissects the history and meaning of popular fronts up to the point of their brief triumph in the heady days after electoral victories in Spain and France. Of special concern in this chapter will be the inquiry into the advantages, disadvantages and false assumptions underlying this turn toward moderation in the quest for allies to the right. I will also explore the somewhat artificially constructed nature of electoral mass support for popular front coalitions by showing how both the French and Spanish electoral arrangements consciously overestimated bourgeois strength at the expense of proletarian gains.

Chapters 7 and 8 represent efforts to address issues which are generally recognized as key determinants of any socialist strategy but which, with equal regularity, suffer from historians' neglect: the degree of reverberation of major events in foreign countries on the shape of politics in, superficially, unaffected states, and the process of interaction between leadership and ranks within each national context. While it is difficult to measure the precise impact of momentous occasions—such as the appointment of Hitler as German chancellor, the Schutzbund rebellion, or the Asturian defeat in October 1934—beyond the borders of the states in which they occurred, systematic searches of the party press, the contemporary literature and other documents generated results which not only highlight the importance of foreign policy events on domestic socialist strategy but, at the same time, support my general thesis of the unique conjuncture of the targeted rebellious years.

My efforts to provide some insights regarding the mutual influence of leadership and ranks, above all in the LSI, led to unexpected results. For, whereas in the transition from fratricide to united fronts the pressure from below played a clearly distinguishable role in forcing their respective leadership bodies to change their tune, no such powerful influences can be discerned in the succeeding move from united to popular fronts. But in the aftermath of its victories in France and Spain, the breach between leadership and ranks, temporarily closed after the adoption of united front tactics across much of central and southern Europe, reappeared in full force. It found expression in the massive waves of strikes and land and factory occupations which signaled the beginning of the end of the popular front experience. I should stress that despite the placement of chapters 7 and 8 toward the end of this book, they represent the most important parts of this study. Indeed, they are so central to my enterprise that I repeatedly attempted to heed suggestions to dissolve them altogether as separate chapters and to integrate my arguments into the remaining portions of my work. The genuine transnational dimension of strategic choices and the symbiotic relationship between leadership and ranks are indeed indispensable conclusions of my research. Yet in the end I decided that to spread these findings throughout the book would detract attention from — rather than concentrate on — the transnational dimension of Europe's socialist movements and the corresponding symbiosis of ranks and leaders. I will conclude with an analysis of contingency in the historical process, general remarks on the heightened relevance of ideology and discourse in moments of societal crises, and an assessment of the origin, impact and fate of such periods of rapid, wide-ranging social transformations.

TWO

The Itineraries of the LSI
and the Comintern

In the years up to 1933 the trajectory of post–World War I European social democracy conformed rather closely to the image of formally Marxist organizations suffused with gradualist principles. Once the turbulent postwar upheavals subsided,[1] most socialist parties were eager to prove their loyalty to the states in which they operated. Of course, part of the rationale for social democracy's commitment to the rules and regulations of interwar democracy was its significant success in utilizing this political free space for the obtainment of concrete social gains. The achievements in the area of social legislation I presented in table 1 are only one manifestation of this seemingly mutually beneficial arrangement. Significant advances in procuring affordable working-class housing in socialist-controlled municipalities are additional concrete gains of the interwar period which have survived until the present day.[2] In three of the five countries under scrutiny—Austria, Belgium and Germany—social democratic parties repeatedly participated in coalition cabinets.[3] The PSOE, after having tacitly supported the moderate dictatorship of Primo de Rivera throughout the twenties, was the only social democratic party of the five which actually occupied government posts the day of Hitler's rise to power.[4] The French Section of the Labor and Socialist International (SFIO) was the sole party which had managed to abstain from governmental participation throughout the entire postwar period. Yet this was not a result of a particularly uncompromising, abstentionist tradition. The SFIO repeatedly helped elect bourgeois governments by the mutual pledge of support between left bourgeois forces and socialists in favor of the strongest candidate in runoff elections. And the SFIO's refusal to enter coalition cabinets was never a matter of principle. In 1932, with an overwhelming show of support by the delegates, the French social democrats drew up a list of demands, the "Cahiers de Huyghens," meant to serve as a bargaining tool in coalition talks with the bourgeois Left. Only bourgeois intransigence, their continued rejection of these measures, prevented socialists from open participation.[5]

While the willingness to enter coalition cabinets alone does not necessarily permit more general deductions about the theory and practice of social democracy in these years, its handling of this crucial issue appropriately reflects the less than combative atmosphere within these parties at the time. Social democrats were by and large no longer enemies of the state. In some cases, as in Weimar Germany or the first Austrian republic, they instead furnished the most committed block of supporters of the democracies then under attack from the radical Right. After 30 January 1933 everything changed, not suddenly, and certainly not overnight, as the full impact of the German tragedy was not felt until months thereafter, but noticeably nonetheless. The general secretary of the LSI had this to say shortly after the SPD was forced to move its headquarters to Prague:

> After the great collapse of the Labour Movement in Germany, we have to investigate with the greatest seriousness *what is to happen in the future*. All the problems of the Labour Movement are raised afresh by the victory of Fascism in Germany. The path to be followed by the working class, the possibilities of the class struggle, must be investigated anew from the beginning. There must be an intellectual clarification in the international Labour Movement which will point the way for the future.[6]

It was the shock of the smooth victory of fascism in Germany, in conjunction with domestic crises, which forced the remaining socialists of Europe, those who could still operate under conditions of legality, to take stock.

The Spanish Crucible

The earliest fundamental revision of an entire party's strategy and orientation occurred in Spain, which was then undergoing civil strife on a scale unparalleled in any other western European country. When military rule collapsed in April 1931, socialists immediately formed part of the new provisional government. And the elections of 28 June 1931 confirmed the coalition of left bourgeois and social democratic parties. The key Ministries of Labor, Justice and Finance were all held by such notable social democratic leaders as Francisco Largo Caballero, Fernando de los Ríos and Indalecio Prieto.[7]

Toward the end of Primo de Rivera's reign the PSOE had undergone a realignment which highlighted the fluid nature of PSOE factionalism. Whereas Prieto had been the main opponent of conciliatory attitudes toward Primo de Rivera, the Basque politician now became a key advocate of socialist support to the republic. In this endeavor he was joined by Francisco Largo Caballero. The moderate Julián Besteiro now became the key opponent of governmental participation, essentially out of concern over the disillusioning effect of socialist responsibility for policies that might not succeed in pacifying the unruly masses.[8] Besteiro's fears were proven right. Not only did Spanish civil society make a turbulent debut, but a new and unprecedentedly radical faction began to emerge within the PSOE itself. At the same time, their bourgeois allies in the republican camp became equally estranged from this first experiment at ministerial collaboration with the socialist Left. Voices calling for an end to this cooperation grew increasingly vocal in both camps, thus amplifying the atmosphere of polarization threatening the stability of this young republic.

In September 1933 Largo Caballero, who quickly emerged as the leader of the nascent left faction, strongly recommended that all compromises established between [the bourgeois] republicans and ourselves regarding the genesis and support for the revolutionary movement [to institute the second republic] shall be immediately discontinued and that, therefore, each political group and each party shall regain its full independence in order to pursue the path they deem pertinent for the defense of their ideals.

The PSOE executive unanimously endorsed such a course.[9] Eleven days later a front-page editorial in the PSOE house organ *El Socialista* elaborated on the meaning of this move, which was ratified by the PSOE national committee on 19 September: "The decisions reached by the national committee signify, above all, this: they are a call to combat. A demand for energy. For what purpose? Not only for defense, but also, and primarily, for attack. Without delay or hesitation, the forces of our party must strive for the complete possession of [state] power."[10] In a front-page interview of Largo Caballero, carried out by the young Santiago Carrillo, in the following Sunday's edition of *El Socialista*, the popular former minister of labor minced no words: "We are currently in the stage of social revolution. Capitalism has furnished everything it could. It does not have the means to resolve fundamental problems such as unemployment." The battle lines were drawn.[11]

As the PSOE-Left included many leading members of Spanish social democracy, all caught up in the whirlwind of Spanish politics, its gradual consolidation in the course of 1933 automatically translated into a changed outlook for the PSOE as a whole. Yet in order to dominate Spanish socialist politics one more hurdle remained to be overcome. The powerful General Workers' Union (UGT) remained a solid point of support for the conservative faction around Julián Besteiro, Trifón Gómez and Andrés Saborit. In a series of deliberations between members of both leaderships, the Caballerist PSOE majority pushed for the removal of Besteiro and his friends from the UGT leadership. When Prieto put forward a ten-point program to be adopted as a common platform of both the UGT and the PSOE, including such far-reaching measures as the dissolution of the hated *guardia civil*, the PSOE executive judged this to be insufficient and added five points of clarification, the first demand running as follows: "Organization of a candidly revolutionary movement with all possible intensity while utilizing all means at its disposal." A compromise worked out between Prieto and Besteiro proved to be of no avail. The Caballerist faction wanted all or nothing, and at a crucial UGT national committee meeting on 27 January 1934 the old executive found itself in virtually complete isolation. Only two union federations supported Besteiro against thirty-three federations in favor of the PSOE position. Two days later Francisco Largo Caballero became the new UGT general secretary.[12]

Now nothing stood in the way of broadening the influence of "revolutionary social democracy." The PSOE leadership embarked on a campaign for united fronts between all organizations of the Spanish working-class Left, although in a hesitant and uneven manner. The UGT and the PSOE constantly reemphasized the need for revolutionary change. And official proclamations often ended with an open call for the conquest of state power.[13] Soon after the removal of Besteiro, a joint commission of representatives from the PSOE, the UGT and the Socialist Youth (JJSS) was set up with the express purpose of preparing for an imminent uprising. An elaborate network of provincial revolutionary committees, complete with codes and passwords, saw the light of day. Instructions were distributed detailing the tasks of armed detachments with great precision. Some sixty provincial committees furnished the national headquarters in Madrid with all sorts of information describing the local state of readiness.[14] Yet in an ultimately suicidal fashion, the social democratic leadership, while seriously stocking arms and issuing secret orders, refused to take the initiative. It chose to tie the outbreak of their insurrection to a decision by the ruling conservative coalition. The signal for armed action was to be the inclusion of the strongest party of the conservative Right, the Spanish Confederation of Autonomous Rightist Groups (CEDA), considered a pendant to Austrian and German fascism by the PSOE, in the governing coalition.

And even then a serious lack of decisiveness characterized the socialists' response. When Largo Caballero learned of the CEDA's entry into government on the night of 3 October, he refused to believe his informants and insisted on seeing the news confirmed in print, and Largo was not the only one in the PSOE's crisis headquarters to lose his nerve. Passivity, confusion and vacillation predestined the eventual, largely spontaneous, armed rebellion to a quick but bloody defeat. After some early successes, particularly in Asturias, the insurrection stalled. Roughly fifteen thousand fighters participated in the various battles. Between sixteen hundred and two thousand people lost their lives. About ten thousand individuals suffered arrests, thus rendering them easy targets for massive and inhumane torture perpetrated by the victors.[15] Yet the world had witnessed the spectacle of an open insurrection by armed civilians led and inspired by the Spanish social democrats. It was the second social democratic armed rebellion in eight months.

Austro-Marxist (In)Action

The inspiration for the Spanish fighters was the armed revolt by the Austrian social democratic paramilitary formation, the Schutzbund, on 12 February 1934.[16] Like the subsequent rebellion centering on northern Spain, the actual fighting did not last very long—less than a week in Austria (and less than two weeks in Asturias). Yet the simple fact of social democratic–led insurrections caused sympathetic and hostile observers throughout Europe and the world to look at social democracy in a different light.[17] For a fuller understanding of the reach and limitations of "revolutionary social democracy's" theory and practice, it is important to note that both upheavals were intended as defensive insurrections, designed to preserve civil liberties and rights increasingly under attack from the forces of the powerful radical Right, although in Spain this reactive revolt was part and parcel of an openly declared campaign to usher in a "new society." More crucially, in both cases the responsible top-level functionaries did not follow up on their creation of a fighting force with an equally decisive, concrete plan of action enabling their forces to take the offensive and to have a chance at victory. The semispontaneous, wildcat manner of the eventual insurrections thus prevented, from the outset, the development of a momentum necessary for any potential military triumph of these ill-equipped civilian fighting forces facing experienced armies.

The hesitations of the social democratic leadership, clearly recognizable in Largo Caballero's desperate attempt to ignore the obvious on the night the CEDA joined the Spanish government, were equally visible in the Austro-Marxists' reactions to the encroaching powers of the bourgeois Right. A dangerous combination of verbal maximalism with self-limiting strategic conceptions restricting concrete actions to, at best, meaningful reforms characterized the political behavior of the Socialist Party of Austria (SPÖ) throughout the interwar period up to February 1934.[18] Small wonder, then, that when the fighting broke out it was due to the desperate decision on the part of a provincial party executive to take a last stand in the face of certain disaster and to force the hand of the Viennese leadership.[19] The latter's halfhearted support led to the same result as the inaction of the leading lights within the PSOE: it merely prolonged the fighting but did nothing to procure victory. Armed conflict erupted in many industrial districts throughout Austria. But only in the Styrian town of Bruck an der Mur were the insurgents on the offensive and able to register territorial gains. In Vienna itself, Schutzbund activists abandoned all attempts to take control of entire districts after the second day of fighting. The last sporadic outbursts sputtered out one week after the initiation of the battle. A total of from ten thousand to twenty thousand Schutzbund fighters had participated in the skirmishes. Two hundred of them died, and almost ten thousand people were arrested in ensuing days and weeks. A passage of a report on the Austrian events by the International Trade Union Federation, itself not known for its radical leanings, summarizes the policy of vacillation in an eloquent manner:

> Every speech made by Christian-Social [the dominant bourgeois party] democrats, who had long ago lost all influence, was used to raise hopes of finding a way out without a fight. Every lie uttered by Dollfuss to hide his real intentions was the subject of lengthy discussions. Every opportunity was taken to get in touch with any member of the Government, which was assured, in and out of season, of the loyalty and willingness to come to terms of the Socialist Party. The Christian-Socials themselves, who had long ago given up any attempts to fight against the tactics of Dollfuss, saw in this continuous attempt to reach an understanding an indication of the Party's weakness. Every warning to give up this purposeless running about after an understanding and instead to show the teeth of the workers and state frankly that the workers would in all circumstances fight for democracy was disregarded.[20]

It was curious, indeed, that the 12 February 1934 insurrection, unwanted by the SPÖ hierarchy, raised the estimation of Austrian social democracy to untold heights within large segments of the LSI. In Austria itself it brought about fundamental changes precisely within the inner life of the SPÖ.

Ever since "Bloody Friday" on 15 July 1927, when a violent protest against a particularly flagrant miscarriage of justice left eighty-five workers dead and many more wounded, new left-wing oppositional currents reemerged within the SPÖ, which itself was considerably left of center within the LSI. Attempting to combat Austro-Marxist fatalism were such diverse figures as Max Adler, Wilhelm Reich and Ilona Polanyi. Their efforts, by and large carried out without much concern for mutual collaboration, finally found massive resonance in the emergence of a left opposition generated by a crisis of confidence within the Austrian socialist youth movement. In 1932 and 1933 this group around Ernst Fischer crystallized into the first major challenge to the hegemony of Otto Bauer and Karl Renner since the experience of the Kriegslinke (War Left), headed by the young Friedrich Adler, during World War I. Their activist highpoint became the last legal SPÖ party congress in 1933.[21]

Their call for an offensive against the creeping clerico-fascist coup, emphasizing the necessity for combative united front tactics, went unheeded by the party's majority. Many oppositionists now took what they regarded as a logical step and, soon after the February defeat, joined the small Communist Party of Austria (KPÖ), some immediately, others after a brief sojourn in an independent organization, the Rote Front. Within Austrian social democracy, then, the events of February 1934, which outside of Austria renewed interest in social democracy as a radical alternative, led to the exodus of large numbers of its radical Left. Yet despite this departure of many of its most vocal dissidents, the lessons of February brought about a powerful shift to the left within the restructured social democratic underground. Their radicalization, despite the departure of Fischer and his friends, is an impressive example of the profound changes affecting (Austrian) social democracy at this time.[22]

Key elements of the politics of the new socialist underground became the open embrace of united fronts and a radical critique of Austrian social democratic strategy and tactics in the past. Two Dutch investigators reported the widespread opinion that "the former leaders, even [Julius] Deutsch [the nominal head of the Schutzbund] and, to a lesser degree, also Bauer, are worn out, and that they can no longer claim the right to consider themselves the leaders of the socialist movement in Austria, because they have failed in every respect."[23] In a meeting between Otto Bauer and leading functionaries in Western Austria, a region previously not known for its oppositional leanings, the delegates even insisted on the removal of any reference to "social democracy" from the subtitle of the new Arbeiter-Zeitung (AZ), and Bauer sensed a silent boycott of the AZ, edited by the exiled party leaders in Czechoslovakia, on the part of the underground leadership, which renamed their organization Revolutionäre Sozialisten Österreichs (Revolutionary Socialists of Austria) (RSÖ) and published their own paper, Die Revolution (The Revolution).[24] While an uneasy truce between the illegal underground and the exiled Socialist Party (ALÖS) in Brünn was barely maintained by the moral authority of Otto Bauer in subsequent years, even the content of the comparatively moderate AZ reflected the momentum to the left. As was the case concurrently in Spain, an entire social democratic party underwent a process of profound, far-reaching realignment.

There was, however, one significant distinction between the outlook of the Spanish social democrats and their Austrian homologues at the point of armed rebellion. Whereas the Spanish socialists openly proclaimed the need for the immediate supersession of capitalist society one year prior to their armed rebellion, prior to February 1934 the Austro-Marxist strategists insisted on the utopian character of ushering in a socialist society then and there. In his last major pre-February programmatic statement in the theoretical journal of Austrian social democracy Der Kampf, symptomatically entitled "On Democracy," Otto Bauer deemed it ludicrous that "a proletarian dictatorship" could survive "even for as little as a fortnight wedged between fascist Germany, reactionary Hungary, absolutist Yugoslavia and fascist Italy." He continued: "No, the decision will be made today not between democracy and the dictatorship of the proletariat, but between democracy and the dictatorship of fascism." "The next goal of our struggle is the reconstruction of democracy. At this point in time all our efforts are concentrated on this aim."[25] This cautious assessment of the geopolitical situation, a mainstay of Bauer's analytical flourish already brilliantly displayed in his defense of Austro-Marxist passivity and self-limitation during the Austrian revolution in the aftermath of World War I, provided the framework for inaction in the months before February 1934.

Austro-Marxist attitudes toward social revolution changed only *after* their defeat. In the fourth issue of the new *AZ*, the same Otto Bauer suddenly discovered the utility of "the weapons of *revolution*." He underscored the necessity for a "*revolutionary dictatorship* of the working class," whose immediate tasks would have to be the expropriation of "landed proprietors, capitalists and the church. . . . Not the restoration of yesterday's bourgeois democracy [but] a true and genuine democracy, [a] socialist democracy is our goal."[26] The underground leadership of the RSÖ, in a memorandum to the LSI, likewise expressed the new strategic turn in novel language: "The Fascist dictatorship in Austria has dispelled all *democratic and reformist illusions*," and the new consensus is the imperative necessity of revolution. "The aim of this revolution, however, can only be the *conquest of the power of the State, the dictatorship of the proletariat*, which must destroy the political and economic foundation of capitalist society in order to realize a classless society, a Social Democracy."[27] Austrian social democrats ultimately arrived at the same conclusion as their Spanish comrades-in-arms. Both eventually proclaimed their goal to be the conquest of state power and the ushering in of a new society in the here and now. Only, in the case of the Austrian socialists, the latter had to undergo a disabling defeat in order to adopt such revolutionary positions.

The contradictory nature of "revolutionary social democracy" in Austria and Spain became increasingly evident. Even in its most militant phase, an ingrained tendency toward vacillation inhibited the full deployment of "revolutionary social democracy's" ideological, political and military apparatuses in the service of its strategic goals: socialist revolution in Spain and the retention of democracy in pre-1934 Austria. Nevertheless, both the PSOE and the SPÖ underwent qualitative political changes in the process of struggle. In Spain the massive shift to the left affected significant portions of the leadership as well as the ranks. In Austria, important numbers of activists radicalized at a quicker pace than most of the leadership team, thus opening up a potentially dangerous ideological rift. However, the call for the removal of traditional party leaders, a commonplace in documents from Austria after February 1934, was first articulated in an uncompromising manner within the German SPD.

Discontent Within the SPD

One of the most respected representatives of the SPD, Rudolf Breitscheid, informed a colleague in the party executive about the mood among his comrades-in-exile in June 1933: "Those people say that no improvement can be expected from those who have led the party up to now. Of course, no one knows how things should have been done and what should happen now. But this mood is a definite reality. I believe that it will only be overcome if Prague [the seat of the SPD in exile up to 1938] begins to work assiduously and aggressively."[28] In early 1934 Breitscheid, who in this phase of his political development still openly supported the course of the SPD executive, assessed the situation in even more pessimistic terms. In a letter to Karl Kautsky he emphasized "that, in general, the people in Prague find no noteworthy resonance whatsoever, either within the socialist emigration, or amongst those who are still in Germany."[29] He reaffirmed this negative assessment of the SPD leadership's policies in April 1935: "There are undoubtedly still numerous individuals within and outside of Germany who identify with the ideas of social democracy, but their opinions on politics and the necessary tactics differ strongly, and I am personally convinced that only a minority is willing to follow Prague."[30] Rudolf Breitscheid was only one of many participant observers to perceive the noticeable disaffection among the party's cadres and the ranks.

The most convincing evidence for the widespread disaffection with the SPD executive-in-exile is provided by the detailed reports by the border secretaries, the individuals responsible for contact with the underground, sent to the Prague headquarters beginning in the latter half of 1933. In their reports, and in other communications to the Prague executive, they frequently furnished detailed insights into the state of mind of party activists in the German underground.[31] In a letter transmitted to the executive by Georg Reinbold, responsible for communications with southwest Germany, a female activist from Unterbaden wrote in September 1933:

> The exiled comrades have to be clear about one thing. In Germany, no Marxist, whether communist or social democrat, deems the question "democracy or dictatorship" worthy of discussion. Here only one opinion prevails. Force can only be broken by force. And to topple the current regime in order to reinstate the democratic state of the past, for this absolutely no one can be found in Germany who would be willing to lift one finger.[32]

One month earlier the SPD functionary Gustav Ferl relayed a reliable report from Magdeburg. The informant noted the extreme reluctance of party activists in this industrial city to work on behalf of the old leadership. "But the very instance that they would be given a new, young leadership, they would be willing, with all the energy at their disposal, to tackle this new task, be it extremely dangerous."[33] Alfred Käseberg, the newly appointed border secretary for parts of western Saxony, in January 1935 summarized the initial response by the activists in his territory during most of 1933 in the following, comprehensive manner:

> The mood of the comrades oscillated like a continuously swaying shock of waves. Fear and hopelessness, annoyance and exasperation over the passive capitulation, complaints about the fact that the party executive went into exile, then a creeping understanding that this was necessary in order to even begin the task of organizing against Hitler, demands for a full accounting, calls for a new leadership, proclamation of a new party as the melting pot for all forces combating Hitler's dictatorship; these were the main points on the basis of which we endeavored to find a path enabling the party to regain its ideological authority.[34]

Hans Dill, responsible for northern Bavaria, reflected on a conversation with two SPD activists from Augsburg in May 1934 that the popular mood had turned against the values of democracy: "People just don't want to hear anything else about the old Weimar Republic. They cannot even tolerate the name 'social democracy.' They laugh at it."[35] The party journalist Franz Osterroth reported after a three-week journey through Germany in the fall of 1934 that opinions regarding the SPD leadership "fluctuate between firm rejection and partial recognition of certain accomplish-

ments," hardly a vote of confidence.[36] And Ernst Schumacher, the responsible official for northwest Germany, noted growing support for an "ideology in favor of a socialist Germany through revolutionary struggle."[37]

Such appeared to be the dominant mood among SPD underground activists that
the aforementioned Hans Dill, whose own informants appeared to be considerably
more loyal, felt compelled to state in August 1934:

> When I hear from other sources that, in their regions, comrades are continuously
> worrying whether we will soon obtain the appropriate leadership for the party, the
> correct program, a new name, that the material emanating from the Sopade is good
> for nothing, etc., and I compare this, then, to what my contacts tell me when I
> meet them; then I would have to say that, if the former are the incorporation of
> activity, the carriers of revolutionary vitality, for some reason I happen to deal with
> nothing but senile dolts, who are good for nothing.[38]

Undoubtedly, Hans Dill's party comrades in northern Bavaria were not the only open
or tacit supporters of the official party line. Starting in 1935, in particular, the border
secretaries' reports give increasing evidence for a moderation of attitudes toward the
leadership in Prague. At the end of 1934 and the start of 1935 a discussion with fifteen SPD members in eastern Saxony led Wilhelm Sander to remark: "The feeling
of hatred toward the emigrants and the party hierarchy gives way to a calm, objective
assessment of the conjuncture."[39] Yet a thorough reading of the numerous documents
now in the SPD party archive suggests that at least in 1933 and 1934 the ideological
hegemony of the party executive must be seriously questioned.

What is particularly significant about the preceding citations is the fact that they
all emanate from party officials faithful to the Prague executive, and the list could
have been extended at will. Naturally, it would have been even easier to cull the
requisite quotations from the communications of left-wing dissident border secretaries, such as Willi Lange, Waldemar von Knoeringen or others. But, as the support
for the various factions within German social democracy in the early years of the
Third Reich remains a hotly contested issue, I deemed it more persuasive to rely on
confidential reports in which the bias is, if anything, to the right.[40] In the end, the
SPD executive's hold on the party, unlike the Austrians' case, was never seriously
questioned. Only a party conference, continuously requested by the oppositionists,[41]
could have contributed to a clarification of the relationship of forces within the SPD.
Such a gathering, for many reasons, never took place.[42]

France and Belgium

A significant shift to the left occurred, therefore, in at least three important sections
of the LSI. In the remaining two countries under scrutiny, France and Belgium, the
gains of the respective parties' Left are less readily apparent. Neither in the SFIO
nor in the Belgian Workers' Party (POB/BWP) did an established left faction gain
the upper hand or seriously endanger a more conservative leadership's control. Yet
in both cases the parties as a whole underwent important transformations that significantly changed their policies in very few months. In that sense, their experience
conforms to the evolution of Spanish social democracy, where almost the entire party
supported Largo Caballero's insurrectionary course. Yet in Belgium and France the

changes never went quite as far. Whereas within the PSOE in 1933–34 there was no room for a left opposition to the leadership, as the executive itself was in the hands of the Left, the leadership teams in Belgium and France continued to face well-organized oppositions, which never gained the upper hand but nevertheless profoundly affected the outlook of their parties as a whole.

In France the opposition grouped around Bataille Socialiste managed to push the SFIO onto a course of firm adherence to a policy of united fronts but failed to effect the SFIO's wholesale adoption of a radical programmatic platform.[43] In Belgium, the left-wing tendency around Action Socialiste witnessed a similar qualified success.[44] As was the case in Spain, Austria and Germany, however, the axis of French and Belgian social democratic politics definitely shifted to the left. In the following three chapters I will demonstrate that the new policy paradigm for the radicalized sections of continental European social democracy was initially the strategy of working-class united fronts. Then, after the dual defeats of social democratic–led insurrections in Austria and Asturias, Continental social democracy moderated its approach and staked its future on an equally novel strategy: popular fronts. But before submitting the theory and practice of united and popular fronts to closer scrutiny, it is incumbent to cast a brief glance at the changing outlook of the Comintern.

United and Popular Fronts in the Practice of the Comintern

Contemporaneous with social democracy's adoption of united and, later, popular fronts, the European sections of the Comintern carried out a similar succession of rapid and far-reaching changes. And it was in large measure the temporal coincidence of communist and social democratic moves toward united and, ultimately, popular fronts which impressed upon all participant observers the sudden and momentous changes in left-wing practice, thus helping to instill confidence in the projects of this seemingly revitalized Left. In this discussion of communist politics in 1934–35, I will focus my attention on the key distinction between united and popular front politics in the theory and practice of the Comintern, as it is the distinction between these two strategies which has been most sorely neglected in the relative abundance of secondary literature on communism in the thirties.

Prior to May–June 1934, the Comintern had pursued an extremely sectarian approach toward other workers' parties, generally declaring its major competitor, social democracy, to be merely one variant of fascism, "social fascism." Communist parties adopted the most strident language in their history; participation in electoral campaigns became a mere sideshow to the extraparliamentary endeavors of party activists and sympathizers; and their trade union members were advised to construct independent, "red" trade unions in open competition to the generally social democratic–led traditional union structures.[45] This communist disdain of cooperation with other forces on the working-class Left was, in a sense, the flip side of the coin of social democratic disinterest in common ventures with parties to its left.

Few historians dispute the sudden willingness of communist negotiators to enter into binding agreements with other parties of the Left, starting in the late spring of 1934. Yet what is particularly striking, given the wealth of new historiographical departures in the study of the communist movement, is the almost universal tendency, present in both national studies and works on the International, to conflate the ensuing united front and popular front strategies into one overarching category, seeing them as variations of a single theme rather than two distinct pathways for social change. As these two alliance strategies constitute the substance of the much-acclaimed Comintern turn in the midthirties, this is wholly surprising and remains to be explained.[46]

The late spring of 1934 is generally regarded as the decisive turning point in the Comintern's sudden move away from open hostility toward other parties on the Left. By contrast, the very first hesitant gropings toward the language of popular fronts did not manifest themselves even in France until well into the fall of that year. Therefore, little controversy exists about the empirical presence of an intermediary phase between the practice of fratricide and the advocacy of disunity on the Left up to May 1934 and the eventual hegemony of popular front discourse at some later date. Yet the nature of this intermediary period has been curiously neglected. Whether they consciously ignore or subconsciously avoid them, historians of communism generally treat these months as a transitional period bereft of deeper meaning, a time span in which communist tacticians, after having finally overcome "Third Period" sectarianism, slowly developed the gradually emerging strategy of popular fronts.[47]

It is my contention that this "intermediary" period, which in my opinion comprises exactly one year, May 1934 to May 1935, needs to be theorized as a distinct period in its own right when communist parties were committed to a strategy of working-class-based united fronts. Starting in the fall of 1934, communist advocates of such united fronts did show a heightened interest in broadening such alliances to include nonproletarian strata around the working-class nucleus. Yet prior to May 1935, this desire to appeal to broader groups of people did not entail major concessions in the programmatic content of these projected alliances or the propaganda of communist parties themselves. The centerpieces of those alliances remained the proletariat per se, and the hopes for attracting other strata were built on the firm belief that a socialist solution to the crisis would likewise be the lowest common denominator for the nonproletarian allies in distress.

The communist language used in this crucial year continued to be a language of united fronts. Inasmuch as communists began to show a keen awareness of the need to include petit-bourgeois strata in their common fight, it may be appropriate to label the second half of this era of united fronts the moment of popular fronts "from below," as their efforts to gain allies outside of the working class as such were *not* geared to include the leadership of petit-bourgeois or bourgeois *organizations* at this time. Only with the open acknowledgment of the need to cooperate officially with petit-bourgeois and bourgeois *parties*, necessitating programmatic changes in the alliances to be built, can the period of genuine popular fronts, popular fronts "from above," be said to have begun. This occurred, for the communist movement, in May 1935. From then onward, communist parties suddenly dropped their revolutionary idiom. Military defense of bourgeois democracies became the watchword of the day. The language of colonial liberation was altered overnight. And a socialist transformation now became no more than a remote long-term possibility.

In sum, rather than intermingling the strategies of united and popular fronts as two constituent parts of an integrated whole, I suggest that these two policy proposals were analytically distinct, emerged at different times and carried substantially different messages. Though they were frequently used in combination, particularly after May 1935, one can clearly distill a temporal distinction between an earlier time span when united front efforts were dominant in communist discourse and a subsequent era when the concerns of popular fronts outweighed considerations of united fronts, which antedated the former. In the following pages I intend to substantiate my thesis, which I propose to defend with the key examples of Spain and France, the two countries where popular front rhetoric ultimately found fertile democratic ground.

The PCF in October 1934

Much of the debate regarding the origins of the French popular front turns on the intricacies of alliance politics in the October 1934 French cantonal elections. In order to support my claim that popular front politics did not become the guiding orientation of French Communist Party (PCF) politics until May–June 1935, it is therefore crucial to submit the events of October 1934 in France to closer scrutiny. In mid-August 1934 Jacques Duclos, a top-level functionary in both the Comintern and the PCF, publicly expressed the opinion in the PCF's monthly journal *Cahiers du Bolshévisme* that it would be possible to support a Radical Party candidate in the upcoming cantonal elections "if a Radical candidate makes a declaration against the government of national unity, against the [repressive] decree-laws, [and] against the fascist groups."[48] Since the "government of national unity" was partially composed of Radical Party luminaries, Duclos's appeal was clearly an attempt to drive a wedge between those Radical Party members critical of their leadership and the party as a whole. It was not an offer of a firm electoral alliance. The proposal was restated in the communists' electoral manifesto of 19 August, and the social democrats followed suit. But the elections of 7 October and 14 October 1934 showed the limited impact of the communists' overture. In the words of the most careful analyst of PCF policy in these months, Daniel Brower: "Not surprisingly, cases of Communist and Socialist support for a Radical candidate were extremely rare."[49] It was a far cry from the open alliance between the respective party leaderships that emerged after May 1935.

On 10 October 1934 Maurice Thorez delivered a speech in Paris in the Salle Bullier which, according to E. H. Carr, was an open "plea for an electoral alliance not only with the SFIO, but with the bourgeois Radical-Socialists." At the occasion of the Radical Party congress in Nantes on 24 October 1934, Thorez repeated his "appeal for an alliance with the Radical-Socialists in a broad anti-fascist popular front," according to Carr, who claims that now the PCF "was openly seeking alliances outside the traditional workers' parties of the Left."[50] If this were true, the PCF maneuver in the fall of 1934 would have been the first instance of a national communist party applying a genuine popular front strategy. It would reinforce the claims of many French communist personalities involved in the elaboration of communist policy that autumn, who insist that the French went forward with their bold alliance policy against the advice of the Comintern leadership.[51] Yet, as Daniel Brower asserts in a close textual analysis of Thorez's speeches between 10 and 24 October 1934: "The popular front was not at that time looked upon as a political alliance which might include the Radical party. Rather, it was intended as a mass movement which would appeal to the liberal politicians and masses." "The new campaign was in general aimed at that floating mass of petty bourgeois which might be influenced by the fascist movements."[52] In short, it was another example of the advocacy of a popular front "from below" in the general context of united front politics.

Another observer of the PCF's evolution during October 1934, Jacques Kergoat, likewise concludes that "the initial objective of the communist party leadership was not the inclusion of the entire Radical party in the popular front, but the hope to bring about a split-off to the left"; yet for Kergoat a qualitative change occurred at a PCF central committee meeting on 1–2 November 1934, where, according to the French Trotskyist historian, "the PCF decided to accept the Radical party program as the lowest common denominator for the fight in defense of 'work, liberty and peace.'"[53] Jacques Duclos concurs in the ascription of the origin of the French popular front to the report by Maurice Thorez at the very same PCF central committee meeting: "The task was [now] to enlarge the already established union between the Communist Party and the Socialist Party, both claiming to represent the working class, in order to extend it to the peasantry and the urban middle classes, of which the Radical Party was, at that time, particularly representative."[54] Yet a close reading of Thorez's report, "The Communists and the Popular Front," casts doubts over the assertion by Kergoat and Duclos that this document constitutes the inauguration of the popular front from above as a mainstay in the propagandistic arsenal of the PCF. Certainly, Thorez quotes approvingly large segments of a recent Radical Party declaration and affirms that these sections "correspond in general to the desire of the French people."[55] "We are adherents of this popular front, which cannot and must not be the same as the entire program of the Communist Party,"[56] thus advertising the willingness of the PCF to enter programmatic compromises in the quest for more moderate allies. But at the same time Thorez underscored that "we are not in the business of establishing a parliamentary program. We want to engender a mobilization which will result in extraparliamentary mass action which, perhaps, may bring about positive results on the parliamentary level."[57] At no point does he call for a top-level alliance between the Radical Party and the working-class Left. On balance, then, even Thorez's central committee report cannot be considered incontrovertible evidence in favor of a French initiative toward a popular front. The stress continued to be placed on extraparliamentary action by the ranks. It was similar to the substance of his 24 October speech in Nantes, where, in the words of Brower, the only concrete proposal for the organization of the desired popular front "was the formation of 'committees elected by all the workers' in the towns and villages" of France,[58] a theme repeated two months later when Thorez emphasized that the offer of collaboration with the middle classes went no further than certain local sections of the Radical Party.[59]

Nevertheless, PCF policy was in a state of flux. The willingness to go the extra mile in accommodating supporters of the Radical Party, and Thorez's 24 October visit to Nantes, where the Radical Party congress was about to begin, show the extent to which the French communists were prepared to compromise in order to enlarge upon the already concluded united front with the SFIO (see later discussion). Also in October 1934, two secret meetings between key officials of the PCF and the Radical Party occurred, which further indicate the direction of intended actions at that time.[60] Yet to interpret this as a unilateral decision by the PCF leadership is hardly credible, as the discussion of open calls for popular fronts "from above" by some Comintern officials as early as August 1934 suggests that such proposals were already debated in leading Comintern circles long before Thorez's overtures toward the Radical Party in October.[61]

The Language of the PCF

One key criterion for the establishment of genuine popular fronts was the extension of common efforts by bourgeois and working-class parties beyond the extraparliamentary terrain culminating in the conclusion of electoral agreements. The first elections after October 1934 were the municipal elections of 5 May and 12 May 1935. In the PCF's daily *L'Humanité*, on 13 February 1935, Maurice Thorez addressed the communists' attitude toward the upcoming elections. At no point did Thorez refer even to the possibility of an alliance with the Radicals, and he directed all his attention to perceived inconsistencies in the social democrats' approach.[62] This stance remained unaltered in the following months.

Between the two ballots, the PCF and the SFIO reached a common agreement to desist in favor of the stronger candidate in the second round, a tactic extended to those "candidates who are partisans of liberty and who are leading against the reaction."[63] This permitted PCF support for select Radical candidates, most notably the victory of the "first elected official of the Popular Front," Paul Rivet, as municipal councillor in Paris.[64] Yet it was a far cry from an open, firm alliance. In Thorez's analysis of the municipal elections, given in a speech on 17 May 1935, he still virtually ignored incidents of tripartite collusion and proudly proclaimed that "we have brought the petty bourgeoisie closer to the working class, which is essential from the point of view of the perspective to combat fascism and to bring about the proletarian revolution."[65] Thus, until mid-May 1935, the PCF, the supposed vanguard in the effort to create popular fronts, was still politically and ideologically unprepared to accept such a turn. According to Albert Vassart, a high official in the Comintern and the PCF, in the early part of 1935 both organizations were actually prepared to accept a breakup of the unity pact with the SFIO. Daniel P. Brower suggests that "Vassart even wrote a pamphlet for use by the French party in which blame for the failures of the pact was placed squarely on the Socialist party."[66] Any interpretation of PCF and Comintern policy as a linear evolution from united to popular fronts should therefore be subject to serious questioning.

Thus far I have consciously avoided references to the most persuasive study of the PCF turns, a recently published lexicometric study of the public discourse of the PCF, Denis Peschanski's *Et pourtant ils tournent* (Indeed, they are turning), subtitled "Vocabulary and Strategy of the PCF (1934–1936)." Placing himself in the tradition of Régine Robin and other proponents of close textual analysis, Peschanski undertook the task of assembling lexicological data emanating from the main front-page editorial of *L'Humanité* in the years under consideration.[67] His findings complement and reinforce the substance of my thesis.

Already in 1968 Annie Kriegel had presented an innovative paper to the Colloquium of the Center for Political Lexicology, in which she analyzed the changing public language of Maurice Thorez during the year 1934. On the basis of this study she concluded that the decisive turn from a politics of united fronts "from below" to that of a united front "from above," as reflected in the discourse of the PCF general secretary, occurred between 27 and 30 May 1934.[68] Between February and late March 1934, Thorez's vocabulary was unmistakably colored by "Third Period" concerns. The desired united fronts were strictly alliances to be built from below. "United fronts are associated with *communism, proletarian revolution*":[69] the language was maximalist; and the openly stated antonym of the wished-for united front was the united front "from above," the dreaded "bloc with social democracy," otherwise referred to as "the counterrevolutionary united front."[70] After a transition period, dating from 27 to 30 May 1934, characterized by confusion and mixed signals, the subsequent language of Maurice Thorez, particularly after 15 June 1934, showed the united front always as a united front "from above." It was far less frequently used as an undifferentiated slogan, and Kriegel concludes:

> Thus it appears to be verified that the study of vocabulary, at least if one is dealing with an institution as scrupulously attentive to language as the communist movement, is one of the techniques that may be substituted, in the absence of other more definitive archival sources, permitting the reconstitution of the chronological process during which, in a hesitant and step-by-step manner, a political discourse takes on shape.[71]

Following Kriegel's first effort at a lexicological analysis of French communist discourse, Peschanski significantly expanded the database and came up with a number of important conclusions regarding the transition from united to popular fronts. He reports a significant, qualitative break in *L'Humanité*'s political vocabulary precisely in the late spring of 1935. Prior to this date, "a vocabulary of class is ever-present," with frequent references to words such as "bourgeois," "proletarian," "workers," "peasants" or "capitalists." Peschanski likewise notes the preponderance of a "vocabulary of combat, with words such as 'revolutionaries,' 'to struggle,' 'revolutionary,' 'outrage' and 'struggle.' The strategy of the Communist Party can be subsumed under the slogan of *united* front [*de front* unique et *de front* uni]."[72] On the other hand, in the subsequent period the class vocabulary is abandoned and "the communist discourse refers to 'the people'" and to other nonclass categories such as "France."[73] "The people" (*peuple*), without any further qualifier, appears sixty-four times in his sample, "but never before June 1935."[74] Peschanski notes that "from now on the dominant strategy is that of a 'popular front' for 'bread,' 'peace' and 'freedom.' Finally, one is struck by the importance of a diplomatic and institutional vocabulary, of articles devoted to the 'Senate' or the 'House of Representatives,'" or similar novel topics. Peschanski exclaims: "What a contrast with the vocabulary of 1934!"[75]

In a series of in-depth studies of major shifts in nuances, Peschanski shows, for instance, the sudden switch from a predominantly offensive use of the word "against" (*contre*) to a primarily defensive application of the identical term.[76] Prior to May–June 1935, *L'Humanité* editorialists appealed for "freedom of the press" (*liberté de la presse*), "the right to demonstrate" (*liberté de la rue*), "the right to assemble" (*liberté de réunion*) and "free speech" (*liberté d'opinion*). After May–June 1935 the word *liberté* is used almost exclusively without a specific referent, in a far more abstract fashion.[77] Whereas the turn toward abstraction in this case denotes a less militant, less demanding posture, quite the reverse is true, for instance, in the more personalized, less hostile manner of referring to Léon Blum, the head of the SFIO, in the later period. Whereas prior to August 1935 twenty-six of thirty-one references do not include his first name, forty-three of forty-nine mentions after that date do so.[78]

Finally, Peschanski studied the frequency of references to key concepts such as "united front" or "popular front." *Front uni* and *front unique* appear on numerous occasions until April 1935, after which they rapidly vanish from sight. By contrast, the term *front populaire* appears first in October 1934, but it is not until May–June 1935 that it makes a massive entry into the pages of the communist daily's editorials.[79] Peschanski concludes: "The class vocabulary so characteristic of the period January 1934 – May 1935 contrasts with a necessarily less rich 'popular vocabulary' [*vocabulaire-peuple*] in the year that follows, for, from that time onward, all nonexploiting social strata and classes are assembled in the concept of 'people,' the eradicator of internal contradictions."[80] Thus, his methodologically challenging study underscores the pivotal break of May–June 1935 in the elaboration of a strategy and corresponding language qualitatively distinct from the preceding period of united fronts.

It is ironic that Peschanski himself suggests that the decisive PCF strategic turn occurred one year prior to the linguistic turn: "Is it not that the major discursive turn of May–June 1935 came about with a one-year delay compared to the strategic turn?"[81] In his conclusion Peschanski responds in the affirmative.[82] His assertion of a one-year time lag between strategic and discursive turns is particularly inappropriate in the case of a subject "as scrupulously attentive to language as the communist movement," in the words of Annie Kriegel.[83] His documentary evidence is far more in tune with my own assertion of the qualitative leap toward popular fronts occurring in May–June 1935. Peschanski's misinterpretation of his data could have been easily avoided had he rejected the notion of *one* strategic Comintern turn and instead accepted the framework of *two* strategic changes: from united fronts "from below" to united front "from above" in May–June 1934 and from united front to popular front in May–June 1935. Peschanski's evidence, combined with Kriegel's analysis of Thorez's language in 1934, suggests the enhanced explanatory power of my own periodization.

Spanish Communism in Transition

The only other European country where political conditions were favorable to the constitution of popular fronts was Spain, and the Communist Party of Spain (PCE) underwent a policy evolution similar to that of its ally to the north. As was the case in France, the Spanish section of the Comintern underwent two turns, one from the policy of sectarian infighting to the advocacy of united fronts (June–July 1934) and another toward the advocacy of popular fronts (May 1935). Paralleling the PCF's course, starting in October 1934 the first feelers toward popular fronts can be detected without great difficulty, but again, as was the case with the PCF prior to May 1935, this broadening of the proposed alliances must be seen as falling within the category of popular fronts "from below," an only slightly modified version of united front politics. As there is relatively little controversy about the abandonment of PCE

"Third Period" politics, I will focus on the latter half of the united front period in order to substantiate my claim that in Spain, as well as in France, motions toward popular fronts prior to May 1935 were merely elaborations of united fronts and that a qualitative shift occurred in precisely the same month as in France.

Differing opinions exist regarding the onset of PCE agitation for popular fronts "from above." Less open to question is the actual dating of the first appearance of popular front rhetoric in PCE documents. Bernhard Bayerlein refers to "the end of October and beginning of November" 1934 as the first moments when the PCE advocated a broad "antifascist bloc."[84] Rafael Cruz dates it more specifically to a PCE circular of 27 October 1934.[85] The timing of the introduction of this new concept is significant in itself, as it further weakens the credibility of claims for French originality in Thorez's initiatives during October 1934. In subsequent months such calls for the constitution of "antifascist blocs" or "popular antifascist concentrations" multiplied. In Spain, first traces of a new vocabulary, analyzed so well by Peschanski for the PCF, also saw the light of day in the six months prior to the second turn.

Already in the October circular which initiated this trend, the central committee's secretariat called on party members to join forces with "socialists, anarchists, republicans, nationalists; everyone in one bloc facing the fascist bloc of the various monarcho-fascist parties of the bourgeoisie."[86] But the well-defined limits of such "popular fronts" were equally apparent from the very inception of this tactical turn. To cite the October circular once more, the most concrete description of the nature of this "antifascist bloc" clearly paralleled the PCF's call for the select inclusion of appropriate allies: "Each party committee should now consider the realization of a broader united front for the struggle against fascism, the task of creating a network of Antifascist Committees, composed of all those elements *who sincerely wish to struggle against fascism* and of all elements opposing the current counterrevolutionary government."[87] This passage likewise suggests that such fronts were not meant to become associations incorporating the leadership of nonproletarian parties, a commonplace of genuine popular fronts. Prior to May 1935, the Left Republicans, Spanish equivalents of the French Radicals, were frequently denounced as disseminators of bourgeois democratic illusions within the laboring population, and calls for united action frequently demanded an end to repression and the respect for civil liberties and rights side by side with a workers' and peasants' government and a Soviet Spain.[88] According to Cruz, "The theoretical consistency of the new proposal was very thin, contradictory and ambiguous."[89] Or, in the words of Manuel Tuñon de Lara: "They continued to consider 'broad unity' as a sort of trap in order to win circumstantial allies to the strategic goals of the party and the working class. . . ."[90]

Whether "trap" or conscious strategy, a purposeful move or a hesitant shift, prior to May 1935 the PCE remained committed to a strategy emphasizing alliances of the proletarian Left with overtures toward other political organizations limited to offers tendered to their ranks.[91] This is further underscored in its attitude toward potential electoral coalitions. In the late winter of 1934–35 rumors thickened regarding the possibility of upcoming municipal elections, the first chance for a public expression of sentiments at the ballot box after the Asturian revolt. These elections never materialized, but the flurry of activities emanating from the PCE confirms its lack of interest in top-level alliances with the bourgeois Left. In a letter from the central committee to its party locals written on 3 March 1935, the PCE referred to a recent platform proposal "which we have presented to the PSOE executive committee and the Workers' and Peasants' Alliance [united front bodies, about which more in chapter 4], in hopes of common electoral action." The PCE leadership continued:

> At the same time we must direct an appeal to all anarchist and republican workers, calling on them to join the united front for the elections. We must aim this appeal at the workers composing the aforementioned groups but not at those parties and groups as such. In those provinces and localities where the Left Republican parties have support amongst the workers and where the situation may arise that it becomes necessary to address those parties *locally*, in this case, before doing so, the [Communist] Party organization must consult the central committee, sending us detailed reports regarding the forces which the respective Republican parties represent amongst the workers of that locality and the opinion of the Party as to the necessity, or lack thereof, to directly consult with the involved [Republican] parties on the issue of common action for the election. *Under no circumstances shall any [Communist] Party organization approach the [Republican] party without prior consultation with the central committee.*[92]

Tuñon de Lara refers to PCE statements with identical content dated 13 March 1935 and 26 April 1935.[93] And in April 1935 the PCE still roundly denounced the PSOE for its "orientation toward collaboration with bourgeois parties, which entails the renunciation of independent, proletarian class politics, while resisting the constitution of a united front of all workers," a declaration its authors ended by stating: "*Only the workers' and peasants' revolution, only the power of soviets, can put an end, and will put an end, to the current regime of misery, slavery and hunger.*"[94] In conjunction with the other information furnished previously, this strongly suggests a close parallel with similar policies pursued by the PCF between October 1934 and May 1935: a strategic orientation toward united fronts supplemented by the tactic of popular fronts "from below."[95]

By mid-May 1935, PCE policy makers initiated a more substantive strategic shift. An internal bulletin, dated 10 May 1935, addresses PCE tactics at potentially imminent elections in telegram style:

> In general to consider the Workers' and Peasants' Alliances as a broad antifascist front. If the Left Republican parties accept our militant election platform, then to establish common lists with them. If the Left Republican parties only accept part of our antifascist platform, but are favorable toward the creation of common lists with us in order to avoid the triumph of the fascist candidates, we must accept that. In Asturias, where the consciousness of the masses is the most mature, we shall only utilize the [exclusively proletarian] Workers' and Peasants' Alliances. In Catalonia, we can extend the united front much further: [Workers' and Peasants'] Alliances, Esquerra, Estat Catalá, Rabassaires, and other nationalist groups.[96]

This "orientation bulletin" is a rare example of confusion tearing at the edges of a seemingly monolithic party. The stress is placed on the proletarian alliance, but common lists with Republican parties are accepted if they make concessions to the communist agenda. In Asturias no such compromises are permitted; in Catalonia, on the other hand, the communists have free rein to include virtually all major liberal nonproletarian parties, for the Esquerra was the most important Catalan equivalent to the Left Republican parties elsewhere in the Spanish state.[97] The guidance document is a rare snapshot of a communist party in motion. Ten days later, on 20 May 1935, the first top-level agreement between the PCE and some Republican *parties* was signed and sealed.[98]

Conclusion

In different ways and in varying degrees Austrian, Belgian, French, German and Spanish social democrats all took part in the general leftward drift of working-class depression politics in these states. The relevance of their verbal committments, the degree to which these parties were prepared to act the way they spoke, may be subject to questioning. Such queries into the seriousness of the social democratic shift may be resolved only through a close-range investigation of the psychology of key individual actors and the participation by the ranks. For the purposes of this study, it may suffice to highlight the *public* shift to the left. As can be gauged from my later discussion of the interactions between leadership and ranks (see chapter 8), it was this openly expressed radicalization — whether a reflection of genuine subjective changes, conscious ploys or a combination of the two — which galvanized the membership and the countries at large. It is therefore only appropriate to do as most contemporaries did and to take social democracy's left turn at face value. The limitations of its switch have been delineated in the preceding pages.

Toward the end of the forty months under consideration, most parties moderated their demands, a point stressed in subsequent chapters, particularly chapter 6. The disintegration of the Belgian Action Socialiste and the French Bataille Socialiste currents, the expulsion of the most vocal opposition from the SPD, the March 1935 decision by the Belgian social democrat Hendrik de Man to participate in a cabinet headed by a Christian Democratic banker, and the eventual waning of the fortunes of Largo Caballero's team were all to be manifestations of this trend. But for several crucial years, important national sections of European social democracy showed characteristics which were radically different from previous and subsequent social democratic politics as usual. The radicalization of social democracy thus highlights the exceptional nature of these years, lived in the shadow of fascism, a growing threat of war and a faltering world economy.

Official communist strategy changed even more dramatically than the public language of the LSI, for the LSI as a whole never ratified the moves toward united and popular fronts. By contrast, Comintern twists and turns were usually carried out in an internationally coordinated fashion. Thus, once the Comintern hierarchy gave the go-ahead for the strategy of united fronts, all sections were bound to concur, though some, notably the German party, did so in an extremely dilatory fashion. The historiography of international communism depicts the evolution of Comintern strategic thinking in the 1930s in a uniform manner: "Third Period" communism, dominant up to 1934, was gradually superseded, in the course of 1934–35, by the politics of popular fronts. On the basis of a close textual analysis of Comintern debates, I have argued in this chapter that the generally neglected "transition period" of May 1934 to May 1935 must be seen as an important period in its own right with a distinct set of policies dominating communist agitation. Focusing on communist discourse in Spain and France, I have suggested that the politics of united fronts guided communist preoccupations in this crucial year and that the politics of popular fronts did not become the watchword of the Comintern until May–June 1935. Given the different dynamics emanating from united and popular fronts, this assessment of Comintern politics sheds new light on the twelve months following May 1934 and thus partially accounts for the volatility of this period and the string of united front agreements I will describe in chapter 4.

THREE

An International United Front?

Hitler's smooth accession to power triggered a profound sense of disorientation within the Social Democratic and the Communist Internationals, thus creating a favorable opening facilitating moves toward unity. Most historians date the beginning of this attempt to reach an international understanding to 19 February 1933, when the LSI bureau published an appeal—"To the Workers of the World"—calling for a cessation of hostilities between the two Internationals and a common effort to counter the growing threat of fascism and war.[1] Yet there is reason to believe that the very first recorded international initiative was a Communist move. According to Jonathan Haslam, "On 13 February, two weeks after Hitler became chancellor, French, German and Polish communist leaders issued a joint communiqué to the social democrats offering a united front of action against fascism."[2] Undoubtedly, the explicit appeal of the LSI raised the stakes considerably higher. It took the Comintern two weeks to respond. When it finally issued its proclamation on 5 March 1933, it rejected any attempt to engage in top-level negotiations and instead called on each national Communist Party to enter separate united front negotiations for each individual country.[3] In turn, the next LSI executive meeting on 18–19 March decided to recommend to its "affiliated Parties to refrain from any separate negotiations . . . until results have been achieved by agreement between the two Internationals,"[4] thereby effectively ending the official moves toward an alliance in times of great need. The Comintern quickly switched back to its tactics of united fronts "from below,"[5] and Aldo Agosti is undoubtedly on the mark when he infers: "The position adopted by the leadership of the LSI could not but have the effect of reinforcing the position of the most tenacious advocates of the theory of 'social fascism' within the leading circles of the Comintern."[6] But an interesting and little-known aftermath of this exchange suggests that the brief rapprochement of the LSI and the Comintern carried more promise than most participant observers suspected at the time. The postscript to the document exchange saw the French writer and political activist Henri Barbusse emerging from the sidelines to enter center stage, if behind closed curtains.

Jocelyne Prézeau draws attention to the fact that, upon the instigation of the German Alfred Kurella and Willi Münzenberg, Henri Barbusse, at precisely this moment, went above the heads of the PCF leadership to contact top officials of the LSI in an effort to break new ground. According to Prézeau, Kurella and Münzenberg's intentions were merely for Barbusse to ask for LSI cooperation in planning for an international peace conference.[7] Yet a number of documents in the LSI archives indisputably show that what actually transpired in the exchange of letters in late March and early April 1933 went far beyond an attempt to convince the LSI of the value of yet another public relations venture.

On 20 March 1933, one day after the LSI's qualified rebuttal of the Comintern counteroffer of national united fronts, Henri Barbusse sent three similarly worded letters to Friedrich Adler, Otto Bauer and Émile Vandervelde.[8] In these letters he laid bare the changed international circumstances and corresponding changes of attitude on the part of both Internationals: "Undoubtedly, after the two appeals of the Second and Third Internationals, there remain obstacles to overcome, but the biggest difficulty, it seems to me, is for one or the other side to carry out the decisive step in order to engage in direct negotiations." Barbusse went on to offer his services to breach the psychological barrier. He stated, "I am genuinely ready to make use of the acquaintances I have in both camps in order to facilitate the establishment of direct contacts," and he proposed to invite, in his capacity as secretary of the conference committee, "several authorized representatives of the two Internationals, so that they may have a first exchange of opinion, not officially, but informally [non officiel, mais officieux]." This letter caused some consternation and a series of deliberations by the three leading figures of the LSI. None of the written responses are on hand, but in a letter by Vandervelde to Adler, the Belgian social democrat intimated that he responded to Barbusse by indicating his agreement with whatever Adler decided to do.[9] Otto Bauer's response appears to have been more openly negative.[10] Adler's initial reply, if there was one, had not arrived at Barbusse's home on the Côte d'Azur by the time Barbusse decided to respond to the indifferent, if not outright negative, letters by Vandervelde and Bauer. In his final attempt to break the ice, Barbusse stressed that he did not mean to impose his services. His proposal was only meant to suggest one concrete solution to the apparent impasse. "The only thing I ask of you is whether you consider such a meeting as possible and whether you are disposed in principle to take part in it."[11]

By mid-April Barbusse's latest initiative had finally come to naught.[12] But Adler's unrecorded decision to reject this mediation offer must have been a difficult one to make. Émile Vandervelde, for instance, while officially responding to Barbusse in a noncommittal manner, privately told Adler, "I would not object to an informal and preliminary meeting."[13] And, upon returning from an extended journey abroad, Vandervelde again wrote to Adler in early May: "It seems difficult to me to tell him [Barbusse] that we do not accept his informal intervention under the conditions he refers to."[14] Nevertheless, Barbusse's united front offensive ground to a halt.

The degree to which Barbusse acted on his own initiative cannot be reliably ascertained. It is perhaps most fruitful to place it in the context of debates and divisions within the Comintern itself. It should be noted that Barbusse acted on the initiative of Kurella and Münzenberg, though the extent of their directives remains unclear, and nothing is known about the degree of their isolation or support within the leading Comintern circles. But in a number of Comintern sections an open political crisis suddenly appeared. Josef Guttmann, the leader of the Czech Communist Party refused to countenance the Comintern switch back to sectarian "Third Period" attitudes, though he found little open support within his party and was eventually excluded.[15] KPD officials Erich Wollenberg, Felix Wolf, Heinz Neumann and Hermann Remmele opposed the Comintern rigidification concurrently with Barbusse's overture.[16] Jules Humbert-Droz refers to a large circle of oppositional German Communists in Switzerland, including Neumann, who were willing to go even further than Humbert-Droz himself in trying to rectify the Comintern line.[17] Finally, the high-ranking KPD official and crypto-Trotskyist Karl Retzlaw informed Trotsky about news he had just learned during confidential Comintern meetings at the occasion of the June 1933 Pleyel conference in Paris. At one of these gatherings Manuilski reported not only that Remmele was about to be excluded on account of his recalcitrant attitude, but that a high-ranking member of the PCF had protested "against the Comintern methods and demanded free discussion. Allegedly several members of the PCF Central Committee concurred. Also, Gottwald of the Czech Communist Party Central Committee is quietly opposing the line."[18] Barbusse's moves in the direction of greater cooperation between the two big Internationals may thus be best explained as part of a more general, though largely uncoordinated, Comintern-wide movement demanding the abandonment of the sterile "Third Period" line, although a degree of personal initiative may also have played a role. Both efforts failed, but in the end these episodes were a first wedge in the seemingly solid front of the Comintern.

As is well known, the moves toward greater openness, which had failed in 1933, finally reached the level of open discussion within the closed circle of the Comintern leadership starting in the spring of 1934. From that year onward, there was no more need for major personal crusades or trial balloons. Efforts at united fronts were the official duty of the Comintern itself, and the Moscow leadership could now afford to openly address the LSI. Now was also the time, however, for the social democrats to show their true colors, as the LSI leadership could no longer use the real or imagined excuse of major uncertainties about the position of the Comintern. As the literature is relatively abundant on the official LSI-Comintern relations, I will only mention in passing the most important moments in this public and open quest for unity: the communist offer of joint solidarity work for the defeated Spanish revolutionaries in October 1934 and the offer of a cooperative alliance against the threat of war at the occasion of the Ethiopian crisis in the early fall of 1935.[19]

Instead, without ignoring these crucial face-to-face meetings, I want to focus on a far less well known aspect of this relationship. For, as it became apparent that the leadership bodies of the LSI would not budge from their antiunitary position, the Comintern undertook a series of high-level efforts to elicit cooperation from that portion of the LSI, which had undergone a considerable radicalization in the past few years and was, in 1934–35, more willing than ever to advocate unity of the two big Internationals. The careful consideration of these furtive meetings between Comintern emissaries and representatives of the LSI-Left show a hitherto unknown dimension of social democratic politics, which go a long way toward explaining seemingly puzzling aspects of the individual careers of such eminent social democrats as Otto Bauer or Theodore Dan. At the same time, the ultimate failure of yet another series of united front ventures with the LSI, or segments thereof, may also help to explain the continual slide of official communist policy from an initial emphasis on working-class united fronts "from above" (June 1934 to October 1934) via the intermediate stage of popular fronts "from below" (October 1934 to May 1935), to the ultimate hegemony of multiclass popular fronts "from above," starting in May 1935.[20]

Pro-Unity Sentiments Within the LSI in Early 1933

The more official character of the 1934 and 1935 initiatives was a result not only of a change of heart of Comintern tacticians but also of major rifts and dissensions within the ranks of the LSI. As a matter of fact, the origins of the loosely organized association of left-wing forces within the LSI can be traced back to the debates surrounding the social democratic and communist resolutions clamoring for greater cooperation in February and March of 1933. A dissident, radical faction had, of course, existed within the ranks of the LSI from the moment of its inception in 1923. Yet its attempt to push the LSI toward more combative positions suffered a qualitative and quantitative blow when, in a period of eleven months between September 1931 and July 1932, the three key elements of this left bloc were expelled, or felt compelled to separate organizationally, from their respective national parties. The break of the British Independent Labour Party, the German Socialist Workers Party and the Dutch Independent Socialist Party with the LSI seriously reduced the base of operations for the remaining oppositional elements.[21]

The continued existence of this amorphous association of left-wing social democrats, however, can be clearly ascertained in the events surrounding the united front overture tendered by the LSI on 19 February 1933. Virtually nothing is known about the debate leading to the initial LSI resolution. The curt introduction to the LSI document merely states: "The Bureau of the LSI met in Zurich on February 18th and 19th and decided to issue the following appeal."[22] No indications are given here or anywhere else about the debates that must have preceded this momentous decision. The official LSI organ was similarly silent on the origins of the LSI's subsequent reversal.[23] Some LSI affiliates later on referred to this second decision as having been reached "unanimously."[24] Yet in this second instance there is reason to believe that not only had there been no unanimity on this issue, but in actuality the LSI executive, in whose name the rejection of the Comintern's response was issued, had voted *in favor of* keeping open the lines of communication by a sizable majority.

This fact clearly emerges from a letter by a member of the LSI executive, the Polish Bund leader Henryk Ehrlich, to Friedrich Adler roughly two weeks after the meeting. In it, Ehrlich complains of several inaccuracies between the content of the actual resolutions voted on at Zurich and their eventual published version. Most of the changes were minor alterations of the texts. "It is different in the case of the united front. The Executive carried on a spirited discussion whether the LSI shall renew its turn toward the communists. This question was answered with a 'yes' in a show of hands (14 votes against 8). Now it is with astonishment that I notice this point missing in the published resolution."[25] Ehrlich went on to state his party's willingness to enter into national negotiations, although he had serious doubts whether such talks would eventually bring forth tangible results. Adler's response is missing.

But what has survived the ravages of time is a draft resolution on the unity of the workers' movement prepared for this very same Executive Committee meeting in Zurich. In this document it is made explicit that, although the Comintern evaded the concrete offer made by the LSI, the LSI turned "once again to the Communist International" and renewed its original offer.[26] This draft resolution, or a similarly worded document, must have been the actual text approved by the delegates in Zurich. Some introductory statements accompanying the publication of the resolutions supposedly adopted at this Zurich meeting provide a clue to the origins of the subsequent distortions. Here we learn that the executive had "instructed the Bureau of the LSI to introduce any additions which might be made necessary by the assembly of the German Reichstag" at a forthcoming bureau meeting in Paris on 27 March. Only one of the resolutions passed in Zurich dealt specifically with the German situation, and the quoted passage presumably is a reference to this German resolution. But it is only reasonable to assume that the Paris gathering changed more than it was empowered to amend, for no "Zurich" resolutions were published until after the subsequent, much smaller bureau meeting, comprising only nine persons compared to the thirty-five delegates in Zurich.[27]

The Paris Conference

Undoubtedly, the LSI-Left's influence in LSI debates in the early months of 1933 owed much to the concrete conjuncture. In this sense its momentary preponderance must be seen as an ephemeral victory. But its forces had reconstituted themselves and were clearly there to stay. Even after the removal of most left-wing oppositionists from the ranks of the LSI in previous years, their presence continued to be felt. Their next big move came in August 1933, at the occasion of the long-anticipated international conference on "The Strategy and Tactics of the International Labour Movement During the Period of Fascist Reaction" in the famous and enduring meeting hall in the Latin Quarter of Paris, the Mutualité. After considerable debate all delegates from the Polish Bund, a majority of the American delegation and a minority of the French, Italian and Menshevik delegates voted in favor of a resolution enjoining the LSI executive to immediately enter negotiations with the Comintern and unaffiliated workers' parties, in order to arrive at a common plan of antifascist and anticapitalist action. On other resolutions the individual vote distribution differed slightly, but the total number of radical minority supporters remained stable.[28] And the officially adopted resolution was by no means openly hostile toward cooperation with the Comintern. While stopping short of an explicit offer to renew the deadlocked exchange of February–March, "the LSI proclaims anew that it will spare no effort in trying to reunite the scattered forces of the working class."[29] A fair number of advocates of concrete united front politics had voted for the vaguely worded majority resolution in an effort to promote internal LSI unity.[30] One such apparent conciliator, Otto Bauer, in his final intervention, railed against a Swedish delegate, Allan Vougt, who claimed the majority resolution explicitly rejected the possibility of direct talks with the Comintern. Bauer pointed to the lack of such strictures in the actual text and underscored the purposeful lack of precision on this point. Joint meetings may become useful at some future date. "The resolution is not in favor of it, but also not against."[31]

This emergency conference turned out to be the ultimate international conference of the LSI. In many respects the antagonisms openly expressed at this gathering prefigured the rift between the major tendencies of the LSI, which later on in the decade came to dominate its life to the extent of completely paralyzing this supreme decision-making body of international social democracy. In subsequent months the fault lines within the LSI began to widen. The moderate sector, essentially composed of the Swedes, Danes, British, Dutch, Czechs and Germans, began to coordinate its activities.[32] But its left-wing nemesis reacted in kind. Little is known about the latter's growth and coordination prior to the August 1933 Paris conference. But in the aftermath of this event, "the comrades of the minority in the International continued to correspond with each other [and] to meet at times, in order to verify the convergence of their ideas in light of new experiences."[33] In the summer of 1934 the LSI-Left issued a joint resolution reconfirming its stand on a variety of issues and calling on new forces to join its "socialist offensive."[34] By this time, though, the signatories showed no increase in support over the past twelve months, although in their text they referred to a favorable evolution within Austrian, German, Polish and Spanish social democracy. And, indeed, by the time the November 1934 LSI executive convened, the forces of the LSI-Left had grown to encompass the entire Austrian, French, Italian, Menshevik, Polish, Spanish and Swiss delegation.[35]

The Stalemate Within the LSI

The catalysts for this qualitative and quantitative growth in power and influence of the LSI-Left were a series of significant events in several European countries, providing a material and spiritual boost to radical activists everywhere. On 12 February 1934 the armed uprising of the social democratic paramilitary organization, the Schutzbund, erupted in Linz, Vienna and a few other locations throughout Austria. Also on 12 February 1934, a general strike and mass demonstrations in support of democratic rights in France fundamentally altered the relationship of forces and the terms of debate within that crucial European country. These two events were, in a sense, the opening shots for the turn toward united front strategies in Europe.

As I will show in chapter 4, the summer of 1934 saw major concrete united front agreements in the Saar, Austria, France, Belgium, Italy and Spain. Pressure on the LSI to address this complex issue in a coherent fashion began to mount as early as the spring. At the 28 May 1934 LSI executive meeting, for instance, Otto Bauer read aloud a letter he had just received from the Central Committee of the Revolutionary Socialists, as the Austrian underground social democrats called themselves after the February defeat, in which the illegally operating activists expressed "the deep longing of the workers for *working-class unity*. In the struggle against the Fascist dictatorship there is no distinction between the Socialist workers and their class comrades organized as Communists." The committee went on to "request that everything be done from the Socialist side to bring about unity. Our minimum demand is that first of all a proposal for the *conclusion of an honorable pact of nonaggression*, which shall apply at least to the Fascist countries, should be made by the Labour and Socialist International to the Third International."[36] When the groundswell for joint actions found public expression in the first major regional or national agreements, the LSI leadership could no longer avoid the issue. Otto Bauer, upon first learning of plans to address this matter at the next executive in August, wrote to Adler in deep despair, for the polarization within the LSI had led to seemingly impenetrable rifts precisely on this question, and Bauer was deathly afraid for the fragile existence of the LSI. As Bauer wrote, "In its time it was absolutely correct to treat the question of the united front on an international level. Today it would be absolutely wrong." Given the fact that national parties, such as the French and the Austrian sections of the LSI, had in effect quietly ignored the dictum of the LSI bureau of 19 March 1933, it would be foolish now to frontally debate the implications of these moves at the upcoming reunion. Bauer continued, "What is supposed to be the result of this session? An injunction against national united front negotiations would be intolerable. Even a declaration expressing tolerance of national negotiations is hardly attainable in the face of resistance by the Pfundblock and the Dutch. Under such circumstances such a meeting can only lead to a dangerous blowup."[37] As it turned out, the LSI bureau of early August deferred the debate to the upcoming executive meeting,[38] where the eventual decision was reached reversing the March 1933 verdict against national negotiations (see later discussion). By that time, however, the uprising in northern Spain had already led to the 15 October 1934 meeting between Adler and Vandervelde for the LSI and Cachin and Thorez for the Comintern.

On 11 October 1934 the LSI received a letter from the two French communists in which they passed on a resolution by the Executive Committee of the Communist International (EKKI) calling upon the LSI to join forces on behalf of the ongoing military action of the Spanish workers.[39] Friedrich Adler happened to be in Prague on that date. In a first informal poll among the present Dutch, German and Czech LSI leaders, no one, except perhaps for Albarda, expressed principled opposition to the Comintern proposal for exploratory talks in Brussels on 15 October.[40] After a consultation with other bureau members, still only a minority opposed such a move,[41] and the historic event took place. The talks in Brussels's elegant Hotel Métropole ended with no concrete agreements, although the Comintern representatives pressed merely for united action in the specific case of defense and support work for the Spanish fighters. Adler and Vandervelde referred all binding decisions to the upcoming November executive.[42] At this crucial executive meeting in the Paris Mutualité tempers flew high, and it almost came to an open split. Acrimonious debates were held on a variety of resolutions and counterresolutions, and, at one point, when the rift appeared insurmountable, Friedrich Adler threatened to resign. Apparently, this ultimatum softened the opposing camps, and the conference adopted a final resolution in the form of an open letter to Cachin and Thorez, in which the LSI officially withdrew its strictures against national united front ventures, while refusing to enter into international arrangements, in effect reversing its stand of 1933.[43]

The LSI-Left

This LSI executive gathering, however, is also noteworthy for the first public emergence of an enlarged left-wing faction within the LSI, given expression by Léon Blum's public declaration of a statement, issued in the name of the French, Swiss, Spanish, Italian and Austrian sections of the LSI, as well as the Polish Bund and the Russian

Mensheviks. In it, the undersigned expressed their satisfaction with their partial success at this conference, but at the same time vowed to fight for the conquest of the majority within the LSI, so that the LSI may renew its 1933 offer of united, international action against the threat of war, for the defense of civil liberties and the defeat of fascism.[44]

To achieve this much, considerable efforts had been expended by some of the major protagonists of this newly reinforced LSI-Left, which now encompassed most of the former conciliatory center. In a letter to Adler, four days after the Brussels meeting with Cachin and Thorez, Otto Bauer spelled out his plans. Bauer knew perfectly well that, at this point in time, the LSI-Left could not hope to persuade a majority of that organization to adopt its views. On the other hand, the LSI, as it existed then, "has become completely incapable of making decisions and carrying out actions," thus creating an intolerable vacuum. "Therefore we should create within the LSI a cooperative association of all those parties favoring united front policies." Bauer went on to propose that a joint committee of these forces be formed "which shall speak with Moscow in our name. We hope to become in this manner a link between the two Internationals, and thereby to prepare a future agreement" between the LSI and the Comintern.[45] Adler responded with a note of caution. His preoccupation remained the avoidance of an open split within the LSI, and he warned Bauer of pushing too far too fast. Adler pointed out that other supporters of a united front initiative within the LSI, such as the Menshevik Theodore Dan and the French Jean Zyromski, were firmly opposed to separate negotiations by only a segment of the LSI. While favoring a turn toward united fronts himself, Adler also added, "I consider it a mistake, if the *initiative* for the release of individual parties from the decrees of the International comes from the Left." He noted the willingness of Albarda to promote such a decentering of authority himself and wrote, "I do not see why it would be in the interest of the Left to assume coresponsibility for such a major step backward, even if, seen in historical perspective, in reality the French took the first step on this path in their own country, without concern for the LSI."[46] Indeed, in a draft resolution for the LSI executive, Albarda had noted "that the Socialist Parties in France and certain other countries have, in view of the special conditions in their countries, commenced joint actions with the Communists." But the executive underscores, continues the text, "that in many other countries the conditions for joint action do not exist. As long as this state of affairs continues, and as long as the Communist International refuses to recognize the democratic principles of the parties affiliated to the LSI, there will be an insuperable obstacle to joint action on the part of the two Internationals, and negotiations to this end will be useless." Inasmuch as Albarda did not explicitly condemn national deviations from the general line, this provided the sought-for opportunity for the Left to develop its own policy unhampered by international obligations.[47]

Very little is known about the cooperation among the members of the group in the ensuing months. The French communist Jacques Duclos notes that the Comintern once approached the "Group of Seven," as the LSI-Left came to be known unofficially, for united actions on the first anniversary of the February 1934 events in Austria and France, only to be met with silence.[48] Perhaps the lack of internal cohesion condemned it to a state of inaction on an international plane. According to a confidential report, the other members of the "Group of Seven" had to go to great lengths in order to convince Léon Blum even to read their declaration at the end of the divisive November executive.[49] Passivity continued to characterize the LSI-Left almost as much as the LSI itself. Even the October 1935 events concerning the Comintern demand for joint antiwar activities led to no new major common initiatives on the part of the LSI-Left as a united body. But, this time, key individuals belonging to this tendency decided that matters had to be taken into their own hands, and they entered into separate talks with Comintern spokesmen. In a very real sense, these efforts in the fall of 1935 constitute the potentially most far-reaching ventures in this quest for united fronts. And for that reason it is only appropriate to end this discussion of international united front initiatives in the 1930s with a description of those contacts as they unfolded in the wake of the VII World Congress of the Comintern.

Otto Bauer and the Comintern

On 13 September 1935 Otto Bauer addressed a long letter to his close comrade-in-arms Theodore Dan. Bauer reported: "I had a conversation with an Austrian comrade, who joined the CP after February [1934], but who remains personally loyal to me. The man was at the [World] Congress in Moscow. I consider his account totally honest. As much of it will be of interest to you, I inform you of the most important parts; but I beg you to treat it confidentially."[50] Thus began the final installment in the circuitous and ultimately unsuccessful route toward a common understanding between the Second and the Third International. It led Comintern emissaries to secret meetings in the West and at least one social democratic emissary to the Moscow offices of the Comintern. In the process, hopes for cooperation were raised to unprecedented heights, only to eventually collapse in the winter of 1935–36 and to vanish into thin air with the beginning of the Moscow purges.

In his letter to Dan, Bauer recounts that according to Ernst Fischer,[51] his interlocutor, the Comintern's turn "is meant sincerely and honestly." "One does not want to put forth offers, which will lead to rejection, in order to immediately compromise the new politics; therefore also no offer to the LSI for right now [sic]. One also has no illusions concerning the possibility to break down the resistance of the English, Dutch and Scandinavians at this time." While rejecting any notions to split the LSI, the Comintern wanted to do everything in its power to "come into very close contact with those parties in the LSI that desire the united front." Bauer likewise informed Dan of Fischer's observations regarding the domestic agenda of the Soviet leadership. Here the key passage referred to sincerely meant desires to carry out far-reaching reforms: "The leading circles of the party are aware of the need to democratize the regime; but one does not know quite yet how to go about it, and they are afraid of the consequences." Finally, Bauer told Dan that Manuilski himself had authorized Fischer to make these statements and to invite Bauer to visit Moscow. As Bauer declined the invitation out of tactical considerations, Fischer informed him that Manuilski would "look for an opportunity to come to the West in order to personally speak" to Bauer and other social democrats.[52] Concurrently with this meeting, Bauer informed Dan, Julius Deutsch, another key figure of Austro-Marxism, was approached by a Russian official of the Red Sports International offering the immediate dissolution of their organization and its entry into the social democratic Workers' Sports International. Dan reacted enthusiastically upon receiving this news. He conjectured that this was a portent of better things to come and declared himself unequivocally in favor of using this new opening in the upper reaches of the Comintern and therefore the very top of the Soviet hierarchy. For Dan this constituted an unprecedented opportunity, "and it is now up to the LSI and its parties whether we are able to place ourselves at the forefront of this stunning historic turn of the workers' movement. I have never felt such a grand inclination to throw myself into the fight for our 'line' to the best of my abilities. . . ."[53]

Five days later it was up to Dan himself to surprise his Austrian comrade with pathbreaking news. A top Comintern official, in a very recent conversation with one of Dan's fellow émigrés in Paris, independently confirmed most of Fischer's observations. The unnamed official further claimed that the key proponents of this "turn" were Radek, Dimitroff and Stalin himself, and that the origin of this reorientation must be seen in the growing fear of imminent war. Soviet officials were planning to democratize their country in order to firm up their popular support and "in order to create better preconditions for the implementation of the international united front." Dan concluded:

> Now is exactly the moment, in which a clear, decisive and systematic influence by you, Adler and Blum can contribute to the formation of real, serious steps in the direction of ending the serfdom [*Entknechtung*] of the Russian workers' organizations and the general democratization of the Soviet regime, and to thereby facilitate an earnest turn, whose truly world historical importance, from the standpoint of the Russian Revolution and of the entire international workers' movement in the struggle against fascism, I hardly need to emphasize to you.[54]

On 27 September Bauer informed Dan of moves by the Comintern to contact Bauer through a non-Austrian emissary,[55] to which Dan responded with the first attempt to theorize this momentous development. In his opinion those domestic and foreign moves grew out of the need for regime stabilization. But this process of stabilization could take on two different forms, a shift toward a Bonapartist dictatorship or moves toward democratization. The first path would correspond to the needs of the capitalist powers, with whom the Soviet leadership sought rapprochements in search of alliances against the war danger, and the second to the desires of the world labor movement. It was now up to "the most fervent advocates of unity of the workers' movement in our ranks, particularly in the 'left' wing of our International," to promote the latter course, for, at the present time, an international, proletarian united front could become as much or more of a necessity for the survival of the Soviet regime as a Kremlin alliance with Western governments, and this was the chance that should not be missed.[56]

The Abyssinian Crisis

By the time the last of these letters were exchanged, the Comintern leadership had already entered the second phase of its latest attempt to entice the LSI into cooperation. On 25 September 1935 the LSI secretariat received a telegram from none other than Georgi Dimitroff himself. In it, the general secretary of the Comintern warned of the danger of impending war in Abyssinia and the Memel region and implored the LSI leadership to consider a less rigid stand. Dimitroff suggested a joint conference and named four Comintern negotiators.[57] The LSI secretariat immediately answered by telegram, telling the Comintern that the upcoming LSI executive would decide on this issue.[58] But in a confidential report to Leon Trotsky, an unidentified informant drew attention to the unusual impact of the Comintern offer by referring to the ambience within the LSI secretariat in the first few days after receipt of Dimitroff's telegram as characterized by "a conspiratorial atmosphere. One only spoke about it by way of suggestions."[59] The Austrian émigré Oskar Pollak described the first reaction to the arrival of Dimitroff's plea in these words: "After D.'s telegram arrived and Fritz [Adler] had initially answered it in a bureaucratic manner, he thought about this affair from all sorts of angles. Of course, I encouraged him not just to say no. (Kathia [Adler] did the same thing, as you can imagine.)"[60] Adler's more considered response became the project of an antiwar congress jointly sponsored by the LSI and the social democratic trade union International under conditions explicitly favorable to Comintern participation. Such a conference would kill two birds with one stone. It would address a specific area of growing concern to everyone, and its limited antiwar focus "would evade the difficulties connected with [more general] united front negotiations."[61] For, as Pollak stressed in his letter to Bauer, any explicit discussion of united front tactics "would probably not result in anything different from previous attempts," as far as the majority within the LSI executive was concerned.[62]

But Adler's project appears to have been stillborn. The all-important Brussels meeting of the LSI executive on 11–12 October 1935 essentially reenacted the November 1934 stalemate. The arguments of the pro-unity forces were blocked by the firm opposition of the Pfundblock. In the end, the assembly voted, with only the Georgian delegate abstaining, in favor of yet another powerless compromise resolution, giving permission to Adler and LSI Chairman Louis de Brouckère to sound out the Comintern emissaries at a meeting on 18 October 1935 but leaving the underlying issue unresolved.[63]

Having anticipated major opposition by the Pfundblock, Otto Bauer used the publication readily at his disposal, Der Kampf, the widely respected journal of Austro-Marxism, to publish a long article addressing the situation of paralyzing equilibrium within the LSI, several days in advance of the executive. To shake itself free from its torpor, he advocated the creation of a concrete link between the two Internationals by means of the now one-year-old "Group of Seven." What he had only dared to advocate in private in 1934, he now aired in public. While, in 1934, he had remained isolated with this plan, now a number of his closest coworkers expressed at least their tentative support.[64] Unsure of the extent of the Pfundblock's opposition to even the slightest tilt toward the Comintern, Zyromski had agreed to read a resolution in the name of the LSI-Left, advocating the establishment of personal contacts with Comintern officials, in case of a complete failure to overcome the resistance of conservative LSI members. But, as the executive had finally permitted an informal meeting between representatives of the two Internationals to take place, this plan became "temporarily obsolete."[65] Bauer drew his own conclusions from the outcome of the executive:

I am not totally discontent with the Brussels meeting. The authorization for the President and the Secretary [of the LSI] to make contact with the Comintern is, in spite of everything, a small step forward. Even more important, however, is the fact that the conservative elements are beginning to realize that something new is happening in the world, and their rigid rejection of any unity of action is no longer advocated with the same clear conscience, the same firm conviction, as before.[66]

Personal Crusades

Bauer's hopes for a gradual change of heart of his more conservative comrades turned out to be unfounded. The subsequent history of LSI-Comintern relations repeated the same pattern of Comintern initiatives, meaningless personal encounters and no practical results.[67] In October 1935, however, Bauer and his cohorts had not yet given up all dreams. Still, most of Bauer's co-players within the LSI-Left had expressed some misgivings regarding his ambitious scheme to utilize the "Group of Seven" as a bridge between the two Internationals. Abramovich, for instance, opposed such a move for tactical reasons but also out of a more general fear that such a constellation would place the LSI-Left at a distinct disadvantage faced with the much more powerful and manipulative Comintern.[68] Theodore Dan, more favorably predisposed toward such an initiative, informed Bauer, after a conversation with Léon Blum, that three of the "Seven"—the French, Spanish and Swiss—probably would not cooperate. "Of the seven parties only four would remain, of which three are émigré parties and two—the Polish Bund and especially our own party [the Mensheviks]—could contribute more to the generation of obstacles to your intended action than to its advancement."[69] Dan, in this note to Bauer, went on to lay out an alternative scenario which prefig-ured the ensuing course of action with amazing precision: "Therefore, in my opin-ion, there is nothing else to do except for you, Adler and perhaps someone else, to personally assume, on your own initiative and at your own risk, the task of informa-tion and mediation, which you intended for the 'seven' parties, as long as this effort remains necessary, while preserving complete loyalty toward our International."[70]

Léon Blum's role in this mediation venture remains obscure. At one point the French socialists had suggested that the LSI leadership leave it up to the SFIO to establish concrete links to the Comintern on the basis of their excellent relations with the PCF at home.[71] But because of the SFIO's crippling passivity in its dealings with the PCF, much criticized by observers inside and outside France at the time, it be-came a less than useful vehicle. For a while it even seemed as if the SFIO was will-ing to fuse with the PCF at the price of leaving the LSI and joining the Comintern.[72] Dan, at that point in almost daily contact with Blum, actually held Blum respon-sible for the relative inaction of the LSI-Left. While refusing to coordinate the activi-ties of the LSI-Left himself, Blum at the same time vetoed any moves carried out without his explicit consent.[73] This forced Bauer to rely on himself since Dan, his closest ally and a key Menshevik politician, was a potential liability in this delicate maneuvering with Moscow. Bauer's main assistant in this venture became Fritz Brügel, who, to date, remains best known as a leading social democratic poet and writer in post–World War I Austria. His activities on behalf of the LSI-Left show him in a different light.

The first personal contact with Comintern representatives subsequent to Bauer's two-day exchange with Fischer in Prague took place in Fritz Brügel's apartment. The KSCz Central Committee member Smeral restated Manuilski's offer for Bauer to travel to Moscow for a personal exchange with Dimitroff and Stalin. Smeral expressed his understanding when Bauer again declined to follow up on this proposal, and he promised Bauer to notify Dimitroff and Manuilski of Bauer's wish for some concessions in the Comintern's attitude toward the pending 18 October 1935 meeting between Adler, De Brouckère and Comintern negotiators.[74] Four days later Bauer met Ernst Fischer again, this time in Böhmisch-Trübau, a provincial Bohemian town.[75] As Bauer was prevented from making a trip to Moscow himself, and Manuilski from visiting the West, Fritz Brügel was eventually selected to visit the Kremlin heights. In his conversation with Manuilski in December 1935, with the latter underscoring Dimitroff's knowledge and approval, the Comintern official pleaded for the cessation of all hostile attacks by both sides. Paraphrasing Manuilski, Brügel reported him as saying:

> We need Bauer, and we wish to live in peace with him." "The turn of the VII [Comintern] Congress is an honest turn and intended to last for years. Things are moving in the direction of war, and [war] is beginning to look like a certainty. If we are left alone, we will be able to realize all those things which Bauer hopes for [viz. democratization] in five years. If war breaks out, perhaps in ten years.[76]

Brügel followed up on his initial report with a letter to Bauer in early January 1936:

> I have the absolute impression that an answer to this conversation [between Brügel and Manuilski] in whatever form is important, and, furthermore, I have the impression that these people definitely want to loyally cooperate with you and your friends. I believe that this opportunity, which seems to be opening up, may develop into a real link. I believe that the future of our project depends on our ability to strengthen this link.[77]

Bauer's answer to Manuilski, transmitted via Ernst Fischer, must have done very little to bridge the gap. Bauer rejected Manuilski's suggestion of a truce. Bauer would never agree to abstain from pointing out serious shortcomings in Soviet society. He even tried to convince the opinion shapers in the Comintern that it was actually in their best interest to have a critical supporter like himself, rather than individuals like the leaders of the SFIO, whose daily newspaper "never criticizes Russia, but only because it never writes anything about Russia."[78] The tenuous link disintegrated rather than strengthened in the ensuing weeks and months. Bauer occasionally still met communist officials, such as Fischer, Koplenig and even Bukharin,[79] but these meetings were no longer as meaningful as in the past. The horrors of the Moscow trials soon closed off the last avenues of hope. Otto Bauer's article "Grundsätzliches zu den Hinrichtungen in Moskau"[80] may have been the final intervention in this one-person crusade to mend relations between the LSI and the Comintern. A conversation with Brügel, serving as a messenger between Fischer and Bauer, in early October 1936 is the last recorded direct or indirect contact between Bauer and the Comintern.[81]

Conclusion

What is the explanation for this ultimate breakdown in communication, and what are the reasons for this whole series of failures? What were the implications for the course which history actually took? As there were several, relatively independent entities involved, it is appropriate to initially address their roles in isolation from each other. Clearly, the immobility of the LSI was a direct consequence of two fundamentally different experiences of the 1930s. A number of social scientists have sketched the rough outlines of the two key paradigms for European social and political developments during the 1930s: class polarization and consensus orientation.[82] For the present purposes it suffices to point out that the formation of camps within the LSI corresponded in rough outline with the type of society the parties were operating in. LSI sections operating in an environment characterized by civil strife tended to favor the Linksblock; those parties benefiting from consensus politics aligned themselves with the Rechtsblock. Both had equally convincing arguments for their respective stances, explaining the decade-long state of unchanging paralysis characterizing the life of the LSI.

The reasons for the trajectory of the Comintern are more difficult to gauge, but in recent years some important new insights have become, if not a commonplace, then at least less readily rejected. The traditional emphasis of Western historiography on the absolute primacy of Soviet foreign policy as the key determinant of Comintern directives can no longer be upheld with a clear conscience. At least in several important instances, it must now be acknowledged that the relationship between major reorientations of Soviet foreign policy and Comintern strategic changes was "not a relationship of cause and effect but one of interaction."[83] At least "for a brief time, roughly 1933–1935, a certain amount of latitude had again been opened up" for the Comintern.[84] The origins of this opening remain obscured and shrouded, but undoubtedly it was closely related to the forceful presence of major oppositional realignments within the Soviet Communist Party precisely within the years under investigation. This new conjuncture created limited free space for the formulation and practical application of significant policy alternatives in the domestic and foreign arenas alike.[85]

For the relationship between the LSI and the Comintern, this moment of opportunity also meant a genuine need for success on the part of the Comintern's key policy makers favoring the turn toward the united front. This may in part explain the sense of urgency with which the Soviet offers were tendered and repeated and the degree to which the Comintern leadership was willing to accommodate the LSI. When the LSI remained unresponsive, the Comintern was forced to look for other allies. In a very real sense, then, the LSI's immobility compounded the relative weight of the ever-present Moscow orientation toward diplomatic cooperation and convergence with other Western governments as the ultimate safeguard rather than toward reliance on the European Left.[86] Foreign policy objectives and Comintern prospects as determinants of Soviet domestic and foreign (re)orientations played different roles at different times. Diplomatic failures as well as Comintern defeats must have lowered the scales in one direction or the other. While the Soviet higher circles were well aware of the potential value of the European working class as allies in their fight for survival, the LSI's cold-shoulder treatment could not but push the Comintern in the direction of a greater reliance on other collective agents. In that sense the LSI leadership dug its own grave.

In the case of the LSI-Left, it must be stressed that this amorphous grouping was anything but a homogeneous force. Some of its internal disagreements have been mentioned in the preceding pages. Apart from the alleged willingness of Jean Zyromski to read a common declaration at the LSI executive of October 1935, the elusive "'Group of Seven" acted in unison only on the occasion of their first public statement of purpose in November 1934, and Léon Blum was extremely reluctant to take even this single step. There are important differences between the LSI-Left of the period prior to November 1934 and the subsequent, enlarged Linksblock. On average, the first, smaller grouping tended to be situated farther on the left within the political spectrum than the later, more influential coalition of convenience. Certainly after November 1934, political opinions between these parties and within each party differed sharply and went all the way from advocacy of the Russian Revolution as universal model to the support of coalition governments with bourgeois parties, from fervent belief in revolutionary defeatism to the defense of participation in the coming war.

This explains the LSI-Left's weaknesses, but what were its strengths? These left-wing social democrats must be counted among the most astute analysts *and* participants in the turbulent events of that decade. Unencumbered by the bureaucratic strictures of the Comintern, which seriously limited the full range of action of such talents as Henri Barbusse and Willi Münzenberg, and with the advantage of a captive mass audience which tended to be the missing link in the otherwise frequently brilliant analyses and guides to action by independent thinkers of the Left or theoreticians of the numerous *Zwischengruppen*, the spokespersons for the LSI-Left were the actual and/or potential organic link to the politicized segments of the European working class during the 1930s. One of the few historic incidents of a positive interaction between leadership and ranks with a radicalizing dynamic could be found within the national structures of the LSI-Left, particularly in 1933 and 1934.

As it happened, this dynamic was arrested in the wake of the Asturian revolt of October 1934, and not just in Spain. This, in turn, reinforced ever-present predilections of most leading left-wing social democrats toward moderation and risk avoidance. The rhetorical radicalism of Francisco Largo Caballero, Otto Bauer and Paul-Henri Spaak, at its height in the summer and early fall of 1934, now came to be overshadowed by a concern for what they perceived to be a realistic assessment of the conjuncture. For these and other reasons, Bauer, Adler and even Dan would never have dared to break with the tradition of the LSI. Ultimately, at the same time that the radicalized masses used the LSI-Left as their sounding board and organizational vehicle, this LSI-Left, not unlike the Comintern, put most of its eggs in the basket of diplomacy and state alliances. The consequences are well known. It was this tension between the demands of an insurgent mass movement and an almost instinctive reluctance to embark on radical adventures which made these groups and key individuals such fascinating, though ill-fated, subjects in their time. Some of the best among them were quite aware of this latent contradiction while they were living it. In the course of their debate about the present and future of Soviet society and the

European workers' movement, Theodore Dan made this insightful statement to Otto Bauer, which illuminates the political personality of Bauer and many other leading representatives of the LSI-Left: "I envision the salvation of Soviet socialism as an effect . . . of the social-revolutionary potentialities of the international workers' movement. You, to the contrary, expect the deliverance of international socialism from the Soviet Union. . . ."[87] Eleven days earlier Dan had expressed his thoughts about the rationale behind the recent groundswell in favor of united fronts in the following eloquent manner:

> You assume as the underlying principle of the unity movement and as its most important goal the "defense of the Soviet Union." In reality the entire unity movement did not arise out of the need of the European working masses to defend the Soviet Union, but out of the need of the masses to avert victorious or threatening fascism and counterrevolution. That is how it happened wherever the unity movement can record positive success.[88]

In the end, then, it was not just the concatenation of a completely paralyzed LSI, a hesitant LSI-Left and a Comintern bent on immediate, tangible successes which closed off this moment of opportunity. This would be to overlook the general turn toward moderation characterizing the forces of the European Left, organized or unorganized, in the wake of several consecutive defeats. Yet it remains equally true that there was no inherent rationale which predetermined this particular disjuncture between the radical dynamic of the mass movement—greatest in 1933 and 1934—and the uneven, but frequently slower, speed at which the major workers' parties responded to this challenge. In this sense, a rare chance to change the face of European politics was missed. All that was left to do was to draw the appropriate conclusions. To quote Dan one last time:

> So much the worse for us, if we failed to utilize this two-year period of united action to at least move a few steps closer to the solution. The impossible now remains impossible; and if we want to continue to passionately work toward achieving unity, then we must register our defeat, analyze its causes, apply the most severe self-criticism to our mistakes, and do everything in our power in the coming period to prepare for the transformation of today's fantasies into tomorrow's feasibilities [die Verwandlung des heute Unmöglichen in das morgen Mögliche].[89]

FOUR

The Era of United Fronts

While most of continental Europe was deeply affected by the ravages of the Great Depression and the accompanying social unrest, no country experienced the process of political polarization quite like Spain. Whereas the volatility of Spanish politics in the 1930s became most visible through the protracted civil war at the end of that decade, in actuality the outbreak of that conflagration can only be understood as a corollary to intense social and political conflicts in the five years preceding Franco's coup d'état of 17 July 1936. Indeed, it is appropriate to characterize Spanish society in the years 1931–37, particularly 1933–34 and 1936, as experiencing an open, prerevolutionary crisis.

After eight years of a moderate dictatorship, the inauguration of Spain's second republic, with the accompanying broadening of civil liberties and rights, ushered in a period of tremendous hopes and illusions for the population, roughly half of which still depended on employment in agriculture.[1] The ruling coalition of liberal republicans and moderate social democrats provided the political environment in which the laboring population felt at least partially protected from the exactions of predominantly Basque and Catalan industrial and commercial capitalists and Andalusian latifundistas. According to Gabriel Jackson, industrial wages generally rose between 1931 and 1935, and agricultural workers' income doubled "between the summers of 1931 and 1932." Yet, at the same time, more fundamental problems of social inequality remained untouched. Measures aiming at land reform were weak and ineffective. And the rapidly rising self-confidence of the Spanish working class found no other social outlet than its manifestation in occasional bloody revolts and ever more radical political demands—demands which the agricultural and industrial elite, handicapped by structural inefficiency and conjunctural decline, could never have fulfilled, even had they wanted to.[2]

The anticlerical heritage of Spanish republicanism, combined with a resurgent Catalan nationalism, likewise served to heat up the political climate of the second Spanish republic. Yet the most decisive ideological factor contributing to the genesis of a prerevolutionary crisis was the strong anarcho-syndicalist presence throughout the regions of Spain. Traditionally, the exceptional strength of Spanish anarchism until the 1930s has been explained by the underdeveloped nature of the Spanish economy and society and the corresponding attractiveness of a "retrograde," "anti-modern," "prepolitical," "millenarian," "peasant- and/or artisan-based" ideology. For James Joll, "the basic assumptions of anarchism are all contrary to the development of large-scale industry and of mass production and consumption. . . . For this reason, much anarchist thinking seemed to be based on a romantic, backward-looking vision of an idealized past society of artisans and peasants, and on a total rejection of the realities of twentieth-century social and economic organisation."[3] Another Anglo-American specialist, George Woodcock, concurs and imagines anarchism floating "like Mohammed's coffin, suspended between the lodestones of an idealized future and an idealized past."[4] And the British Marxist Eric Hobsbawm likewise concludes: "Classical anarchism is thus a form of peasant movement almost incapable of effective adaptation to modern conditions, though it is their outcome."[5]

This view of anarchism, predominant outside of Spain for many decades, has recently given way to a more nuanced assessment of the origins and impact of anarchism in the modern world. Works such as Temma Kaplan's *Anarchists of Andalusia, 1868–1913* have underscored that rural peasants in the south of Spain were guided by rational concerns and objective observations to the same extent as their supposedly more modern neighbors to the north. And even the "sociological" labeling of anarchist movements as peasant-based or peasant-influenced is no longer accepted as a foregone conclusion. Emphasizing the varied social background of the Barcelonan anarchist workers, Michael Seidman, for instance, points out that the French or German working classes were likewise "partially composed of former peasants, but their sociological composition cannot explain French anarchosyndicalism or, for that matter, the lack of anarchosyndicalism in Germany."[6] Focusing on the Spanish anarcho-syndicalist National Confederation of Labor (CNT), Seidman underscores the distinctly modernist trends in anarchist thought and shows their keen interest in questions of large-scale economic organization. Instead of opposing "industry, science, or progress in general," anarchists criticized the bourgeoisie's ineptness at fostering growth of the productive forces. "Indeed, few were more fervent believers in progress and production than Spanish anarchosyndicalists."[7] The Spanish workers' penchant for anarchism is seen, instead, as a perfectly rational response to a political system frequently relying on violent repression and military rule coupled with the existence of a Marxist current, social democracy, thoroughly mollified by decades of complicity with the ruling regimes.[8]

This decidedly radical, anarchist tradition played a crucial role in the shaping of the political unrest characterizing the second Spanish republic. Together with the sudden shift to the left by Spanish social democracy in the second half of 1933, described in chapter 2, this restiveness manifested itself in a rising tide of localized individual, then industry-wide and, finally, citywide strike movements, which enabled proletarian class formation to make giant strides forward within very few years. The corresponding reaction on the part of their bourgeois opponents, the tighter organization of employers' associations and the standardization of their response in turn heated up the political and social climate of the Spanish state to the point where open conflict became an accepted mode of operation for both sides of the class divide.

TABLE 4   Labor Unrest in Five European Countries

Country	Year	Number of Strikes	Workers Involved (1 = 1,000)	Days Lost (1 = 1,000)	Labor Force Involved (%)
Austria	1932	30	7	80	0.22
	1933	23	6	65	0.19
Belgium	1932	63	161	520	4.29
	1933	86	35	664	0.93
	1934	79	34	2,441	0.90
France	1932	362	72	1,244	0.33
	1933	343	87	1,199	0.40
	1934	385	101	2,393	0.46
Germany	1932	648	172	1,130	0.53
Spain	1932	435	444	3,590	4.80
	1933	1,046	937	14,441	10.16
	1934	594	742	11,103	8.04

Source: The information in the first three columns is taken from B. R. Mitchell, *European Historical Statistics,* *1750–1970* (London: Macmillan, 1975), pp. 178–181, except for the number of days lost to industrial disputes in Belgium, which I have adapted from Peter Flora, *State, Economy, and Society in Western Europe, 1815–1975,* 2 vols. (Frankfurt: Campus, 1987), 2:694. In order to compute the percentage of the labor force actively involved in strikes, I have relied on the figures for the total labor force provided by Flora for Austria (1934), Belgium (1930), France (1931) and Germany (1933) [Flora, 2:454, 466, 503, 517] and Mitchell's figures for Spain (1940) [Mitchell, p. 161], and then made my own calculations. I have only included the years in which the labor movement in the respective countries could operate under conditions of relative freedom. In assessing the 1934 figures for Spain, one should note that political conditions in Spain after October 1934 were such as to preclude major incidents of labor unrest for the rest of that year.

Only this atmosphere of extreme tension can explain the decision of Spanish social democracy to embark upon a plan of military insurrection.[9]

Table 4 shows the exceptional degree of class conflict in the Spanish state compared with the other four countries under scrutiny. From 1932 to 1934 Spanish strike statistics underscore the qualitatively distinct level of social discord. With the important exception of Belgium in 1932, when the militant actions of Walloon miners shook up the bilingual state to the north, Spanish strike activity far surpassed that of any other surveyed country. The first successful efforts at working-class united fronts anywhere in Europe were born out of this atmosphere of intense class hatred and despair.

The Peculiarities of Catalonia

Whereas this Spanish prototype of proletarian united fronts became most famous as a result of its role in the October 1934 Asturian revolt, its origin can be traced to the political cauldron in the northeastern reaches of the Spanish state: the region of Catalonia. Within the already unique political conjuncture of Spain, Catalonia added yet another twist to the story of Iberian peculiarities. Combined with the strength of the Catalan economy, a centuries-long tradition of political and cultural autonomy — in the thirties far stronger than any other nationalist movement in Spain, including the Basque—favored liberal republican, though pro-Catalan, sentiments through-out that Mediterranean region.[10]

Within the Catalan workers' movement it was not so much the virtual monopoly of anarcho-syndicalism which accounted for the difference with the rest of Spain, but the near-total absence of the social democratic PSOE and the virtual eclipse of Third International communism within an already marginalized communist Left. The strongest Marxist currents in Catalonia up to 1936 were a dissident communist grouping, the Workers' and Peasants' Bloc (BOC), expelled from the PCE in 1930, loosely allied with the Comintern's international Right Opposition, and a Catalan dissident offshoot of Spanish social democracy, the Socialist Union of Catalonia (USC), expelled from the ranks of the PSOE in 1923.[11] The strong moral authority of the key spokesman for the Trotskyist Communist Left of Spain (ICE), the Catalan Andreu Nin, was an additional factor in this kaleidoscope of Catalan Marxist organizations.[12]

Finally, an important and frequently overlooked evolution within certain sectors of Catalan anarcho-syndicalism played another crucial role in Catalan politics, particularly in the genesis of the Catalan united front. Spanish anarcho-syndicalists had always insisted on the virtues of abstaining from the political process as manifested in party politics and elections. This attitude kept the CNT as a whole relatively immune from reformist aspirations, but it also signified an ambivalent attitude on the part of the CNT leadership toward the movement to overthrow the dictatorship of Primo de Rivera. And, in most elections under the second republic, the massive refusal of CNT members to go to the polls helped skew the electoral outcome in favor of the Right.

In reaction to this increasingly self-defeating refusal to alter time-tested anarchist doctrine, and in response to equally harmful continued insistence on insurrectionary tactics by the political leadership of the CNT, the hard core of the Iberian Anarchist Federation (FAI), a CNT national congress in June 1931 witnessed the momentary preponderance of more pragmatic currents within the anarcho-syndicalist movement. Yet in subsequent months the anarchist cadres of the FAI managed to isolate the less doctrinaire syndicalists within the CNT. In the second half of 1932, most of the re-form-oriented CNT locals and individual thinkers were expelled, particularly in Catalonia, and by March 1933 an umbrella organization of the expelled syndical-ists—the Libertarian Syndicalist Federation (FSL)—began to coordinate the work of the Sindicatos de Oposición.

While a small minority current within anarcho-syndicalism even within Cata-lonia, the FSL continued its evolution away from anarchist doctrine and became increasingly open to aspects of Marxist political theory, eventually culminating in the creation of a seeming contradiction in terms, a syndicalist party—the Partido Sindicalista—in March 1934. By this time, however, Angel Pestaña had gone far beyond the limited opposition sentiments of most dissident anarchist comrades or-ganized in the numerically far more important Sindicatos de Oposición. Yet in the course of 1933, the FSL and the Sindicatos de Oposición played a crucial role in the creation of the very first united fronts within the Spanish state: the Workers' Alliance of Catalonia.[13]

The Catalan United Front

The simultaneous presence of several widely recognized but minoritarian dissident tendencies within the Marxist and anarchist Left—the BOC headed by Joaquín Maurín, the ICE led by Andreu Nin, and several unorthodox anarchist organizations—constituted a critical mass out of which new ideas could easily emerge. By themselves, however, these subjective "domestic" factors were necessary but not sufficient elements favoring the growth of novel solutions to the impasse facing the Left. The outside stimulus acting as a powerful catalyst to the construction of united fronts was the victory of fascism in Germany. As elsewhere on the Continent, the swift and efficient neutralization of the German Left triggered a heightening of actions, only in Catalonia it found expression in the sudden relevance of united front politics, at least for the most flexible and creative thinkers on the Left. With the exception of the numerically insignificant Spanish Trotskyists, the BOC and FSL were virtually the sole organizations of the Spanish Left to draw attention to the rise of fascism in other European countries even prior to January 1933. After Hitler's victory they redoubled their efforts. One recurrent theme of their agitation was the centrality of united front tactics as the only adequate response.[14]

In the second half of 1932 the BOC had begun its first concrete efforts at alliance politics with the creation of the Barcelona Unemployed Workers' Council. The principal partner in this venture was the USC. Yet at the main public event sponsored by this council, a conference on 12 February 1933, BOC dominance within this group was painfully evident and few activities were recorded thereafter.[15] The next BOC initiative met with far more success. Out of a private meeting between Joaquín Maurín and Tomás Tusó of the BOC and Joan Comorera and Joan Fronjosà of the USC in early 1933 emerged the call for a "Workers' Alliance Against Fascism." Publicized in a joint meeting of the BOC, the USC and Pestaña's FSL in March 1933, the first major organizational meeting on 22 April 1933 saw representatives of the Communist Party of Catalonia (PCC), the Communist youth organization, the radical nationalist group Estat Català, the Sindicatos de Oposición and the Trotskyist ICE sitting side by side with the original organizers in the facilities of the Barcelona workers' cultural center, the Ateneu Enciclopèdic Popular.[16] The first public manifestation of the newly created workers' alliance occurred on Friday, 28 July 1933, when eight thousand workers filled the meeting hall, La Bohemia, to capacity. Speakers representing the BOC, the FSL and the USC addressed the audience. Flushed by success, the "Workers' Alliance Against Fascism" now set out to spread its message to other Catalan population centers, always making sure to provide speakers from all three political tendencies.[17] Two unexpectedly successful strikes by Barcelonan power and office workers in the fall of that year, both under the political leadership of the BOC, reinforced the moral and political authority of the Catalan dissident communists.[18] By November 1933 the Catalan federation of the PSOE formed a common list together with the BOC in the upcoming federal elections.[19]

Throughout Spain, the November elections resulted in a resounding defeat for the badly splintered Left. In Catalonia the anarchists' active campaign for an abstention further skewed the outcome in favor of the Right. This unfavorable evolution of forces suddenly turned the proposal of a working-class united front into a promising solution to the crisis of the Left. On 10 December 1933 the founding document of the Workers' Alliance of Catalonia was published in the area's workers' press. Signed by representatives of all workers' organizations in and around Barcelona, except for the CNT and PCC, it warned against the rising tide of right-wing reaction throughout the Continent and Spain:

> Workers of Catalonia and of Spain! Do as we have done! Lay aside the disputes which separate you from your comrades-in-exploitation, without abandoning all efforts at defending your own doctrinal points of view, in order to constitute local and regional antifascist committees in opposition to the advance of reactionary forces, so that, having synthesized and unified your desires and aspirations in a representative national organization, we may counterpose to fascism and reaction the insurmountable wall of our will and our desires![20]

For the first time in the history of Spain and Europe, forces originating in the three main branches of the European workers' movement—social democracy, communism and anarchism—had overcome their deep divisions in an entire region.

After several months of preparatory work, the Catalan united front carried out its first major project: solidarity actions with a militant general strike in the capital city of Madrid. On 13 March 1934 the Catalan Alianza Obrera declared its own general strike in solidarity with its beleaguered comrades in Castile. Before that date no organization other than the CNT had ever been able to paralyze Catalonian economic life. The success of the Catalan united front's call to action symbolized the power of newly found unity and reinforced its ranks. Outside of Barcelona proper the strike was virtually 100 percent successful and proved to be one of the most militant actions in years. Even within Barcelona, the real stronghold of the CNT, the strike was solidly heeded in all those sectors of the labor movement under the leadership of the BOC and the FSL.[21] Yet the road ahead was perhaps more difficult than the path already traversed, for Catalonia was only one among many regions of Spain. The peculiarities of the Catalan Left were without parallel anywhere else. And, as exemplified in the mid-March labor action, the dominant force in Catalan working-class politics, the CNT under hard-line FAI dominance, steadfastly refused to join.

The Absence of a National Structure

Word of the creation of the Workers' Alliance of Catalonia spread throughout Spain. Letters of support arrived at its Barcelona headquarters from all corners of the state, and soon Alianzas Obreras were set up in Córdoba, Granada, Jaén, Madrid, Santander, Seville and a host of smaller towns and villages.[22] The unitary sentiment was strong enough to influence the PCE briefly to abandon its Third Period sectarian tactics months before the official Comintern turn. On 20 January 1934 the party's national newspaper, *La Lucha*, printed an open letter to the highest bodies of all important Spanish workers' organizations—including the PSOE, UGT, CNT and FAI—calling for the formation of united fronts in defense of civil rights and for drastic improvements in the lives of the toiling population.[23] And four days later the Communist youth group extended a similar invitation to the leadership bodies of all major left youth organizations, including the Republican youth.[24] As a result, local workers' alliances in several towns, including Valencia, Murcia, Cartagena, Seville, Alcoy, Mieres, Sama and others, included representatives of Third International communism at least for a brief period.[25] But after several weeks of such exceptional openness toward top-level alliances, in early March 1934 the PCE executed another 180-degree turn, expelled the most "compromised" central committee member, José Antonio Balbontín, and rejoined the fold of Comintern parties dedicated to uphold the banner of "Third Period" sectarian approaches.[26] In some cases the dissensions within the PCE brought about the forced removal of the PCE from the ranks of local alliances even prior to their renewed rigidification in early March.[27]

Compared with Spanish Third International communism, Spanish social democracy was a far more stable participant in the creation of united fronts. At virtually every location where workers' alliances sprang up, the PSOE local formed an integral part of their operations. Of the social democratic leaders, Largo Caballero in particular liked to present himself as a supporter of united fronts, a theme he repeatedly mentioned in his many speeches delivered at that time. On 21 January 1934, for instance, the closing section of a major address in Madrid was devoted to the construction of united fronts: "If there is concord and all proletarians desire unity, who can in all sincerity be against it? No one! . . . There are those who say that in a successful united front we would be victims of the anarchists. But let me tell you, for those who say such things, that if I have to be anyone's victim, I would prefer to be a victim of the anarchists rather than a victim of shameful fascism."[28] Yet whenever the PSOE national leadership debated the necessity and utility of a centralized national workers' alliance structure, the answer was invariably negative.

The issue was first brought to the attention of the PSOE executive committee on 25 November 1933 by Largo Caballero, who had received a delegation of Pestaña's syndicalists. The official minutes record: "The executive [merely] takes note of this information as it is impossible to accept such collaboration without the accord of both [PSOE and UGT] executive committees and without official solicitation by responsible elements."[29] On 3 January 1934, replying to a similar request by the Trotskyist ICE, the PSOE executive went into more detail in justifying its negative response:

> The executive committee believes that one can and must maintain cordial relations with every single element which sees the necessity to organize forceful actions against the constant provocations emanating from the Right; but at the same time the executive committee believes that no joint commissions of any kind should be formed and that, instead, each group shall organize those they represent; and the moment we encounter the common enemy, the control of each trade union or political faction will be exercised by those individuals elected to the respective leadership bodies.[30]

This became the standard PSOE reply. Local and regional united fronts were tolerated, but the line was drawn when it came to the issue of a national center. Even by mid-June 1934, the executive, including Largo Caballero, still hid behind the supposed lack of information regarding the stance of other workers' organizations on the issue of a national workers' alliance structure.[31] Clearly, the PSOE leadership did not cherish any potential opposition to its own prominent position within the kaleidoscope of the Spanish Left. Largely because of social democratic resistance to effective coordination, Spain never experienced a national united front.

The Asturian Commune

As was the case in Catalonia, the anarcho-syndicalist CNT abstained from all workers' alliances throughout the Spanish state, with one important exception. In the northern province of Asturias, the CNT leadership had historically been less inclined to follow the hard-line course of the national confederation and, when in 1931–32 Angel Pestaña expressed his opposition to the suicidal course determined by the FAI, the Asturian regional federation openly sympathized with the syndicalist leader. Yet it refused to follow Pestaña's course of an organizational rupture with the CNT as such, preferring to pursue its goals within the anarchist umbrella organization.[32] On 18 March 1934 a potentially pathbreaking accord was proposed between the two regional union federations in Asturias. The opening statement of this document left little doubt as to the direction of their moves: "The undersigned organizations, UGT and CNT, are in agreement that, given the economic and political situation of the bourgeois regime in Spain, it is imperative to undertake common action on the part of all proletarian sectors with the exclusive object to promote and bring about the social revolution."[33] On 31 March 1934 the only slightly revised text of the founding statement of the Asturian Workers' Alliance was signed and sealed by the representatives of the CNT, the UGT and the PSOE. Rarely had the forces of the majoritarian Left agreed to resolve their differences in such a clear-cut, forward-looking manner. Rarely, if ever, had social democrats joined forces with anarchists to bring about such fundamental changes. Soon they were joined by other sectors of the Asturian Left. As time was of the essence, they immediately set out to achieve their goal.

In the years under review, as noted earlier, Spain was the most conflict-ridden country of Europe. Within Spain, Asturias led the way. A rapidly ascending spiral of layoffs, strikes, wage cuts and anguish had thus prepared the way for the first united front between the most important sectors of the Left in an industrial region of Europe.[34] The resources of the entire Asturian Left went into the organization and strengthening of the Alianza Obrera de Asturias. With the aid of the regional social democratic daily, *Avance*, now effectively transformed into the organ of the Asturian united front, the following months witnessed the consolidation of their work. Meetings, demonstrations, strike support work and other efforts to achieve concrete economic gains and to promote solidarity characterized the work of the Asturian alliance.[35]

In the first three weeks after the signature of the Asturian pact, more than fifty thousand workers were involved in labor disputes in Asturias alone, providing fertile ground for the mushrooming of local Alianzas throughout this mountainous province. Despite the fact that it was called on only two hours notice, the first public meeting of the Oviedo united front, for instance, filled the spacious local labor center to more than capacity, a vivid reminder of its popularity, repeated in many locations throughout Asturias. By 1 May 1934 the stage was set for a powerful expression of the will of the unified Asturian working class. The inevitable general strike was 95 percent successful. Eighty thousand workers participated in countless local meetings and demonstrations, and the ensuing months witnessed continued organizational advances of the Asturian united front. In mid-May a strike by eleven thousand miners erupted over a local incident in El Sotón, effectively shutting down the Nalón valley southeast of Oviedo. Over the protests of local activists, the miners' union executive soon called a temporary retreat, but this was less a sign of weakness than a decision based on sober calculations. Heavily engaged in the Alianza's preparations for a revolutionary strike, the miners' representatives were unwilling to sacrifice their overall designs for a local skirmish, for in the course of this strike repression was severe, and a spiral of violence threatened to prematurely ignite the Asturian powder keg. Local socialists and anarchists soon began to intensify the procurement of weaponry necessary for their ultimate plans. Established channels of contraband trading and thefts by workers in munitions plants soon amassed a considerable array of weapons, including machine guns. It was a logical response by the Asturian working class to the frequent total or partial suspensions of constitutional rights by the Radical government in Madrid and its local representatives.

In June a general strike by the socialist National Federation of Agricultural Laborers (FNTT) polarized the entire nation. In Asturias most farming was carried out by small *minifundista* property owners. Given the political climate reigning in Asturias, they nevertheless heeded the call by the provincial FNTT leadership for solidarity actions. Proving that the Alianza Obrera could count on solid support among the lower middle class as well, Asturian farmers, especially in the central agricultural zone in areas close to the mining districts and industrial cities, stored their produce and refused to sell on the open market. By mid-June a renewed strike wave erupted throughout the mines of central Asturias, taking on even more massive proportions than the earlier strikes in May. The catalyst for this work stoppage was the decision by mine owners to reemploy a company guard whose provocative antiworker attitude and actions had triggered the first round of strikes in May.

Throughout July the Asturian socialist youth emerged as a leading force in the campaign against "fascism" and for a new society. Between 8 July and 29 July 1934, every important population center in Asturias witnessed public meetings organized by the young socialists exhorting the audience to persevere, and this campaign was extended into August. Suddenly young socialists undertook excursions into the countryside; they were, however, not designed to offer distractions from the summer heat but furnished the occasion for the familiarization of activists with the illegally procured weaponry and the holding of small-scale maneuvers. On the return trip from one of these outings, a pistol fight erupted between young socialists and right-wing activists in Infiesto, leaving behind two injured "fascists" and one wounded socialist. The regional forces of order responded by detaining seven members of the radical Right (all released the following day) and twenty-four young socialists who had been present at Infiesto, among the latter seven female activists. Similar events took place throughout the region.

On 1 September 1934 the women's section of the social democratic youth organization in the mining community of Sama held a march and rally against fascism and war. Male activists consciously stayed away from the assembled crowd in order to minimize the risk of altercations with the *guardia civil* deployed throughout the city. Still, shortly after the march began, the forces of public order stopped the demonstration and began to bludgeon the demonstrators. Soon the first shots fell, and, in the end, one female socialist was killed, two others were gravely injured, as were three onlookers and one policeman. Repression was severe. In response, however, a powerful general strike paralyzed the entire province on 8 September 1934.

For a number of weeks the radical Right had planned an important act of propaganda for 9 September 1934 in the Asturian town of Covadonga at the foot of the highest mountain range in northern Spain, the Picos de Europa. Therefore, the Alianza Obrera de Asturias declared the continuation for another day of the general strike called for 8 September to protest the bloody repression in Sama, now meaning to draw attention to the dangers of the CEDA rally. Despite massive mobilizations by CEDA supporters, Gil Robles's audience was smaller than expected, as most trains and many buses heading for Covadonga never reached their destination. Pistol-wielding left-wing activists stopped some trains; in other instances the rail lines were destroyed by explosive charges; buses were delayed by a well-coordinated campaign of covering most major roads leading to Covadonga with nails and other sharp devices.[36] This frenzied atmosphere of violence, repression and countermobilization, then, was the reality throughout Asturias in the months and weeks prior to the actual insurrection by the unified forces of the radical Left. On 11 September 1934 the PCE central committee finally decided to enter the long-established workers' alliances. This meant that the Asturian united front was virtually complete.[37] When the call for a "revolutionary general strike" emanated from the Madrid Comité Revolucionario in the PSOE national headquarters on 4 October 1934, it was small wonder that the Asturian region responded in full force.

The summer and early fall of 1934 witnessed the high point of united front politics within the Spanish state. In subsequent months the PSOE became noticeably cooler toward continued involvement in workers' alliances even at the regional and local levels. This left both Third International and dissident communists as the main proponents of continued orientation toward united fronts, spelling an uncertain future for their project, as they were marginal elements within the defeated Spanish Left. By mid-1935 the politics of popular fronts had clearly gained the upper hand.[38]

Moves Toward Unity in the Austrian Underground

As we will see in chapter 7, Austrian social democrats were the explicit model for the Spanish revolutionaries. The mountain state in central Europe had undergone a similar evolution in the past few years. It witnessed rising political instability, a creeping clerico-fascist coup and finally a last-ditch effort at armed rebellion by the Left. But whereas in Spain united fronts were part and parcel of the political culture prior to the armed revolt, in Austria they only became a widely discussed concept on the Left after their defeat. Prior to February 1934 the Austrian social democrats organized in the SPÖ had an almost complete hold over the hearts and minds of the Austrian workers. The sole competitor, the KPÖ, had never managed to gain more than a toehold of support. This changed dramatically in the weeks and months after the February defeat. As was mentioned in chapter 2, within Austria the Schutzbund uprising had a completely different effect on the reconfiguration of the Left compared with its international echo. For most combatants the events of mid-February led to a deep-seated alienation from the SPÖ leadership, which was perceived to have deserted the ranks at the moment of greatest need. One of the ramifications of this suddenly emerging gulf between social democratic leadership and ranks was a massive wave of resignation from the SPÖ, with many disappointed socialists joining the KPÖ.[39] This sudden growth of the KPÖ forced the rapidly disintegrating SPÖ to seriously address the proposals and ideas of its newly emerging competitor.

The KPÖ initially saw few reasons to change its course. Mired in the thicket of "Third Period" regulations against joint action with "social fascists," it expected time to work in its favor and unity to occur within the ranks of the KPÖ.[40] The social democratic underground was initially preoccupied with analyzing its own failures and drawing the lessons of the most recent past. But by June 1934 a sudden change occurred. Joseph Buttinger left behind this description of the mood characterizing the social democratic ranks:

> To aggressive shouts against the "peaceful methods" of the old party were added, in April, the defamations of their leaders and, in May, the estrangement from and renunciation of Brünn [the headquarters of the exiled leadership]; the heads of the "new beings" [Buttinger's caustic description of the radicalized social democratic underground] were still full of this agitation when, in June, suddenly the call for "unity" drowned out all other demands, and this new fever took hold of the young organization. Of all magic formulas none other had managed to obtain such power over the "new beings" as the newly discovered formula of "proletarian unity." Even before the chimera and truth of this slogan grabbed hold of the masses and left ideologues of socialist movements in other countries, the illegal activists of all tendencies in Austria had slavishly surrendered to it.[41]

The decidedly critical assessment by the Carinthian socialist vividly captures the rapid learning process within the Austrian underground.

Local efforts at united fronts could be noticed, with increasing frequency, starting in 1933.[42] After the qualitative breakthrough of the united front idea in the late spring and early summer of 1934, a series of negotiations finally led to an agreement for joint action between the RSÖ, the KPÖ and the then nominally autonomous Schutzbund. United actions, accordingly, were not only permitted on a central level but were likewise recommended for all district and local instances.[43] One year after the February defeat, united front committees existed, apart from the central Viennese organ, in many locations throughout Austria and, on a regional level, in the states of Carinthia, Salzburg and Tyrol.[44] Then, suddenly, soon after the relatively successful anniversary actions, which saw demonstrations and a series of coordinated ten-minute strikes, the RSÖ leadership pulled back. In a lengthy document entitled "Guidelines for Our United Front Politics," the RSÖ decided to gain a greater independent profile and to abandon "our passive stance" vis-à-vis the KPÖ. Citing repeated severe breaches of conspiratorial precautions on the part of its communist partners, the RSÖ announced that henceforth all united front activities would be centrally directed or not be permitted at all. For all practical purposes, it was the end of the agreement reached in July 1934.[45]

Whether the carelessness of the communist underground activists alone would have been sufficient to bring the period of united fronts to an end may be subject to doubt. In a 1936 letter to Otto Bauer devoted to a host of contentious issues, Karl Hans Sailer, a leading member of the RSÖ, questioned the usefulness and rationale behind this move. Sailer asserted that "back then there existed absolutely no conflicts, and the sudden break and sharp aggression [against the KPÖ] must have felt like a bolt from the blue. We ask ourselves in vain until today what purpose this abrupt course correction was supposed to have served."[46] One of the changes accounting for the tactical switch was a certain consolidation of the RSÖ which was then no longer losing members to the KPÖ and was steadily gaining ground. Lending credence to KPÖ complaints of RSÖ duplicitousness in this affair, the social democratic activist and historian Otto Leichter, years later, summarized the united front episode in the following cynical terms. Through efforts at united fronts the Austrian social democrats "gained time and room for maneuver in order to develop their own politics unhindered by communist attacks."[47] In March 1936 a new united front agreement was signed by the RSÖ and the KPÖ, but the unitary dynamic was broken. The March 1936 pact never became more than a pale shadow of its 1934 model.[48] Yet from the summer of 1934 to the spring of 1935, united front politics had been the cornerstone of the Austrian Left's realignment.

United Fronts in Germany

As was the case in Austria, the German Left never seriously addressed the question of united fronts prior to illegality; yet, unlike Austria, this was not for want of a glaring need for such a rapprochement. In fact, in Germany more than anywhere else the open hostility between social democracy and communism, both organizations with massive memberships and public support, played a particularly detrimental role in the continued division and ultimate defeat of a once vibrant, model Left. Apart from occasional and momentary advances, the two hostile parties were as estranged from each other on the day of Hitler's rise to power as they had been in the preceding several years. Only in the very last months and weeks before 30 January 1933 could one detect some individual initiatives within both the SPD and the KPD to build a bridge.[49] Yet it was too little too late.

The KPD had been most closely associated with Comintern "Third Period" tactics of unremitting hostility toward cooperation with social democracy. Not until January 1935 was the entire KPD leadership brought into line with the subsequent Comintern policy advocating nonsectarian united fronts. Already in the course of 1934, however, a number of regional and local KPD organizations softened their stance on fraternal cooperation with social democracy.[50] Once the KPD adopted the united front orientation, it quickly became evident that German social democracy was no more prepared to enter serious united front negotiations than the KPD had been up till then. The high point of top-level attempts to forge an underground united front was a gathering in November 1935 between Friedrich Stampfer and Hans Vogel for the SPD and the KPD's Walter Ulbricht and Franz Dahlem in the social democratic headquarters in Prague. The meeting further underscored the insurmountable gulf and led to no agreement.[51] Two months after the Prague summit, the SPD executive issued a circular to its cadres forbidding all joint activities with communists: "The party executive obliges all border secretaries, local representatives [Vertrauensleute] and heads of base operations [Stützpunktleiter] to reject all organizational connections with communists, especially arrangements and agreements concerning common actions with communist delegates or organizations."[52]

But, as elsewhere in continental Europe, leadership decisions did not necessarily reflect the mood of many of the ranks. Once the KPD leadership carried out its turn toward united front politics, the pressures for such alliances only increased for social democrats, especially on a local level. Starting in the second half of 1934 and all through 1935, a series of united front agreements were reached between SPD and KPD organizations on a regional and local level in Hesse, Thuringia, eastern Saxony, Baden, Württemberg and several western cities, such as Wuppertal and Lüdenscheid.[53] Perhaps the most important pact of this nature was signed on 16 June 1935 between representatives of the Berlin SPD and KPD, an agreement for mutual aid which lasted until January 1936.[54]

On the whole, however, full-fledged united fronts were the exception and not the rule. A major reason for the absence of stable agreements was the character of the KPD's underground work. The KPD's clandestine operations often entailed breaches of the most basic conspiratorial rules, leading to repeated massive arrests of KPD activists. As a result of such carelessness on the part of communists, members of the SPD underground, though often in principle sympathetic to cooperation with the KPD, frequently refused to engage in common action to avoid infiltration by Gestapo spies.[55] In one region of Germany, however, an open and viable united front exemplified the potential impact of a successful surmounting of hostilities. On 2 July 1934 the first regional united front accord anywhere in Europe outside Spain was reached between the Saar region's organizations of the Second and Third International. While its ultimate demise in early 1935 proved that unity alone did not necessarily entail victory, it was widely regarded and commented on as an example to be followed by the European Left.[56]

In the wake of the German defeat in World War I, the Saar region had been declared technically independent from Germany and placed under the supervision of the League of Nations. This status was to be maintained for fifteen years, after which a referendum was to decide on three pre-given options: unification with France, reunification with Germany or continuation of the postwar status as a quasi-independent entity under the authority of the League of Nations. Up to 1933 there had been few doubts as to the outcome of this referendum; all major parties clearly favored the German option. After Hitler's rise to power this unanimity began to unravel. For those political parties in opposition to the Nazi state, it became increasingly suicidal to advocate a return into the German fold. By early 1934 the Saar SPD openly rejected the annexationist option. Not before June, however, did it agree on the final formulation of its call for the upholding of the status quo as the recommended option for the referendum taking place on 13 January 1935.[57]

The KPD, for its part, kept insisting on the validity of its slogan, "For a Red Saar in a Soviet Germany," for much of the first half of 1934. But the pressure building from below, in combination with the derigidification of the Comintern line, forced the Saar KPD to finally abandon its increasingly ludicrous official position.[58] Already on 7 May 1934, the Comintern executive committee had officially abandoned the demand for the "repatriation" of the Saar.[59] On 3 June 1934 a Saar communist delegation to the League of Nations headquarters in Geneva published a declaration calling for the maintenance of the status quo.[60] This announcement had a catalytic effect. In a communication to the KPD politburo, Hermann Schubert, the designated successor to Ernst Thälmann in the post of party chair, described the echo of this public turn:

> News of our declaration was like a bombshell; at least among the working class it had a very good response; it creates the basis for the mutual rapprochement [Sammlung] of the working class. Judging from the statements in the Volksstimme and the Freiheit [the two papers under Saar SPD dominance], we can expect that they will come forth with a united front proposal; at any rate, the mood among social democratic workers is extraordinarily propitious.[61]

In the following days and weeks an intense debate arose within the top-level leadership of the KPD regarding the appropriate intervention in this volatile situation, culminating in the 29 June 1935 proposal by the Saar KPD to its social democratic counterpart for a united front in favor of the status quo in the upcoming referendum battle. Three days later an agreement was reached.[62] Between July 1934 and January 1935, countless meetings, demonstrations and other highly visible means of propaganda by the working-class united front in favor of the status quo heated up the referendum battle in the Saar.

Apart from the favorable sentiment among the ranks of the organized and unorganized Saar proletariat, about which more in chapter 8, the swift ratification of this pact was also due to the radical proclivities of the Saar SPD, headed by Max Braun. Already in the final years of the Weimar Republic, the Saar district SPD had been a notable opponent to the passive toleration by the German SPD of the gradual dismantling of Weimar democracy. After 30 January 1933 this opposition course to the SPD executive in Berlin, and later Prague, intensified, leading to the open secession by the Saar SPD at an extraordinary congress of the Saar social democrats on 12 November 1933.[63] One of the hallmarks of left-wing opposition to the German SPD executive had always been the advocacy of united fronts. Thus, on the occasion of the Austrian Schutzbund uprising, the Saar SPD reiterated its stance in favor of unity on the Left. "The Sozialdemokratische Landespartei Saargebiet declares its readiness to cooperate in the united front of workers' organizations at any given moment. The only preconditions are the cessation of hostilities [dass der Bruderkampf eingestellt wird] and that all insults of [our] organization and leaders are discontinued."[64] The concatenation of a radical social democracy and a flexible KPD leadership in conditions of extreme duress thus accounts for the first successful creation of a united front of major importance outside Spain. While it provided a stimulus for forces favoring unity not just in the Saar, its impact on the Prague SPD executive was negligible, leaving one left-wing opponent within the Prague decision-making body to utter in despair to one of his more conservative colleagues:

> Whereas in Germany and the world new understandings are beginning to gain the upper hand, and whereas each socialist observes the turn, which may lead to the ending of proletarian fratricide and to the unity of revolutionary action, in a state of utmost excitement [mit Herzklopfen], you continue to fixate relentlessly on those forces, which you have left behind since your last coalition, and you continue to expect salvation from another, class-extraneous world [von einer anderen klassenfremden Welt].[65]

United Fronts in Belgium, France and Italy

In Belgium united-front politics assumed the form of radical planism. As I will demonstrate in chapter 5, the planism of Hendrik de Man and his generally left-wing army of supporters should be regarded as a unique trajectory of united front politics, which rose and fell parallel to the successes and defeats of united front politics elsewhere on the Continent. As such it will be the subject of a separate section of this work. The sole instance of "traditional" united front agreements between social democrats and communists in Belgium was the 11 August 1934 united front agreement between the social democratic, communist and Trotskyist youth organizations of that country for international solidarity, against repression in Belgium, for concrete economic demands and against militarization. Apart from the Spanish Alianzas Obreras, which often included Third International communists side by side with anarchists and dissident communists *after* the PCE decided to join the already functioning institutions in September 1934, the Belgian pact was the sole recorded agreement of major importance which included official and dissident communists. And, more importantly, it was the sole instance anywhere where "the right of asylum for all victims of international reaction *and in particular for Trotsky*" was included in the founding charter. As such, it was a testimony to the moral authority of Leon Trotsky and his supporters at this time.[66]

Because of the pivotal role of France in the European constellation of forces, perhaps the most important united front pact came to be the 27 July 1934 "Unity of Action Agreement" between the French sections of the Second and Third Internationals. This pact took on particular importance for the communist movement as the French Communist Party was the sole western European communist group with aspirations to become a mass party. While gaining only 8.3 percent of the vote in the 1932 elections,[67] it was a force to be reckoned with on a national scale. Another particularity of the French situation was that, because of the relatively underdeveloped membership structure of the SFIO, the gulf between the popularity of social democrats and communists was less substantial than in most other national contexts. For these and other reasons, the signing of the pact in late July meant a considerable reinforcement of the pro-unity forces, and not just in France.

As the unity agreement is rightfully regarded as an important milestone on the road to the eventual creation of the French popular front, it is generously referred to in the literature on popular fronts. Likewise, the literature on the Comintern's 1934 turn pays much attention to the French unity pact, as the two developments were intricately connected. For these reasons, it would be redundant to enter into any great detail on the genesis and birth of the French united front. It may suffice to mention that the foundation for eventual moves toward unity was laid in response to a right-wing riot in the center of Paris in early 1934. On 6 February, in a series of altercations, several buildings, including the navy ministry, went up in flames, 15 people died and 1,500 were wounded in a semispontaneous assault on the institutions of the French Third Republic. In response, the French Left temporarily overcame its deeply ingrained mutual distrust and mobilized in unison against this thinly veiled threat against the survival of democratic institutions. On 12 February 1934 the badly fractured French Left marched shoulder to shoulder in an act of solidarity and defiance of the Right. The Paris demonstration, which numbered three hundred thousand strong, was an overwhelming success. Throughout France, 1 million demonstrators took to the streets. A nationwide general strike had the active support of 4.5 million workers.[68] Yet the 12 February unity in action initially proved to be an isolated, though promising, event. In the ensuing weeks and months, infighting once again won out over advocacy of cooperation. Yet by late May a flurry of high-level meetings between social democrats and communists in France and top-level consultations with the Kremlin leadership by French communists paved the way for the eventual united front agreement.[69]

In the present context I merely want to underline the signal importance of the French agreement for the promotion of similar efforts elsewhere. A leading Italian social democrat, Pietro Nenni, reflecting on the reasons which enabled the Italian sections of the two Internationals to sign their own unity pact several weeks after the French, highlighted reasons peculiar to the dynamics within the Italian Left but underscored the crucial impetus of the French example: "But nothing would have been done without the realisation of unity of action in France, which has created the psychological conditions favorable for a gathering of the working-class forces."[70] Pietro Nenni, in the introduction to the same article, suggestively subtitled "From the Anti-Fascist Concentration to Working-Class Unity of Action," eloquently describes the political atmosphere created and reinforced by the Continental movement toward united fronts:

> The Italian political emigration has just reclassified itself in accordance with the facts of a situation which continues to evolve in spite of its static appearance. Our Socialist Party is still the pivot around which turn the forces in opposition to Fascism. *But the place of the axis has been moved in a distinctly working-class direction.* The Anti-Fascist Concentration, which was organised in Paris at the beginning of our exile, and which grouped around the Party the Republicans and Democrats, has been dissolved. The alliance of the Party with the "Justice and Liberty" movement has come to an end. These alliances on the right have been replaced by a limited and circumstantial agreement between the Socialist Party and the Communist Party for working-class unity of action against Fascism and war.[71]

Conclusion

As can be inferred from the preceding, united fronts are essentially alliance structures among two or more organizations representing or claiming to represent working-class forces in a given location, region or state. As will be shown in chapter 8, particularly on a local level it appears that petit-bourgeois organizations were not infrequently a constituent part of such institutions, although, as I will argue, this did not make them precursors of popular fronts. All major pathbreaking regional or national agreements took care to define the working-class character of the agreed-upon united fronts. Thus, for instance, the original charter of the December 1934 Workers' Alliance of Catalonia added a note of clarification to the agreement: "This being an exclusively proletarian front, the political organizations and parties which are not of [working-]class origin may only express their agreement morally; they cannot become effective members."[72] This near-exclusive orientation toward a working-

TABLE 5   Important Regional and National United Front Agreements

Country/Region	Date of Signature	Key Forces Involved
Catalonia	10 December 1933	BOC, FLS, PSOE, USC, ICE
Asturias	31 March 1934	PSOE, CNT, UGT
Saarland	2 July 1934	SPD, KPD
France	27 July 1934	SFIO, PCF
Austria	Late July 1934	RSÖ, KPÖ
Belgium	11 August 1934	JGS, Communist + Trotskyist Youth
Italy	17 August 1934	PSI, PCI

class constituency had far-reaching consequences, which were not always clearly discernible from the clauses of the respective pacts.

Looking at the texts of united front agreements, most documents simply focus on a limited set of concrete tasks. They generally include an array of regionally or nationally specific demands, such as the April 1936 Austrian call for "the redemption of all unpaid taxes for cottagers, small tenant farmers, small- and medium-sized farms, as well as small craftsmen and tradespeople accrued up to December 1935";[73] the Belgian youth's summons for joint activities "against the steps prejudicial to the young unemployed taken under the Plenary Powers Act of 1933";[74] or the retention of the status quo in the Saar. Yet there are a number of underlying themes which can be found in virtually all important regional and national agreements I was able to consult.[75] One repeated demand was the call for a united response to the repressive acts of the respective regimes, be they dictatorial or democratic. Thus the first public declaration issued by the newly created July 1934 united front in Austria demanded, among other items, "the liberation of the jailed participants in class struggle";[76] the founding document of the Workers' Alliance of Catalonia emphasized the need to repulse the attempts of the central government to move toward dictatorship;[77] and the French agreement likewise underscored the urgent need "to defend democratic liberties" then increasingly under attack.[78] Equally visible was the wish to combat the growing danger of a second world war. The French and Italian agreements, the 1936 Austrian pact, the Belgian youth alliance and the founding statement in the Saar all referred to the concrete fear of war as one crucial reason for the creation of these fronts. The first published documents emanating from the 1934 Austrian and Asturian alliances likewise highlight their opposition to potential wars.[79]

Yet the most common denominator of this wave of united front agreements from Vienna to Gijón was the solid determination to resist the onslaught of fascism. The Catalan, Saar, Austrian, French, Belgian and Italian agreements all focused on the fascist danger as a central threat. For a number of them it was the most important obligation and the raison d'être for the pact, as in the case of the French, where the opening sentence ran as follows: "The Central Committee of the Communist Party and the Permanent Administrative Committee of the Socialist Party are animated with the will to defeat fascism."[80] Only the original 18 March 1934 clandestine Asturian agreement ignored the question of the fascist danger in its text. Yet the open letter to Asturian workers, issued less than two weeks later by the same body, highlighted the need to oppose the fascist threat and thus showed that it was just as central to the concerns of the alliance of social democrats and anarcho-syndicalists in Asturias as to their allies elsewhere on the Continent.[81]

Combating repression, war and fascism was the central focus of these supraparty alliances. Regardless of whether they operated in bourgeois democracies, as in France or Belgium, in a state of tenuous legality, as in Austria prior to February 1934 or in Spain for much of 1934, or under clear-cut dictatorships, as in Italy, Germany or post–February 1934 Austria, these common features were crucial characteristics of united fronts. Their almost uniform occurrence across much of continental Europe was an eloquent testimony to the similarity of issues and concerns across national frontiers. United fronts were institutions meant to amplify the defensive actions already engaged upon by each individual component prior to the pact. Unity of action was thus more than an empty phrase designed to placate fearful souls. United fronts grew out of the lived experience of a divided, fractured Left increasingly on the defensive and with rapidly diminishing options. The call for, and extension of, united fronts became the most promising formula available to the European Left in this difficult conjuncture.

Alongside the mutual reinforcement of defensive measures by each participating organization emerged an additional feature of united fronts. To the extent that their successes permitted a less pessimistic view of the present, united fronts also tended to foster a more optimistic perspective on the future. The gathering of strength and the growth of self-confidence resulting from a series of victorious exploits, or even simply from the fact that such seemingly utopian agreements for unity in action were now concrete realities after years of bitter strife, enhanced the value of these mutual assistance pacts beyond all measure. In previous years, disunity had further undermined an already weakened working-class Left. One of the social democrats most concerned to foster united front experiences, Otto Bauer, was only one of many keen observers of the nefarious effects of fratricide between the major parties on the Left: "The heated competitive infighting between social democrats and communists over the leadership of the working class has destroyed the feeling of class solidarity. . . . In this manner, the attractive force of the ideas of socialism was terribly diminished."[82] Now, with the momentum in their favor, the previously fragmented forces on the Left began to express their hopes and aspirations in a less defensive manner. They began to believe in what had, for many years, been merely a distant dream. Out of the movement for greater coordination of defensive measures reemerged the confidence in the timeliness of the socialist perspective.

This heightened concern for the relevance of socialism was in many cases directly translated into the language of united fronts. An agreement between the RSÖ and KPÖ in the industrial Floridsdorf district of Vienna demonstrates their recognition of unity as the missing link permitting the satisfaction of both concrete, limited demands and the attainment of their long-term goal. In the preamble, after pledging their utmost efforts, they underscore the fact

> that only a unified working class can successfully defend its interest; moreover, that only a unified working class can beat back the attacks of fascism and permit a counterattack. Also, the victory of the working class over capitalism can, in the end, only be attained by means of the political and trade union unification of the work-

ing class. *For this reason*, the representatives of the RSÖ and KPÖ in the Floridsdorf district, in the course of their joint consultation, have developed the following plan for common work. . . .[83]

The Floridsdorf Marxists went on to outline ten concrete demands, none of them necessarily transcending the limits of bourgeois democracy. What was already recognized, yet only implied, in the Floridsdorf pact became the sole programmatic highlight of the Asturian united front. Here the first plank of the nine-point agreement merely stated: "The undersigned organizations will work together toward the triumph of the social revolution in Spain and toward the conquest of political and economic power for the working class, as concretized in the immediate creation of a Federal Socialist Republic."[84] The remaining document was an enumeration of the workings of this plan. In its singular orientation toward the short-term perspective of a socialist revolution, the Asturian united front was truly exceptional. By contrast, several other pacts did not mention a socialist agenda even for the distant future, although some referred to their long-range goal in the preamble. Does this suggest the existence of two types of united fronts, one of primarily defensive nature and another of offensive use?

Such a premature conclusion would, on the one hand, have to ignore the existence of hybrid pacts of the Floridsdorf type where the signatories expressed their awareness of the relevance of the socialist perspective but focused exclusively on demands objectively attainable under capitalism. The 1936 Austrian agreement, for instance, also starts out by proclaiming the goal of its pact to be "the restoration of complete unity of the Austrian working class on a revolutionary basis" but then goes on to list five demands realizable in any bourgeois democratic regime. On the other hand, a seemingly moderate covenant, such as the French pact, specifically mentions the need to restrict its focus to "clearly defined objectives" but then goes on to list a host of demands which, while not specifically socialist in orientation, in essence could only be fulfilled by a radical societal change clearly beyond the capacities of any bourgeois government at that time.

I therefore argue that the creation and consolidation of united fronts wittingly or unwittingly unleashed a dynamic toward socialism. Successfully operating united fronts developed in an upward spiral of partial conquests, leading to more far-reaching goals which, if obtained, further stimulated the imagination of the actors involved. It was this inbuilt dynamic which Léon Blum referred to at the all-important November 1934 LSI executive committee meeting by describing the impact of the unity agreement with the PCF on the working class throughout France:

> I do not hesitate to present as the first undeniable result [of the pact] the fact that, as soon as it was signed and sealed, a kind of electrical current of fervor and of hope arose among the masses, such as we have never seen before. Not only in the Parisian region, where the communist forces are equal to, if not superior to, ours, but also in regions like that of Toulouse, where there are hardly any communists, the idea of the union of proletarian forces, the distinct feeling that now, in France, not a single impulse of the workers' energy will any longer be wasted on fratricidal struggle, has brought about an incalculably favorable reaction.
>
> Everyone of us knows perfectly well what it was like to go speak before large crowds in the past and what it is like today. Previously, large gatherings invariably

ended in heated polemics which left behind the peculiar flavor of profound division playing into the hands of our enemies; now they are substituted by meetings where the common desire of the French proletariat manifests itself in a twofold direction: to resist fascism by any means necessary and to prepare for the socialist society.[85]

This inbuilt momentum toward an offensive, forward-looking application of energies set free by unity of action in defense of concrete, hard-won achievements of the past was once more given expression by a Spanish delegate, Indalecio Prieto, at the same gathering of social democratic world leaders in Paris. Reflecting on the recent Asturian events, the Basque politician proclaimed: "The masses went into the battle in a spirit of defense against fascism; although, naturally, I must not deny that, had we won, we would have undertaken legitimate efforts in order to go beyond the positions acquired at the beginning of the [second] republic, and we would have tried to install a socialist regime."[86] The existence of such a dynamic would have had major repercussions had it occurred in merely one national context at any one time. But the conjuncture of a series of parallel strategic turns executed by the leading forces on the Left in a number of important countries in Europe engendered a particularly volatile alignment of political forces on a quasi-Continental scale, which the Left experienced simultaneously as an existential threat from the Right and a bountiful moment of opportunities. That this process transpired in an atmosphere of heightened interest in the lessons of experiences outside of national frontiers, about which more in chapter 7, only served to further raise the stakes.

Some of the most brilliant contemporary participants in, and observers of, this rapid shift to the left were well aware of the possibilities inherent in this fluid situation. The Russian Menshevik Theodore Dan, in rejecting arguments against cooperation with the Comintern, emphasized that the movement for unity was developing in the context of a "gigantic process of political, ideological and psychological transformation of the broadest sectors of the working class. On account of this experience, the unity movement is developing its own momentum which, in the end, will win out against all detractors from within, as its general direction conforms to the expectations of revolutionary, democratic socialism."[87] Dan spoke from experience, having been a firsthand witness of the spontaneous birth of the French united front in the days after the attempted right-wing coup on 6 February 1934. The major programmatic statement of the German left-wing opposition to the course of the SPD Prague executive was a lengthy document characteristically entitled "The Path Toward a Socialist Germany: A Platform for a United Front." In its pages the authors exhibited a similarly delicate understanding of the inner dynamics of united fronts: "[A] revolutionary socialist united party . . . will not be the result of mechanical unity negotiations. The path to the united party leads via the construction of the united front. But the united front can only become reality via united actions. But at the beginning of unity was the unity of the deed."[88] The final word in this enumeration of prophetic claims will be given to a key individual within the left wing of French social democracy, Jean Zyromski, who together with Marceau Pivert was extremely influential in propagating united front politics among the ranks of his party. Shortly after the ratification of the unity pact, he wrote a position paper in which he discussed the role of various factors in the genesis of the agreement. He then went on:

Whatever the case may be, an excellent result has been achieved. Unity of action has become a reality in our country. It has taken shape on a vast terrain: against fascism; against the politics of the National Union government; and for peace and the defense of democratic liberties. The Communist Party has clearly concurred on this last point in a manner which gives us full and total satisfaction. This achievement, which will hopefully set an example for other countries, has given rise to considerable emotion within the bourgeoisie. It will increasingly call forth an intensification of the already declared struggle and the formation of two antagonistic blocs: *bourgeoisie versus proletariat*, which is within the logic of capitalist evolution and the march toward socialism. This is the true battlefield cleaned of all impediments and barriers.[89]

Of course, the historical process in the thirties never permitted the full development of Dan's favored "ideas of revolutionary, democratic socialism," and neither did a "revolutionary socialist united party" see the light of day, at least not in the shape envisioned by the German socialists cited previously.[90] Class polarizations were rarely expressed on a "battlefield cleaned of all impediments and barriers," at least not on a national scale. It was ironic for the fate of the radical Left that the cause of radicalization—the national and international advance of fascism—simultaneously served to blunt the socialist edge. After an intense flurry of activity, instead of moving forward to achieve its goal, the unity movement began to lose its momentum and, in the course of 1935, was largely superseded by a turn toward popular fronts. The October 1934 Asturian defeat, a lost battle in precisely that region of Europe where an unparalleled alliance on the Left had given rise to the most far-flung hopes anywhere at the time, constitutes a symbolic turning point in this rapid pace of events. That it came to this defeat was as much a result of the uneven support for united fronts in the rest of the Spanish state as the logical outcome of the absence of serious movement toward unity on an international scale throughout these years.

FIVE

The Promise of the Plan

On Sunday evening, 23 August 1931, an extraordinary assembly of men and women gathered in the Amsterdam Koloniaal Instituut for a conference which was to last until Friday morning, 29 August 1931. Economic experts arrived from all five continents to participate in the deliberations of the meeting, called to debate "World Social Economic Planning: The Necessity for Planned Adjustment of Productive Capacity and Standards of Living." While the topic was certainly not a standard theme for international congresses at the time, and whereas the geographic spectrum represented lent an unusual dimension to this gathering, what was perhaps most remarkable was the breadth of social and professional interests represented at this meeting.

Economists and industrialists, statesmen and trade unionists, journalists and architects, factory inspectors and factory owners, engineers and communists; a remarkable assortment of individuals hailing from every imaginable social and professional background assembled in the Koloniaal Instituut for what became known as the 1931 World Social Economic Planning Congress. Among the well-known personalities present were Rudolf Wissell, the former German secretary of labor; Fritz Naphtali, the head of the German trade union research association; Friedrich Pollock, a leading member of the Frankfurt Institute for Social Research; French journalist and politician Bertrand de Jouvenel; Dutch social democrat F. M. Wibaut, the éminence grise behind Amsterdam's exemplary municipal housing development project; Albert Thomas, the director of the Geneva International Labor Bureau; the Brookings Institute economist Lewis L. Lorwin; Valeri V. Ossinsky, the leading Soviet economic expert; H.S. Person, the managing director of the American Frederick Taylor Society; and leading industrialists from many countries. It was an unprecedented meeting of minds concerned about the state of disarray of economies and societies in 1931. Person formulated the concerns of the participants in the following manner: "We have come to the conclusion that individualistic enterprise has indeed constructed a magnificent and efficient economic machine, but that it has finally reached a stage of evolution in which individualistic industry is unable to keep it in order and operate it properly. We have come to the conclusion that a regulating mechanism must be added to it—*social economic planning*. . . ."[1] For six days the conference participants were united by their common goal to strive for rational solutions to the crises of their times. There was no question in the minds of virtually all participants, whose comments were recorded, that some form of governmental planning was direly needed to surmount the economic and social obstacles. Even the need for a systematic, all-encompassing and worldwide approach was repeatedly underscored. It was perhaps symptomatic that a factory owner, Dr. F. Meyer zu Schwabedissen, partner in the Bielefeld firm of Bertelsmann and Niemann, made one of the most eloquent defenses of the necessity to regard "national economic planning [as merely] a first step toward the planning of the world economy."[2]

As Alfredo Salsano highlights in an important article entitled "Engineers and Socialism,"[3] the 1931 Amsterdam Koloniaal Institute congress occurred at an extremely important conjuncture for social democrats, social scientists and "social engineers" in the interwar period. The conference took place at exactly that moment when the scientific debate, which for much of the preceding decade tended to concentrate on technical aspects of rationalization, shifted and began to focus on the problems of economic and social disturbances then affecting the concrete conjuncture. For a brief moment economists, industrial sociologists, social democrats and entrepreneurs were united in their vision of a technocratic, though not necessarily antidemocratic, solution to the social dislocations resulting from the Great Depression. Utopian projects of five-year world plans were seriously put forth and debated by the assembled crowd in Amsterdam and elsewhere. The participants were convinced that macroeconomic dilemmas were no more invincible that the microeconomic problems they had conquered in preceding years.

This discovery of large-scale economic planning as social panacea made headway throughout the early 1930s. For several important years a different vision of planist politics captured the imagination of economists and social democrats. Within social democracy most strongly in the Belgian state, but with powerful reverberations in France, Switzerland, Holland, Great Britain and even Austria and Spain, planist politics was put forth as a concrete alternative to traditional reformist practice, which had, in most of continental Europe, arrived at an impasse. The most prominent individual in this enterprise to rejuvenate European socialism was the Flemish activist, philosopher and industrial psychologist Hendrik de Man.

Hendrik de Man

Hendrik de Man, born into a prosperous family residing in Antwerp, after a brief flirtation with Proudhonian anarchism joined the Belgian Socialist Young Guards (JGS) on May Day 1902. Three years later, during a brief visit to Germany, where he was sent to report on the SPD's Jena Congress for the Belgian social democratic daily *Le Peuple*, he decided to remain abroad. He began to work as an assistant at the *Leipziger Volkszeitung*, the most important press organ of the radical faction in the SPD, then directed by Franz Mehring. Among his acquaintances at this crossroads for Europe's left-wing social democrats were Rosa Luxemburg, Karl Liebknecht, Robert Michels and Leon Trotsky. Soon he began to take courses at the University of Leipzig, leading to a dissertation on the medieval cloth industry in Gent, supervised by the economic historian Karl Bücher. He rapidly began to take an interest in international affairs and became a cofounder of the Socialist Youth International in 1907. Fluent in four languages, he frequently worked as a translator at international gatherings of European social democracy, exposing him to the whole gamut of opinions within the European Left. He was an orthodox Marxist up to 1914. His decision to volunteer for the Belgian army in World War I and the experience of trench warfare in his native Flanders shook up his belief system, and he began to embark on a course leading him in a variety of novel directions, clearly distinguishing him from most other interwar social democrats.

De Man spent the last months of World War I on a mission in America, sponsored by the Belgian government, which was to report on the impact of Taylorism on industrial relations in view of the Belgians' plans for postwar reconstruction. While most participants of this mission spent their time at top-level gatherings with American "experts," Hendrik de Man made contacts with employers and trade unionists, worked on a Detroit assembly line for several days and, after his return to Europe, published a study of the social consequences of "scientific management," entitled *Au pays du Taylorisme.* In 1919 he set out once more on a journey to the New World, taking on odd jobs in Canada and the United States, spending a summer in a colony of Industrial Workers of the World (IWW) syndicalists in Puget Sound and ending his brief sojourn in America as a lecturer in social psychology at the University of Washington. When an offer arrived from Émile Vandervelde asking de Man to build up and direct an ambitious project of adult workers' education in Brussels, the École Ouvrière Supérieure, de Man returned to Belgium.

A speech at an institute for workers' education in Cologne, delivered in March 1922, put an end to his career as managing director of the École. De Man had publicly opposed the continued occupation of the Rhineland by foreign armies, a move which earned him massive protests in the Belgian press and found few defenders even in the ranks of the BWP/POB. In the fall of 1922 he moved to Germany, teaching at the Frankfurt Academy of Labor, before finally taking on a lectureship in social psychology at the University of Frankfurt. De Man took pride in emphasizing that this post was, to the best of his knowledge, the first such position anywhere on the Continent.[4] It was during his stay in Frankfurt, which ended with the Nazi takeover, that de Man elaborated his most lasting contributions to the development of Marxist theory, industrial psychology and socialist practice.

Hendrik de Man was never prone to abstract theorizing. He once expressed his sentiments by stating, "I attach more value to the building of a new sewer in a working-class neighborhood or to the placing of a plot of flowers in front of a working-class tenement, than I do to a new theory of the class struggle."[5] And he was fond of paraphrasing an English colleague who once described German theoretical sociologists as people who "continuously pack suitcases, but never leave on a voyage."[6] Undoubtedly his lifelong interest in workers' education and his activism in the socialist movement instilled this healthy dose of skepticism as to the role of theory in social struggles in de Man. Nevertheless, he set out to write two major treatises on Marxist social theory, which have been largely neglected in the historiography of twentieth-century Marxism but were widely regarded as important contributions by contemporaries from Thomas Mann to Antonio Gramsci.

His first work, *Zur Psychologie des Sozialismus*, was immediately recognized upon publication as a major questioning of orthodox Marxism; indeed, upon recommendation by Benedetto Croce, the Italian, French and Spanish translations of this work carried the title *Beyond Marxism*. This choice of words was not a reflection of de Man's wish to abandon an outmoded ideology but was meant to convey the Hegelian sense of *Aufhebung*, or "negation" through incorporation and further development. The main target of this book, written and first published in German in 1925, was the determinist legacy of Second International Marxism. Incorporating insights gained from his empirical studies of industrial relations, the labor process and their socio-psychological effects on the blue-collar proletariat, de Man's critique of orthodox Marxism was simultaneously a defense of the voluntarist dimension in political thought and social practice. Thus de Man became one of the few important social democrats to criticize his socialist colleagues severely for their one-sided appropriation of the Marxian legacy. His critique paralleled simultaneous moves within communist circles, most visible in the works of Georg Lukács, Karl Korsch and Antonio Gramsci. Yet in 1925 all indications seemed to point in the direction of a moderation of his political project, even though he explicity castigated specific aspects of social democratic reformism and patriotism.[7] After the publication of *Zur Psychologie des Sozialismus*, de Man continued to join theory and practice in his work on industrial psychology, resulting in *Joy in Work*,[8] his 1927 study of the relationship between workplace conditions, work satisfaction and the creation of proletarian subjective identities.

The publication of Marx's *Economic and Philosophical Manuscripts* in early 1932 reconfirmed de Man in his insistence on the importance of the nondeterminist legacy of Marxism. Whereas de Man generally kept aloof from the Institute for Social Research at the University of Frankfurt, the cradle of the "Frankfurt school," he used this opportunity to approach Max Horkheimer and suggested a presentation on the "Humanist Phase of Development in Marx's Thought." He delivered his speech in the institute's main auditorium on 27 May 1932.[9] Four weeks earlier, de Man had seen another one of his creative ideas come to fruition in a Frankfurt auditorium. Together with members of the Frankfurt workers' cultural club and others, de Man had spent over a year preparing for the *Festspiel Wir*, which had its premiere on May Day 1932 with two thousand participants and an audience numbering eighteen thousand. Utilizing avant-garde techniques of minimizing the division between players and audience, it was a multimedia production including choirs, orchestral music and film projections. After its Frankfurt success, *Wir* was performed in other German cities and abroad.[10] Subsequent plans to produce a film, based on animated pictures in cooperation with the Flemish wood engraver Frans Masereel, were never realized.[11]

The Socialist Idea

While laboring to extend the realm of cultural politics in defense of socialist ideals, de Man's major intellectual project became *Die Sozialistische Idee*, a work whose original German edition had the misfortune to be published in March 1933, at the very moment of closure of freedom of the press. In this volume de Man set out to paint in bold, imaginative strokes the paradigm shifts of cultural history from the philosophies of the ancient world via Christian moral ethics to bourgeois humanism. And, most importantly, de Man postulated the advent of a new paradigm shift: the move from the epoch of bourgeois cultural hegemony to the predominance of "the socialist idea." De Man once again proved his erudition and his mastery of philosophical literature, just as he had earlier demonstrated his acquaintance with many shades and variations of the socialist heritage.[12] Yet what made this 1933 work stand out, compared with his 1926 *Zur Psychologie des Sozialismus*, was not only its more constructive, and less critical, approach but the combination of theoretical innovations with an orientation toward the practical application of the insights gained. De Man himself explained his growing interest in the political dimensions of theory as paralleling the rise of the Great Depression and the corresponding failure of reformist practice.[13]

For de Man the economic and social crisis underscored that it was high time for the definitive supersession of the bourgeois epoch. His final chapter, entitled "The Realization of Socialism," was entirely devoted to the elaboration of this task. De Man criticized prevailing pessimism and suggested that the contemporary crisis should also be seen as a promise and a chance to finally carry out the long-expected social transformation. Yet to carry out this project, reformist measures had to be abandoned. Citing R. H. Tawney, who had written that the current programs of European workers' parties were like "a forest full of brilliant Christmas trees with gifts for everyone, instead of action plans for what must be, to all intents and purposes, a bitter struggle," de Man proclaimed the first step to be the suppression of "the difference between the practical minimum program and the theoretical maximum program."[14] Daily practice and visions of the future should no longer be treated as separate entities but as parts of an organic whole. And de Man continued by arguing for the abandonment of all hitherto existing programs in favor of the adoption of a *plan*: "The plan as the expression and symbol of the new phase of socialist action signifies that the surmounting of the system of production itself must, from now on, become an immediate and direct task."[15] As a consistent advocate of united front politics, he drew the attention of his readers to the necessity of a new approach in order to break the deadlock which kept the main bastions of the European Left in hostile camps. "The united front of the working class cannot be realized without *another* kind of socialism and *another* kind of communism. Therefore, the creation of a new socialism; this is the task of socialists today."[16] The practical conclusions of *Die Sozialistische Idee* were still cloaked in a somewhat abstract language, which was appropriate to this theoretical treatise but insufficient as a concrete guide to action. They were written at the very moment when de Man was preparing to reenter practical politics, a field he had abandoned for several decades.

The End of the Reformist Era?

Under the impact of the Great Depression, Hendrik de Man was only one of many individuals whose attention was redirected away from the specifics of industrial relations and the impact of Taylorism toward a focus on more general concerns. As a matter of fact, his first contribution to the literature on planist thought, *Refléxions sur l'économie dirigée*, was precisely an intellectual assessment of the proceedings in the Koloniaal Instituut. Criticizing the utopian project of the Industrial Relations Institute, which largely ignored fundamental differences separating the participants, de Man nevertheless underscored that, "on all sides, American engineers, Soviet functionaries and European socialists, one is convinced of the bankruptcy of the free enterprise regime."[17] In late 1931, Émile Vandervelde once again asked Hendrik de Man to return to his native Belgium. This time de Man was to launch and direct an institute for social research in Brussels linked to the Belgian labor movement and funded by an industrialist. While the Office of Social Studies (BES) was not founded until the summer of 1933, the idea of a research organization in the service of the Left soon began to take on great importance for de Man. In an October 1932 letter to Vandervelde he forcefully restated his interest in this affair, while stressing that his primary interest was a focus on the international dimension and only secondarily the case of Belgium.[18]

Still teaching in Frankfurt and a member of the SPD, Hendrik de Man often went on lecture tours of German cities and abroad. A frequent stop on his lecture circuit was Hamburg, which he had visited every year since 1926. His speeches usually addressed the conundrum of disunity on the Left. When, in 1931, he defended the idea of a positive campaign for immediate socialization as a method to overcome the fratricide between communists and socialists, he still encountered, in his own words, "the determined opposition of a large majority" of listeners; "in December 1932 I found the reverse situation. This time the overwhelming majority of the assembly expressed its assent to my conclusions and expressed the hopes that the social democratic party congress, scheduled to take place in March 1933, would comment on my theses in an affirmative way."[19] De Man's hopes to have an impact on the reorientation of the SPD vanished after 30 January 1933. He returned to Belgium, became the single most important factor behind the reconfiguration of Belgian social democracy and fully developed his planist ideas. A series of articles published at the end of 1932 in the Hamburg SPD daily *Hamburger Echo*, detailing his emerging ideas, provide a convenient point of departure for an analysis of his opinions at the moment of creation of the Plan de Man. Portions of these essays were incorporated into the final chapter of *Die Sozialistische Idee*.

The central thesis of his exposition was the realization that a new era of fundamental changes had begun. He wrote, "the era of reformist socialism is past; it is time to practice the politics of socialization, i.e., the revolution [Umwälzung] of the system of production."[20] Reformist politics, useful and appropriate in previous years and decades, had now become counterproductive obstacles on the road to social emancipation. "If the working classes want a larger piece of the pie, they must *bake another pie*; for, the existing capitalist pie is continuously shrinking."[21] This was not meant to cast aspersions on *all* attempts at defensive efforts. Quite to the contrary, de Man even envisioned the possibilities of partial conquests. Yet de Man took care to emphasize "that even the *defensive struggle* for the retention of acquired gains can only lead to success if it is carried out as an *offensive struggle* for as yet unachieved, or not even yet demanded, objectives." Defensive postures should merely be preparatory moves for a large-scale offensive. For contemporary socialism, "the task of this defensive struggle is exactly the same as the tasks of digging and constructing trenches for a fighting army, which is preparing itself for the *transition from a war of position to a war of maneuver* [*vom Stellungskrieg zum Bewegungskrieg*]."[22] "Given the revolutionary situation of today, nothing is more *inopportune* than that which was called *opportune* up to now; *now, the only things that are possible and practical are what appeared, yesterday, as impossible and impractical.*"[23] Hendrik de Man closed with the affirmation of the necessity of a united front on an anticapitalist basis to encompass not just the warring factions of the proletariat but the peasantry, intellectuals and the middle class.

The Plan de Man

Already in early 1932, Hendrik de Man began to design a research program for the planned BES in Brussels. The earliest outline of activities can be dated to February–May 1932; it clearly pointed in the direction of studies on the contours of planned economies.[24] Yet the real work on what became known as the Plan de Man did not begin to take off until the establishment of the BES in July 1933. The think tank created at the BES oversaw the elaboration of the plan, which took on shape in the course of the late summer and fall of 1933. The Seminar on Economic and Financial Studies of the University Association for Social Science, a slightly enlarged group of sympathetic economists which served as a first sounding board for the projects of the BES, met regularly from September 1933 until March 1934, the period of gestation of the plan.[25] Starting on 24 September 1933, the columns of the daily BWP/POB paper *Le Peuple* carried weekly articles explaining the meaning of the emerging project. In mid-October the leading figures in the Belgian socialist trade union movement openly proclaimed their assent, concurrently with the approval of the upper echelons of the BWP/POB. In late December 1933 the Christmas congress of the BWP/POB voted by an overwhelming majority for the adoption of the Plan de Man.[26]

What was the novelty of the Plan de Man? To what extent did the plan break with previous traditions of social democracy and the European Left? To judge the content and the meaning of the plan, it is incumbent to assess a series of thirteen articles which Hendrik de Man published in *Le Peuple* between September and December 1933. They were republished as a brochure entitled "Pour un plan d'action."[27] The preface to this series promised a thorough renewal of socialist strategic thinking. Synthesizing his conclusions drawn in previous months and years, Hendrik de Man asserted "that we are facing the task of closing a chapter of the history of the workers' movement, a chapter which opened approximately two or three generations ago." Not only the methods but "above all, and especially, the objectives of the movement" are in dire need of a "fundamental revision. . . . I believe, to say it in a nutshell, that *the socialism of the coming generation will be, under pain of total failure, as different from the socialism of our fathers as their socialism differed from the Communist Manifesto.*"[28]

Drawing on his firsthand experience of Germany, de Man went on to criticize the false antifascism of contemporary social democracy. In his view, social democrats banked on a self-defeating strategy of containment of the fascist danger by means of defensive struggles for the retention of democratic rights. Two methods were employed in their traditional undertaking: parliamentary maneuvering and the countering of the fascist street gangs with the construction of a social democratic paramilitary force. For de Man such strategies were necessary but insufficient to bring about success; "the fundamental error has been the refusal to recognize that to overcome an evil one must attack its root causes and not concentrate to fight against its symptoms."[29] The four sources of fascism's success were, for him, the discontent of the middle classes resulting from proletarianization; nationalist frenzy amplified by international economic competition; the weakness of parliamentary institutions; the feeble response by the socialist Left, which continued to focus on the blue-collar proletariat as its salvation; and a Left which, instead of working toward "a new order," tended "toward the defense of established institutions."[30]

In subsequent sections of his argument, de Man underlined the ongoing differentiation of the salaried workforce and, particularly, the creation of a "new" middle class and the stagnation, if not absolute diminution, of the traditional blue-collar proletariat. De Man also observed that in the ranks of the traditional "old" middle class a fundamental ideological evolution changed the premises for social change. Whereas petit-bourgeois anticapitalist sentiment in the nineteenth century was directed first and foremost against the spirit of free enterprise, their contemporary anticapitalism targeted, above all, the monopolistic tendencies in twentieth-century capitalism and in particular the machinations of finance capital. Yet it would be wrong to postulate the disintegration of specifically petit-bourgeois sentiments under the pressure of proletarianization. As a matter of fact, in a quasi-instinctual rearguard reflex action, "the more they feel threatened in their identities and the more they become fearful about the persistence of their proper social values, the more they attempt to consolidate their [particular] position." Because of such sentiments, it would be wrong to seek conjunctural alliances with the middle classes "in struggles for [limited] immediate interests." For such particularistic struggles are apt to reinforce divisions; they would merely oppose "farmers who sell their products to urban dwellers who consume; the small shopkeepers who are crushed by taxes to the unemployed battling for the maintenance of their indemnities. . . ."[31] "In other words, for common action of the working class and certain middling strata to emerge out of their joint opposition to the monopolistic power of finance capital, *this action must be aimed at far more radical reforms of the economic system than those pursued by socialism up to now.*" Referring back to his earlier argumentation in favor of the abandonment of a "war of position" and its replacement by a "war of movement," de Man suggested that socialist strategy must give up its orientation toward "reforms of redistribution" and concentrate on "structural reforms."[32]

The outline of such structural reforms promised not sudden wholesale nationalization of private property but a threefold approach to capitalist enterprises. Monopolies were to be socialized immediately. Those sectors of the economy which could be, in some sense, described as functioning on the basis of free competition were spared from expropriation but subject to governmental directives. Small-scale enterprises, where the division between ownership and labor force was nonexistent or ephemeral, were to be encouraged. "This pluralistic conception of socialization seems to me appropriate to the extent that it is the sole means by which we can, at this point in time, avoid the choice between two evils, to substitute the oppression by private monopoly with oppression of a totalitarian state, i.e., of an all-powerful bureaucracy."[33] State directives in the realms of fiscal, commercial and social policies were to ensure a renewed economic takeoff and the absorption of the unemployed within very few years. Countering objections by detractors of his plan, some of whom regarded it as far too limited in its demands, Hendrik de Man expressed the irony of such reproaches by stating that "it is amusing to hear complaints of excessive moderation directed at a plan of action which, for the first time in the history of socialism in Belgium, envisions nationalization measures as tasks for immediate realization, measures which, up to now, were relegated to that part of the socialist program more concerned with theory than practice."[34] De Man closed his series of articles with an affirmation of the internationalist mission of the Belgian Plan of Labor, as the Plan de Man was officially termed. While the circumstances of European politics required the elaboration of this plan within the confines of the Belgian state at first, this should not be regarded as a renunciation of its global message. "We are simply carrying out what can be done in the framework of one nation," without waiting until international conditions are ripe for the broader reaches of such a plan.[35]

In sum, the Belgian Plan of Labor was a dynamic device to shake up Belgian social democratic practice. Setting out to overcome traditional divisions between reformist practice and revolutionary goals, it constituted a transitional program for the alleviation of concrete social ills and the advent of a new social order. Conceived of as a measure to combat the lack of unity on the working-class Left, it went beyond other efforts at united fronts by consciously attempting to mobilize nonproletarian strata in pursuit of common, future goals.

Popularizing the Plan

After the adoption of the Plan of Labor at the December 1933 BWP/POB congress, the labor of popularizing these ideas commenced.[36] On 10 January 1934 the formation of a National Bureau of Action for the plan was announced. Propaganda and agitation in favor of the Plan de Man was to be carried out in three successive waves. In the first stage, cadres were to be educated in the principles and methods of the plan, cadres, which, in turn, were to mobilize workers and the unemployed in a second phase of the plan's implementation. Finally, the third wave was to result in a vast popular movement, transcending social classes and political parties and ultimately leading to the constitution of a new government whose sole task was to be the launching of the plan. For, as planist propaganda continuously hammered home, supporters of the Plan de Man were to abstain from any coalition whose actions were not guided by the *full* adoption of the plan. To facilitate the work of propaganda in favor of the plan, the chief directors created a massive distributional apparatus, consciously attempting to integrate the latest methods in media work with the active participation of countless supporters. Or, in the words of José Gotovitch, "the campaign constituted a totality—today one would call it a multi-media affair—in the service of an idea, of a positive program around which one was to rally public opinion."[37]

Initially, study courses and retreats were the methods used to spread the word among a core of activists. Then mass meetings for a socialist audience were carried out, at the same time that teams of bicyclists crisscrossed the Belgian countryside in an effort to introduce the Plan de Man to a rural audience. In March 1934 the first issue of a special French-language weekly devoted to the propagation of planist thought appeared. In May the Flemish counterpart was launched. A series of pamphlets and brochures, frequently directed at specific audiences, were put into circulation.[38] Apart from the print media, radio programs, theater productions, "plan cabarets," mass meetings with songs and speaking choruses and even a film were developed to create a powerful image of impending success and a dynamic toward the embrace of planist ideology on the part of the majority of the Belgian population. Playing on insights gained from the study of mass psychology and propaganda techniques, planist activists set out to instill an emotional identification with planist goals in those portions of Belgian society previously untouched by socialist appeals.[39]

Part of the dynamism underlying propaganda for the plan was due to the level of support emanating from the left wing of the BWP/POB. Elements of the radical left-wing faction Action Socialiste and the youth movement organized in the JGS were in the forefront of planist activity. As de Man explicitly stated at a planist conference in Paris on 10 December 1934: "Despite the fact that, since its inception, after only several weeks, it [the plan] had conquered the majority of the Belgian Workers' Party and the allied trade union movement, the planist movement is essentially a movement of the Left, even the Left within the Socialist Party, and a movement of young people."[40] Action Socialiste was a mainstay of the left faction within the LSI with close ties to the independent left socialist and dissident communist groupings of their time.[41] The JGS was then undergoing a rapid radicalization which led, in the course of 1934–36, to the brink of severing all relations with the social democratic Socialist Youth International.[42] Their energetic mobilization in support of planist politics imparted a particularly militant flavor to their common cause and was a constant source of potential conflict over the meaning and direction of the Plan de Man, for the officially adopted planist project clearly committed the advocates of Belgian planism to a legalist approach. The official resolution prescribed "that the Belgian labor party will immediately undertake an offensive for the conquest of power *by all constitutional means* in order to realize this plan"—an unequivocal statement at odds with the spirit of de Man's invocations of the end of the reformist era.[43] In his major speech to the December 1933 BWP/POB congress, de Man defended the more cautious approach, but he added a proviso: "If, because of some contingencies, the action of the capitalist class, by means of the abandonment of legality, takes away our legal means of propaganda, which we need in order to conquer the majority, then we must defend ourselves by any means necessary, even if, in order to do so, we ourselves must abandon legal ways of action."[44] One year later, in Paris, he again emphasized his reticence with regard to extralegal ventures: "It is no longer by means of the revolution that one can arrive at [state] power; it is via [state] power that one can arrive at the revolution."[45]

This open renunciation of the insurrectionary road caused some consternation in the ranks of the Plan de Man's supporters. The spokesperson for Action Socialiste, Paul-Henri Spaak, in his congress intervention, expressed his misgivings about the superficial way in which the party appeared to treat the question of legality. Spaak asked for a clarification of how exactly the party was planning to defend itself in case of the imposition of dictatorial rule. Referring to the events in Italy and Germany,

Spaak suggested that such questions were far from purely theoretical concerns: "We do not ask you to tell us here which means, which forces and which methods you will employ. That is a matter of confidence between the party leadership and that portion which one terms the Left of the party." But Spaak pressed for concrete preparations.[46] Apparently the doubts were largely allayed, for, apart from a small minority of the Brussels federation, which abstained in the final vote, all other BWP/POB federations voted unanimously in favor of the Plan de Man.[47] Yet the near unanimity behind the adopted resolution merely constituted a thin veneer over ongoing deep disagreements between the party leadership and Action Socialiste. For the left-wing forces, the attractiveness of the Plan de Man lay not only in the concrete measures advocated but also in the dynamic generated by united action. As Spaak emphasized in a series of articles in *L'Action Socialiste*, their weekly paper, prior to the December 1933 congress: "For years our position was defensive and negative. We prevented, or attempted to prevent, our adversaries from pursuing their offensives victoriously; we wanted to keep the conquests gained by our elders; we repulsed attacks."[48] Now, "for the first time in its history, the POB poses *the transformation of society as its immediate task*."[49]

Activists of the socialist Left appropriated planist politics into their arsenal of methods for the immediate revolutionary transformation of society. The main reporter at the November 1934 JGS national congress, the JGS national secretary Fernand Godefroid, when addressing potential contradictions between planist politics and the perceived necessity of a revolutionary path, stated: "The Plan clarifies the situation, specifies our objectives, but it does not eliminate revolutionary contingencies. To the contrary, we believe it calls for them!"[50] Walter Dauge, the popular left-wing activist from the Borinage, once publicly declared that when he "conditionally" joined the planist effort, he did so on the basis "of what was new, bold and revolutionary in it," and he would have nothing further to do with it if its message were to be watered down.[51] De Man himself, in an open letter to Spaak, referred to articles in *L'Action Socialiste* which proclaimed that "the preliminary act before the realization of the Plan is the revolutionary conquest of power," something which de Man expressly distanced himself from.[52] The Belgian Plan of Labor therefore generated much enthusiasm, a vast propaganda effort, but also contradictory interpretations of the meaning of the plan. Carried forward by elements of the radicalized socialist Left, it imparted a spirit of readiness for action into the towns and countryside of the Belgian state. With increasing efficiency, the well-oiled planist propaganda machine galvanized the country more than any other political project in recent memory.

Echoes of the Plan de Man: Germany, Austria and Spain

One of the close collaborators of de Man, Léo Moulin, in a recent communication describes the impact of the plan on Belgian public opinion in the following words: "The Plan of Labor was a nuclear explosion in the party and in all of Belgium. People truly believed that one had found a solution in order to escape the crisis." And this sentiment was by no means restricted to socialists, including "many Catholics; many Catholic trade unionists, et cetera, even liberals; bourgeois individuals; intellectuals;

the audience of Hendrik de Man was infinitely larger than that of a simple socialist theoretician."[53] The popularity of Hendrik de Man also transcended national boundaries.

In Germany, the place of origin of the plan, interest in planist thought was of necessity restricted after the end of legal avenues toward change, for a key prerequisite for the success of planist action was the presence of a legal framework for maneuvers. In its absence, interest in the Plan de Man was largely restricted to party intellectuals. Jakob Marschak and Emil Lederer were two prominent economists of the pre-Hitler era who followed through on their active interest in planist ideology.[54] Fritz Tarnow, one of the originators of the 1932 German trade union's work creation program, likewise pursued such lines of thought for years thereafter.[55] Yet in these cases their interest in planist schemes may have had little to do with the Belgian model.[56] In several other instances these links were explicit. Wilhelm Hoegner, some ten years later the first prime minister of Bavaria, in March 1935 expressed his admiration for the ideas of Hendrik de Man, particularly in regards to the latter's efforts to overcome the narrow orientation of social democracy to the blue-collar proletariat only.[57] Alexander Schifrin, active on the left fringes of German and European social democracy in these years, in a programmatic article in Hilferding's *Zeitschrift für Sozialismus*, a retrospective assessment of the defeat of the German Left, bemoaned the failure of belated efforts at united fronts just prior to 30 January 1933. He noted the beginning of a convergence between planist ideology and strivings for united fronts and reasoned: "If the coup d'état of 30 January had not interrupted these promising developments, the German labor movement could have reached, on the basis of its own experience, the first stage of its ascent [to power]; the liquidation of the reformist epoch would have occurred spontaneously and organically."[58] Curt Geyer, in the leadership of the Prague SPD, then momentarily under the influence of the massive shift to the left within international social democracy, wrote a front-page editorial in the SPD's *Neuer Vorwärts* on the BWP/POB's December 1933 congress and called for emulation: "The work of the Belgian comrades is more than the drawing up of a program. It is a renewal of the will [to act]. In this sense we too must work programmatically—and we will do so."[59] By no means everyone, of course, supported the trajectory of the Plan de Man. Most social democrats remained silent and continued to adhere to the tenets of orthodox Marxism, personified by Rudolf Hilferding's continued mockery of any and all attempts at governmental intervention in the economy short of total nationalization.[60]

Echoes of the Plan de Man were likewise audible in the Austrian republic. Yet here, too, the slide into dictatorship, barely six weeks after the publication of the Belgian plan, rendered the political circumstances less than appropriate for the wholesale application of planist ideology. Pushed by the concerns of socialist trade unions, Austrian socialists had already begun in the course of 1933 to pay serious attention to the propagation of a jobs creation program as a solution to the economic crisis.[61] Yet the more radical Belgian variant of planist politics was also no stranger to the Austrians' debate. The left-wing social democrat Oskar Pollak, in particular, repeatedly published articles on Belgian planism and de Man in the pages of the Austrian socialist daily, underscoring the system-transforming dimension of the Plan de Man. In a review of *Die Sozialistische Idee*, Pollak highlighted the activist and utopian dimension in the thought of Hendrik de Man. He approvingly cited de Man: "The correct solution [to the lack of proletarian unity] is to reintegrate the utopian element into socialism, but in a manner that one may recognize the utopia as the point of departure, instead of as the ultimate goal; or, in other words, as contemporary psychological reality instead of a future foundation for society."[62]

Even in faraway Spain, reverberations of the Plan de Man found their way into socialist discourse. As I have repeatedly mentioned in preceding chapters, the PSOE underwent a process of rapid radicalization in the year prior to October 1934. In the midst of its tactical and strategic reorientation, a leading member of the PSOE, Fernando de los Ríos, suggested at an executive committee session in December 1933 "that several members of the executive travel to Brussels in order to familiarize themselves with the Plan of Labor which the Belgian socialists are in the process of creating." This initiative, however, was immediately defeated when Francisco Largo Caballero said that, "if time would be no object, he would favor the trip to Belgium but, in his view, the problem at hand demands an immediate solution."[63] It probably did not help the course of Spanish planism that the most active proponents of planist politics, Julián Besteiro and Andrés Saborit, were located in the moderate spectrum of PSOE politics.[64] Yet the radiation of planist ideology into Spain was not restricted to moderate socialists.

Already in 1931 and 1932, the syndicalist magazine *Orto*, directed by dissident anarcho-syndicalists around Angel Pestaña and Valeriano Orobón Fernandez, the same forces that were in the forefront of united front politics within the ranks of Spanish, and especially Catalan, anarchism, carried articles by the onetime Comintern instructor Lucien Laurat, then active in the SFIO, on the politics of planned economies.[65]

"Planomania" in France

It was no surprise that a French author introduced the ideas of planist politics into Spanish debates, for it was in France that the strongest wave of sympathy arose in favor of another national version of the Belgian Plan de Man. Throughout 1934 a veritable fascination with the notion of a plan gripped French politicians from all walks of life, leading one observer to note that, "everywhere, plans are sprouting like mushrooms in the rain."[66] One strong advocate of planist thought in France was the aforementioned Lucien Laurat. A longtime specialist in economic affairs, Lucien Laurat had already published several brochures on aspects of a planned economy when he first met Hendrik de Man in April 1933. It was probably a mutually satisfying encounter as de Man utilized a private conversation to question Laurat on the experiences of the Soviet New Economic Policy in 1923–27, a period Laurat had experienced first-hand.[67] In the fall of 1933 Laurat began to edit a monthly journal, *Le Combat Marxiste*, a major source of information on planist politics for the next several years.

The second major influence behind the rapid spread of planist thought in French socialist circles was the small group of young intellectuals who had first gained public attention with the publication of *Révolution Constructive*, a book devoted to the problem of the intellectual renovation of French socialist thought, whose title gave the group its name. Among the eleven authors were Georges Lefranc, who was to

TABLE 6   Membership versus Electoral Support of the BWP/POB and the SFIO

Party	Membership	Electoral Votes	Percentage of Total Electorate
BWP/POB	559,000	869,486	37.1
SFIO	137,684	1,975,593	20.0

Source: Werner Kowalski, ed. *Geschichte dere Sozialistischen Arbeiter-Internationale (1923–1940)* (Berlin: Deutscher Verlag der Wissenschaft, 1985), Appendix: "Tabelle zu 6.3." Figures are for 1932, except for the BWP/POB total membership, which dates from 1931.

become a prolific historian of the French labor movement and radical politics; Robert Marjolin, one of the architects of the post–World War II European Community; and Claude Lévi-Strauss. Convinced of the relevance of planist politics for their own project, this group of activists became a key distributor of planist ideas in France.[68]

Yet the appeal of planist politics rapidly spread beyond the narrow limits of these two core groupings. Key figures in several factions of the SFIO embraced some version of planist politics. Portions of the trade union movement took on the task of popularizing its ideas. In early February 1934 several dissident factions within the SFIO joined forces behind a common planist resolution which sought a fundamental reorientation of SFIO politics in accordance with the Belgian example. Georges Lefranc reports that "entire [cantonal] federations adopted the text almost unanimously, notwithstanding the objections formulated by their elected representatives. A groundswell of revolt animated the activists, especially the young."[69] Because of the 6 February 1934 Parisian émeute, the impending Lille congress of the SFIO was never held. While it is unlikely that the motion "For a Socialist Offensive" would have garnered a majority of party delegates, it was reasonable to assume that "a strong minority" would have spoken in favor of this plan, thus creating favorable conditions for the reinforcement of the inner-party offensive.[70] As it happened, the dynamic toward radical planism was undercut by the rival strategy of united fronts, which began to exercise an enormous attraction for socialist activists in the wake of 12 February 1934. Planist politics continued to sway large numbers of people, within or without the socialist Left, and even played a certain role in the elaboration of the French popular front. But, in a trajectory far different from that of the Belgian Plan de Man, the original impetus of planist politics vanished parallel to the rise of the united front as a concrete, tangible alternative. Why was this so?

In Belgium, classic united front politics, the joining of forces of social democrats and communists, was never on the agenda. The forces of Third International communism were minute compared to the numbers organized in the POB/BWP. Belgian social democracy exercised a virtual monopoly within the socialist Left. Table 6 shows that while electoral support exceeded socialist membership, the membership base of the BWP/POB was perhaps the strongest of all European social democratic parties, given the small size of the country. In France, by contrast, SFIO membership was minute compared with electoral votes received, leaving French social democrats far more vulnerable to rapid swings in the popular mood. Thus, when the call for joint action between socialists and communists became the watchword of the day, the SFIO had little room for maneuver.

With the meteoric rise of united front discourse after 12 February 1934 in France, particularly among the social democratic Left, the competing ideology of socialist planism rapidly lost ground. Themselves favorable to united front politics, advocates of French radical planism were not strong enough to leave their imprint on the shape of the emerging united front. The absence of key leadership support within the SFIO and disunity within the planist ranks engendered a situation where French planism became a key intellectual current within French left-wing economic thought through-out the 1930s and beyond but was unable to become the dominant paradigm within socialist debates. The proliferation of plans throughout 1934 and 1935 was there-fore as much a sign of weakness as an indication of support. A front-page manifesto published in *Bataille Socialiste*, the journal of the SFIO-Left, was on the mark when it stated in early January 1935: "A large number of 'plans' have come to light in recent days, testifying, by their multiplicity, simultaneously to the revolutionary character of the current situation and to the general state of disarray of contemporary think-ing."[71] The final death knell of French socialist planism was sounded with the super-session of united front politics with the discourse of popular fronts. For, by then, all attempts at qualitative transformation of the social system had to make way to the efforts to enlist the support of the Radical Party to the defense of democratic rights. This limited agenda left no space for the experimentation with planist ideology in pursuit of socialist goals.[72]

The Sudden Fall of the Plan de Man

Meanwhile, in the Belgian state the promise of the Plan de Man underwent its own peculiar evolution. In December 1934 the third wave of planist agitation began to captivate the nation. As an editorial in *Plan* proudly announced:

> Whenever we organize meetings on the Plan of Labor, we see crowds that we have never encountered before, even in the course of the most heated electoral cam-paigns. The organizers of these meetings, who are quite familiar with the people in these respective localities, are every time astonished to see the large proportion of nonsocialists who come to listen to our speakers. Most frequently, a third or half of the audience is composed of small shopkeepers, white-collar employees, mem-bers of the liberal professions, civil servants, artisans and farmers from all walks of life.[73]

On 7 February 1935, the association of shopkeepers and artisans in Liège became the first independent petit-bourgeois association to officially adhere to the Plan of Labor.[74] All eyes were now directed toward a national demonstration in support of the plan, called for 24 February in the capital city of Brussels.

Meanwhile, the popularity of Hendrik de Man steadily increased, to the point that it acutely embarrassed de Man, whom Léo Moulin describes as "a man devoted to his studies; a man who felt at home in libraries; a man who, besides, loved the outdoors; who certainly was not a man at home in labor centers and socialist clubs."[75] A passage in de Man's autobiography graphically depicts his enormous popularity and his sense of intense unease:

The more the people treated me as a kind of saviour, the heavier did this burden my conscience. I recall a typical winter night's scene when I arrived in a small Flemish industrial town, where I was expected to address a meeting. From the railway station to the meeting hall I was surrounded and almost carried along by a crowd which shouted: There he is. There he is! Women kissed the lines of my overcoat, others held up their children for me to touch. Far from relishing in it I trembled, and when my travelling companion wondered why I was so dismayed by this impassioned reception, I answered him: But it is awful! I am no miracle doctor! And how difficult will it be not to disappoint these poor folk![76]

Events in the traditional hotbed of Belgian working-class activism, the mining region of the Borinage, soon brought the political atmosphere to a boiling point.

Large-scale unemployment and the attendant social misery had polarized this southern province of the Belgian state. When the conservative government, headed by Georges Theunis, decreed the lowering of unemployment benefits and pensions, the crisis point was reached. Hendrik de Man, together with Paul-Henri Spaak and a local deputy, Achille Delattre, a former miner himself, on 19 January 1935 addressed a large crowd assembled in the mining community of Quaregnon. De Man later recalled:

I will never forget the formidable and sombre spectacle. Towards sunset, we witnessed from the speakers' platform, erected on the main square of the village, enormous dark columns from all directions filling up the square, without a single banner, without fanfare, not a single shout. It was as if all of the rage of this miserable planet had suddenly gathered there for one last silent warning.

During the course of the speeches, some voices clamoring for a general strike could be heard, but they belonged to a minority in the assembled crowd; "far more impressive was the silence of the masses, who, after having listened to our speakers, disappeared into the night."[77] This experience was a signal event in the political evolution of Hendrik de Man and Paul-Henri Spaak, his main political ally behind the planist surge. That evening, upon their return to Brussels, de Man penned an impassioned editorial for *Le Peuple* entitled "Impressions from the Borinage: It Is Five Minutes to Midnight," in which he exclaimed:

To hell with weekly articles! To hell with professorial dissertations, statistics, traditional arguments of economists and patient explanations of the Plan of Labor! I've had enough of continued explanations of the Plan. The moment of explanation is past; the moment of applications has sounded. From now on, we need to be less concerned with arguments than with solutions. After more than a year dedicated to the exposition of particulars, the moment has arrived to make decisions.[78]

The sullen anger of the crowd at Quaregnon impressed upon de Man the necessity for quick, decisive action. He realized that the experience in the Borinage exemplified the popular mood throughout the land.

Léo Moulin remembers Hendrik de Man returning "truly frightened" from his visit to Quaregnon. The point had been driven home to the head of the BWP/POB that something had to be done soon.[79] Hendrik de Man's son recalls his father's anguish over the alternative either to engage in open rebellion, "which would entail the responsibility of many deaths," or to avoid bloodshed by means of forming a moderate coalition and entering a new government.[80] This was exactly the alternative which Hendrik de Man posed to the public in the aforementioned editorial. He believed that, while a social explosion was imminent, there was still the chance to spare the country the dissensions of a general strike and the accompanying social unrest, and to create a parliamentary majority which would respond positively to the desperate calls to attention by the victims of the crisis. Yet, at this point de Man was profoundly uncertain over the prospects of the latter course, for, as he expressed it in his editorial, "a hungry stomach does not have ears." It was ultimately "hunger which propels the masses to desperate solutions." It was a race against time.[81]

Three days later, the headline of yet another one of his editorials sounded a more moderate tone. "The Hour of the Plan Must Come Before the Hour of the General Strike" was the title of this piece, in which he counseled patience and hope in a peaceful solution to the crisis.[82] But when the Theunis government outlawed the plan demonstration scheduled for 24 February, a hastily called joint emergency conference of the BWP/POB and the socialist trade unions debated the merits of a general strike. A motion favoring the general strike was narrowly defeated in a vote of 581,412 to 481,112, with 23,619 abstentions.[83] This strike vote became a major turning point in the year-long dynamic toward a planist alternative.

On 18 March 1935 the Theunis government was forced to resign in the middle of a financial panic gripping the nation. The BWP/POB leadership immediately dropped its insistence that they would consider participation in a government only if that government *wholly* adopted the Plan de Man. The foundations were laid for the entry of social democrats into a coalition government. Starting in the fall of 1934, Hendrik de Man had come to the conclusion that the original idea of coming to power on the crest of popular support for a planist regime entailed certain dangers and that the BWP/POB alone was a less than certain vehicle on the road to success. He believed that, instead of banking on a gamble of all or nothing, a more certain way out of the crisis would postpone qualitative social transformations but would lead "fairly rapidly to the absorption of unemployment and the end of the crisis." Beginning in November 1934, in a series of private negotiations with a Christian Democratic banker, Paul van Zeeland, an economist favorable to mild forms of planist interventions, an accord was reached on a governmental program along such moderate lines.[84]

On 26 March 1935 a new coalition government of Christian Democrats and social democrats, headed by van Zeeland, was announced to the public. Two of the socialist ministers were Hendrik de Man and, to everyone's even greater surprise, Paul-Henri Spaak, the former spokesperson for Action Socialiste. The second extraordinary congress of Belgian social democracy in less than six weeks, called for 30 and 31 March 1935, despite bitter recriminations sounded by members of the left wing and the youth section, sanctioned the party's decision with an overwhelming majority of 519,672 to 41,902, with 18,928 abstentions.[85] Thus the Belgian experiment at radical social transformation by means of planist politics, which had set out to break the back of finance capital, ended with the participation of de Man and Spaak in a government headed by a vice governor of the Banque Nationale. The veteran socialist Fernand Brunfaut, in his conference declaration, criticized the congress decision and, comparing it to previous enthusiastic votes in favor of joining coalitions, noted:

"I rediscover once again, right here, the atmosphere of previous congresses that opted for coalitions in 1919, 1921 and 1925: same arguments and pretexts, but also the same illusions. . . . By opting for this road, which the POB is taking in 1935, in a process identical to that of certain other elements of social democracy on the decline, I fear the most terrible consequences."[86] One of the immediate consequences of the BWP/POB entry into the van Zeeland cabinet was the de facto abandonment of the Plan de Man. After fifteen months of continual agitation in favor of "The Plan; All of the Plan; Nothing But the Plan," only minor portions of the planist arsenal were taken over by the new coalition, essentially countercyclical measures meant to shore up the sagging economy but not to challenge the social order. While the BWP/POB continued to pass pious resolutions in favor of continued agitation for the plan, in practice such statements of intent remained inconsequential.

Conclusion

At the important 10 December 1934 Sorbonne conference featuring de Man, Georges Lefranc and René Belin, the adjunct general secretary of the French General Confederation of Labor, Hendrik de Man openly proclaimed that the aim of the planist movement was "to obtain power legally" and that "planism remains gradualist." In the same speech, however, de Man also mentioned "that one can best symbolize the dynamic unity of structural reforms with the improvement of the conjuncture by referring to it as a combination of the objectives of Lenin and of Roosevelt."[87] This was certainly an ambivalent statement open to varied interpretations. Earlier on, in the first stage of the genesis of the plan, de Man was more explicit. In his final chapter of *Die Sozialistische Idee*, his vision of the planist potential was less openly devoted to the gradual road. When discussing ways of reaching socialism, he asserted that socialist ideals "can no longer be obtained by a movement which is devoted to operate within the constraints of capitalism; they can only be obtained through a movement *against* capitalism. The existing social order becomes increasingly intolerable every day. It can no longer be ameliorated; it only deserves to be overturned [*renversé*]."[88]

The contrast between de Man's statements of early 1933 and late 1934 suggests, on the one hand, a certain evolution of his thought. On the other hand, this innate ambivalence enabled the forces of the radical Left within social democracy to gain a point of entry into the planist movement, which official plan propaganda could not efface. For, as I pointed out earlier, in Belgium one of the motor forces of the planist movement was to be found among the revolutionary socialist youth and the left-wing supporters of Action Socialiste. This was clearly recognized by leading planist ideologists even after the BWP/POB's entry into the van Zeeland cabinet. As late as November 1935, Max Buset, a key figure behind the Plan de Man and himself an earlier sympathizer of Action Socialiste, wrote in an open letter to the socialist youth, when trying to revitalize planist agitation: "You will discover that the planist conception is, given the circumstances in the Belgian state and of our forces, the conception of the true Left within our party."[89]

The identification of the socialist Left with planist ideology was perhaps even stronger in France, where few leading party stalwarts even formally embraced the plan. Jules Moch and Vincent Auriol were some of the few centrist leaders of the SFIO to openly identify with the planist project at some point during their careers. Léon Blum, by contrast, authored a series of articles in the SFIO daily Le Populaire criticizing planist ideas precisely at the time of its highest acceptance in French socialist circles. Blum, who, like many social democrats, could envision no alternative other than full nationalization under socialism or small remedial measures under capitalism, ignored the transitional dimension of radical planist thought. Thus, for Blum, planism fell short of the socialist goal but was too radical to take effect under capitalism.[90] Within the SFIO-Left, by contrast, planist sentiment was far more widespread throughout 1934 and 1935. The planist resolution drawn up for the Lille congress of the SFIO, the congress which, on account of the events of 6 February 1934, never occurred, was signed and supported by leading members of three party factions situated on the left: Bataille Socialiste, the traditional faction of the SFIO-Left; Combat Marxiste; and Révolution Constructive. The leading spokesperson for Bataille Socialiste, Jean Zyromski, in the period preceding the next party congress in Toulouse (May 1934), was a determined advocate of planism but with a radical bent. In mid-April 1934 he asserted in a front-page editorial in Bataille Socialiste that "the march toward socialism by means of democratic, legal, peaceful evolution" has been rendered irrelevant in the current situation, and he argued for the "necessity of specifically revolutionary action by the working class." And, in this undertaking, the advocacy of a concrete plan played a key role: "The conquest of power and the Plan are, to me, two closely connected notions. Power, all power, for the realization of the plan, for the enforcement of the Plan; this, I believe, is the terrain on which we shall operate."[91]

Members of Révolution Constructive debated the merits and demerits of a plan in similar fashion. Pierre Boivin once suggested "I do not pretend that planism necessarily implies, or even prefers, recourse to insurrection or the general strike. What I do not understand is how it is supposed to exclude it."[92] Robert Marjolin, in December 1934, argued that, "taken in isolation from socialist action and revolutionary goals, the Plan loses all significance and leads straight toward organized capitalism, as undesirable as the capitalism of free enterprise which it would supersede."[93] And in January 1935, Claude Beaurepaire was still contesting the supposed irrelevance of a link between the "Plan and insurrection" in the pages of their journal.[94]

Social democratic planism appeared in many shades and variations, particularly in the years 1933–35. I have focused on its most radical portion, yet, with equal ease, European social democrats frequently adopted more moderate proposals too.[95] This reflected the polymorphous nature of the planist project at the same time that it underscored the tremendous potential inherent in the plan, for its rise to prominence within Belgian and other European socialist movements graphically displays the desperate scramble for effective solutions then preoccupying social democrats everywhere. In its more radical incarnations, particularly in Belgium and France, it briefly emerged as a coherent alternative not only to the social crisis of the day but to the entire social order. It was this interpretation of the planist movement as an emancipatory, and not merely ameliorative, project which accounts for at least part of the vast popular approval in the Belgian case, and for the solid support given to the plan by many left-wing social democrats.

The measured vagueness of the Plan de Man on questions of state power, important for the initial obtainment of broad support expressed at the December 1933 BWP/POB congress, also served to seal its fate. For, when push came to shove, when it became apparent that the moment had come to take decisive measures, the plan leadership refused to countenance open rebellion and was content to join a center-left coalition in pursuit of limited objectives. Hendrik de Man, Paul-Henri Spaak and others, in late March 1935 thus replicated the vacillation characteristic of other left-leaning European social democrats in 1934—witness the hesitations of the Austro-Marxist leadership faced with the spontaneous Schutzbund revolt or the similar paralysis afflicting the leaders of the PSOE in early October 1934. This is not to say that an open insurrection would have led to success or even that a majority of the Belgian party would have favored such a course. Clearly, the massive approval of the decision to form part of the van Zeeland cabinet suggests otherwise. But this incident equally clearly suggests the limits of the planist surge. As a strategy for social transformation, given its initial success, it sooner or later had to confront the task of a qualitative break with the prevailing social order. Once the decision was taken to moderate the course, the upward momentum, the inner dynamic accountable for much of the plan's success, was irreversibly broken.

There are interesting parallels between the timing of the Plan de Man's rise and fall and the fate of the sole other contemporaneous alternative strategy to capture the social democratic imagination in the months between early 1933 and early 1935: the orientation toward united fronts. The virtually identical trajectory of the two political projects suggests close political affinities. And, indeed, as I explicated previously, Hendrik de Man conceived of his plan as a means to overcome divisions on the Left. The experience of disunity in Germany was the single most important factor behind his reimmersion in socialist politics after an almost two-decade-long absence. But de Man paid close attention to middle-class concerns, a cornerstone of later popular front strategies. Can the Plan de Man, then, be considered a precursor of subsequent popular fronts?

As I argue elsewhere, the lack of attention to middle-class concerns was a serious drawback of most united front initiatives, although this was not a cardinal rule. Where united fronts differed from popular fronts regarding the question of middle-class allies—apart from their *relative* disinterest in this topic—was in their contention that one need not compromise one's socialist goals under the assumption that such espousal of radical ideas would frighten potential middle-class allies. Instead, proponents of united fronts argued that only a sufficiently radical solution to the crises of their day would be able to win over middle-class allies to the common cause. As we have seen, it was precisely the view of Hendrik de Man that only unusually deep-seated measures would attract petit-bourgeois victims of the Great Depression to the camp of the socialist Left. The planism of Hendrik de Man must therefore be considered, for all practical purposes, a variant of united front strategies.

Both explicit united front practices and the project of the Plan de Man were at their peak in the months of 1934 and vanished in the course of the first half of 1935 in order to give way to more moderate approaches. As I argue elsewhere, the negative repercussions of the Asturian revolt in October 1934 marked the beginning of the end of united front strategies everywhere in Europe. It is undoubtedly more than just coincidental that Hendrik de Man began his secret negotiations with Paul van Zeeland in November 1934. While I have no hard evidence to establish a firm link between de Man's personal and political evolution and the increasingly ominous national and international trajectory of the socialist project in the aftermath of the Asturian October, the parallel moves toward moderation, starting in the fall of 1934, clearly suggest more than nationally specific causes. They were symptoms of a rapidly worsening world situation, coupled with a growing sense of doubt regarding the applicability of socialist united fronts.

As just mentioned, the strategy of radical planism is clearly distinct from united front proposals in one all-important way. Whereas most advocates of united fronts paid little or no attention to the plight of what were then generally referred to as "the middle classes," all planist projects paid close attention to the fate and the needs of social groups and classes far beyond the limited numbers of the blue-collar proletariat. In that sense the planism of Hendrik de Man and other radical plans, despite their inner contradictions, laid out the broad contours and, in some cases, detailed specifics of a nonreformist path for social transformation, arguing the necessity for transitional solutions in order to effect a broad cross-class alliance for socialism. It was the most coherent, all-encompassing and therefore radical proposal for qualitative social change to emerge during the thirties.

Clearly, as a socialist project it failed. The experience of Belgian, or for that matter French, planism is now a largely forgotten episode in the national histories of the countries concerned. There was little awareness of the planist potential present in the post–World War II Left.[96] Yet radical planism deserves recognition not solely for its relevance to debates about radical social change; radical planist experiments were also important manifestations of a larger paradigm shift affecting European societies and economies at that time. They were integral elements of the move toward governmental intervention in economy and society which Karl Polanyi, in 1944, eloquently described as *The Great Transformation*. Social democrats, but not only social democrats, were some of the first actually to attempt the implementation of such bold plans, which then captured the imagination of economic experts and politicians on all five continents. Socialists, wittingly or unwittingly, thus helped shape the contours of post–World War II Europe. Not least of all in this more limited, yet also more global, sense, the experiments in Continental social democratic planism deserve a wider hearing.

The awareness of an impending paradigm shift in the history of the modern world was already present at the 1931 World Social Economic Planning Congress in the Amsterdam Koloniaal Instituut. It was perhaps most clearly and evocatively articulated by Goetz Briefs, the head of the Institute for Industrial Sociology and Industrial Relations at the Berlin Technical University, who began his presentation with the following words:

> Let us imagine that we would live one hundred years ago, and this assembly hall would be filled with people whose task it was, three generations ago, to discuss the economic problems of their times. I am sure that then we would all say: "We must put an end to this economy bound by limits imposed by the state and by the guilds, and we must move forward to free enterprise [*hinein in die Konkurrenz*]!" We would have spoken in favor of absolutely free competition with similarly convincing

arguments as they are put forward today in defense of planning. And we would have asserted that free enterprise would bring about economic harmony. Three generations were convinced that free enterprise would lead to welfare and social harmony. But now, at this congress, we have heard very few voices who consistently defend the idea of laissez-faire capitalism.[97]

Charles Maier, in his seminal 1970 article "From Taylorism to Technocracy," underscores that the utopian dimension of the fascination with rationalization, a dimension not uncommon in the first post–World War I years, vanished with prosperity and disappeared during the Great Depression.[98] The 1932 Amsterdam congress belies this judgment. Yet, more so than the strange alliance of social democrats and social engineers gathered in the Koloniaal Instituut, it was the experience of social democratic radical planism in 1934 which was the culmination of this period of hopes and illusions. At the same time that it was the summit and supersession of the juncture between social democratic and technocratic visions of utopia, the 1934 planist surge once again suggests the unique character of this moment in European history, when socialist, but not only socialist, ideologies were in a constant state of flux.

SIX

The Nature of a Popular Front

Hendrik de Man was crucially aware of the necessity to win allies to the working-class-based socialist ideal. Yet, contrary to received revisionist wisdom, the Flemish social democrat refused to link this search for a broader social base to a softening of the social agenda of the multiclass movement he hoped to construct. Essentially, de Man pursued a pragmatic approach, with strategies and tactics changing in accord with the overall political conjuncture. In times of relative social peace, "in order to envisage an alliance with the middle classes, or propaganda among the midddle classes, one needed to pour water into our wine," meaning that socialists would have done well to tone down their social message; "today, when we are dealing with revolutionized [*révolutionnées*] middle classes, even if they are not yet revolutionaries, we need to add wine to our water, if we want to win them over!"[1] In the concrete circumstances of the 1930s, the Flemish social democrat banked on the inbuilt dynamic of a forward-looking, radical approach when attempting to win "the middle classes" to the side of the socialist movement. In fact, de Man refused to see a difference between social democratic alliance politics regarding nonproletarian strata and the question of the proletarian united front: "This opposition which some would like to establish between, on the one hand, unity of the working class and, on the other hand, the alliance with the middle class is a false opposition. The truth is that the conditions for a rallying of proletarian forces are exactly the same as those for the rallying of proletarian and nonproletarian anticapitalist forces."[2] The way out of the seeming impasse of the Left appeared to lie, then, in the simultaneous attempt to unify the splintered working-class constituency and to draw the disaffected elements of the "old" and "new" middle classes into the forward motion of a rejuvenated, radicalized social democracy. The way to gain petit-bourgeois support, for de Man, seemed to lie in the installment of hope and the resurrection of an optimistic perspective. And this, so he argued, could only be achieved by the promotion of a fundamental break with the prevailing social order. United front politics was held to be the answer to the threat of social and political dislocation. A concrete socialist perspective was regarded as the missing element in social democratic politics not just for the gathering of (blue-collar) working-class forces but also for the retention or conquest of potential middle-class support. This rationale guided radical activists throughout the era of united fronts.

Few proponents of the united front approach, however, were as consciously aware of the necessity to address the specific concerns of potential middle-class supporters, be it within the framework of a socialist perspective, as Hendrik de Man. As I demonstrated in chapter 4, united fronts were, as a rule, specifically designed to be associations of working-class unions and parties only. As I will show in chapter 8, on a local level it was not uncommon for middle-class organizations to actively participate in their actions and deliberations. Yet it is undeniable that, as a matter of principle, united fronts were conceived of and regarded as primarily working-class alliances, which did not reject middle-class support but which also refused to undertake specific efforts to draw in nonproletarian strata in the common fight. It was felt that the force of their example would be sufficient to draw firm middle-class support in their wake. Nothing is more telling in this regard than the relative lack of explicit concern for middle-class affairs in the charters and deliberations of the numerous united fronts constituted throughout Europe mainly in 1934.

Yet the almost mystical belief in the striking force of the proletarian united front suffered a major blow in the wake of the bloody defeat of the October 1934 Asturian Commune and a series of other disappointments and setbacks. Combined with the increasingly gloomy international political conjuncture, which made prospects of impending war seem less improbable, the stage was thus set for a greater attention to alliance politics on the part of the increasingly less self-confident workers' movement, for in the hour of danger it became imperative to seek out support. Small wonder, then, that the forces of the Left began to pay more attention to the needs of potential allies. Out of this concern for a reinforcement of their ranks, out of this growing need to combat fascism and war, arose the third new strategic proposal in less than two years to capture the attention of the European Left: the call for popular fronts. For it was only logical to assume a more decisive impact on the ranks of potential middle-class allies, if more direct considerations were bestowed on their concerns.

This strategic turn did not occur overnight. In chapter 2 I described the slow and faltering evolution of communist policy toward the adoption of a popular front orientation starting in the fall of 1934. Again, it is important to realize that many, if not most, united fronts did in some fashion address the participation of middle-class representatives. Indeed, one of the topics of debate at the very first meeting of the Workers' Alliance of Catalonia on 22 April 1933 was precisely the issue of middle-class representation.[3] The novelty of popular fronts was therefore not so much the explicit interest in middle-class concerns, though this was an important element, but their orientation toward a policy of top-level alliances with nonproletarian, democratic parties, primarily the Radical and Republican Parties of southern Europe. Popular fronts were explicitly designed as multiclass alliances incorporating working-class, petit-bourgeois and bourgeois *organizations* in defense of democratic rights. While the stated short-term objectives of popular fronts were frequently similar to the goals of united fronts, the broadening of the political bases of these alliances necessitated a blunting of united fronts' radical edge.

Radical democratic parties had been a recurrent feature of nineteenth-century Europe. According to Robert O. Paxton, "They had been radically committed to the nineteenth-century struggle for universal suffrage, universal free public schools, separation of church and state, and curbs on professional armies. Vigorous anti-clericalism kept them militant after their other goals had been achieved";[4] and they survived into the twentieth century in predominantly Catholic Latin Europe. Radical parties were staunch defenders of private property, and their social base, as much as can be ascertained, consisted of a solid block of middle-class supporters.[5] One of their French spokespersons, Fernand Buisson, described their character in the following terms. Focusing on the Radical-Socialist Party, Buisson described this organization as "a bourgeois party with the soul of the man in the street [*d'un petit peuple*]." Radical Socialists are "property owners who work and workers who own property"[6] — an apt categorization for a party which, by the twentieth century, despite its name, was neither radical nor socialist. A less benign observer had this to say about the French Radicals: "The Radical Socialist Party represents that political instrument of the big bourgeoisie which is the best adapted to the traditions and prejudices of the petty bourgeoisie."[7]

With the onset of the popular front orientation, the hopes of advocates of greater unity on the Left turned to this agglomeration of antisocialist, left bourgeois parties. As these parties, more than any other political vehicle, appeared to represent the varied components of the "democratic middle class," the desire, on the part of the socialist Left, to build a firm alliance with nonproletarian forces translated into an orientation toward close cooperation with the *parties* of the bourgeois Left. This decision necessitated a softening of the social message of the previously existing united fronts, seriously restricting the dynamic of such fronts. While popular fronts were an organizational extension and enlargement of united fronts, they simultaneously represented a qualitative reduction in the professed or implied goals of unity on the Left. This was the price to be paid for the inclusion of openly antisocialist, nonproletarian organizations in the broader, all-inclusive democratic bloc.

French Socialists Debate the Popular Front

In France the popular front emerged as an organizational extension of a previously existing well-established united front. As I mentioned in chapter 2, the first communist moves in the direction of a popular front date back to the fall of 1934. Yet neither communists nor social democrats initially succumbed to the temptations of such a broader, *though more moderate*, multiclass front. One early defender of such a novel strategy was Louis-Olivier Frossard, a former leading communist and, by 1934, on the right fringes of the SFIO. Picking up on conciliatory comments in the French communist press directed toward the French Radical Party in October 1934, Frossard went on the offensive and demanded that his party comrades fall in step with the communists' apparent turn. Frossard declared himself a supporter of the united front but wondered aloud why one should not "extend unity of action to all those individuals or parties that have identical preoccupations and the same determined resolution to block the road for fascism." He went on to explain:

> I have the impression that Maurice Thorez has clearly understood the insufficiency of an excessively narrow alliance. The other day he spoke of a "popular front," and he suggested a program of positive and practical reforms. A "popular front"? What

does that mean? One will reply to me that Thorez is thinking about the middle classes. I am aware of that. To be sure, one needs to count on the support of the middle classes as we do on the peasantry. But a large fraction of the middle classes and a major portion of the peasantry belong to the party of bourgeois democracy, on which Zyromki [a spokesperson for the SFIO-Left] has declared war. Let us be frank: they vote Radical. Are we going to push them into the enemy camp? Are we distinguishing between the leaders and the ranks? Certainly. Prior to the "united front," the communists also distinguished between the socialist leaders and the troops! But experience has taught them that the troops did not agree to separate from their leaders in response to exhortations from outside. It is important to consider the Radical Party in its entirety—without committing the stupidity of trying out maneuvers to disintegrate their ranks which upset us when we were the target.[8]

Frossard's bold attack in the discussion column of the SFIO's national daily newspaper caused a brief flurry of responses, accusations and counterattacks. The first to join the fray was Jean Zyromski, the only one Frossard had referred to by name. Zyromski pointed out that it was hardly a stroke of genius to call for an open alliance with a party which was a mainstay of the conservative National Union government at that time. On the other hand, Zyromski continued, there is nothing wrong with a conscious orientation toward the middle classes as such. Zyromski declared this "an urgent and necessary task" but refused to identify the middle classes with the Radical Party:

> To the contrary, we will not gain the following of the "democratic" masses, which still follow the Radical Party out of habit and tradition, if we do not employ a vigorous, clear and simple policy, which will lay bare the total inconsistency of the Radical Party's social conceptions, faced with the crisis, and its failure to deal with the enemies of bureaucracy. . . .
>
> Our role is another one: we must carry out a great effort of propaganda and penetration among these intermediate social categories; we must show them that fragmentary remedies are illusions; we must show them that only the march toward socialism will bring about concrete solutions.[9]

Five days later it was the turn of an SFIO centrist, Jean-Baptiste Lebas, to accuse Frossard of a lack of realism. Lebas, the editor of *Le Populaire*, also argued for a radicalization of the SFIO's policy rather than a moderation of its course. Even for a centrist like Lebas, the united front agreement of July 1934 was actually too soft on the future of big business. In its failure to include specifically anticapitalist demands, it was in dire need of a general overhall: "[A]lready its insufficiency is clear to all our militants."[10] This only served to further stimulate debate. Frossard retorted by once again underscoring the value of the agreed-upon united front. But he remained steadfast in his wish to see it enlarged:

> I am far from denying the dynamism of united fronts [*unité d'action*]. I am delighted to see these great mass gatherings, whose success is assured by unity of action; I am delighted to see the enthusiasm which it unleashes in the working-class quarters. I know that if the circumstances demand it, the proletariat will fight, and it will fight well. I do not doubt either its capacity for action or its courage. But I am less concerned with battles than with victory. After Italy, after Austria, after Spain, it is not enough for me to maintain dignity.[11]

Frossard went on to demand SFIO readiness to join forces with the Radicals in a coalition government to defend democracy.

On 7 November, in the midst of a governmental crisis, the SFIO executive unanimously passed a resolution declaring its willingness to take on governmental responsibilities. But no one asked the SFIO to help form a government at that time.[12] Apart from this significant interlude, Frossard's crusade for an alliance with the bourgeois Left went largely unheeded. In the following weeks the discussion column in *Le Populaire* continued the debate. But, for most of the first half of 1935, the question of a popular front remained a nonissue within the SFIO. Only after May 1935 did the issue reappear, but this time with almost instant success. Nevertheless, I deemed it useful to refer extensively to the debate of October–November 1934, for the discussion arose before the actual implementation of a popular front and the participants in the debate could therefore argue free from, and unencumbered by, the divisive and emotionally charged problems of living reality. The necessary degree of abstraction serves to highlight the strategic underpinnings of the popular front project and the designs of its left opponents at the time.

Six months later, at the June 1935 SFIO congress in Mulhouse, French social democracy carried out a radical turn. With majority support from the delegates, it prepared the way for the creation of the rapidly ascending popular front. What had happened in the meantime to lay the groundwork for this switch? Certainly, there were plenty of concerns regarding French domestic policy which served to raise the fears of socialists in France. Several violent incidents involving right-wing paramilitary groups brought home the reality of the fascist danger. Prime Minister Flandin, on the way home from a commemoration of the victims of the right-wing émeute one year earlier, was roughed up by the fascist leagues on 6 February 1935. In mid-April the SFIO's Paris and Lille headquarters were ransacked by the Croix de Feu.[13] But the most decisive influences on the SFIO were, in all likelihood, only indirectly related to the French domestic scene. The greatest force for moderation came to be the rapidly worsening international constellation of forces endangering the survival of democracy throughout Europe and the world.

Karl G. Harr Jr., in his recently published 1950 dissertation, points out "the tremendous if not decisive influence of external events upon the relationship of the parties of the Left" in this crucial period of flux. Harr's analysis benefited from close personal contact with leading personalities of the French popular front. "The question of which arrangement would affect most favorably the ability and determination of France to resist German aggression, although it became uppermost in Communist aims after the Franco-Soviet Pact and also was an important consideration of the Socialist leaders, was never an explicit part of the negotiations" between the PCF and the SFIO, but was ever present nonetheless.[14] The growing threat and fear of war form a constant backdrop to socialists' efforts to revitalize their tradition. Harr's section "Mulhouse, June 1935" provides an excellent account of the impact of the international conjuncture on the deliberations of the SFIO's thirty-second party congress. One year earlier, at Toulouse, the road had been cleared for the SFIO to undertake a bold experiment in united front politics. At Mulhouse there were plenty of defenders who still favored strengthening the working-class alliance with the ultimate goal of "organic unity" (i.e., organizational fusion) with the PCF. "However, for each delegate who retained the plea for organic unity there were several who, in one form or another, saw the advantage of the Popular Front." The party leadership emerged victorious. "The spirit of the resolutions taken a year before at Toulouse had been reversed. Stress was no longer laid upon the pure proletarian policy of the party, but rather upon the use of all means 'without rejecting anyone' to combat fascism."[15]

In the following weeks and months the dynamic toward a popular front took on concrete dimensions. Seven days after the end of the SFIO congress, on 19 June, the Radical Party top leadership agreed to cosponsor and participate in a mass demonstration in defense of the Republic on the French national holiday, 14 July 1935. Two hundred thousand marchers assured the success of this first show of force of the emerging popular front. In October 1935 the Radical Party congress ratified the decision of 19 June. On 11 January 1936 the parties of the working-class and bourgeois Left published their common platform. The two rounds of elections, on 26 April and 3 May, gave the newly formed coalition a resounding show of support. On 5 May 1936 it became clear that the head of the SFIO, Léon Blum, would become the next prime minister of France.[16]

The Waning of the French Radical Party

In the next section on Spain, I will closely examine the mechanism of power *within* a popular front. While there undoubtedly exist many crucial differences between the French and Spanish versions of the popular front, the basic contradictions and problems at the heart of these alliances were roughly the same. Both popular fronts were primarily composed of left bourgeois, social democratic and communist supporters, with a host of smaller groups adhering to the respective pacts. The heightened degree of radicalism in Spanish politics accounts for much of the difference in the intensity of the conflict within the Spanish popular front compared with the French counterpart. The Spanish case thus serves as a better barometer of the social pressures tearing at the edges of a fragile bloc. In the remainder of this assessment of the origins and character of the French popular front, I will therefore concentrate on only one crucial dimension of the turn toward multiclass alliances: the frequently repeated claim that, short of a moderation of the working-class Left, the supporters of French Radicalism would not have come around to support a socialist bloc. While to some extent a counterfactual argument beyond reasonable proof, there are indications that the hold of Radical politics over a substantial portion of French voters began to seriously erode in the course of the nineteen months between October 1934 and May 1936.

The three most important general elections taking place in those months were the cantonal elections of 7 and 14 October 1934; the municipal elections of 5 and 12 May 1935; and the national elections of 26 April and 3 May 1936. All three elections occurred after the PCF-SFIO united front was signed and sealed, meaning that the dynamic of newly developed unitary politics on the socialist Left had an important impact on behavior at the polls. Only in the case of the 1936 national elections was the Radical Party a component part of a larger democratic bloc. But, as I will show, even here the electoral outcome supported rather than contradicted the claims of those advocates of a turn toward the middle classes, who believed that a radical rather than a moderate approach would enable socialists to gain a hearing within their midst.

The October 1934 cantonal elections were a clear victory for the working-class Left. Accounts of the results differ in the number of seats gained or lost, largely because of the multitude of independent or semiindependent candidates, who were oftentimes difficult to classify. But all observers agree that the PCF and SFIO were winners, whereas the Radicals saw diminishing returns.[17] Results from the May 1935 elections were, in one sense, less conclusive. The socialist vote remained stable, although, due to a different constellation of forces, socialists gained control of a number of important city councils, including Marseilles, Nantes, Perpignan, Agen, Colmar and Calais, while losing the majority in only one previous stronghold, Grenoble. The communists continued their upward swing and doubled the number of representatives. Among the parties of the future popular front only the Radicals were left without a reason to celebrate the results. While their losses were minor and supportable, the Radical leaders grew increasingly uneasy about their "disquieting stagnation."[18]

Both elections took place when the Radical Party was still a part of the National Union government headed by Doumergue (October 1934) and Flandin (May 1935). By May 1935, however, the Radical behavior prior to the vote already differed significantly from October 1934. In the fall of 1934 there were few actual cases of Radical cooperation with socialists. By contrast, in May 1935 a common list with socialists was a frequent occurrence, though not yet the rule. Berstein notes "the extraordinary confusion of electoral alliances in which Radicals took part."[19] Nevertheless, in both instances the Radical Party was seen to suffer from the drawbacks of intimate association with the National Union government. All signs seemed to point in the direction of the ascending electoral weight of the working-class Left. Starting in June 1935, the Radical Party threw in its lot with the latter camp.

The national elections which brought victory to the popular front were a further devastating blow to the fortunes of the bourgeois Left. Depending on the count, the Radicals lost between four and six hundred thousand votes and fell below the already disappointing results of the 1928 elections. Whereas the PCF's parliamentary representation jumped from 10 to 72 and the SFIO added 49 to its previous total of 97 for a strong showing of 146, the Radical Party, in most counts, lost 43 of its previous 159. While it thus kept at least second place within the popular front coalition in terms of its parliamentary representation, the defeat was even worse when judging the popular vote. From its prior position of hegemony compared with the SFIO and the PCF, it fell to third place. Even the PCF had garnered more votes than the Radicals.[20]

The balance of the Radical showing at the polls, therefore, tended to support the viewpoint of those among the working-class Left who felt that middle-class voters would not necessarily refuse to support socialists. For, regardless of whether Radicals supported the moderate Right (October 1934 and May 1935) or whether they were part of an alliance with the Left (spring 1936), the traditional party of the French middle class appeared destined to disintegrate, and a significant portion of its electorate now supported the socialist Left. Certainly, one could say that the stunning 1936 defeat of the Radicals occurred only *after* the socialist Left had moderated its appeals. Why, then, did formerly Radical voters switch party allegiance even after the Radical Party became part of the popular front? If fear of socialism would have been a decisive factor in their electoral behavior, nothing would have been safer than continued allegiance to the party of the middle class. Also, the Radical Party had already lost its momentum prior to its entry in the popular front.

In this context it is highly instructive to follow Berstein, the definitive author on the history of French Radicalism, in his analysis of the 1936 results. He notes the gravity of the defeat and points out that, in sixty-six out of ninety *départements*, the Radicals lost votes. Significantly, in the vast majority of the twenty-four continued strongholds, the Radicals' strong showing was due to the hostility of the designated candidate to the project of a popular front. Berstein concludes:

> [T]he electorate of the Radical Party turned away from it in those locations where it appeared clearly as one of the components of the popular front coalition, be it because the supporters of the Left abandoned a party which, in their eyes, was too timid and which had entered too many compromises in the era of National Union, or be it because its moderate clientele refused to sanction its alliance with the extreme Left. In contrast, where the Radicals presented themselves as a barrier against the Rassemblement Populaire, they benefited from the support of moderate voters that compensated — or more than compensated — for the votes lost to the Left.[21]

What had occurred, then, was a classical case of voter polarization benefiting the more determined advocates of clear strategic alternatives, the socialist Left and the more conservative Right. France was undergoing the same process which had previously whittled down electoral support for moderate centrists in other European states — witness Germany toward the end of the Weimar Republic. Therefore, to proclaim the election results of 1936 a victory of the moderate approach toward gaining middle-class support is, given the circumstances, a rather questionable and contradictory hypothesis. Daniel Guérin, for instance, puts forth the claim that the Radical Party's defeat would have been even more stunning had the workers' parties formed an electoral bloc without the Radicals. Based on his calculations, the Radicals would have lost an additional thirty-five seats to the SFIO or PCF if the latter organizations had not entered the electoral pact with the Radical Party.[22] Yet, beyond the shadow of a doubt, the victory of the popular front was perceived as a radical turn by all sectors of French society, particularly after the extent of realignment within the popular front coalition began to emerge. For prior to 3 May 1936 it was generally assumed that the Radicals would lead a popular front coalition government, if not govern alone. This expectation had to be rapidly shelved. The victory of the French popular front followed on the heels of the 16 February 1936 victory of the Spanish *frente popular*.

The Genesis of the Spanish Popular Front

In my explanation of the genesis of the Rassemblement Populaire, I have emphasized the threatening international conjuncture as one major element favoring the extension of the working-class united fronts. The same factors played a role in the constitution of the Spanish popular front, yet, unquestionably, in the Spanish case domestic factors were decisive. Inasmuch as they were the outgrowth of a working-class defeat, the October 1934 uprising, they were nevertheless part and parcel of a sobering and disillusioning international climate. Ricard Vinyes i Ribes, in his magnificent study of the Catalan popular front, describes how this multiclass alliance grew out of a truly popular response to the Madrid government exactions against the vanquished fighters of October 1934. Catalan forces had themselves participated in the October events, though to a minor extent. Similar to the combatants in Asturias and elsewhere, their endeavors had been crushed. Resulting from this mutual defeat, an emotional identification with the victims of repression, most severe among the Asturian working class, grew to encompass vast sectors of Catalan public opinion. Immediately after the October defeat, Catalan forces began to collect donations for the prisoners of the state; and the April 1935 arrival of a trainload of children, sons and daughters of imprisoned, killed or laid off Asturian workers, further reinforced the wave of solidarity transcending class boundaries.[23] Other authors concur in this assessment of the origins of the Spanish popular front. Manuel Tuñon de Lara extends Vinyes's analysis to the rest of the Spanish state and likewise underscores that the Spanish multiclass alliance "evolved out of a defeat." And, whereas in Catalonia public opinion was also strongly influenced by nationalist concerns, the demand for amnesty for political prisoners was the universal rallying cry and focus of early efforts at popular fronts. Compared with the French bloc of the democratic Left, "[t]he Spanish Popular Front was decidedly more of a drama than a festival."[24]

Prior to October 1934, apart from isolated instances of tentative contacts between moderate social democrats and the bourgeois Left, the entire spectrum of the working-class Left was committed to the project of united fronts. The Asturian defeat reversed this trend. With the important exception of the social democratic youth federation, resistance to a broadening of the alliance to the right disintegrated in the following months. High-level talks between individual members of Spanish social democracy, organized in the PSOE, and the bourgeois Left became increasingly common and accepted modes of operation. Indalecio Prieto became the social democratic mastermind behind this strategy. In numerous meetings with Republican politicians in Paris, Brussels and Oostende; with a spate of publications directed at lingering social democratic doubts about this turn; and through other means of overt and subtle pressure, the Basque politician once again proved his flexibility as a party tactician.[25]

An important factor favoring the move toward popular fronts was the state of near-total paralysis which befell the formerly hegemonic left-wing PSOE leadership faction, headed by Francisco Largo Caballero, after the Asturian defeat. With virtually all of its leaders incarcerated, their activities were, of necessity, severely curtailed. Nevertheless, given the relaxed conditions of imprisonment granted to Largo Caballero and his team, they were able to partake in PSOE deliberations. As a matter of fact, a number of PSOE executive committee meetings took place within the Madrid Carcel Modelo to facilitate their active participation. Yet despite the concrete possibilities for debate, the PSOE-Left was remarkably passive in the face of Prieto's offensive. By the late fall of 1935, still incarcerated, the circle around Largo Caballero sanctioned the first organizational efforts at a popular front.[26]

A key indicator of the waning fortunes of the PSOE-Left was the ideological evolution of its Asturian branch. As I indicated in chapter 4, the Asturian federation of the PSOE threw itself wholeheartedly behind the project of united fronts and the military upheaval. After the signing of the Asturian united front agreement, the Asturian social democratic daily *Avance* became the journalistic mainstay of the Alianza Obrera de Asturias, although several key leaders continued to harbor misgivings about this overtly revolutionary posture. This change in political orientation from moderate reformism toward advocacy of a working-class united front by Asturian social democrats had come about as suddenly as the parallel turn to the left by the PSOE as a whole.[27] After the Asturian defeat, the previous model federation of the socialist Left became the most solid mainstay of support to Indalecio Prieto's moderate course. And, by doing so, the Asturian socialists "were really returning to a position with which they were most comfortable." In countless interventions by party members in and out of jail, Asturian socialists defended the broadening of the socialists' appeal and their participation in the emerging popular front.[28]

The Electoral Manifesto

The actual pact inaugurating the popular front was initially conceived of as a purely electoral arrangement between the bourgeois Left and the PSOE. Only at the insistence of Largo Caballero did the PSOE negotiators succeed in including other forces of the Left, most notably the PCE, in the provisions of the pact. The actual negotiations, however, remained the sole domain of the bourgeois and social democratic Left.[29] On 16 February 1936, five days after the announcement of the French pact, the programmatic manifesto of the Spanish popular front was published in the daily press. It is one of my contentions, enlarged upon in chapter 4, that proletarian united fronts possessed an inbuilt dynamic toward radicalization, regardless of the actual terms of the agreed-upon pact. To gauge the dynamic of the popular front it is instructive to begin by studying the actual negotiations between representatives of the bourgeois and working-class Left. As mentioned earlier, in the Spanish case the talks were the exclusive domain of the social democrats and the Republican Left. The actual composition of the electoral committee included two social democrats and three representatives of the Republican parties participating in the popular front: the Republican Left (IR), the Republican Union (UR) and the National Republican Party (PNR).[30]

The archives of Spanish social democracy, repatriated from the Soviet Union in 1981, contain the abbreviated minutes of the actual proceedings of the founding sessions of the popular front. They are a stunning example of the near-total ideological dominance of the Republican negotiators over their social democratic allies. On every single disputed point, the PSOE members were forced to accede to the Republican point of view. It was a first indication of the inherent dynamics of the Spanish popular front. If the broad alliance was to survive, the working-class partners had to capitulate on all important points of doctrinal difference. The negotiations underscore the fact that popular fronts were alliance structures designed to accommodate the most conservative members. The axis of such a coalition was bound to be the lowest common denominator: the position of its most moderate adherent.

As was the case throughout interwar Europe, paramilitary organizations of the Radical Right were a characteristic feature of Spanish society. The working-class Left had a vital interest in their elimination, just like their wish to dissolve the hated *guardia civil.* Therefore, it was no surprise that one of the first points raised by the socialist delegation was precisely the "dissolution of the *guardia civil* and other armed institutions hated by the people." The Republicans stepped in immediately. The minutes record "that the Republican delegation declared in decisive terms that it could not accept such a claim" and that such measures should be "reserved for the estimation of the government and should likewise be extended to cover all armed organizations and all centers of antigovernmental conspiratorial centers."[31] This answer was a barely concealed attempt to fudge the issue and a concerted effort to place equal blame for the difficulties of the Republic on both the Right and the Left. According to the minutes, the PSOE negotiators insisted "on the creation of a popular armed militia, made up of Republicans and select workers and suggested by the respective parties; a measure which the Republican delegation flatly rejected"; the minutes conclude, "in view of the adduced reasons, the socialist delegation abandoned its claim."[32] This procedure of socialist claims, Republican vetoes and PSOE surrender became a standard during the entire talks.

The socialists initially demanded an amnesty for all political prisoners, including those who had been sentenced for common crimes during the upheaval. This was an important proviso, given the judicial tendency to blur the distinction between common and political crimes and to focus on the former. The Republicans naturally expressed their disagreement and successfully demanded that, "of those crimes qualified as common crimes by the law courts," only those may be included in the amnesty "which, in effect, had the character of politico-social crimes," a vague formulation to say the least.[33] Regarding the issue of the countless workers who, in the wake of the October revolt, had been fired from their places of employment and continued to be unemployed, the social democrats demanded full reinstatement. The Republican negotiators retorted that, while on principle not opposed to such a solution, they were far more concerned with "the legitimate interests of those workers occupying the positions of the suspended and of employers who had acted without any political resentment." To which the socialists replied that, whereas there may certainly arise certain problems, they could not budge from the principled position in favor of full restitution.[34] In the end, the published manifesto proposed a solution which, once again, underscored the dominance of the Republican Left in the emerging multiclass alliance. Whereas all unduly punished civil servants and salaried employees (*funcionarios y empleados*) were to be fully reinstated, a different fate was reserved for the blue-collar victims of governmental and employer repression. Only those workers who had been part of the public sector workforce were promised reinstatement. In the case of the private sector, the recommended solution left much to be desired. Their cases were left to be determined by an arbitration committee.[35]

On four points of contention the socialists were determined not to give in: their demands for the nationalization of land and its free distribution to the peasantry; the introduction of unemployment compensation; the nationalization of the banking system; and the institution of measures of workers' control. Yet on all these crucial issues the eventually agreed-upon terms were the positions of the Republican negotiators. On all four points the electoral manifesto promised certain improvements but fell far short of a qualitative rupture with the prevailing social system. The most the Republicans were prepared to accept on these central concerns was the mention of unstated doctrinal differences among the coalition partners in the respective clauses of the pact, but with the text listing solely the more moderate demands.[36] And, indeed, it would have been surprising had the bourgeois Left agreed to support a programmatic platform which would have run counter to the interests of at least a portion of its electoral clientele. Thus, the total domination of moderate Republican concerns was the price to be paid by the working-class Left in order to obtain the agreement. The history of the genesis of the popular front manifesto bode ill for the future of the alliance.

El Acoplamiento

Yet the story of the powerful electoral committee of the Spanish popular front had not yet come to an end. It was also destined to play a determining role in securing a solid Republican plurality of candidates for the slates of the popular front advocates in the coming elections of 16 February 1936, for the next task assigned to the highest decision-making body of the emerging popular front was the adjudication of disputes arising in the course of the determination of the alignment of candidates in each electoral district of Spain. Here, again, the story is essentially one of socialist concessions and Republican gains. During the deliberations leading to the publication of the electoral manifesto, suggestions had been made to enlarge the delegation of the working-class Left on the electoral committee for the next stage of its proceedings. Quite to the contrary, when the moment came to tackle the assignment of candidates throughout the regions of Spain, the Republican, and not the social democratic, membership was significantly enhanced. After a personal éclat by Sánchez Román, head of the PNR, led to the demise of this particular formation of the bourgeois Left, he was replaced by the undisputed leaders of the remaining bourgeois formations, the IR and the UR, Manuel Azaña and Diego Martínez Barrio, respectively. Thus, the PSOE influence on the committee "was not only not enhanced but, in relative terms, it diminished."[37]

The original idea behind the *acoplamiento*, the distribution of posts among the allied parties on the Left, was to have the national center decide on the exact proportions for all of Spain. The dominant personalities behind the *frente popular*, the Republican Manuel Azaña and the PSOE centrist Indalecio Prieto, were in agreement that disproportional representation should be given to the parties of the Republican Left, for everyone agreed that, in case of the popular front's victory, no workers' party was to participate in the formation of the popular front goverment. Instead, they were to form a supporting bloc in parliament assisting the labors of a purely Republican cabinet. For Prieto and Azaña, the easiest way to assure the workings of this plan was the securing of a comfortable winning margin for the Republican component of the popular front.[38] Doing so, however, became a far more contentious and bitter task than the literature has recorded up to now.

Ricardo Miralles reports difficulties in the Basque province of Vizcaya, leading to the intervention by the Madrid watchdog committee of the popular front. What was unusual in this respect was the arbiter's decision in favor of the working-class Left.[39] Juan-Simeón Vidarte, one of the two PSOE representatives in the all-powerful electoral committee in Madrid, feigned surprise upon learning that the candidate

list for the *frente popular* in Badajóz was made up of six socialists, one communist
and four Republicans, although in the 1933 elections the PSOE had received, in
Badajóz, 139,000 votes compared with the Republicans' mere 8,000.[40] The same
glaring disproportion was apparent in Valladolid, the major urban agglomeration
between Madrid and Asturias. In 1933 the Republicans garnered 8,755 votes against
the PSOE's 153,661. Nevertheless, by 1936 the PSOE and IR were both told to
put forth two candidates each in the upcoming election. The author of a history of
popular front elections in Valladolid, Marcia Concepción Marcos del Olmo, with
the aid of simple arithmetic thus concludes that each socialist candidate needed
76,830 votes to gain a post, a Republican candidate only 4,377.[41] The comparison
with the 1933 election was the official standard reference for the rough proportions of party strength in early 1936. On the basis of the 1933 returns, the PSOE
local in the city of Madrid demanded eleven candidates for itself, of which it was
willing to offer one to the PCE, with the two remaining posts for Republican forces.
The Republicans stonewalled. Reconsidering their demands, the Madrid PSOE
was willing to concede three posts to Republicans, only to meet the same negative
response. Even the offer of four posts, after the intervention of the PSOE executive, did not soften the resolve of their bourgeois "allies." Finally, the Republican
Left graciously conceded to be satisfied with five candidates. It was only one less
than the original Republican request but far more than warranted by the actual
relationship of forces.[42] In my own research I have collected evidence from Murcia,
Alicante and the province of Madrid. It further testifies to the gross inequality determining the process of *acoplamiento* on the Left, and it underscores my argument
regarding the ideological and political hegemony of the most conservative forces
participating in popular fronts, regardless of the actual relationship between their
constituent parts.

On 27 December 1935 Juan-Simeón Vidarte, one of the two PSOE representatives on the electoral committee, had sent a questionnaire to the PSOE's regional
federations asking them to report on (1) the number of candidates that, in their opinion, the socialists and Republicans should obtain in their district; (2) how many places
on the electoral slate the PSOE federations may be willing to concede guided by the
spirit of "maximal benevolence" toward the parties of the bourgeois Left; (3) how strong
the PCE was in each locality and whether or not it should obtain a post; and (4) a
general indication of the prospects of the impending electoral contest.[43] In its reply to
the PSOE circular of 27 December 1935, the Federación Provincial Socialista de
Madrid answered the questions by asserting that the Republican forces are not sufficiently developed to assure the election of a single candidate. Nevertheless, "out of
our own goodwill [*con un criterio de benevolencia*]" the local PSOE activists would
consider giving them one position on the candidate list.[44] Eleven days later they
informed the PSOE executive of a series of bitter negotiation sessions in which the
Republicans insisted that they should rightfully occupy three out of six positions ear-
marked for the *frente popular*. The socialists stressed that, on the basis of the 1933
results, the Republicans deserved a maximum of one, which "produced a violent refusal
by the Republican delegation, who refused to continue the talks, whereupon we
modified our proposal, leading to our maximum concession of four socialists and two
Republicans."[45] All this was to no avail. The Republicans won out in the end, and,

shortly after the elections, the provincial federation informed the PSOE national executive of the election of six popular front candidates, evenly divided between the bourgeois and social democratic Left. The federation's secretary once again high-lighted the injustice underlying this disproportion imposed by the upper reaches of the *frente popular*: "In the electoral arena, we were able to observe that the political influence of the allied parties of the Republican Union and the Republican Left scarcely had an impact [*apenas cuentan una muy escasa fuerza política*]."[46] The other two examples of *acoplamiento* on the Left refer to incidents on the Mediterranean littoral.

The Murcia local's recommended candidate distribution for the city of Murcia was one socialist seat and two Republicans. For the province of Murcia, the appor-tioned seven posts were to include five socialists and two Republicans. The commu-nists were deemed too insignificant to obtain a single post.[47] On 20 January 1936 all parties of the popular bloc met in the offices of the local labor center, the *casa del pueblo*, to resolve their differences. The candidates for the city list were determined in due course. The sole dispute was the insistence of a minor bourgeois formation, the Federal Democratic Republican Party, on obtaining one post; after pressure was applied, it gave up on its request.[48] Things became rather more complicated when the negotiators began to address the makeup of the provincial candidate list. The UR demanded three posts, the IR another three, the PRDF one, the communists one, and the socialists five. As the total number of available posts was no higher than seven, this meant that someone had to give in or a standoff would occur, leading to possible overall losses at the polls. Two UR spokespersons, Juan Antonio Méndez Martínez and Diego Jimenez Castellano, delivered lengthy speeches, listing the supposed strength of their parties in many locations throughout the province and repeating their demand for three seats. Biedma Hernández, for the IR, cast asper-sions on the UR's claims but was himself willing to reduce the total number of de-sired IR posts to two instead of three. The PRDF and PCE, however, continued to insist on one post each. Aurelio López Doblas, for the socialists, affirmed that in the 1933 elections the PSOE had received 63,000 votes, compared with 10,000 for the IR and 22,000 for the UR. Yet, to show its magnanimity, it was willing to reduce its request to four posts. Biedma Hernández countered López Doblas's claim of a mere 10,000 votes for the IR with the assertion that, indeed, the IR's vote had been closer to 20,000. Méndez, for the UR, reconfirmed that union's own request for three posts, and the meeting became a sounding board for mutual recriminations and sharp accusations. The most accommodating voice was that of Eusebio Serrano for the PCE, who, at one point, indicated his willingness to rescind his party's demand for one post "if this would bring about a solution, but, as this does not appear to be the case even with such a concession, they insist on their one seat." The meeting resolved to ask for assistance from Madrid.[49] As could be expected, the Madrid committee decided in favor of the Republican side. The combined total of ten posts for the popular front candidates in the province and city of Murcia was to be divided in a manner giving a paltry four to the PSOE, with the remaining six going to Republi-can formations. The Murcia PSOE local responded with a mixture of critique and resignation, pointing out the "lamentable impression amongst all comrades" created by this recommendation.[50]

Finally a glance at the situation in Alicante. On 31 December 1935 the Alicante socialists informed their national center that, in the 1933 elections, the PSOE had received 57,020 votes, the two parties that now formed the IR 24,718, and the PCE 3,755. As there were eight positions to be filled, a generous appraisal would suggest five socialist candidates and three for the IR. The UR was, in the province of Alicante, as weak and insignificant as the PCE. The Alicante local of the PSOE went on to imply that it was willing to reduce its claim to four seats, "not in recognition of the [alleged] forces of Republicanism in this province, but in order to facilitate the labor of this [Electoral] Commission and with the hope that the [Socialist] Party will receive appropriate compensation in the course of the *acoplamiento* in other provinces."[51]

On 21 January 1936 the Alicante socialists informed their headquarters in Madrid that, in a joint meeting with the PCE and Pestaña's syndicalists, they had agreed upon a total number of five posts for the working-class Left, with one seat for the communists. At a subsequent meeting with the bourgeois Left, the Republicans countered with their own demand for five representatives. At a second negotiating session the Republicans lowered their request to four, but the PSOE-PCE bloc was unwilling to reduce its own request, and asked for intercession by Madrid. In a letter to the PSOE leadership, the bloc emphasized that, in the 1933 elections, the PSOE got three seats and the bourgeois bloc had been too weak to receive a single seat. "If we obtain four seats in the coming elections, we would have advanced by a total of one and the Republicans by four, a situation totally beyond reality."[52] When the decision favoring the Republican request for four posts was handed down from Madrid, the Alicante social democrats were dumbfounded: "We consider this absurd." They predicted that this was "bound to produce a most disagreeable reaction among our provincial organizations." Furthermore, it would lead to fratricidal conflict with the PCE, for the reduced total number of seats for the working-class Left narrowed the room for maneuver below any tolerable minimum.[53] Yet the national popular front leadership stayed its course. A 30 January 1936 letter by the Alicante socialists expresses the extent of their disappointment. But, surprisingly, the devastating decision by Madrid did not lead to a renewed bout of conflict with the PCE. Quite to the contrary! In a joint meeting with the Alicante PCE, the social democrats report, the communists aired "their disgust in a somewhat unfriendly manner" but then went on to pledge allegiance to their cause and promised loyal cooperation.[54]

In the end, due to similar maneuvers and deceit, the national leadership of the popular front managed to increase the share of the bourgeois Left in the candidate selection process beyond all reasonable proportions. Santos Juliá emphasizes the vast discrepancy between the fact that the IR alone got 108 seats against the PSOE's 124, compared with the 1933 results of more than 1.7 million socialist votes and, at most, 300,000 votes for the IR. Or, from another angle, in order to qualify for one candidate in the 1936 elections, a Republican needed 6,084 votes in 1933, a communist 8,552, and a social democrat 12,775.[55] This was the process and one result of the creation of the much-heralded Spanish popular front.

Electoral Victories in Spain and France

The Spanish national elections of February 1936 brought victory to the popular front coalition and radically changed the political landscape of Spain, still suffering from the aftereffects of the October 1934 Asturian uprising and defeat of the working-class Left. According to Javier Tusell, 72 percent of eligible voters cast their ballots. Of these 72 percent, 34.3 percent favored a candidate of the popular front; 33.2 percent voted for the Right; and 5.4 percent chose Center parties or the regionally important Basque nationalists.[56] Due to the relative disunity of the right and center-right parties, and because of the provisions of Spanish electoral law favoring coalitions by giving 80 percent of seats in each electoral district to the coalition gaining more than 50 percent of the local vote, the popular front alliance emerged with a majority of 263 parliamentary seats against 210 for the center-right groups.[57] The popular front was thus voted into office by a minority of votes cast. Compared with earlier elections, conservative parties had lost little, if any, voter confidence and were relegated to second rank only because of electoral provisions which in 1933, for instance, had operated against the forces of the Left. It was a conflict-laden election result that boded ill for the incoming Republican government.

The French "winner-take-all" election system was similar to the Spanish in giving disproportionate advantages to the strongest coalition on the national scale. According to the estimates least favorable to the *front populaire*, in the first round of elections in late April 1936 a total of 5,515,446 voters cast their ballots for the Left and 4,325,297 for the Right.[58] Yet only 174 out of 598 local races were determined in the first round. Results for the second round on 3 May were less favorable to the Left, yet their lead remained sufficient to gather a total of 376 seats versus 214 for the Right.[59] While not overwhelming in terms of the popular vote, it was a sounder victory than the earlier success of the Spanish *frente popular*.

In comparing the French and Spanish results, it is also important to underscore significant differences in the relationship of forces within each popular front, as expressed in the distribution of parliamentary seats between the various components of the respective alliances. Whereas in both France and Spain arrangements had been made to give disproportionate weight to left bourgeois candidates, this was far more pronounced in Spain than in France. In France, then, the combined number of seats by social democrats and communists amounted to 219 versus 109 seats for the bourgeois Radicals (with lesser amounts to smaller formations), whereas the Spanish bourgeois Left garnered 151 parliamentary seats versus 112 for the working-class Left.[60] Whereas the Spanish working-class vote was probably as significant as in neighboring France, and whereas Spanish left-wing politics—given the strong anarchist presence, which found no reflection in the composition of the popular front—was considerably more radicalized than to the north, the parliamentary representation of the popular front did not reflect this Spanish peculiarity. Indeed, the Spanish popular front's representatives in parliament constituted a far more moderate bloc than was the case with their homologues in France. The particularly pronounced disjuncture between Spanish left-wing politics and moderate parliamentary representation added to the volatility of the postelection period.

Contradictions Within the Victorious Popular Fronts

In early June 1936, the Federación Socialista Murciana once again addressed a letter to the PSOE national leadership in Madrid, this time complaining about what it rightfully perceived as unacceptable behavior on the part of the newly appointed governor: "We agree with the [PSOE] national committee that we must maintain the Popular Front; but it is impossible for it to continue functioning in Murcia, as the position of the Unión Republicana obstructs it." The Murcia socialists complained of the absolute partiality of the governor, "who throws up all sorts of obstacles to the normal development of the associations affiliated with the UGT [the socialist trade union federation]." The popular front committees throughout the province were reported to be stacked with "reactionary elements and allies of the perennial exploiters [*los eternos caciques*]"; and the governor continues to "unconditionally protect" the employers.

> And in the local labor exchanges, which are run by members of the UR, they only hire his friends, for, in this manner, they believe the working class will flock to his political associations. . . . We need his immediate impeachment . . . in order to avoid that, one day, we may have to bemoan tragical events. We need a governor who acts in accordance with the Popular Front, nothing more.[61]

Already in mid-April, a PSOE local in a small town in Murcia province had complained about UR influence peddling. With the governor's complicity, the local UR strongman had made it a habit to give out rifle permits only to known supporters of the ultrarightist CEDA and similar elements. The social democrats from Alhama de Murcia implored their national leadership to contact one of the UR members of parliament from the city of Murcia and to press for changes. A clash was possible at any moment; "no one should be surprised, for it would be justified."[62]

The demand for top-level intercession by the PSOE leadership on behalf of their provincial supporters is a recurring theme in the extant correspondence. On 28 March 1936 the Agrupación Socialista de La Roda on the high plains of La Mancha notified the PSOE national committee of "the profound disloyalty displayed toward us by the Izquierda Republicana to the extent that we do not foresee a continued coalition in the approaching struggle."[63] On 14 May the La Roda socialists went one step further. They announced that

> because of the perfidy of the Izquierda Republicana we were forced to break off all political relations with that party. Because of this step, the president of the town council is persecuting us just like in the worst times of the ancient monarchy [*de la fenecida monarquia*]; making life for our representatives almost impossible in the city council; jailing young socialists; and, with the help of six members of the *guardia civil*, detaining ostentatiously the vice president of our local [and] transporting him to Albacete [the regional center]. We have lodged energetic complaints about all these exactions with the provincial governor, the government secretary and, at the same time, comrade Prat [a PSOE member of parliament from Albacete]. How do the authorities respond to all this? They ordered a truckload of assault guards to the next session of the town council, thus provoking a feeling of intense unease among the local population.

What caused the La Roda socialists to write this letter, however, was the most recent decision to hold town council meetings at ten o'clock in the morning on a workday, which effectively prevented the PSOE councillors from attending, "for, as manual workers, they need to earn their bread." When one present PSOE councillor expressed his disagreement with this measure, he was promptly arrested by the *guardia civil*, expelled from the session and dragged to the police inspectorate.[64] In this case the archives contain a response by the PSOE in Madrid, which immediately contacted the IR's national committee. On 26 May the IR responded to the PSOE's request and mentioned that it had instructed the regional party authorities to rectify the wrongs. The PSOE headquarters forwarded this letter to La Roda.[65] Three weeks later nothing had changed for the better. Instead, the La Roda socialists reported that, "if, up to now, they assaulted our party for defending the politics of the Popular Front, today they are assaulting the entire population in general by means of the dictatorship imposed upon them by the IR." The PSOE councillors had decided to brave all odds and to forgo a part of their meager income in order to attend the town council meetings. In response, "the dictatorial mayor [*este alcalde dictadorzuelo*]" simply canceled all council meetings.[66] Similar tales arrived at the PSOE headquarters from all corners of the Spanish state.

One frequent complaint was the massive and premeditated entry of known members of the right-wing parties, including the fascist Falange Española, in the ranks of the Republican Left. This was not necessarily the fault of the respective local organizations, which may have opposed this move, but when the other parties of the popular front complained to the regional federations of their bourgeois allies, as did the PSOE in Ciudad Real, the authorities promised to amend the situation, but no changes were forthcoming.[67]

Undoubtedly, the divisive acts of bourgeois notables mentioned thus far were not a uniform occurrence throughout Spain. The PSOE archives contain the occasional effusive account of harmonious cooperation between all members of a local popular front, such as the report of a successful commemoration of the Day of the Republic in the village of El Provencio (Cuenca):

> The council, which leads the destiny of this municipal administration, composed of members of the Izquierda Republicana, Unión Republicana and the Socialists, desiring to add luster to the festival which took place on the 14th [of April] at the occasion of the fifth anniversary of the glorious Republic, ordered all businesses to close, and, with the authorities leading the way and a numerous public, the magnificent band marched through the streets of our village intonating the National Anthem, which was received with great enthusiasm by the population. Afterward, and in full view of the crowd gathered in the Plaza de la República, several dozen strange balloons [*glovos grotescos (sic)*] rose into the air, which the honorable mayor Don Fabricio Huedo Martínez had prepared to this effect. . . . In the late evening several films were shown in the theater, with free admission, which was a smashing success.[68]

Short of a more systematic search of the archives and the local press, it is impossible to generalize from the adduced evidence. Yet what should be underscored is that I have only referred to cases where the offending party was clearly a member of the popular front. It would be easy to list cases of injustice committed by government organs of the popular front but where it is difficult to pinpoint the exact source of the tensions. After all, generally only the top-level administration could be replaced by the incoming popular front government, and the remaining old-regime supporters were only too keen to cause problems.[69]

The Two Dynamics of Popular Fronts

It appears that there subsisted at least two inherently contradictory interpretations of the nature of popular fronts among their supporters in both France and Spain. One was a vision of the broad alliance as an enhancement of united fronts, the other a pragmatic assessment of it as an extension of previous center-left coalition governments entered into by social democrats in earlier decades. The former tended to be predominant among the working-class ranks, the latter among the leading echelons of most participating organizations. This partially hidden contradiction had important consequences for the course of the popular front. As soon as victory appeared certain, a tremendous wave of popular enthusiasm and activism swept the countries concerned. In Spain, spontaneous mass demonstrations "opened the prisons and released the workers detained since 1934, without waiting for the amnesty decree to be signed."[70] A wave of strikes and land occupations, carried out against the desires of the Republican government, polarized the entire state. Long before the eruption of the civil war and the attendant social revolution in Catalonia and Aragon, "the majority of the electors of the Popular Front now constituted an explosive force over which their leaders no longer had any control."[71] In France the popular front's victory likewise instilled added confidence in working-class activists. Two strike waves, the first one in May and the second, stronger one in June, shook up an archaic system of class relations and assured the smooth passage of Léon Blum's reform legislation. Yet here, too, quite like Spain, the movement of strikes and factory occupations emerged, on the whole, spontaneously and was only tolerated, and not encouraged, by the popular front government. For Jacques Kergoat, "the movement of June 36 can be defined simultaneously as a movement against the dictatorship of the employers and as a conscious means of exerting pressure on the government's performance."[72] Clearly, a victorious popular front created the preconditions for a radicalizing dynamic similar to the case of united fronts. For many among the working-class Left, the victory of the popular front meant more than the guarantee of certain tangible, immediate improvements. But, unlike the case of united fronts, this view was shared by an increasingly diminishing number of party policy makers.

This discrepancy of opinion within the working-class Left accounts for the overriding difference between the dynamic underlying united and popular fronts. In the case of the former, there occurred a common convergence between the desire of the ranks and the designs of the respective party leaderships. Even if the terms of a given united front proposal were limited to the defense of democratic rights only, it was generally accepted that the agreed-upon united front was the opening shot in a concerted move toward socialism then and there. In the case of the popular front, this degree of harmony in the expectations from the future began to rapidly disappear. The gulf between the leadership and ranks, temporarily closed in the heyday of the united front, began to reappear as leading social democrats, and later communists, began to share governmental responsibilities for a regime unable and/or unwilling to break with the prevailing social order.

Two contradictory dynamics operated under popular fronts. One was the inbuilt mechanism which assured the ideological hegemony of the most conservative partners *within* a popular front; the other was the moral impetus for a more far-reaching assault on the precepts of the capitalist social order, instilled within the supporters of this alliance. The former was, above all, the domain of party strategists; the latter the terrain of operation by the ranks. Both are important aspects of popular fronts. But only the former can be rightfully considered an inherent principle underlying the constitution of such fronts. The latter emerged, to a certain degree, as unintended consequences of the actual operations of the fronts. For this reason I will address this second dimension of popular front politics in far more detail in my chapter on the interaction between leadership and ranks, as it will provide an opportunity to compare and contrast the impact of united and popular fronts on the respective workers' parties. Presently, I am primarily concerned with the place of popular fronts in the strategic reorientation of the European Left.

Conclusion

The signal contribution of the politics of popular fronts was its mindful problematization of alliance strategies beyond the realm of the working class alone. For whereas united fronts did not reject the support of other social forces in the pursuance of their aims, they generally did not conceive of middle-class support as a crucial stepping-stone toward success. Popular front advocates went the extra mile in their quest for allies. Rather than treating middle-class support as a helpful but not necessary means to an end, they realized the importance of this task and set about to search for solutions. With the notable exception of radical planism, united front activists only began to pay serious attention to the conundrum of the middle class *after* the theorists of popular fronts began to air their views. This did not have to spell the end of the era of united fronts. It became apparent that united fronts could easily encompass members of the middle classes, if only the latter would adopt the basic principles animating the recently created united fronts. As a matter of fact, it was argued, the most certain way of making allies among the intermediary strata would be to give them a perspective of radical societal change. Given the enormous crisis of the prevailing social system, only a fundamentally different solution could have sufficient appeal to attract the disaffected middle classes to a democratic, socialist solution instead of to the only other highly visible alternative in the 1930s, antidemocratic authoritarian regimes. And, as I have attempted to show with the example of French Radicalism, it appears that such opinions were not without cause. Yet by the time proponents of united fronts began to recognize the need to offer a clear perspective for potential middle-class recruits as well, the stage was already set for the eventual breakthrough of popular fronts.

As I will argue in chapter 7, the bloody October 1934 defeat of the Spanish Left, in conjunction with the increasingly ominous storm clouds on the international political horizon, played a crucial role in intensifying the search for allies in defense of increasingly tenuous civil liberties and rights. While some working-class proponents of popular fronts agreed that, eventually, the middle classes may be won over to the side of the socialist Left, they grew increasingly afraid that such a switch would come too late. After the Asturian defeat and the loss of the Saar, they decided on what they perceived as a shortcut to middle-class support. Advocates of popular fronts reasoned that, rather than banking on the eventual disillusionment of middle-class supporters with the traditional parties of their choice, a quicker way of gaining middle-class allies would be to convince the actually existing middle-class-based organizations of the usefulness and value of a common project. As it turned out, this was a realistic assessment. In the course of 1935, the Radical and Republican Parties of France and Spain became pivotal elements within broad coalitions in defense of democratic rights and in pursuit of concrete goals—but at a price.

Champions of united fronts considered the bourgeois Left part of the overall problem they were eager to remove. The Radical and Republican Parties would never agree to fundamental social changes leading in the direction of the supersession of the prevailing social order. Therefore, advocates of united fronts proposed to circumvent existing bourgeois *parties* and to focus on the ranks instead. Working-class supporters of popular fronts likewise realized that existing left bourgeois parties would never accede to socialist demands, but they regarded the need to win these parties as an indispensable condition for victory. Hence champions of popular fronts argued for the need to moderate the outlook of such multiclass alliances. And, if, for one reason or another, socialists entered the negotiations with more far-reaching demands than their bourgeois allies were willing to concede, the former were always willing to accommodate the latter for the sake of greater unity. In this chapter I have demonstrated the mechanism of negotiations for a common pact in Spain. This process of wholesale capitulation to the demands of the most conservative forces in a popular front was repeated in France. The literature is replete with comments on how the social democrats of the SFIO were forced to drop virtually all their socialist demands in the face of a curious coalition of Radicals and PCF clamoring for moderation. Jules Moch, a prominent SFIO politician at the time, remembers the negotiations as the moment "when the 'miracle' of the collusion of extremes occurred, with the Radicals and communists opposing the socialists."[73]

In the end, popular fronts were alliances between working-class and middle-class organizations based on a programmatic platform acceptable to the bourgeois Left. Perhaps the most appropriate definition of a popular front, therefore, would be its designation as an alliance strategy *for* the middle classes rather than as a proletarian strategy for close cooperation *with* the middle class. This is not to deny that the working-class component of a popular front stood to benefit, and indeed benefited tremendously, from the victory of a popular front. But one must not lose sight of the fact that many achievements of "the popular front" were in actual fact obtained as a result of unforeseen vast social movements developing in the wake of the popular front's victory but *against* its declared goals. On balance, then, as an alliance strategy, a popular front filled the need for a broad coalition of forces in order to obtain or retain crucial democratic rights in a time of prevailing defeats. Rather than enhancements of united fronts, popular fronts were consciously constructed moderate alternatives.

SEVEN

Transnational Consciousness Within the European Left

Since its inception, social democracy has been an international phenomenon, organized in national sections but with multiple links and avenues of exchange connecting the varied strands across political frontiers. Regular international congresses were held to coordinate the political responses to the challenges of the day, although, in practice, it remains to be determined what, if any, impact the decisions reached at the international gatherings had on the daily practice of national parties. Certainly by the 1930s the social democratic International was little more than an empty shell. Yet some form of international center continued to exist, and regular meetings of the LSI executive and bureau were held in frequent succession. The memoirs of Adolf Sturmthal, a key employee of the LSI in Zurich and, later, Brussels, are a fascinating reminder of the impressive international contacts maintained between social democrats in Europe up to the outbreak of World War II.[1]

Personal contacts were, however, only one dimension facilitating potential intellectual cross-fertilization and exchange. A well-developed network of social democratic publications reinforced the public committment to an internationalist perspective. In each of the five countries under review, social democrats controlled a plentiful and generally lively party press with, in each case, one national daily newspaper as the informational backbone, at least for as long as conditions of legality prevailed. A network of foreign correspondents kept each national section abreast of information from abroad. German, Austrian and Spanish social democracy furthermore published important theoretical journals with significant attention to international events. Rudolf Hilferding's *Zeitschrift für Sozialismus* (ZfS) provided a much-needed forum for reflections on the tragedy of German labor. As much of its readership was dispersed among the few remaining democracies in Europe, there existed more than purely intellectual reasons for heightened attention to what used to be considered "foreign affairs." Theoretical analyses of fascism, the changing nature of the state and the strategies of united and popular fronts stood side by side with up-to-date assessments of the latest Comintern twists, politics in Spain and the most recent programmatic innovations of the British Labor Party. Rudolf Hilferding was himself a transplanted Austrian who had become a leading figure in interwar German social democracy and who spent his exile years in Denmark, Switzerland, Czechoslovakia, then Switzerland again and finally France, where he was eventually interned by the Vichy regime and, together with Rudolf Breitscheid, delivered to the Nazi executioners.[2] Major contributors to his journal were Arthur Rosenberg, Richard Löwenthal, the Mensheviks Alexander Schifrin and Georg Decker, together with more mainstream SPD luminaries such as Curt Geyer.[3]

The Spanish monthly journal *Leviatán* paid even more attention to international politics than Hilferding's *ZfS*. Luis Araquistain, the director of *Leviatán*, had been the Spanish ambassador to Germany from April 1932 to May 1933, an eventful thirteen months which resulted in Araquistain's complete overhaul of his strategic conceptions and which catapulted him into becoming the éminence grise behind the massive swing to the left of the majority of the Spanish section of the LSI, the PSOE. To judge the impact of his German tour of duty, it may suffice to contrast his speech at the occasion of handing his credentials to the head of the German state, Paul von Hindenburg, on 1 April 1932 with the lessons of the German tragedy he expanded on in several interventions after his return to Spain. In the spring of 1932 he stressed the influence of German traditions on Spanish democracy from the time of the 1873 first Spanish republic to the most recent example of the Weimar constitution, which stood as one important model for the drafters of the 1931 Spanish constitution. After witnessing the rise of Nazism, Araquistain's views on democracy and socialism underwent "a radical inversion." He now castigated the evolutionary determinism of the German SPD, and he went on to note the lack of a voluntarist dimension as one of the reasons for the SPD's defeat. Significantly, he demanded a policy of working-class united fronts as one crucial consequence of the German defeat, where unity had been a distant dream until it was forced upon the factions of the working-class Left behind the barbed wires of the early concentration camps.[4] When *Leviatán* was finally launched in May 1934, it immediately became a powerful ideological weapon in the arsenal of Spanish left-wing socialism. Surveys of fascist and authoritarian regimes and movements throughout Europe, articles on international communism and socialism in Europe and the world, including analyses of social democracy's advances in Great Britain, Belgium and Scandinavia, were as much of its standard fare as assessments of the Asturian Commune or the fate of the Spanish economy.

Yet the most respected and admired journal of interwar social democracy was the Austrian *Der Kampf*. Published in Czechoslovakia after February 1934, it continued the tradition of critical Marxist analysis exemplified by *Die Neue Zeit* (NZ) in the glory days of Second International socialism prior to August 1914. NZ lost much of its intellectual appeal after the 1917 removal of Karl Kautsky from its editorial board, which he had been part of for nearly thirty-five years, although the journal itself survived as a colorless magazine until 1924.[5] *Der Kampf*, launched in 1907, took over where NZ had left off and developed into a lively medium of intellectual exchange. Under the influence of left-leaning Austro-Marxism, its monthly editions included articles covering the entire spectrum of European socialism, with preference given to its left critics. As the correspondence in the Otto Bauer papers, housed in Amsterdam, reveals, it was not only the focal point of attention of the LSI-Left around Otto Bauer, Theodore Dan and Léon Blum but was dutifully studied in the Kremlin as well. In the absence of a viable and functioning International, it was *the* medium for the remaining believers in the internationalist mission of social democracy and the entire working-class Left. Yet only a small minority of party activists followed the debates carried on in the pages of the aforementioned journals. Most party members and sympathizers received their information from the parties' daily press or educational conferences or speeches delivered by visiting party lecturers.

The German Tragedy in European Perspective

Regardless of the exact sources of their knowledge and beliefs, European social democrats, as a rule, were vitally concerned with the rapidly shrinking terrain for legal operations of their movements and concerns. Inasmuch as the conciliationist attitude of German social democracy regarding curbs on Weimar democracy was the subject of debate within the LSI even prior to 30 January 1933, warning voices about the SPD's course of action were not uncommon even then. To cite just one example, Frans Liebaers, the national secretary of the Belgian textile workers' union and leading activist within the International Socialist Antiwar League (ISAOL), wrote in September 1932: "The Italian experience [the victory of Mussolini], rich in lessons, has had absolutely no impact on German social democracy and its trade union organization, and the entire International acts as if all of this is without importance." Criticism of their German comrades fell on deaf ears, and only words of encouragement were permitted. Liebaers concluded his planned speech to the Belgian Trade Union Commission, which he never got the chance to read: "There is nothing surprising in all of this. To the contrary, it is entirely natural, for by defending German social democracy, you think about your own defense."[6] Indeed, German social democracy had been the shining example of a successful and theoretically astute national section of an international current for many decades. The Menshevik Alexander Schifrin, in December 1933, drew the attention of his readers to this supposed German model for the other parties of the LSI:

> "To speak German"—this meant, within the international workers' movement before the war, the construction of a centralized political mass organization, legality and the struggle for democracy. "To speak German"—in the postwar period this meant the positive, successful, practical work of construction and the integration of the workers' movement in the democratic state.

The impact of the Nazi success can be measured in the very next sentence in Schifrin's survey of the changed configuration of the LSI: "'To speak German'—today this means the martyrdom of concentration camps. . . ."[7]

The demise of German social democracy was not fully comprehended overnight. The extent of the SPD's defeat became clear only in the spring of 1933. In mid-April Rudolf Hilferding, still in the middle of assessing the impact of the most recent events, wrote to Karl Kautsky: "Everything is so charged and full of meaning that, despite the fact of having had ample time for reflection, I am still unable to form a clear image of what historical meaning our defeat will have and which consequences to draw from it. I do believe, however, that these consequences will be far-reaching and affect a number of our basic principles."[8] Rudolf Hilferding was not the only social democrat suspended in midair by the sudden Nazi victory. An excellent barometer of the changing contours of the LSI throughout the interwar period were the surviving structures of the exiled Russian Menshevik Party.[9] In a long and detailed letter to the aging Karl Kautsky, who remained in close personal contact with many European socialists until his death in 1938, Peter Garwy listed the varied responses by key individuals within Menshevism to the German defeat. The underlying lesson for virtually all factions operating under the Menshevik umbrella was the necessity of a viable united front. Theodore Dan now regarded it as "the task of the hour" and hoped for the eventual reunification of the Second and Third Internationals. Olga Domanevskaia even regarded the merging of communism and social democracy as an immediate perspective, whereas Abramovitch, who likewise considered "the surmounting of the division within the workers' movement a necessity of life," was far more skeptical about the chances for success of this perspective. Garwy, who himself saw unity as a distant dream, regarded Alexander Schifrin as representing "a peculiar position"; Schifrin pleaded for a reorientation of the LSI's foreign policy perspective. Instead of a policy favoring disarmament and reconciliation, efforts should be undertaken to fashion a bloc of democratic powers against the menace of Nazi fascism. Peter Garwy closed his outline of Menshevik responses to the victory of Nazism with the following words: "I have sketched for you all these voices of opinion because it may be of interest to you. You can gather from this how extensive the agitation [Gärung] is even within the ranks of the Russian comrades, triggered by the German events."[10]

The advocacy of movement toward united fronts characterized the responses of most social democrats throughout continental Europe reflecting on the triumph of Nazism. In Spain, for instance, the loss of German democracy played a crucial role in the early construction of united fronts. The launching statement of the electoral bloc between the dissident communists of the BOC and the regional federation of social democracy in November 1933, the immediate precursor of the Workers' Alliance of Catalonia, referred in explicit terms to the lessons of Germany.[11] The first speaker at a mass rally in favor of united fronts in the mining town of Mieres (Asturias), just prior to the launching of the Alianza Obrera de Asturias, implored his audience to heed his warnings. In his view, the terror afflicting the workers' movement of Italy and Germany should be constant reminders of the nefarious consequences of fratricide and disunity on the Left.[12] An editorial in the Spanish socialist daily El Socialista drew the following conclusion in view of several defeats: "Has socialism failed? By no means." The blame should instead be placed on the individuals who attempted to carry out socialist politics. "That which failed were the people, who, in Italy and Germany, were very much inferior to the ideals [of socialism]."[13] This somewhat simplistic rendering of recent occurrences was amended by the end of the year, when the PSOE halfheartedly embraced united front politics. An El Socialista editorial now suggested: "We hope that the lessons of the German events may serve to, from now on, attenuate hostilities between the workers, not only here [in Spain], but everywhere."[14]

This transnational consciousness of the significance of Hitler's victory did not remain the sole property of leadership levels within the LSI. Two documents emanating from two different regions of Spain may serve to exemplify the fashion in which the SPD's defeat translated into concrete motion elsewhere. On 19 October 1933 four members of the social democratic youth organization in the Basque industrial city of Bilbao sent a letter to the local executive committee asking for consideration of a proposal for a national antifascist united front to be introduced at the upcoming regional federation's congress. The motion ran as follows: "Given the consequences which fascism would entail for our country, and given the very significant lesson [*la lección tan grande*] of Germany, where, even more so than the triumph [of Nazism] itself, it was the enormous lack of unity between the so-called Marxist workers, which expedited the path [for fascism] and enabled it to easily establish itself," the National Federation of Young Socialists should devote all efforts to the construction of an antifascist united front.[15] In the midst of the PSOE campaign for insurrectionary action, the president and secretary of the PSOE local in the tiny Andalusian town of Nerva (Huelva) sent a letter to the national center pledging its support to Largo Caballero's revolutionary course. The entire letter went as follows:

> Designated to carry out the leadership function for the year 1934 at the last general assembly of this PSOE local, a task we have assumed today, we wish our first decision to be the unconditional support of the party's politics and its press organ *El Socialista* in its magnificent campaign in the spirit of Marxism and, most definitely, the theses advocated by our comrade Largo Caballero, for our local believes that, in the present moment when the period of legality is coming to an end (or, to be more precise, has already come to an end), a conformist position would annul the fighting spirit of the working masses and, as a logical consequence, would lift the spirits of those forces that, more or less insolently, help to bring about and actively prepare the fascist Corporate State.
>
> *Comrades in the executive*: Make sure that we do not have to take upon us the responsibility of treachery which is the hallmark of German social democracy.[16]

Whether interpreted as lack of initiative, passivity in the face of mortal danger, or outright treachery, the (in)action of German social democrats affected socialist discourse throughout most European states. In France, however, the reaction was considerably more divided than was the case in Spain.

In France, advocates of radical responses immediately went on the offensive. They regarded the German defeat as bitter testimony to the inefficiency of governmental collaboration as the means to defend democracy. As one leading member of the eclectic radical group Révolution Constructive proclaimed at the April 1933 Avignon congress of the SFIO in response to the conservative wing's demand to drop the opposition to participationism: "One cannot deny that, for ten years, you have told us: 'Look at the German comrades; they do not share your scruples; they agree to share power; they are realists.' We have just seen where this realism led them to." The minutes record sustained applause after this particular segment of the intervention by Pierre Boivin.[17] At the July 1933 SFIO congress in Paris, one of the spokespersons for the SFIO-Left, Marceau Pivert, defended the creation of a self-defense organization as one of the lessons of Germany. Yet one incident during his speech exemplified the mixed emotions generated by the SPD's demise, for the SPD had possessed a strong party militia, the Reichsbanner, and was nevertheless unable to stem the tide of fascism. When Pivert expounded on the value of such a paramilitary body, an unnamed delegate interrupted the speaker: "And the German comrades, where are they at today?"[18] Those in the emerging rightist neosocialist current, soon to be expelled from the SFIO for breach of discipline, drew a different set of conclusions from the continued reverses suffered by the European Left, yet they started out from similar assumptions about the impasse of traditional social democratic precepts. In their defense of moderation and Keynesian policies *avant la lettre*, they wrote the following explanation of how the worsening world situation affected their judgments: "The point was forcefully driven home that, in view of these frightening events, changes in the tactics and methods of the Party were becoming necessary, calling for things other than recourse to [time-worn] rites and formulas. . . ."[19] "It is true that we have spoken a language which appeared to be new." But by doing so, they expressly wanted to remain within the socialist tradition and merely wished "to advocate active solutions" and to highlight "the uncertainties which have resulted from the fall of several parties of our International under the blows of brutal reaction."[20]

As I have underscored in chapter 5, the German tragedy was *the* catalyst for the rapid ascent of radical planism in the Belgian state, itself racked by the rise of unemployment and the radical Right. Hendrik de Man repeatedly referred to the lessons of Germany in his push for Belgian social democracy's acceptance of the Plan de Man. Indeed, he had initially hoped to convince the German SPD of the virtues of his plan, and only after the Nazi takeover agreed to focus his attention on reforming the BWP/POB. Those who criticized the Plan de Man from the left were no less aware of the catalytic role of 30 January 1933. For them, however, the reorientation of social democratic strategy did not go far enough. In the words of Frans Liebaers: "The Plan du Travail was adopted as an innovative charter by the Belgian Workers' Party because the German example had taught it quite a bit, but it [the Plan de Man] was also adopted because the POB had not drawn the [additional] lessons of the defeat of the German workers' movement, that it is not new charters or novel programs that the workers' movement needs, but a [radically different] orientation. . . ."[21] But, whether moderate, radical or revolutionary critique, the Nazi triumph caused a flurry of rethinking on the social democratic Left. Certainly, up to a point, the strategic thinkers in the ranks of social democracy were only expanding on lines of argumentation developed prior to Hitler's legal coup. Émile Vandervelde was not mistaken when, in his opening address to the last international conference of the LSI in August 1933, he suggested that "socialists who do reflect, who ponder over the events in Germany, have, despite everything else, the tendency to search for arguments regarding the tactics and strategy of socialist democracy which they already previously espoused."[22] But, as has hopefully emerged in my discussion of the evolution of European social democracy in chapter 2, on balance a distinct shift to the left affected most continental European socialist parties in the course of 1933–34 and set the stage for a noticeable radicalization in the five countries under review.[23] The next landmark in the evolution of interwar European socialism was the February 1934 Austrian Schutzbund uprising.

The Schutzbund Uprising

This last-ditch effort in defense of Austrian democracy had an effect on the parties of the LSI similar to the Nazi takeover in Germany. While it tended to reinforce prior prejudices within both the conservative and radical camps of the LSI, the overall result was a further slide to the left among most Continental LSI sections. Combined with the French example of a successful movement toward united fronts, it ultimately paved the way for the substantive enlargement of the LSI-Left, described in chapter 3. That the Austrian revolt would have major repercussions for the remaining sections of the LSI was clear to everyone involved. As an unsigned article, published one month after the uprising, in the German *Sozialistische Aktion* put it:

> The defeat of the Austrian workers opens up a whole sequence of deep-seated problems, which must be reflected on, and solved by, the entire international workers' movement. For, the defeat in Austria is a defeat of the entire workers' movement: the lessons of the Austrian struggle are determinants for the tactics of *all* parties, regardless of whether they are operating in fascist or nonfascist countries.[24]

For the LSI-Left the issue was simple. René Dumon, the head of the French Young Socialists and, in this capacity, a leading element in the radicalization of the Socialist Youth International (SYI), informed the general secretary of the SYI that the rising tide of fascism had convinced Dumon's cothinkers "that the old parties have failed and that the young generation cannot easily agree to remain prisoners of formulas which have proven to be ineffective in the defense of the proletariat against fascism."[25] Stressing the positive aspects of the Austrian revolt, the ubiquitous Alexander Schifrin wrote: "For the first time in the history of the revolutionary struggle of the proletarian and the popular masses in Europe, the vanguard of the proletariat has taken up arms in a *counterrevolutionary* situation." Previous revolts all took place in moments of revolutionary fervor. "The courage of the participants in the Austrian uprising therefore takes on extraordinary importance. . . . Austrian social democracy shall now become the spokesperson of central European revolutionary socialism: the quality of its leadership, its moral authority and its revolutionary experience bestow upon it the necessary mandate."[26]

Two days after the outbreak of hostilities in Linz, the editors of the Saar SPD's daily, *Deutsche Freiheit*, had already drawn their conclusion: "It is presently uncertain how the fighting will end. What is certain, however, is that the courageous and determined attitude of Austrian social democracy will revive the belief in the seriousness of the fighting spirit of socialists, which was severely shaken by the German collapse."[27] The following day's lead article concluded despite the obvious defeat: "The battle for freedom in Austria has ended in glory. Now begins the struggle for the socialist dominance over Europe in new forms and with new methods of combat."[28] The usually moderate official paper of the German exile SPD, *Neuer Vorwärts*, felt compelled to editorialize: "Your freedom, your self-determination, your part of life; those things which belong to you; you must defend them against rapacious fascism, if need be, with weapons in hand—that is the lesson of Vienna! . . . Vienna! It will forever live within our memories. . . . Force against force will be the way to conquer freedom."[29] Even Léon Blum, usually more of a centrist than a leftist critic of the LSI regime, wrote an inspired editorial extolling the virtues of his Austrian comrades four days after the outbreak of the Schutzbund revolt and after it became clear that the Austrian Socialist Party would lose:

> Yes, the loss is as enormous as the suffering is cruel. Yet, nevertheless, I do not recognize this as a defeat for international socialism. Socialism is beaten, some-

times irretrievably, when it gives in without struggle. When it fights back, as the admirable combatants did in Vienna, grouped around Julius Deutsch and Otto Bauer until the last moment; when, through heroism and sacrifice, it creates a glorious legend; then one massacres it without having won.[30]

As mentioned earlier, in Belgium the Nazi takeover was the explicitly recognized catalyst for the adoption of the Plan de Man. It had taken major efforts at persuasion to convince Paul-Henri Spaak, the leading spokesperson for the powerful left-wing faction within the BWP/POB, to join the planist project. In the late spring of 1934 major quarrels erupted between the moderate supporters of planism, including Hendrik de Man, and the radical forces who had joined the planist bandwagon for their own purposes. It came to an exchange of hostile open letters between de Man and Spaak in the pages of L'Action Socialiste. Spaak publicly complained:

> You know better than anyone else, citizen De Man, the enormous concession which I made by accepting the political position of the Plan; you know how strongly I believe it to be insufficient. You also know the reservations I expressed when I officially joined the common effort. Since then there have occurred the events of Austria and Paris. How can you expect that, every now and then, I would not remind you that there exist entirely different forms of struggle other than those permitted within the framework of bourgeois democracy.[31]

The combination and identification of the Austrian defeat and the successful united front demonstrations on 12 February in France as two expressions of the changing contours of European social democracy in the age of fascism were likewise dominant themes in the writing of those Belgian left-wing critics of the BWP/POB, who had taken a neutral position toward the Plan de Man from the outset. The predominantly Flemish ISAOL reasoned: "Vienna teaches us that an insurrectionary movement which is not sufficiently based on mass participation cannot win against the powers of the state. Paris incorporates exactly the positive image of the Austrian negative."[32] Six weeks later Herman van der Goes emphasized in the pages of Het Liga Sinjaal: "Vienna signifies the end of the passively accepted destruction of European socialism. For the first time in decades workers have resisted till the end. [However,] the radiance and greatness of Vienna lies not in having taken up arms." Instead, it was the timing of their action which proved "that socialism is again something for which one can die." For, in recent years the prevalent and cynical belief was "that socialism was something to be betrayed and to abandon for battleships, national defense and the hoax of the League of Nations."[33]

The tendency of left-wing critics within the LSI to interpret the Schutzbund defeat as an inspirational act of defiance was perhaps most pronounced in the ranks of Spanish social democracy, which was then engaged in a full-scale assault on the prevailing social order and in the midst of preparations for an armed uprising. Spanish social democrats, however, were also the least inclined to interpret the Austrian events as an inspirational, heroic gesture without concrete lessons for the future conduct of armed insurrections, for what was at stake was nothing less than the future of their own designs. Under the headline TRAGIC WARNING the PSOE daily El Socialista drew the attention of its readers to several choices of the Austrian social democrats in the year prior to the uprising which had paved the way for their ultimate defeat.

The continued concessions in the face of a relentless adversary and the insistence on legal measures of defense had prepared the ground for the weakened position of Austrian socialists, said the Spanish critics. On 14 February 1934, while the fighting still raged in the municipal housing projects in Vienna, the Spanish socialists drew parallels to the situation at home and concluded their first assessment of the Austrian events with the following words: "All of Europe has its eyes fixed on Austria. And, more than anyone else in Europe, this is the case for the Spanish workers, who have understood the tragic warning."[34]

Two days later the editorialists of *El Socialista* further underscored the nefarious effect which the excessive concessions of their Austrian comrades had had on the outcome of their struggle, once they were forced to take up arms. Having adopted defensive postures all along, they had given away all initiative and the advantage of an offensive course. To choose the right moment for the insurrection unencumbered by legalist concerns, "to decide upon the [optimal] psychological moment with maximum rigor"—this was the lesson of Austria driven home with increasing conviction by the Spanish socialists witnessing the destruction of Austrian democracy.[35] The inspirational example of the Austrian fighters, however, was emphasized in the following day's editorial, headlined THE CASE OF AUSTRIA: A DEFEAT WHICH WAS NO DEFEAT: "This much is axiomatic: German social democracy has perished forever, whereas Austrian social democracy is today more alive and powerful than two weeks ago."[36] On 18 February 1934 the major front-page article reinforced this conclusion:

> The truth is that the events in Austria, regardless of their outcome, have raised the estimation of socialism which, after the fascist victories in Italy and Germany, has suffered terrible moral disintegration to the extent that many militants have asked us [in the past] whether the role which misfortune reserved to socialists was that of abandoning the field of struggle before the battle had commenced.[37]

Spanish young socialists were rather more scathing than their elders in the PSOE in their analysis and critique of the Schutzbund uprising. Increasingly disaffected with the passive stance of international social democracy, they questioned their international leadership:

> What idea has the [LSI] executive of what a revolution really is? And how do they envision conflict with the fascist movement? We draw little hope from the most recent [August 1933] conference in Paris; that, however, which we [absolutely] cannot fathom is the complete incapacity to defend oneself. If it would depend on the leading circles [of the LSI], we will soon have to transfer the [seat of] the International to Africa, driven by the fascist hordes.[38]

However, this low opinion of the LSI did not preclude the Spanish young socialists from recognizing the exceptional courage and idealism of the Austrian fighters. The same issue of *Renovación* proudly proclaimed in its front-page banner headline: THE DEFEAT OF AUSTRIA IS A STIMULUS FOR OUR TRIUMPH.[39]

The supposed lessons of Austria were continuously hammered home by Spanish propagandists of revolutionary action in the months and weeks before the October uprising centered on Asturias. The Asturian social democratic daily *Avance*, for instance, suggested in September 1934, in an editorial entitled "The Only Disastrous Revolution Will Be the Revolution Which Is Not Attempted": "We are, then, confronted with a situation where the attempted revolution in Austria has been less dangerous than the nonexistent one in Germany; where those who opted for force in Austria have not gravely compromised the working class, contrary to those who, in Germany, continuously postponed hope and [practiced] submission."[40] Spanish socialists combined the inspiration of the Austrian defeat with a distinct set of lessons in order to avoid a repetition of the ultimately unsuccessful efforts of the Schutzbund militants. The editorial on the very last page of the last issue of *El Socialista*, prior to its fourteen-month suspension in the wake of their revolt, ended with the following call to action: "The firm and unwavering decision of the Spanish proletariat, today more united than ever, is that Spain will not become a second Austria, in whatever sense of the word."[41]

Not everyone, of course, saw the Austrian defeat in a similarly glowing light. Whereas many social democrats viewed the lesson of Vienna as the reinforcement of a revolutionary course, more moderate observers drew the opposite conclusion. In a crucial SFIO national committee debate on the pros and cons of united action with communists, Marx Dormoy, two years later secretary of the interior in the cabinet of Léon Blum, invoked the Austrian example as proof "that class unity is not sufficient to prevent Fascism from advancing" and cautioned his comrades against a premature alliance with the PCF.[42] The social democratic economist Alfred Braunthal criticized the one-sided interpretation of the Italian, German and Austrian defeats and went on to call for a more nuanced assessment of the actual events:

> It should be material for reflection that the same defeat has been suffered in three countries with such different attitudes of the socialist movement as is the case in Germany, Austria and Italy. Especially a comparison between Germany and Austria suggests that the previous analyses of the German defeat have been inadequate; for, the mistakes, which the German movement accused itself of up to now, have by and large been avoided in the Austrian movement.

Braunthal saw the underlying weakness of social democracy in the lack of attention to the dire need of revamping its "proletarian class strategy." In his opinion, social democrats should begin to orient themselves toward other social groups and classes.[43] Karl Kautsky took the initiative to write an entire pamphlet, "The Limits of Force," in which he railed against the increasingly popular interpretation of the Austrian defeat as inspiration for redoubled revolutionary action:

> We also count the Viennese February events among the spontaneous mass actions, which one must understand and not condemn, even if one wishes that they had not occurred. What we are against, however, is the view which wishes to reinterpret a defeat as a victory and which may seduce others to, perhaps, again unleash a fight to the bitter end, even if the ultimate defeat is crystal clear from the beginning.[44]

The undisputed leader of Belgian socialism, Émile Vandervelde, had this to say about the Austrian defeat:

> The other day, speaking of France, we cast doubts on the willingness of bourgeois leaders of the liberal persuasion to defend democracy. We [now] note, once again, that the energies [which are absent in the liberal camp] can be found

among the reactionary bourgeoisie, when the task of the day is the strangulation of democracy.

On the other hand, if there still were among us some younger comrades, whose romanticism found expression in the idea of the insurrectionary road to power, the Austrian events have brought about the irrefutable proof of the truth, which Marx and Engels proclaimed already seventy years ago: the impossibility of victorious street battles against armies equipped with modern weapons if the latter do not pass, in whole or in part, on to the side of the revolution.[45]

On balance, then, the impact of the Schutzbund revolt was twofold. For representatives of moderate socialism, like Kautsky and Vandervelde, the Austrian defeat reinforced their refusal to advocate revolutionary means to power and their predilection for consensus politics and coalitionism. This reaction was most pronounced among social democrats operating in countries largely unaffected by domestic fascist movements, primarily the northern European states.[46] In much of continental Europe and among the LSI-Left in particular, the Austrian defeat was regarded as an inspiration and a stimulus for heightened radical action. The battle over the meaning of the Schutzbund revolt drastically underscores the seemingly unlimited possibilities for varied interpretations of the very same events. Yet the universal struggle to extract meaning from experiences elsewhere also graphically depicts the heightened attention of European socialists to the lessons of the day. Living through an unprecedented existential crisis, socialists began to look for solutions in the remotest corners of the Continent. Forced against the wall by fascism, European socialists began to regard their continent as a unit, although most had never visited a foreign country other than in times of war.

The Radiance of Asturias

The next important test of socialist strategies was bound to take place in Spain, where class relations had heated up in the course of 1933 to reach a point far beyond the level of industrial action in other European states (see table 4, p. 55). As it happened, the hostilities broke out in early October 1934. The outcome of the Spanish revolution would determine the course of action for the European Left for the remaining years of relative peacetime up to 1939. For as the Austrian socialists, then operating in illegality and exile, stressed in their analysis of the October events:

Our Spanish brothers have fought under far more propitious circumstances than we did. The Spanish workers were not as isolated as we were; on their side stood a part of the radical bourgeois intelligentsia, a part of the landless peasantry, and the Catalan and Basque population fighting for their national independence. . . . One has frequently reproached Austrian social democracy that they had hesitated far too long before they called to action.

This "mistake" was consciously avoided by Spanish social democrats. "Their tactics were dominated by the concern *to engage in battle before it was too late*."[47] In short, the fighters of the PSOE consciously set out to avoid the "errors" of their Austrian comrades. Under the remarkable slogan "Better Vienna Than Berlin," Spanish socialists attempted to learn from the perceived mistakes of their Austrian models, while following their example. What became known as the Asturian Commune took on all the characteristics of a decisive test for insurrectionary strategies, now immensely popular after the inspirational Schutzbund revolt.

The defeat of the Spanish fighters marked the real and symbolic turning point in the radicalization of continental European social democracy and the Left as a whole. The origins of the moderation of the European Left, its reorientation away from a policy fixated on the promise of a working-class united front and toward the advocacy of multiclass popular fronts, can be traced back to the devastating impact of a second clear defeat of the insurrectionary course in less than nine months. After the initial February action of the Schutzbund fighters in Austria, which was widely understood as an inspiration and not a defeat, the renewed failure of an openly revolutionary strategy injected a heavy dose of caution into the deliberations of a European Left desperately searching for effective solutions to their existential crisis. The Asturian Commune of October 1934 marked the high point of the reemergence of revolutionary politics in the European theater after a ten-year hiatus following the end of the 1917–23 central European cycle of working-class rebellions. Perhaps most remarkable about the 1934 conjuncture, in contradistinction to 1917–23, was the leading role of social democratic parties. Whereas revolts occurring in the aftermath of World War I were generally instigated and led by the newly emerging communist parties, and social democrats had played a passive or even counterrevolutionary role, the year 1934 saw the first and last instance of traditional social democratic parties at the forefront of armed revolts. Similar to the earlier attempts at insurrection, however, this year witnessed nothing but defeats. The Asturian Commune thus closed a brief and unique chapter in the history of the European Left. It played a role similar to the abortive October 1923 revolution in Germany. How did social democrats outside Spain react to the second defeat of an armed insurrection in less than eight months?

The Belgian socialist intellectual Louis Piérard had never been affected by the radicalization of European, and Belgian, social democracy in the years leading up to October 1934. After the Asturian defeat, his voice of moderation gained increasing currency within the circles of the BWP/POB. A frequent visitor to Spain, Piérard used the opportunity proffered by the defeated Asturian Commune to air his point of view. In an open letter to Paul-Henri Spaak, the spokesperson for the Belgian left-wing critics of the party's course, Louis Piérard expressed his admiration for the fighters in Asturias. "But the real question is whether this campaign was necessary, whether it was inevitable, if it was necessary to expose the Spanish working class to this bloody defeat?" Piérard argued for the existence of a real, and more promising, alternative: parliamentary maneuvers to detach at least a part of the bourgeois Left from the project of conservative authoritarianism. And, he stressed, there were some even within the radicalized PSOE who advocated precisely this course of action. "But these very comrades were not listened to. The mystique created by the *united front* carried the day. No one dared to react against it."[48] For Louis Piérard this was not a sudden revelation. Like others in the moderate wing of social democracy, he was merely restating his long-standing personal conviction. To judge the full impact of the Asturian defeat on Left rethinking, it is more important and persuasive to concentrate on expressions of doubt in the validity of a revolutionary course of action among those forces that had become caught up in the radicalizing momentum after the sudden loss of Germany and the inspirational actions of the Schutzbund activists.

Claude Beaurepaire had been a sympathizer of the PCF during the 1920s. Within the SFIO, he earned a reputation as a member of the eclectic but nonconformist current Révolution Constructive before joining up, in 1935, with Marceau Pivert's militantly left-wing Gauche Révolutionnaire. A supporter of radical planism, he drew the following pessimistic conclusion in an article on planism and insurrection:

> Vienna and Asturias: may these memories, which are still so close to the present day, give rise to uncertainties! There will certainly be those who will explain that, in Austria, there was a lack of leadership with a revolutionary mentality and that, in Spain, one witnessed anarchist treachery; we will undoubtedly ask ourselves whether, in Paris, there will also be some element about which one will say, after the defeat, that, without it, victory would have been assured.

Beaurepaire went on to demand a more realistic assessment of reality than some of his comrades were willing to carry out. While unwilling to abandon *all* insurrectionary perspectives, he called for a firmer preparation of the necessary, militant course.[49] The pages of the social democratic *Le Combat Marxiste*, a journal edited by the erstwhile Comintern functionary Lucien Laurat and his companion Marcelle Pommera, were a sounding board for a variety of approaches to the strategic questions of the day. Arguing against the age-old mystique of the insurrectionary general strike, Pommera referred to the examples of "Vienna and Asturias . . . which should be the occasion for reflection before [re]launching this slogan, which may be inspirational for a handful of devoted and determined militants, but [will prove ineffectual] for the masses which adopt a wait-and-see attitude."[50]

Austrian socialists, who had been catapulted to the left by their February defeat, drew the conclusion from the failure of the Asturian Commune "that an armed insurrection can only be victorious in a truly revolutionary situation," when significant elements of the armed forces themselves have joined the rebels en masse.[51] After referring to the stimulating effect of the Schutzbund rebellion, Austrian young socialist had this to say about the impact of Asturias:

> The developments of the year 1934 taught more reasoned observations [*kühlere Überlegungen*]. The July putsch of the Nazis [a failed coup attempt in Austria] and the battles of the Spanish workers showed that a revolution cannot be successful if the state apparatus is not ripe for collapse. The Austrian working class [now] remembered historic experiences: it realized that the revamping of society cannot be successfully undertaken overnight and that it will have to prepare itself for a longer struggle.[52]

Many of the more determined advocates of radical action within the ranks of European social democracy merely moderated their approaches by degrees. Some continued to believe in the applicability of insurrectionary tactics, though now generally tempered by appropriate cautionary remarks, as in the case of the Austrian socialists or Claude Beaurepaire. Others went much further in the abandonment of a revolutionary perspective. One example of a more decisive renunciation of the leftist heritage was the Belgian Raymond Bottelberghs, a onetime activist in the BWP/POB's left-wing faction Action Socialiste and a noted journalist.

In a June 1935 article in *Le Combat Marxiste*, in response to allegations that the BWP/POB had betrayed its own committment to radical planism by joining, literally overnight, the coalition government of a Christian Democratic banker, Paul Van Zeeland, at the end of March 1935, Raymond Bottelberghs developed the following scenario. Had the architects of the Plan de Man refused to take up the offer of taking up posts in the Van Zeeland government, he argued, the likely course of events would have been the constitution of an openly reactionary government which would have declared social democracy a seditious force in order "to crush it in open battle." Perhaps social democracy would not have been outlawed right away, but, in a piecemeal fashion, the BWP/POB would have arrived "at a quasi-total state of powerlessness, as in Spain, Hungary or Poland."[53]

The moderating influence of the Asturian events was most apparent in the deliberations of the crucial November 1934 LSI executive meeting in Paris debating the future of the international united front. Whereas the Schutzbund battle had given rise to a whole mythology of revolutionary action for the Left, the Asturian defeat resulted in the opposite extreme. Indalecio Prieto, himself a moderate centrist throughout 1934, insistently defended the October uprising against conservative detractors: "When debating unity of action I believe I heard some delegate say that the Spanish movement was the best possible proof of what he considered dangerous about the adoption of united front tactics." Another Spaniard present in the Mutualité, Julio Alvarez del Vayo, mentioned in a confidential report: "For my part, I had to intervene repeatedly with the sole purpose of correcting erroneous interpretations of the October movement formulated by those who wished to recognize in the Spanish events a decisive argument against unity in action."[54]

An interesting debate erupted in the German SPD's newspaper *Neuer Vorwärts*, in the aftermath of the Asturian October. Viktor Schiff, a prominent party journalist, reported from Barcelona on the consequences of the Spanish defeat. In a survey of responses to previous setbacks elsewhere in Europe, Schiff stated: "Partially out of revolutionary romanticism and partially out of hateful prejudices against 'reformism,' one has been unwilling to draw the necessary consequences from the collapse of the German working class. Then came Vienna. Has one at least learned something from the Austrian events? Look at Spain!" Schiff concluded by highlighting what he considered the senselessness of military action short of the assured neutralization of the army.[55] The first response to Schiff came from Karl Böchel, the spokesperson of the Revolutionary Socialists of Germany, who was soon to be expelled from the ranks of the SPD. He castigated the refusal of his more moderate party colleagues even to consider military action without a prior guarantee of certain success:

> There we have finally arrived at the point where the German example of passive capitulation, which can be explained by a multitude of factors, but which supposedly was not desired by anyone, slowly turns into an act of reformist political brilliance. It is a manifestation of monstrous arrogance [*von aufpeitschender Arroganz*] to see how the pragmatic message of the German example is invoked as a model [*Lehrmeister*] vis-à-vis the "petit-bourgeois" ideology of the Austrian and Spanish workers, who staked their lives for their socialist beliefs.[56]

Subsequent interventions by Victor Schiff, "Fred War," Friedrich Stampfer and, again, Karl Böchel reiterated their opposing viewpoints. In the course of this debate it became obvious that, in some respects, the spokespersons for the LSI-Left moderated their approach and began to sound warnings against ill-considered military action, not very different from the words of caution offered by more moderate socialists all along. But, in practice, it became equally obvious that the words of admonition by Kautsky, Stampfer and other advocates of sobriety and prudence were, in actuality, meant to prevent any and all insurrectionary moments. This much the left-wing critics were not prepared to concede. The debate was symptomatic of the state of affairs within European social democracy after October 1934.

While some continued to point to the Asturian and Austrian revolts as supporting evidence for the validity and necessity of a revolutionary course of action, based on a united front approach,[57] the general tendency of reactions to the latest course of events went in the direction of moderation. This was clearly recognized by the proponents of the radical alternative. In December 1934 the Austrian underground socialists suggested that "out of the experience in Austria and Spain, which we interpret as signs of increasing revolutionary disturbances of the capitalist system, major portions of the international proletariat draw the conclusions that the revolutionary path is momentarily impassable and that, for that reason, we must maintain democracy *at any price*."[58] The moderating effect of the failed revolts of 1934 and other disillusioning news from abroad could even be felt in the isolated German underground. The SPD's border secretary for eastern Saxony, Wilhelm Sander, in referring to the increasingly less hostile attitudes of party activists toward their conservative Prague exile executive, mentioned "that the comrades themselves point to Austria, Spain and the executions in Russia" as the reasons for their turn.[59] A corollary of the Asturian defeat was the changed assessment of the Schutzbund revolt. As can be gauged from many of the foregoing citations, the Austrian insurrection was now no longer regarded as an inspiration but as a defeat. What had been a hallmark of conservative evaluations starting in the immediate aftermath of the February revolt now became the common property of much of Europe's embattled Left. It was a sign of changing needs.

The Victories of Popular Fronts

In the preceding sections on the transnational ramifications of national disasters in Germany, Austria and Spain, I have solely utilized citations that explicitly mention the impact of these three "foreign" events on the state of mind of the respective national or international workers' movements. In my surveys of the party press and other communications within social democracy, I have found few specific references that explicitly link the atmosphere of growing disillusionment after October 1934 with the simultaneous process of the rising popularity of popular fronts. Yet I believe that evidence adduced thus far clearly demonstrates the transnational significance of the Asturian Commune for European social democratic rethinking. In light of this and my argumentation in chapter 6, one would be hard-pressed to deny the circumstantial link between the repeated failures of an insurrectionary course and the rapidly ascending discourse of popular fronts. One experienced socialist who drew the explicit connection was Louis-Olivier Frossard. Perhaps this is the moment to cite, once again, a lengthy paragraph from his November 1934 personal crusade in favor of a French popular front. It may stand as a symbol for the rapidly changing contours of socialist politics in the midthirties:

> I am far from denying the dynamism of united fronts. I am delighted to see these great mass gatherings, whose success is assured by unity of action; I am delighted to see the enthusiasm which it unleashes in the working-class neighborhoods. I know that if the circumstances demand it, the proletariat will fight, and it will fight well. I do not doubt either its capacity for action or its courage. But I am less concerned with battles than with victory. After Italy, after Austria, after Spain; it is not enough for me to maintain dignity.[60]

The victories of the Spanish and French popular fronts powerfully reinforced the image of such an alliance as *the* hope for the future and the long-sought-for answer to the search for middle-class support. Upon learning of the victory of the *frente popular*, the LSI secretariat greeted the news with obvious relief. The lead article in the LSI's home journal, *International Information (II)*, announcing "Victory in Spain," stressed the importance of this event for Spanish politics while simultaneously highlighting its "great *international significance*." For the LSI leadership, "the victory in Spain represents a fresh defeat for Fascism from an international point of view and a new hope for all those countries, which are still languishing under despotic rule today."[61] The veteran French socialist Auguste Bracke reported a similar sense of elevation among the members of the LSI's executive assembled in Brussels shortly after the electoral victory of the French popular front. Upon arrival, the French delegation "was greeted by an atmosphere simultaneously characterized by joy and confidence in the immediate aftermath of the elections which have instilled the greatest hopes in all countries."[62] Both reactions were remarkable expressions of solidarity by an organization, the LSI, which never took a stand on the pros and cons of popular fronts throughout the years of the latter's greatest influence.[63]

Understandably, the respective electoral victories in Spain and France triggered outpourings of contentment and cheer on either side of the Pyrenees. The Spanish victory was greeted by the SFIO centrist Paul Faure in the pages of *Le Populaire* with effusive words of enthusiasm: "Yes, the horizon becomes clearer, and reactionary forces are retreating all along the line."[64] For Marceau Pivert, the left critic and soon-to-be media expert in France's own popular front government, it was nothing less than "the socialist Republic [which] appears on the horizon."[65] Spanish socialists were following the electoral contest in France as closely as the French. Three days before the first round of elections in France, *El Socialista* declared the contest to be one "over the most direct path toward *European-wide* peace and *international* justice."[66] When the favorable results of this first round trickled in, *El Socialista* entitled its editorial column "The French Elections Are the Defeat of Fascism," and went on to declare: "For good reasons, the domestic contest in France took on an international character and quality: because of the repercussions which it may have by means of the solutions which will be applied [by the incoming government] in the coming days to difficult problems currently preoccupying all of Europe."[67] In the editorial announcing the resounding victory in the second round of elections in France—characteristically entitled "Hosannah to Our Brothers in France!,"—the author(s) concluded on a theme continuously repeated in succeeding weeks and months: "The consequences of the new direction which French politics will take on starting today do not need to be feared. One also need not fear the repercussions which it will, of necessity, exercise on our politics. For good reasons there has always existed, and this is reaffirmed today, massive cross-fertilization between the Left of the old and the Left of the new Latin Republics."[68]

Yet the most telling testimony of the moral impact of the popular front was the reception of its victory in countries where matters never came to the constitution of a popular front. The underground RSÖ was adamantly opposed to popular front politics in Austria. Nevertheless, when news of the Spanish victory reached Vienna, RSÖ members, including a significant portion of its leadership, then incarcerated in a Viennese prison, opened their jail cell windows, gave speeches and intonated the "International."[69] The following issue of the *Arbeiter-Zeitung (AZ)* started out with reminiscences of the 1893 Belgian general strike which had brought the Belgians universal male suffrage: "Back then the Belgian example inspired the Austrian working class, which was still completely excluded from all political rights. The demand 'We want to speak Belgian!' reverberated through the meeting halls back then." This was the beginning of the Austrian struggle for the enlargement of the franchise. "As did the Belgians then, now the Spanish are our shining model. Today we must learn *to speak Spanish*."[70] In a similar vein, the victory of the French popular front was greeted by the Austrians as "a defeat for *European* fascism."[71]

Reports from the German underground likewise paint a picture of sympathetic approval of popular front victories, although here the element of resignation, ever present in socialist circles after more than three years of continuous Nazi terror, was a noticeable factor too. Franz Bögler, in April 1936, reported discussions on popular front politics "in Spain and France" among his contacts in Silesia.[72] Gustav Ferl reported from the Rhineland an interest in the politics of popular fronts: "In general the events in Spain have aroused the curiosity of the people. Those developments and the Spanish popular front have left behind major impressions and instilled new hopes in many a person."[73] In May of 1936 Ferl relayed news he had received from Aachen: "The electoral victory of the Left in France was only hesitantly announced. However, once the loudspeakers announced the results at noon on Monday, the fourth of May, news of the victory spread like wildfire through the factories. . . . The workers were busy discussing the returns."[74] Party members favorable to the project of a German popular front were naturally quite fascinated by victories abroad and immediately realized the potential Continental impact. Thus Alexander Schifrin, already in mid-1935, grasped the significance of the newly forming popular fronts and reasoned: "French domestic politics today takes on European-wide importance."[75] Commenting on the May 1936 success, Heinrich Ehrmann, the member of Neu Beginnen, (NB) wrote: "Not only for the fate of French socialism, but for the fate of European socialism as a whole, the next months of French developments will be of utmost importance."[76]

Given the fact that popular fronts were an organic outgrowth of Continental politics, the apparent interest in, and sympathy toward, popular fronts by other Continental actors is not exactly surprising. Even in the cases of left critics of such a strategic orientation, the feeling of relief and satisfaction at the news of electoral victories is fully understandable, for the fate of *any* project of the Left was intricately connected to the ups and downs of all the others. Given the heightened importance of popular fronts starting in the summer of 1935, any major setback to this particular alliance strategy would have spelled doom for the proponents of *all* alternative responses to the rise of fascism and the ravages of the Great Depression.

Conclusion

Formally, in the mid-1930s, European social democracy was an increasingly compartmentalized agglomeration of largely independent national parties. Until its resurrection as the Socialist International in the aftermath of World War II, the August 1933 Paris conference on the assessment of responses to the fascist danger was the last representative international gathering of the LSI. As I underscored in chapter 3, subsequent to this event the LSI became an increasingly paralyzed organizational shell which survived into the years of World War II only thanks to its refusal to decide on any issues of importance to the workers' movement as a whole. Because of this abstentionist stance, essentially permitting each national organization to pursue its own individual path, LSI bureau and executive meetings became important forums for the exchange of ideas but were devoid of any larger significance for the movement they were set up to direct.

Yet, precisely at this moment of minimum authority for the supreme directorate of international social democracy, Continental developments within European society and politics took on extraordinary importance. The future of social democracy, and democracy in general, was increasingly challenged, and the wave of fascist victories and threats narrowed the room for maneuver for any opposition to this course. In much of continental Europe, a series of radical revisions of accepted social democratic theory and practice captured the imagination of socialists from Seville to Berlin: united fronts, radical planism and popular fronts. The initial shock triggering a momentum to the left came as the irreversibility and significance of the Nazi takeover in Germany became crystal clear to everyone concerned. The February 1934 Austrian Schutzbund uprising further reinforced this trend away from ministerial collaboration and disinterest in close cooperation with other parties of the Left toward advocacy of united fronts and a heightened interest in radical, if not insurrectionary, tactics. The summit and supersession of this radical response to the spread of fascism and the persistent Great Depression came to be the Spanish insurrection of October 1934 centered on the Asturian Commune. The failure of this most militant adventure of European social democracy to date caused a renewed bout of rethinking among social democrats desperate for workable solutions. The defeat of the Spanish revolutionaries, following on the heels of the Austrian February revolt which met a similar fate, underscored the less than certain promise of the united front alternative. The search for additional allies in the fight to stave off the Right ultimately brought about the creation and the surge in popularity of the popular front.

In chapters 4–6 I traced the evolution of national and international debates on the strategies under review. While focusing on the specific national trajectories of the respective orientations, the transnational parallels were always suggested, if not openly implied. The move to united and, later, popular fronts occurred at roughly the same time in many locations across continental Europe. Yet specific references to the experiences of other countries faced with similar problems are generally absent in the documents most crucial for the historiographical reconstruction of the respective national debates. Given the simultaneity and similarity of the different debates, the search for the smoking gun is, I believe, a less than necessary task. The parallels between the evolution of social democratic political thought in Austria, Belgium, France, Germany and Spain are strong evidence of the transnational character of this experience. Yet to show the explicit impact of "foreign" events on the consciousness of national actors can only strengthen my point. It is for this reason that I have chosen to demonstrate the effect of four key turning points in the history of the European Left during the thirties on European socialists irrespective of frontiers: January 1933 in Germany, February 1934 in Austria, October 1934 in Spain, and the victories of popular fronts in Spain (February 1936) and France (May 1936). I believe this chapter shows the acute awareness of international events among the member parties of the LSI. Events in distant countries, which, for most social democrats, were essentially worlds apart, were perceived and interpreted as important lessons for their actions at home. There is no better symbol for this process than the guiding slogan of the Asturian revolt, "Better Vienna Than Berlin."

In most instances where historians, or other social scientists, have studied the impact of key events in other countries on domestic constituencies, the project is exactly that. The relationship between the geographic entities involved has usually been interpreted as a relationship of cause and effect rather than of dynamic interaction.[77] And, of course, in a very real sense, at the moment of, say, the Asturian revolt, the vagaries of military action in the valleys of Cantabria were far more influential on developments abroad than, say, the simultaneously occurring cantonal elections in France or debates about tactics in the Austrian underground. Taken in isolation, each event may be understood as an independent variable with specific results. Placed in sequential order, the reference to relationships of cause and effect becomes an increasingly meaningless interpretive device. Instead, what emerges very clearly is the transnational character of the lessons to be drawn and the ongoing cross-fertilization between social democratic movements faced with a common threat. The perceived lessons of each event become part of a Continental intellectual heritage influencing the next steps of the movement as a whole. In turn, subsequent experiences reinforce future realignments and prescribe further actions. Only in this manner can the Continental drift from coalitionism and fratricide to united fronts and, ultimately, popular fronts be adequately understood.

Socialists' reactions to key turning points were never uniform. I have repeatedly highlighted the divergent reactions by the two main tendencies within the LSI, the radical Left and the moderate Right. The same events were usually interpreted in dramatically different ways by members of the same International. In this specific, limited sense one has to recognize the existence of at least two distinct voices of international socialism throughout that decade. Yet both camps were jolted into action by identical concerns, and, in continental Europe at the very least, a distinct pattern of responses can be traced in relation to the four major experiences shaping socialist politics: an ascending curb of radicalization up to October 1934 and a sobering of expectations after the Asturian defeat. This policy evolution occurred in all five countries under review. In short, the evolution of European social democracy in 1933–36 is a classic case of dynamic interaction on a quasi-Continental scale long before the advent of a Europe without borders even in the limited sense implied by the expansion of the Common Market at the present time. Precisely at a moment when national divisions affected European politics more deeply than at any other peacetime period in the twentieth century, the experience of European social democracy marks the transnational dimensions of national politics.

EIGHT

Piston-Box and Steam

Innovative ideas, in and of themselves, lead nowhere fast. Novel strategies on the road to social emancipation take on greater relevance only if the social climate is propitious. Concepts of united fronts, for instance, were bandied about within the small circles of independent left socialist and dissident communist groupings for a number of years prior to 1933 without any major consequences.[1] What had to happen for such new ideas to attain positions of importance within the mainstream European Left was a sudden wave of questioning of traditional ways of thinking and action within mass parties and their peripheries. In this process the interplay of party leadership and ranks took on primordial importance.

No definition of the terms "leadership" and "ranks" will satisfy all possible doubts. As a matter of fact, the mere use of the term "leadership" is highly suspect, if only because it already implies some notion of primacy over the second concept, "ranks." Furthermore, given the layered structures of mass political parties, a person wielding a certain degree of political or moral authority in a small-town party local will be on the receiving end of party circulars emanating from the party's regional federation; the regional federation, in turn, is subject to national directives; but, ultimately, the national leadership may be democratically removed by what is sometimes termed a rank-and-file rebellion. It is precisely one of my aims in this chapter to emphasize the interdependency and mutual reliance on each other of each element in this conceptual pair. Thus, if I employ the word "leader" or "leadership," it should be understood in the sense of one or several individuals who, by virtue of training or circumstance, exercise some front rank or guiding function, be it in the furtherance of intellectual pursuits or the application of theory to practice.

At the same time that it is advisable to exercise caution in the utilization of such terms, I believe that such concepts have a distinct usefulness in the clarification of historical processes, particularly in mass movements. Not all segments of a social group or a social movement move with equal speed or in the same direction. And this is no less true within the daily practice of mass parties with tens or hundreds of thousands of members and an even larger circle of sympathizers. Ultimately, the ensuing pages are the product of a double dissatisfaction with the literature to date, for it seems that many students of working-class history fall into the trap of highlighting one or the other element of the conceptual pair employed. Victories and defeats are frequently attributed to accomplishments or shortcomings of either leadership or ranks. By contrast, I will argue that strategies become successful if and when there exists a certain degree of overlap between novel ideas and popular sentiments, by no means a natural or frequent occurrence. One such moment of convergence was the spring and summer of 1934.

Unity in the Provinces: France, 1933

Concerning the genesis of united fronts, some available data in the case of France suggest that it was precisely at the grassroots level that relationships between the various organizations of the European Left may have been the least antagonistic, even prior to the beginnings of the first national united fronts. Whereas party offices in the Parisian headquarters of the PCF and the SFIO cultivated attitudes of mutual disdain, activists on the local level frequently made common cause. Michel Brot, in one of the rare cases of a regional study of the united and popular fronts, repeatedly refers to moments of official cooperation between the PCF and the SFIO in the Alpes-Maritimes prior to the national breakthrough in the summer of 1934. Brot reports several instances of fraternal action in the Mediterranean coastal town of Nice in early 1933. One such action, a joint meeting in late February 1933, may have been a local manifestation of the brief international thaw between communism and social democracy I referred to in my earlier chapters. But another occasion, a joint May Day celebration, falls outside of the narrow time span of semiofficial truce. Brot claims that the May Day 1933 demonstration in Nice was the sole instance of social democrats marching shoulder to shoulder with communists and other forces of the Left anywhere in France.[2]

Yet information culled from other sources casts doubts on Brot's assertion of the singularity of the Nice action. An equally rare regional study of the PCF in the eastern reaches of the Pyrenees by Michel Cadé relativizes Brot's claim. In Rivesaltes, the canton with the highest proportion of communist votes in Pyrénées-Orientales, the PCF and the SFIO similarly marked May Day 1933 with a joint celebration.[3] In the predominantly rural *département* of Lot, May Day 1933 was also celebrated in unison. It was an important enough event that the SFIO delegate from that area, speaking at the July 1933 SFIO national congress, referred to this experience in highly favorable terms. He reported on the success of their joint meeting with the PCF and the two rival trade union federations at the local labor exchange: "Whereas in previous gatherings, organized by either the communist or the socialist party, only a few diehards bothered to show up, on that day [May Day 1933] the labor center was filled to the brim and a delirious crowd was present to applaud workers' unity."[4]

The existence of three unitary meetings on May Day 1933, all in southern France, is not meant to suggest that local unity was the rule. At best this is impressionistic evidence that a unitary course of action was a distinct possibility, even at a time when the respective party hierarchies were opposed to such fraternization. And, indeed, special circumstances may have very well played an important role in these exceptions to the rule. Rivesaltes had witnessed a major working-class defeat in 1929, which, Cadé suggests, taught local activists a lesson.[5] The Nice local of the SFIO, according to Brot, "was a bastion of the extreme Left within the SFIO."[6] And the Lot federation of the SFIO, at the July 1933 congress, voted unanimously for the motion of Révolution Constructive. In a joint statement of the Lot federations of the SFIO, the PCF and their respective trade union affiliates, dated 25 May 1933, the four organizations pleaded for official cooperation of their national leaderships as a first step toward an eventual merger, once more underscoring the exceptional conditions prevailing in their *département*.[7]

Another notable contravention of official hostility between the parties of the French Left occurred in the summer of 1933 in and around the Alsatian capital of Strasbourg. A construction workers' strike in late June was unusual in that communist, socialist and independent unions joined their forces, formed a common strike committee and issued a call for solidarity strikes when, by late July, the employers still refused to budge. By early August 10,000 workers were on strike, and massive demonstrations contributed to the polarization of the town. On 3 August 1933 it came to violent confrontations resulting in 145 injured demonstrators and 75 arrests. Two days later the city had come to a halt, and the strike movement was beginning to spread to other areas of Alsace.[8] In the end the strike wave receded without any satisfaction of the original demands. Yet, despite the ultimate defeat, the Strasbourg riot of the summer of 1933 was a vivid reminder of the potential power of a unified Left and of the possibility for such unity to arise in the course of struggle. As was the case in the Alpes-Maritimes, Pyrénées-Orientales and Lot, however, the unusual political configuration of the Alsatian Left played a crucial role in this early manifestation of a practical united front. For, unlike many areas of France, the communist trade union was dominant in Strasbourg, and, significantly, the communist movement was under the political leadership of French followers of the International Right Opposition. In the summer of 1933 Strasbourg's mayor and member of parliament were members of the Alsatian Communist Opposition, the former Alsatian federation of the PCF.[9]

While those four cases may have been exceptional—although further research would perhaps significantly augment the number of "exceptionalisms"—they simultaneously point to some of the crucial elements necessary for the eventual breakthrough of the unitary trend. The presence of left-wing critics of the official party line and the bitter lessons of a previous defeat were of vital importance in the ultimate construction of the French united front, ratified in late July 1934. Yet another necessary ingredient for the ultimate attainment of unity in France and elsewhere was prominent in at least one of these cases. It is highly symptomatic that the May Day gathering in Cahors, the capital of Lot, was portrayed as *unexpectedly* large and *surprisingly* enthusiastic. As we will see, similar reports abound regarding the origins of unity elsewhere. And, whereas next to nothing is known about the background to this action in Cahors, given the subsequent joint statement by the leaders of the local workers' parties and union federations in favor of national unity, it is very plausible that at least part of the success of the Cahors united front must be ascribed to an unusual combination of prescient local leaders and a responsive party membership at large. The events of February 1934 confirm this view.

Unity in the Provinces: France, 1934

The unitary mass demonstrations of 12 February 1934 in the east end of Paris, the opening shot in the tortuous campaign toward nationwide unity in action between French socialists and communists, only became a reality in the final moments of the event itself. The PCF national leadership had hesitated even to announce a march for that date until 11 February, and then they mobilized for a separate communist feeder march to the Place de la Nation. The possibility for clashes to occur upon the final merging of their ranks was an openly debated option on both sides of the divide. As it happened, the meeting of socialists and communists at the Place de la Nation became a joyous celebration of unity in action and a spontaneous expression of the similarity of aims. It is for that reason that much of the discussion on the origins of French unity begins with this admittedly momentous occasion on the afternoon of 12 February 1934 in Paris.

Yet a look at the February days in the provinces of France suggests that, while unity at the summit in Paris may have been the crowning event, in many locations throughout France the groundswell of opinions favoring common action made itself felt in unequivocal ways prior to, and independent of, the eventual concurrence of the Paris leaderships. Antoine Prost, in a meticulous study of the February days outside of Paris, reports that already on 8 February, four crucial days earlier than the Parisian march and rally, at least eleven provincial towns witnessed unitary demonstrations jointly organized by the SFIO and the PCF, among them the dockworkers' stronghold of St. Nazaire.[10] Additional local and regional demonstrations for an end to fratricide on the Left occurred on 9–11 February. According to Henri Heldman, the cities of Amiens, La Rochelle, Nîmes, Le Mans, Chambéry, Lyon and many other localities saw common actions by the PCF and the SFIO prior to the change of heart by the PCF central committee.[11]

Yet, even in the provinces, the big breakthrough occurred on 12 February 1934. Antoine Prost documents 346 actions in defense of democratic rights that day, not counting numerous meetings and marches in Paris and its immediate environs. Of these actions 161 can be clearly identified as cooperative ventures comprising the PCF and the SFIO; in the vast majority of the remaining cases the pertinent information does not furnish sufficient data for such a conclusion, although it is probable that most would have conformed to the general trend.[12] At first sight this may suggest a temporal coincidence of province and metropolis. Prost, however, effectively argues for the independent, and earlier, move toward unity in the provinces on the basis of several indicators. First, L'Humanité's call for a march on the 12 February, published on 11 February, had little effect on the course of events in the country at large. Plans for joint demonstrations outside of Paris had long since been decided upon. Second, L'Humanité, in Paris, had called for a separate march of communist ranks. In the provinces, by contrast, the vast majority of demonstrations were unitary demonstrations where, from the beginning and by conscious design, socialists marched shoulder to shoulder with communists.

The ultimate proof, perhaps, of the irrelevance of L'Humanité's belated and halfhearted call are those rare cases where provincial socialists and communists were unable to come to an agreement and where, on 12 February 1934, the local population witnessed separate marches by the hostile groups. In Roubaix, Lille, Lyon and

Saint-Étienne, for instance, despite the last-minute call to action by the Paris hierarchy, "the communist switch [in Paris] was of lesser importance than traditions of antagonism or the excessive belief in [long-established] theories on the part of activists."[13] But in many locations throughout France, the turnout for these demonstrations exceeded the most optimistic expectations. In several large cities—Bordeaux, Toulouse, Limoges, Lorient, Brest, Cherbourg, Calais, Mulhouse—at least 10 percent of the entire local population joined the marchers. In some locations up to a third participated.[14]

Soon after the day of unity, 12 February 1934, the PCF retracted from its advocacy and practice of united fronts, and top-level negotiations between the SFIO and the PCF stalled until the late spring and early summer, when, given the green light from Moscow, PCF luminaries suddenly rediscovered the virtues of unity and, on 27 July 1934, signed a national united front agreement with the SFIO executive. On a local level, however, elements of continuity with the unitary experience of February are far more manifest. Henri Heldman, sorting through police reports in the Archives Nationales, found impressive evidence suggesting continuing movement in favor of unity between the PCF and the SFIO in many locations throughout France. Heldman reported unitary demonstrations in at least seven *départements*, outside of Paris, between March and early June. And eighteen *départements* witnessed public meetings sponsored by the local party leaderships, in open contravention of national directives.[15] In a candid statement to an assembly of representatives from the party's departmental federations, the SFIO general secretary Paul Faure told his audience in mid-April:

> The [SFIO] executive committee and the general secretary have acted in accordance with their belief that, faced with the events of the past several months, it became unnecessary [!] to rigorously apply congress decisions concerning rank-and-file contacts with the Communist Party [which were officially frowned upon]. There are moments when one must not move against the popular current, for, in that case one would risk being swept away.[16]

The French experience with united fronts prior to the ratification of the national pact suggests the strong presence of a grassroots current of opinion favoring such a strategy and partially circumventing the more reticent party hierarchies. Whereas, throughout the first half of 1934, neither the SFIO nor the PCF officially favored such a turn, in many locations throughout the country the necessities of local circumstances engendered powerful, if perhaps frequently ephemeral, instances of united action between the PCF and the SFIO. Added together, they constituted a powerful impetus pushing the parties' hierarchies toward the official sanctioning of such a turn. Given the higher degree of centralism determining the inner life of the PCF, this popular sentiment had a far more difficult time gaining a hearing in the top-level decision-making bodies of the communist movement than was the case within the SFIO. The existence of a Comintern directorate as an additional constraint on the PCF further complicated this intricate web of interactions between different levels of the party hierarchy.

Within the SFIO, Paul Faure's admission to the assembled heads of the party's federations graphically demonstrates the impact of grassroots sentiments on party policy. Ultimately, the SFIO's adoption of the united front orientation would not have come about in July 1934 without the prior groundwork having been laid at the local level in previous months. For the PCF the same holds true, if to a lesser extent, for here the indispensable factor in the course toward a united front was the Comintern's approval. Yet, ultimately, the Comintern's abandonment of "Third Period" politics in May–June 1934, and the concurrent adoption of united front tactics, must also be seen as a reaction to the fact that unity within the European Left was beginning to become reality in France and elsewhere, regardless of party directives. This dynamic toward unity was recognized by many observers at the time. Léon Blum, writing in his party's daily, described, perhaps more elegantly than most, this sudden shift in attitude:

> That there is enthusiasm is undeniable, and I note at once that it has been noticeable not only in Paris and its vicinity. In the most diverse and distant parts of the country, the same current of electricity has made itself felt. The desire for unity, the will to unity, latent no doubt for many a long year, has suddenly come to the surface under the shock of the fascist aggression of 6 February. . . . After 6 February, the masses of the people felt instinctively that, in France as elsewhere, the unity of the workers, enabling a defensive action or a counteroffensive to be waged with all the strength of the workers, was the surest safeguard against the fascist menace. This natural reaction arising from the instinct of self-preservation is in accord, too, with reasoned examination of the facts of the situation. We are therefore in the presence of a powerful movement, all the more powerful because it is spontaneous, which no one can or should refuse to recognize. . . . One feels, in spite of oneself, as if one were on a steep slope and being carried down rather by the force of gravity than of one's own volition.[17]

Grassroots Unity in the Saar

Similar observations about rapid motion toward united fronts have been made in other European countries at an almost identical time. Joseph Buttinger, in his colorful memoirs, describes the sudden hold of pro-unity sentiment within the recently defeated Austrian socialist underground in June of 1934.[18] Reports from the Saarland, where social democrats and communists had entered a united front in early July, repeat the same scenario. A lead article in the social democratic daily *Deutsche Freiheit* recounted the events of a major united front rally in the industrial town of Burbach and highlighted "the magnificent expression of support by the masses, which suddenly fused into one unit." The same report went on to offer an explanation of the origins of this rapidly emerging united front sentiment: "After the hard school of overwhelming terror, which Saarland social democrats and communists had undergone in the past year, the will to create a proletarian united front began to stir, initially not within the leadership but among the ranks, and within days this desire emerged victorious."[19] The presence of a social democratic regional leadership, which was highly critical of the Prague SPD executive, and the simultaneous pro–united front attitudes of the KPD in the Saar ensured that this grassroots movement toward unity rapidly became translated into concrete agreements.

Precisely this popularity of united fronts emerged as a major source of worry for more conservative members of European social democracy, who were not always on principle opposed to cooperation with communists but generally rejected permanent arrangements. Wilhelm Sollmann, a leading SPD functionary in the Weimar Republic and now a liaison between the Saarland federation and the Prague executive, reported to Paul Hertz on the inherent dynamics of rank-and-file unity in the Saar:

> If one mixes up one's regiments in struggle in such a manner, it will be difficult to ever get them apart again. To this one must add that we [the social democrats] are of course more chivalrous than the others [the communists]. I have repeatedly listened to our speakers greeting an audience with the shouts "Freedom" [*Freiheit*, the preferred slogan of the SPD] and "Red Front" [*Rote Front*, the communist salute], but I have thus far never witnessed a communist speaker returning the favor by shouting "Freedom." On the other hand, I have repeatedly observed social democratic comrades, whom I greeted on the open street with raised fist and "Freedom" reply with "Freedom" while at the same time raising the arm in the manner of the Red Front salute. This is perhaps only a trifle, but it sets me thinking.[20]

Mechanisms of Unity in Spain

Similarly, in Spain, united fronts sprang up throughout the country once the idea was launched in Catalonia. Andreu Nin, the Catalan Marxist and member of the executive of the Catalan united front, reported one month after the formation of this front:

> News of its constitution had enormous repercussions throughout Spain. In the executive committee of the Alianza we received every single day letters from workers' organizations throughout the country, expressing their support and encouraging us to continue the initiated project. Not only in Catalonia, but in all of Spain, sentiments in favor of the united front rapidly expanded and translated into the constitution of numerous local committees.[21]

The minutes of the PSOE executive committee meeting in early February 1934 likewise recorded a flood of letters from local affiliates "inquiring about the significance of committees that are springing up in order to construct united fronts. . . ."[22] Paco Ignacio Taibo, in his magnificent illustrated history of the Asturian Commune, includes a picture of a large meeting hall in the regional capital of Oviedo filled to maximum capacity. His caption underneath the photo reads: "The first meeting of the united front in the Oviedo Labor Center. Completely packed with only two hours prior notification."[23] Other accounts confirm the Oviedo experience.

Yet the Spanish case is particularly instructive in regard to the critical balance between an open-minded leadership and a willing rank and file in order for the construction of a united front to become reality. For united fronts were favorably regarded in almost every part of Spain, but only some regions and localities ever experienced a viable united front. All available evidence points to the crucial role of the subjective factor in the genesis of the Spanish united front experience. Victor Alba, in the only book-length study of this phenomenon, summarizes the mechanism by which united fronts became reality: "As the idea was in the air, as it responded to a necessity and to a general sentiment within the working class, all that was necessary was that either an activist with sufficient prestige or an organization began to agitate in favor of united fronts and to suggest its formation in a given locality."[24] Alba and others emphasize the role of Spanish dissident communists and Pestaña's syndicalists in the propagation of such fronts. In the province of Alicante, for instance, where dissident communists had few local supporters, the map of viable united fronts parallels the local implantation of dissident federations of the anarchist CNT under Pestaña's influence.[25] In Asturias the particular concatenation of a radical social democratic federation and a CNT federation sympathetic to, though not part of, Pestaña's opposition course was a crucial ingredient in the success of the Alianza Obrera de Asturias.

Perhaps a series of letters exchanged among Basque left-wing organizations in the industrial center of Bilbao and their regional and national directorates best exemplifies the interplay of instinctive interest in united fronts by a broad audience and the necessity for an outside catalyst to get the process started. In early August 1934 a letter arrived at the Bilbao headquarters of the JJSS, written by spokespersons for the Trotskyist ICE and the Federation of Tobacco Store Owners in Bilbao. The letter reported that the two organizations had recently decided to take the initiative to form an Alianza Obrera in order to combat fascism "in all its manifestations and to prepare the working class for the institution of a Socialist Republic of Spain as the indispensable condition for its total liberation." The Federación de Tabaqueros and the ICE were now turning toward the PSOE, its youth organization and the social democratic trade union federation (UGT) for an extension of this front.

In normal times it is more than likely that such a request from a fringe organization of the political far Left and a small shopkeepers' association, the latter probably under the influence of the ICE, would not have been taken very seriously. And the archives do not yield any information on the response by the PSOE and the UGT. But the JJSS, for its part, immediately composed a letter to its regional federation, for the Bilbao young socialists were uncertain how to react. It is quite apparent from the letter that they were favorably inclined toward the initiative by the ICE and the Federación de Tabaqueros. In their letter to their regional leadership, they expressed their wish to receive a speedy response so that they might soon begin to actively participate, if this was also the recommendation of their superiors. The Vizcaya federation of the JJSS was equally uncertain on how to proceed. Thus, it forwarded the Bilbao local's request to the national leadership in Madrid and suggested to its Bilbao comrades to inform the Federación de Tabaqueros that an answer would be forthcoming in a circular from the Madrid leadership. Two days later Santiago Carrillo, the JJSS general secretary, wrote back to the Vizcaya federation in the affirmative. He included some words of advice: "The united front exists for the essential purpose of organizing the revolutionary struggle toward the conquest of a *República Social*. That is the essential basis. And each participating organization retains its special identity and independence to carry out its propaganda." He promised to send more detailed instructions within a few days.[26]

Ricardo Miralles, in his study of Basque socialism under the second republic, does not mention whether it ever came to the constitution of a united front in Bilbao, the largest industrial city in Vizcaya. He does suggest that, prior to October 1934, no *regional* united front ever came into existence in Vizcaya despite some preliminary meetings to this effect.[27] But, whether or not it ever came to the constitution of a viable Bilbao front is less important than the fact that a simple initiative by a fringe organization could have had such wide-ranging reverberations. The request by the

ICE and the Federación de Tabaqueros not only was taken seriously by the Bilbao JJSS but likewise preoccupied the Vizcaya regional federation of the JJSS; and its national leadership, in the person of Santiago Carrillo, immediately penned a report with recommendations and a promise of more detailed instructions. This series of communications demonstrates the favorable climate toward united fronts in 1934, as well as the importance of the subjective factor, that is, the presence of a nucleus of individuals whose initiative, limited though it must have been, was able to begin a process which, in certain times and in certain places, perhaps not in Bilbao, eventually resulted in important consequences. The experience of neighboring Asturias, of course, shows that such a catalytic impetus could equally well emanate from within the traditional mass organizations of the majoritarian Left.

Sources of PSOE Radicalization and Paralysis

The literature on the radicalization of the PSOE under the second republic is replete with references to the key factor of rank-and-file militancy in propelling the PSOE leadership toward the open embrace of an insurrectionary course eventually culminating in the October 1934 uprising. Paul Preston, in his pathbreaking study of revolution, reform and reaction in 1931–36, traces the leftward evolution of the PSOE's undisputed leader, Francisco Largo Caballero, to two factors—"a growing awareness of the spread of fascism" elsewhere in Europe and Largo Caballero's "response to the mood of the rank-and-file, rendered impatient by the slowness of reform and by the success of right-wing obstruction of its application."[28] At the same time, Preston underscores the somewhat halfhearted and rhetorical nature of Largo's radicalization, which ultimately led to the isolation of the revolutionaries battling in the mountain valleys of Asturias.

One of the reasons the uprising was so successful in Asturias was precisely a highly developed sense of identification between the regional leadership and their subordinate ranks. "Yet it is significant that, even in Asturias, the revolutionary movement did not start in the stronghold of the party bureaucracy, at Oviedo, but was imposed upon it by outlying areas—Mieres, Sama de Langreo and Pola de Lena." Preston continues:

> Left-wing critics of the PSOE have pointed out that the revolution was strongest where the party bureaucracy was weakest: thus, in the Basque country, for instance, the workers seized power in small towns like Eibar and Mondragón, but Bilbao, the capital, was relatively quiet. There can be little doubt that it was spontaneous rank-and-file militancy which impelled the local PSOE leaders to proceed with the revolutionary movement.[29]

The PSOE turn toward revolution had been gathering steam in the second half of 1933 and was openly launched in the party press by January 1934. A stream of support statements immediately arrived at the Madrid headquarters of *El Socialista*. Some were typewritten statements of varying eloquence; many were handwritten, with orthographic mistakes and a labored script indicating the infrequency with which the writers used a pen. All of them were enthusiastic acclamations of the party's leftward movement. The handwritten letter by the president and secretary of the Workers'

Society La Unión in the agricultural community of Gabia Chica in the Andalusian province of Granada—addressed to "The Comrade Editor" of *El Socialista*—may stand as symbol of the popular identification with this radical trend. The somewhat cumbersome diction and the frequent spelling errors of the Castilian original text dramatize the authenticity and spontaneity of this pledge of support.

> The undersigned, José Martin Baena and Francisco Gil Pedrosa, president and secretary of the Sociedad Obrera la Unión de Gabia Chica, bring to your attention that, in an extraordinary general assembly on the twenty-ninth of January, agreement was reached with absolute unanimity and great enthusiasm, leading to cheers for the workers' united front and cheers for social revolution, to adhere to the slogans of the Spanish Socialist Workers' Party. We are ready to act upon its orders in order to bring about the realization of its entire program in which figure all of the peasantry's aspirations, and we are ready to defend it under the red flag of the General Workers' Confederation and the Socialist Party.

Between the two signatures of the Workers' Society officers, the organization's stamp was prominently affixed. In a postscript the secretary informed the "comrade editor" that, on 21 January, that is, in the midst of this hectic campaign for changes, a new name was added "to the civil registry of this township, a child of our comrade president, by the name of Manuel," undoubtedly interpreted as a sign of hope for a brighter future for the socialists of Gabia Chica.[30] This letter from a small-town workers' organization in the province of Granada, and many similar ones, strongly suggests that the leftward motion of the PSOE leadership was welcomed by the party's ranks.

Despite its practice of verbal maximalism, the PSOE leadership was never a consistent supporter of united front initiatives even prior to October 1934. Throughout 1935 it remained officially uncommitted to this approach and gave little, if any, informative replies to inquiries by party locals on how to respond to the constitution of such fronts. As the alternative proposal of a popular front did not emerge as a major contender until the summer of 1935, and as the PSOE did not sanction this new approach until the end of 1935, the official politics of the PSOE leadership was a politics of paralysis. Unable or unwilling to reach a binding decision, the PSOE leadership preferred to give contradictory suggestions or no guidelines at all. The result was massive confusion at the lower echelons of the party structures and a growing sense of discontent. Two examples may illustrate this state of confusion by party members favorable toward participation in united fronts, who were willing to follow contrary directions but above all frustrated at the lack of decisiveness within the top-level leadership.

On 17 August 1935 the PSOE regional federation of Seville, a stronghold of the PCE, addressed a letter to the head of the party's parliamentary faction, Ramón Lamoneda. The Seville socialists bitterly complained of inconsistent directives by their Madrid leadership, paralyzing work within the Seville province's united front. In January 1935 they had received the go-ahead to join this formation. When two workers were assassinated by the forces of the radical Right, the Alianza leadership called for a meeting to be addressed by a speaker from each political tendency. After this decision was taken, a joint PSOE-UGT circular arrived from Madrid, counseling against joint meetings with other political tendencies in the campaign against repression. Four weeks later, another letter from Madrid was more ambivalent but not a clear directive. Now, one day prior to the long-awaited meeting, Seville socialists were understandably confused. They indicated that they would go ahead and send a speaker but ended their letter to Ramón Lamoneda by emphasizing the "great confusion and unquestionable damage to our cause, which we hope to remedy as soon as we are able to clarify what has happened, to which effect we have already written to the [PSOE] executive."[31] One month later, the Madrid Association of Labor Centers sent a similar letter to the headquarters of the UGT:

> With respect to public meetings [of the Madrid united front], the Party [i.e., the PSOE], which we have asked for directions, told us that we could do as we pleased; but in regard to our permanent presence within its [the united front's] structures, we do not know what to do. For some time now, we have not participated [in these bodies]. Since they consistently invite us, we would like to know what shall be our position.[32]

The PSOE's ranks, then, were clearly prepared to follow directives. While certainly not without opinions of their own, they recognized the need for a coordinated approach. Consequently, what frustrated them the most were nebulous or nonexistent pieces of advice. The state of PSOE top-level indecisiveness continued throughout most of 1935 and equally affected its attitude toward the construction of popular fronts.

The Meanings of the *Frente Popular*

As early as March 1935, several PSOE locals, including the organizations in the cities of León and Valencia, asked their national leadership for an opinion on the advisability of forming electoral alliances with sections of left Republicanism.[33] At this point the party leadership was still leaning, though reluctantly, toward exclusive cooperation with the working-class Left. Thus, when, four weeks later, other PSOE locals asked for permission to send speakers to joint meetings with Republicans, such acts were dubbed "premature" by the PSOE executive.[34] By December 1935 the PSOE leadership as a whole gave in to the combined pressures of its centrist faction and demands by communists to their left and Republicans on their right and finally sanctioned the course toward the popular front. This shift from united to popular fronts entailed a number of significant changes for the actions and goals of the working-class Left. In my earlier chapter on the popular front, I alluded to the emergence of a growing gulf between the policy of popular fronts as understood by the party hierarchy and as practiced by the rank and file. This holds true for both Spain and France. A satisfactory account of this dangerous dynamic would require a far more detailed narrative and a concentration on the social history of popular fronts, which I am unable to offer within the limited framework of this study. Nevertheless, I deem it fruitful to briefly address this issue, for it will throw additional light on the intricate relationship between various levels of party politics.

There is little evidence to suggest a stronger opposition to the politics of popular fronts by rank-and-file members compared with the attitude of party functionaries *prior* to the victory of this alliance. In Spain and France, prior to the spring of 1936, an aversion to this course was strongest in those portions of the leadership and in those party locals where a left-wing faction continued to hold sway. But there is little apparent correlation between the drift toward popular front politics and the political predominance of particular levels of the parties' hierarchies. As I have emphasized in chapter 6, the movement from united to popular fronts coincided with the desire of vast popular strata to forge broad alliances in pursuit of concrete political goals which had generally escaped the reach of previously existing united fronts. In Spain the popular front was generally understood as a tactical tool in the battle against repression carried out by the conservative government in the wake of the Asturian Commune. In Asturias itself the identification of the popular front with the battle for amnesty was virtually complete. The historian of the Asturian Commune, Paco Ignacio Taibo, writes:

> According to all eyewitnesses which I was able to interview, perhaps because this was what influenced them most profoundly, perhaps because this was what they most wanted to hear or because this was what they heard when they listened to the speakers, the fact is that all of them remember amnesty for the prisoners of October as the exclusive center of the electoral campaign.[35]

Apparently, Asturias was not unusual in this image of the popular front as the harbinger of amnesty.[36]

The problems and dissensions started on the morrow after victory. Once victory was assured and the prisoners released, it gradually became apparent that, on the grassroots level, the popular front was decidedly not regarded as an alliance strategy significantly different from the earlier united fronts. On the leadership level, as exemplified by the programmatic manifesto analyzed in chapter 6, the political content of the Spanish (and French) popular front was determined by the limitations imposed by its most moderate components. In the popular neighborhoods and at the base of the popular front committees, however, there was little tolerance expressed for the self-limiting strategy imposed from above. Again, the case of Asturias may exemplify this trend. Adrian Shubert contends that two factors proved most crucial for the vitality of the Asturian popular front. The first was the degree of local activity developed by popular front committees; the second was the extent to which activists were able "to turn it into a vehicle for working-class demands and actions." Basing his analysis on the local press, Shubert argues that, already in the period of electoral campaigns, agitation for the popular front was not single-mindedly oriented toward achieving amnesty. While this was a crucial interest, "it was not the sole point of attraction. During the campaign speakers at Popular Front rallies associated the coalition with local issues of interest to the working classes." This focus on proletarian demands powerfully influenced their activity after victory. While organized activity of popular front committees was "both localized and sporadic," where it did occur it was hardly distinguishable from united front concerns. According to Shubert, the Trubia popular front committee, for instance, "snubbed a number of local businesses under the banner 'Comrades: Boycott Those Who Live Off the Proletariat and Betray It.'" Other local committees saw their task as the defense of "the cause of the workers and the Republic," as did the committee in Figaredo cited by Shubert.[37]

This was far from the intention of the architects of the Spanish popular front, and it openly contradicted the spirit and the letter of the popular front manifesto, the programmatic guideline for the *frente popular*. Combined with the massive semispontaneous social movements affecting many reaches of Spanish society after electoral victory of the popular front, taking on aspects of a quasi-social revolution, it would therefore be far-fetched to posit a basic congruence between the official charter of the popular front and the radical interpretation by the working-class ranks. Shubert concurs: "The incipient transformation of local Popular Front committees into independent political protagonists pressing working-class demands ran counter to the determination of Azaña and Prieto [the respective spokespersons for pro–popular front tendencies within Spanish Republicanism and the PSOE] to resume traditional parliamentary politics and to assert the power of central government."[38] Likewise Manuel Tuñon de Lara, himself formerly a communist youth activist during the thirties, in an important contribution to the understanding of the Spanish popular front argues that "it is possible to demonstrate that the Spanish popular front developed from a defensive tactic into a defensive strategy and, later on, keeping in mind the historical conjuncture of the year 1936, into an offensive strategy which outflanked the narrow conceptions of every organization." Tuñon de Lara argues for the close connection between antifascism, the struggle for democracy and the move toward socialism, and refers to this interlacing of "democratic conquests and revolutionary implications" as the "dialectic of the Spanish Popular Front."[39]

The existence of such a dynamic in the struggles of the 1930s is a clear and present element, and not just in Spain. But Tuñon de Lara's abstract references to Spanish reality leave out the most important aspects of this process of the semispontaneous subversion of the popular front: the actual mechanisms of this dynamic. And here, I believe, closer attention to the interaction between leadership and ranks will result in the growing realization of a gap between the respective entities' political visions. On balance, I would argue, one was more likely to find supporters of the official program and the codified meaning of the popular front in the higher echelons of the party bureaucracy than among rank-and-file activists. Conversely, the push to deepen the social impact of the popular front, to achieve maximum gains for the agricultural and industrial proletariat of the Spanish state, was strongest and most lasting within the lower reaches of the socialist hierarchy. The same tendency to regard popular fronts as tactical enhancements of united fronts could be seen in operation north of the Pyrenees, where a popular front agreement had been reached a mere five days after the signing of the electoral manifesto in Spain.

The Meanings of the Rassemblement Populaire

In France, as elsewhere, it is important to recognize that local united front initiatives frequently included elements of the non-working-class Left, including their political organizations, in this case France's bourgeois Radical Party. Short of a detailed examination of these local attempts at broader unity, it is difficult to judge their political content and the ideological direction of their operations. The most detailed history of local united front initiatives is the annex to Jacques Doriot's open letter to the Comintern, where he lists eighty-six examples of local united fronts throughout France at the occasion of the massive demonstrations on 12 February 1934. In fifteen cases they included the Radical Party of the given location. Some of these localities were important regional centers, such as Châlons-sur-Marne, La Rochelle, Narbonne, Orléans or Troyes.[40] Most of these united front initiatives may have remained ephemeral episodes, forged in the heat of the moment. How many of them survived the February days and how many local united fronts may have reemerged in the wake of the July 1934 national agreement between the SFIO and the PCF is impossible to judge. What is certain is that the presence of the Radical Party in local alliance structures had little influence on the overall direction of national efforts at united fronts. As a matter of fact, in the case of the Secular and Republican Youth, a fifty-thousand-member-strong youth organization associated with the Radical Party which closely cooperated with the Marxist youth organizations even prior to February 1934, and which in the spring of that year decided at its national congress to support unity efforts of the working-class Left, it appears that it joined the campaign for unity without imposing any programmatic restrictions whatsoever.[41]

The situation changed with the open attempt by the PCF and the SFIO to woo the national leadership of the Radical Party itself, starting in the summer of 1935. As was the case in the Spanish negotiations between the PSOE and the Republican Left, the inclusion of the French Radical Party hierarchy in a broad alliance considerably altered the meaning of unity for the working-class Left. From a point of departure for offensive actions threatening to undermine the capitalist order, unity on the Left now became an alliance specifically limited to the defense of democratic rights and the attainment of a series of reforms. Yet in France as in Spain, the changed perspective of unity at the political summit did not necessarily translate into an equally changed understanding of these qualitative changes among the lower echelons of France's Marxist parties. There is insufficient information on the interpretation of the popular front at the rank-and-file level to warrant definitive conclusions, but some of the limited evidence suggests that the switch from united to popular fronts was seen in a different light by activists at some distance from the parties' executive committees.

The lack of information on local popular front committees is identical in France and Spain. A systematic investigation into their structure and activities would undoubtedly cast more light on the rank-and-file understanding of the popular front. In France they appear to have been fostered especially by the Communist Party. While, on the one hand, pushing for the self-limitation of the popular front's political demands in order to assure the adherence of the Radical Party as a whole, the PCF repeatedly called for the creation of local popular front committees, dominated by the working-class Left. To what extent they were successfully created is unknown.[42] But it was not only the PCF which argued for the creation of local popular front committees. Elements within the SFIO were equally alert to the importance of such grassroots organizations for the future of the popular front. Such voices within the SFIO were situated on its left wing, and their statements clearly imply that their particular understanding of the meaning of the popular front was qualitatively different from the SFIO hierarchy.

At the SFIO party congress held between 30 May and 1 June 1936, a few weeks after the victories of the popular front, several regional delegates spoke out in favor of an orientation toward the creation and extension of popular front committees. The delegate from the Rhône argued that, "vis-à-vis the popular front committees, we cannot take an attitude of distrust; but, to the contrary, we shall become their creators and energizers,"[43] thus frontally opposing official SFIO discouragement of involvement in such local structures. Durel, the delegate from the *département* of Lot-et-Garonne in southwestern France, was even more straightforward in upholding a different interpretation of the meaning of the popular front, compared with the official understanding of the message of this alliance. Pointing out the limited impact of the electoral victory in and of itself, Durel enjoined his audience: "If we limit our horizon and our view of life in general to what goes on within the walls of Parliament, don't you think that we are risking the creation of sentiments and hopes which are simultaneously confining and deceiving?"[44] Durel, frequently interrupted by applause, then argued for full support to "these popular front committees, which have appeared to the surprise of everyone, and whose veritable origins, perhaps, History will attempt to explain. . . . The people are beginning to consider taking charge of their own affairs!"[45] Durel went on to deliver a ringing defense of these committees, which, in some *départements*, were under the political dominance of the SFIO and provided an excellent recruitment tool for socialist activists over and above their function as an instigator of popular initiatives:

> Popular front committees: an original force, an incipient force. It is up to you to either condemn them and leave them up to their own resources, with all the unknown they harbor within themselves, or, by contrast, to seek them out, to be present within them, always following their inspirations, to gather information, to make the socialist point of view be known, and to perhaps assure the success of the appeal which the socialist government will launch toward them when the day of difficult decision comes, which we must anticipate. Do you believe it appropriate to break the link with this incipient force?[46]

This vision of the meaning of the popular front meshed quite easily with the view put forth by left-wing dissidents within the SFIO. Jean Zyromski, in 1934 a firm supporter of united fronts, rallied to the cause of popular fronts in the summer of 1935. Initially, at the very least, his understanding of the popular front was that of a popular movement, in liaison with, but independent of, governmental combinations. In June 1935 he regarded the popular front as a "great popular movement, which is developing throughout the country, in the midst of which the political organizations and trade union organizations of the working class are simultaneously the energizers and the axis." Zyromski continued by stressing that

> just as much as this popular movement can transform itself into a governmental coalition in which, as a mirror image of the country at large, the parties of the working class will assume the direction, authority and majority; just as much we continue to remain resolutely and flatly opposed to those forms of ministerial collaboration, to those governmental combinations, that are determined by the numerical strength of the parliamentary factions and which lead to the belief in the possibility to realize a common program with different elements, disparate elements, incapable of combating a crisis.[47]

These images of the popular front as relying on mass participation and initiative were rebuked by the May–June 1936 SFIO congress. The contrast between the foregoing citation and the official course of the SFIO clearly emerges from the keynote speech by Léon Blum, who was preoccupied with the calming of tempers and the reining in of expectations heightened in the course of the massive strike wave which erupted in the aftermath of victory. Addressing trade union concerns, Blum warned against the radical dynamics unleashed by social movements of such major proportions: "Whatever the case may be, we must, on our part, be careful to act in such a manner that they do not escape and outflank the control by the leadership of trade union organizations." He went on to argue for the clear distinction of the "exercise of power" in the framework of capitalist society and the "revolutionary conquest of power," one of his favorite themes since the 1920s, insisting that only the first was possible at the moment. "Is there not reason to fear that the working class will mix up one with the other?" Blum repeatedly emphasized that the necessity to make workers realize the limits of their power was the socialists' basic problem and primordial task: "And that we must accomplish, all of us together, by all means of persuasion that we can muster. . . ."[48] It would be a task beyond the limits of this study to engage in a critique of Blum's assumptions. It is indeed questionable whether the social movements of May–June 1936 were ever powerful enough to threaten the capitalist social order. But there is a difference between realizing the limits *of* a popular movement and the active attempt to impose limits *on* a popular movement. To some extent Blum's proposals virtually ensured that it would never come to any widespread attempt to institute a different social order. Blum's response to social unrest was designed to inhibit even the possibility that qualitative social change could have been put on the agenda.

The PCF leadership embarked upon a similar course. While, in contrast to the SFIO, it was openly supportive of the idea of popular front committees, when faced with increasing militant rank-and-file demands and actions it began to sound a retreat as well. Maurice Thorez's famous dictum "One must know how to end a strike" is only the most well known symptom of this particular aspect of communist politics.[49] In this context much attention has been devoted in the relevant literature to the role of the PCF in instigating and controlling the strikes. The argument concerns the importance and the limits of spontaneous rank-and-file activity during the strikes. Some argue for the relevance of spontaneity in the initiation of the strikes.[50] And it speaks in favor of this thesis that the first rumblings of discontent announcing the strikes could be noticed in the provinces and not the Parisian center,[51] thus paralleling the course of events in October 1934 in Spain. Others point to the importance of the presence of a layer of, primarily communist, militants in the initial movement toward a strike but especially in the organization and coordination of such strikes once they broke out.[52] Raymond Hainsworth, in his study of the miners' strikes in the Nord and Pas-de-Calais, points to the existence of a layer of rank-and-file miners, some of them recent recruits to the PCF, who had been catapulted into the forefront of action in the course of the strikes, who followed the directions of the PCF but, as soon as the party sounded the retreat, refused to heed the calls for moderation. In a rather paternalistic manner Hainsworth describes what he regards as the motivations of such individual leaders:

> Somewhat intoxicated by what they had experienced in the course of a week during which they had encountered no opposition to their activities at the point of production, they came to believe in themselves as the sole artisans of their success, forgetting in the process that it was undoubtedly the union leadership which

had given the movement its cohesion and obtained the satisfaction of demands from the employers.[53]

Here, of course, one is confronted with a similarly insoluble question as earlier in the case of Léon Blum's call for moderation. Clearly, not all action will lead to success, and the most militant action is not necessarily the most productive. For the sake of the larger picture, of the overall direction of a given social movement, it will oftentimes be necessary to limit a specific action or a whole series of moves. Such decisions will inevitably be questioned by part of the leadership structure, by voices within the ranks or by a combination of the two. My point in adducing these instances of dissension is thus not to render judgment on such acts, although in some instances, such as Blum's fear of the "unruly masses," I have been tempted to pronounce such a verdict. Instead, I mainly want to highlight the existence of multiple and competing currents of opinion within the camp of supporters of popular fronts, particularly within its working-class components. And, if anything has emerged from the preceding, it is hopefully the image of the popular front as contested terrain. The battle over the meaning of the popular front *within* the popular front was perhaps almost as significant as the struggle to create and retain majority support for this alliance within the general population.

Conclusion

Up to 1934 the working-class Left in Europe was seriously divided. Then, primarily in the spring and summer of that year, a sudden rush toward unity characterized the political landscape. Here, I argue, what was needed for this process to occur was the simultaneous presence of a popular desire for unity and the presence of some individuals who could articulate this shift. Where this mixture was present, a simple call for the constitution of a united front was often massively heeded and led to success. Wherever authoritative voices on the Left advocated unity, unity was established. Wherever these voices were lacking, unity remained a dream. The mosaic of united fronts in Spain, their presence in some towns and regions and absence in others, can largely be explained by the presence or absence of such catalysts, although the last word can only be spoken after a more representative series of local and regional studies. In France and in Spain, united fronts were eventually superseded by popular fronts. On the level of party leaderships, this change entailed strategic shifts and favored moderation. The second half of this chapter has been devoted to the questioning of the reality of this strategic moderation at the rank-and-file level of the concerned workers' parties. Evidence suggests that, for many party members, the switch from united to popular fronts entailed no changed perspective. Party militants, who saw united fronts as levers in their quest for a new society, regarded popular fronts in a similar light. The activities of popular front committees differed in few respects, if any, from efforts at united fronts, although it is important to stress the limited and impressionistic evidence available to date.[54]

My sympathies, clearly, lie with the workers' ranks. As a result, much of the foregoing discussion may perhaps be wrongly interpreted as a sentimental invocation of the mythical purity of workers' instincts, contrasted with the pragmatic tendency toward compromise by seasoned party bureaucrats. Perhaps this is the moment, then, to close with the story of an election campaign meeting in Torrubia del Campo in the province of Cuenca on the high plains of Castile. Five days prior to the elections of 16 February 1936, the socialists of Torrubia del Campo had organized a meeting with two popular front candidates as featured speakers. As is apparent from other election campaign reports throughout Spain, local activists of the PSOE relied on prominent outside speakers as powerful propaganda tools for their common cause. Cuenca was a stronghold of the Right, so the socialists were facing an uphill battle. Much organizational effort and skill went into arranging this event, for Torrubia del Campo was in the middle of an agricultural region with a decentralized and widely dispersed workforce. The handwritten letter of the secretary of the Association of Landless Laborers addressed to the PSOE executive in Madrid tells what happened on that night. The labored handwriting and the disregard for punctuation or spelling suggest that, for this letter writer, recourse to such action was a desperate act of last resort. The letter was written on the day after the scheduled event:

> *Estimados companeros Salud!* We are communicating to you the fact that we have been betrayed by Comrade Almagro and Don Lopez Malo, candidates for our district. As you can tell by the enclosure, on 11 February we celebrated an act of electoral propaganda in an atmosphere that we have never before witnessed in this community. Already at five in the afternoon one could note the heightened state of animation among the present workers; at six the hall was filled to maximum capacity. But at seven the speakers still did not show up, and neither did they at eight, nor at midnight or thereafter, and still the workers hoped for the arrival of our comrades, but these comrades never came. . . .

Apparently, the slated speakers had come to within seven kilometers of Torrubia, when they were overtaken by fatigue and decided to skip the meeting. The letter was intended as a call for an official reprimand to these two men and for the dispatch of alternate speakers, for the flop had entailed major consequences for the socialists in Torrubia. "Given the disaster of this meeting, the rightist forces have taken advantage of their propaganda. Up to this moment, they had been unable to make their presence felt, given the [political] ambience we were able to maintain." Now, apparently, they had made a showing.[55]

What is the meaning of this event? Leaving aside the actions of the two speakers, I believe that this unadorned rendering of a campaign mishap demonstrates in clear-cut fashion the reliance upon, and the high expectations of, party leaders by the party's ranks. Lacking sufficiently experienced and skilled orators, the socialists of Torrubia banked on the cooperation of their superiors within the PSOE.[56] At the same time, the devastating results of the abortive meeting suggest the extraordinary degree to which skilled propaganda affected the electorate. Perhaps the letter writer exaggerated the sense of loss for the prospects of the Left engendered by this mishap, and the forces of the Right did not experience the sudden popularity the letter implies. After all, the letter was written on the day after the failed meeting. Yet, even if the writer expressed only his subjective beliefs, this personal assessment by a leading local activist is a useful reminder of the powerful bonds between leadership and ranks. The story of Torrubia del Campo may thus stand as a symbolic counterpoint to my earlier prevailing emphasis on the radical instincts of the ranks, for the relationship between leadership and ranks was one of mutual dependence. Or, as a noted revolutionary and a historian of revolutions once observed:

> Only on the basis of a study of political process in the masses themselves can we understand the role of the parties and leaders, whom we least of all are inclined to ignore. They constitute not an independent, but nevertheless a very important, element in the process. Without a guiding organization the energy of the masses would dissipate like steam not enclosed in a piston-box. But, nevertheless, what moves things is not the piston or the box, but the steam.[57]

NINE

Contingency in the Historical Process

The various strategies discussed in preceding chapters were, for the most part, regarded as pathways toward a noncapitalist, democratic and socialist order. United fronts, radical planism and popular fronts were widely considered to be means to obtain this socialist goal. It was that aspect of these strategies which caught the attention of contemporaries and which ensured the meteoric rise of these novel propositions to positions of national and international prominence. This was most unabashedly so in the case of united fronts and planism. Both pathways to social change were regarded, quite often explicitly, as clearly identifiable socialist projects. In the case of popular fronts, I argue, this was less decidedly so. Here, a gulf began to emerge between the popular identification of popular fronts as a socialist project, the "popular front in combat," and the views of popular fronts as an exercise of power rather than "the conquest of power," prevalent among the upper levels of the party hierarchies associated with this scheme.

Much of the attention of historians of Europe's Left has hitherto been devoted to the communist tradition, and the radical achievements of European social democrats have been neglected in the process. Partially responsible for this case of historical amnesia, of course, has been the prevailing view of social democracy as a gradualist and steadily moderating political force, a view encouraged by, among others, post–World War II social democracy itself. By contrast, I argue that the driving force behind these strategies for social change was continental European social democracy. To be sure, not all Continental social democrats identified with this socialist project at that time, and not all supporters of this socialist project were social democrats. Yet, by 1934, a majority of Continental social democrats favored a path of radical societal change, and they were by far the most numerous Continental political force on the working-class Left.

In preceding chapters I have repeatedly referred to communist collaboration in the struggles of the day. Indeed, the central strategy of this period, the notion of united fronts, presupposed unity in action to achieve the common goal. Yet, generally speaking, social democrats were far more prominent than their communist rivals in the elaboration and the practical application of such novel strategies. Even in the case of the popular fronts which are, in collective popular memory, frequently associated with communist moves, it is evident that they were the product of changing national and international political climates and, at best, only indirectly the result of specifically communist interventions. The Spanish popular front was created and consolidated without much noticeable input by the PCE. Even in France, where the Communist Party was more numerous and influential, the contributions by the PCF to the creation of the Rassemblement Populaire cannot be said to outweigh the actions of its social democratic rival or, indeed, the bourgeois Radicals. The simultaneous moves by the PCF, the SFIO and the Radical Party in the direction of cooperation were, if anything, a perfect example of the confluence of national and international political factors pushing the working-class Left in the direction of moderation and some bourgeois formations into a tactical alliance with this newly reformed Left. Three such moderating factors were the continuing series of defeats suffered by the Left throughout the Continent, the rise of the radical Right and the increasing likelihood of war. As such, these three elements were closely interrelated and mutually reinforcing. In the end they served to end this brief moment of opportunity for the European Left in which, for the first time since the immediate post–World War I era, a socialist outcome to the crises of European societies appeared possible.

Social Movements and the Historical Process

Historians of social movements have long recognized the cyclical nature of their outbreak and peak influence. In a recent attempt to assess overall patterns of their recurrence, Andre Gunder Frank and Marta Fuentes found clusters of social movements occurring in the decades of the 1820s, 1830s and 1840s; the last decade of the nineteenth and the first decade of the twentieth century; and the years from the 1960s onward to the present. While they are unable to account for this peculiar pattern, the evidence is incontrovertible. Social movements appear, rise and fall in clearly distinguishable cycles, the origins of which, however, Frank and Fuentes assert, are impossible to pinpoint. What is empirically striking, in addition to their bunched occurrence within each nation, is the high degree of temporal overlap, especially in advanced industrial countries and in the two most recent waves.[1]

Whereas Frank and Fuentes do not venture a guess as to the origins of these successive waves of social movements in the modern age, others have attempted such judgments. Sidney Tarrow, generalizing from a model first developed by Peter Eisinger for the specific context of American urban protest movements, suggests that changes in the "political opportunity structure" of a given locality or state may account for the sudden emergence and perseverance of any number of such movements. Tarrow points to "the openness or closure of formal political institutions, . . . the stability or instability of political alignments within the political system [and] the availability and strategic posture of support groups" as key determinants fostering or prohibiting the emergence and success of social movements, a category which, for Tarrow, includes labor movements side by side with other "newer" forms of protest groups.[2]

Karl-Werner Brand, by contrast, focusing exclusively on middle-class-based social movements of the past two hundred years, suggests "that the mobilization waves of new social movements and their predecessors appear in phases of a general cultural crisis, in an atmosphere conducive to a spreading critique of modernization in its various forms." These protests may be forward-looking or nostalgic critiques. Regardless of their precise character, however, Brand contends, references to the changing contours of political opportunity structures are necessary but not sufficient explanations for their recurrence. For Brand, "these political opportunity structures are embedded in, and influenced by, the prevalent cultural climate."[3]

Brand, Frank and Fuentes demonstrate the lack of any correlation between the cycles of social movement protest and the long waves of capitalist economic development, the so-called Kondratieff cycles. Whereas the first and the most recent of the three waves of protest in the past two hundred years occurred at a Kondratieff downturn, the social movement cycle around the turn of the century occurred toward a peak.[4] Although Tarrow is equally hesitant to draw firm conclusions, he suggests that *some* economic crises, "but not others," may influence political opportunity structures and thus facilitate the emergence of social movements.[5] What contribution, if any, may my own study make toward the understanding of the origins and trajectory of social movements?

Here, I believe, attention to the factor of contingency in moments of historical crises may prove useful in comprehending the sudden, widespread emergence of popular protest movements. First, however, it is important to understand that, contrary to Brand, Frank and Fuentes, I am specifically concerned with a movement based on working-class mobilization, although some of my conclusions may just as well apply to middle-class-based social protest movements. As he includes both types of movements — working-class-based and middle-class-based protest movements — Tarrow is perhaps more amenable to consider the impact of economic crises on protest cycles than are his colleagues. Yet working-class protest and radicalization in the 1930s did not occur in *all* countries where the political determinants and economic indicators permitted and encouraged protests to occur. In chapter 1 I pointed out the glaring lack of correlation between the severity of the economic crisis and the depth of protest cycles. Political polarization and economic crises do not overlap. Some of the countries with the highest unemployment rates throughout the thirties witnessed the least amount of radicalization.

The Origins of Interwar Dictatorships

Following Ekkart Zimmermann, I classify European states of the 1930s into two broad categories: countries with a high degree of national consensus formation, facilitating cross-class alliances in defense of democracy, and countries suffering from political polarization around both extremes, racked by protest cycles organized by both the radical Left and the radical Right. As Zimmermann is, above all, concerned with the survival and collapse of democracy, he includes France and Belgium in the camp of the former, whereas I find it more useful and appropriate to focus instead on the incidence and severity of protest movements rather than on the ultimate outcome as the primary classification mechanism. Thus, France and Belgium, for instance, conform more closely to the pattern of Spain, Germany, Austria and Italy prior to the onset of dictatorships in these countries than to the relatively staid political climate of Sweden, Denmark and the Netherlands.[6] Zimmermann's thesis on the importance of national consensus formation for the absence of system-threatening political polarization is closely related to Gregory Luebbert's notion of the relevance of class alliances in the transition to mass politics. For, in both Zimmermann's and Luebbert's schemes, the nationally specific configurations of affinities and hostilities between and within social classes play the primordial role in predicting policy outcomes for the nation as a whole. Certain class alliances engendered certain outcomes. Fascism in Germany and the beginnings of the welfare state in Sweden were results of specific class configurations within the respective states.

While these are important insights, in one sense they merely beg the question. If the specifics of class alliances determine pathways toward consensus politics or class polarization, what, in turn, influences the parameters of class alliances? Here Luebbert has gone the farthest in the search for an overall answer. In a broad sweep of several decades, from the late nineteenth century to the Great Depression, and a survey of a large number of states from Norway to Spain, Luebbert proposes a new answer to a question that has plagued social scientists ever since the Continental spread of fascism in the 1930s and 1940s underscored the need for a comparative study of this phenomenon. Whereas Alexander Gerschenkron and Barrington Moore ultimately viewed the survival of old agrarian elites as primarily responsible for the genesis of fascist authoritarianism in some parts of the Continent, Luebbert's broader survey of the Continent as a whole proposes that social democracy's attitude toward landless agricultural laborers was the decisive criterion. Wherever social democracy engaged in active support and defense of agricultural workers' livelihood, such efforts antagonized the crucial layer of middle peasants and set off a whole series of chain reactions, ultimately creating the preconditions for a fascist outcome to the given countries' political and economic crises.[7]

This is not the time and place to subject Luebbert's proposition to a balanced critique. Similar to Zimmermann, Luebbert single-mindedly focuses on regime outcomes as indicators of the success of class alignments and thus tends to ignore massive contrary evidence. Luebbert, for instance, lumps Britain, France and Switzerland into one particular category based on the "comparative continuity" of democratic institutions and claims that, in all three cases, "class conflict was mitigated, contained and dissipated by the legacies of pre-war liberal hegemony and Lib-Labism."[8] To suggest, however, that class conflicts in France between 1934 and 1937 were "mitigated, contained and dissipated" in ways similar to Switzerland is surely stretching the point. Likewise, Luebbert creates a category sui generis for the Dutch and Belgian states, characterized by a compromise between confessional parties and the working class.[9] Yet the Netherlands was far more prone to lean toward consensus politics than its neighbor to the south, where the language of class and conflict was far more relevant to the nation's political course, particularly during the 1930s. Most importantly, Luebbert's focus on structural continuities within each country's system of political coordinates leads him to an utterly deterministic conclusion. Luebbert essentially proclaims that political traditions and long-range historical experiences left no measurable leeway for political actors. Certain sets of preconditions inevitably resulted in predictable outcomes. Luebbert writes, "One of the cardinal lessons of the story I have told is that leadership and meaningful choice played no role in the outcomes."[10] Was this really so?

The Relevance of Contingency

Curiously enough, in support of another line of argument, which need not concern us here, Luebbert furnishes some elements of a critique of his own thesis. Arguing against the view that social polarization must be held primarily accountable for the breakdown of democracy in interwar Europe, Luebbert makes the following observation about the discontinuities inherent in patterns of polarization: "One country that became authoritarian, Spain, was in fact conspicuously depolarized at the beginning of its democratic experiment in 1931. Some countries that became democratic — in particular Norway and Sweden — were, in contrast, if strike activity indicates class polarisation, amongst the most polarized societies in Europe [throughout the 1920s]."[11] And, perhaps, the absence of clear-cut explanations for the differences between national trajectories of interwar European social democracy is one of the key results of my own research. For, in trying to assess the origins of the radicalization of social democracy in the five countries under review, it is exceedingly difficult, if not impossible, to suggest any overall explanatory patterns that permit inferences as to the origins of the divergent paths of what may be termed continental and northern European routes.

Certainly, as I point out in the body of my work, the direct or indirect threat of the radical Right, the reverberations of the German defeat and the inspiration of the Schutzbund uprising, singly or combined, must be held accountable for the leftward drift of much of Continental social democracy, the genesis of united fronts and the outbreak of two social democratic–led military revolts within eight months. In other words, I do recognize the validity of *certain* explanations across *some* national frontiers. Yet why did such events trigger the leftward evolution in some countries and moderation in others? Take, for instance, the case of Belgium and the Netherlands. Both countries experienced, by the midthirties, moderately successful indigenous fascist movements. The proximity and latent threat of Nazi Germany were of equal weight in both countries as well. Yet in Belgium the social fabric of the nation was continuously rent by massive strikes — and even some military mutinies — culminating in the June–July 1936 strike wave encompassing a fifth of the entire workforce, an even higher proportion of strikers than generated by the May–June 1936 protest cycle in neighboring France. The Netherlands, by contrast, were an island of relative social peace.

But even the countries included in the moderate, northern tier of European states experienced incidents of grave social conflict. Luebbert's reference to the social polarization of Sweden and Norway in the 1920s, before the relative quiescence of the thirties, points to important discontinuities in the pattern of political protests there as well. In 1933 and 1934, politics in the Netherlands was profoundly affected by two incidents which appeared to polarize the nation. A mutiny on a Dutch naval ship in the East Indies resulted in the murder of twenty-three sailors, and, closer to home, July 1934 saw bloody riots in the streets of Amsterdam as a result of the lowering of unemployment compensation by the state.[12] In calm and proper Switzerland, the November 1932 military suppression of an antifascist demonstration in

Geneva resulted in thirteen dead protesters and sixty-five injured.[13] But in the cases of the Netherlands and Switzerland the severe repression meted out in the three cited cases did not result in the further polarization of the respective societies but had the opposite effect, including within the forces of social democracy.

Prior to November 1932, Swiss social democrats had adopted political measures much closer to what I term the Continental pattern of socialist responses to the Great Depression and the rise of the radical Right than the pattern of their northern comrades. Oskar Scheiben then demonstrates how the Geneva massacre triggered a profound reorientation of Swiss social democracy in the direction of moderation and alliance building to their right. Within very few months after November 1932, Swiss social democracy abandoned its class struggle orientation and advocacy of united fronts in favor of cooperation with more moderate middle-class representatives.[14] Peter Jan Knegtmans posits a similar turn toward moderation by Dutch social democrats, although, in this case, it came as less of a surprise since Dutch social democrats had never embraced a radical course prior to their opening to the right. In the Netherlands the triggering event was the electoral defeat suffered by social democracy in the wake of its open expression of sympathy for the mutineers of the Dutch navy. An anti-social democratic smear campaign by conservative opponents had ensured the social democrats' resounding defeat. The mutiny of De Zeven Provinciën and the negative impact at the ballot box then initiated a similar turn toward moderation and alliance building with the middle class, as witnessed earlier in Switzerland.[15] Thus repression and concomitant defeat, which, I argue, in most of continental Europe triggered, if anything, a course to the left, had the opposite effect on at least two social democratic parties and set in motion an orientation toward alliance building with moderate forces and consensus politics.

What do these "patterns of discontinuities" suggest? I believe that an explanation for the varied patterns of political responses must be sought in the heightened role of contingency in the historical process, particularly in "moments of opportunity" when sudden, rapid shifts in political orientation and allegiance patterns are bound to occur. In such moments of opportunity older patterns of political behavior are suddenly abandoned in favor of more promising approaches. And novel solutions, if found wanting, are prone to be as suddenly jettisoned as they were once adopted. The element of contingency above all else, certainly better than most structural or other factors, may explain why Dutch and Swiss social democrats moved to the right when experiencing repression and defeat in 1932–34, at the very same time other social democrats drew opposite conclusions.

Patterns of Discontinuities

What structural or other factors can satisfactorily explain what I believe are random variations within the experience of continental European social democracy in the five countries under review? There are worlds of differences, for instance, between the social structures of the five targeted states. What degree of commonality existed between Spain, where semifeudal latifundistas still exerted powerful influence, and Belgium, the oldest industrial nation on the European Continent, where the peasantry, in any of its manifestations, was a dwindling and politically insignificant force?

In terms of ideological traditions within and between the working classes of these states, there was little that united the Spanish proletariat, strongly influenced by anarchist practices and splintered into many factions, with, for instance, the Austrian working class, organized almost as a body within the Austro-Marxist SPÖ. The only consistent pattern distinguishable within the five countries under review, and the other European states, is that, faced with the loss of previous certainties, confronting a social, political and economic crisis, social democrats were forced to make difficult choices. Previous patterns of decision making and policy orientation were found wanting, and new ones waited to be explored. The precise choices that were ultimately made were essentially unpredictable and contingent on any number of factors that can be reconstructed by painstaking and detailed work but that follow no particular pattern.

Consider, for instance, the stubborn insistence by the German SPD leadership in Prague to abstain from any efforts toward united fronts within the German underground and exile. If there ever was one instance where the "objective" and "subjective" circumstances warranted such a course, the German case would have been it. Repression was severe, the isolated underground groupings frequently practiced the politics of united fronts regardless of what their executive said and, after 1934, the KPD actively promoted such a course. But Otto Wels and the majority of the Prague SPD leadership consistently rejected such offers. Or, consider the patchwork of united fronts throughout the regions of Spain. The most persuasive reason for the prevalence of united fronts in some localities and their absence in others was the presence of some nuclei of activists with sufficient authority among the larger ranks and willing and able to carry out the task of propagating and constructing such united fronts. Evidence adduced for France suggests similar contingent reasons for the early appearance of united fronts in some locations prior to the national breakthrough of 1934.

On a Continental scale, then, social democracy was forced to make certain choices. In some countries it turned toward the promise of united fronts, in others toward cooperation with the middle classes. In a few instances, notably Switzerland, it tried both in rapid succession, and in some sense the ultimate turn toward popular fronts in Spain and France and the almost simultaneous abandonment of radical planism in Belgium in favor of a renewed experiment in classical ministerial coalitionism are expressions of the eventual victory of the moderate track in almost all of Europe, preparing the ground for the postwar social compromise.

Constraints on Contingency

The notion of contingency, however, only goes so far. Whereas choices, I argue, are not predetermined, they are limited. Whether social democrats opted for the routes of moderation, radical planism or united fronts also depended on the availability of such options. Clearly, the range of possibilities was restricted by the menu offered. For instance, radical planism, by definition, could not have been an option prior to its elaboration in the course of 1933. Once shaped into a coherent strategy, its popularity rapidly grew. The presence or absence of a body of ideas thus powerfully influenced the range of choices and delimited possible outcomes.

Yet not only is the availability of competing ideologies or, in this case, strategies a strong determinant of contingent results; the character and quality of proponents of alternative ideologies likewise influence the decision-making process. In chapter 5, for instance, I cited evidence suggesting that in early 1934 Spanish social democrats briefly discussed the relevance of the Plan de Man within the Spanish context. Given the heightened degree of social tension at that time, it is not surprising that, instead of forming a commission to investigate the potential role of planism for Spanish socialists, the PSOE executive embarked upon a campaign of military insurrection. But, regardless of the concrete circumstances, the identification of planist ideology with the conservative figures of Julián Besteiro and Andrés Saborit was an additional handicap and could not but adversely affect the prospects of planism in Spain.

Similarly, as I just mentioned, the patchwork of Spanish united fronts was, if anything, a function of the presence of individuals committed to this approach rather than a reflection of structural dispositions or anything else. The opposite trajectory taken by the Austrian social democratic exile executive in Brno, compared with their German comrades in neighboring Prague, was likewise primarily a result of the individual qualities and predispositions of the personalities within the respective leadership bodies rather than a logical outcome of differing political traditions, although the latter undoubtedly played a role. Both Austrian and German leaders, after their respective defeats, were subject to a campaign of vilification and emotional expressions of distrust by many members of their respective parties. Yet the Austrian exile leadership proved itself to be far more flexible and responsive to such criticism than its German counterpart. Again, the most convincing explanation for this divergence must be sought in the subjective qualities of the individuals concerned.

Contingency, agency and ideology are three key notions for an approximate understanding of the historical process in the 1930s. For social democracy to start in new directions, alternative ideologies or strategies had to exist, advocated by sufficiently popular and authoritative agents so that choices could be made. The precise choices could rarely be predicted. What does all this have to say about the relevance or irrelevance of structural continuities, be they of "material" or "ideal" provenance? Does this depiction mean free rein for free choice? What are the limits imposed on this array of competing ideologies and strategies waiting in the wings to be adopted? Or are there no limits?

The Conjunctural Importance of Contingency

Several social scientists, among them Marshall Sahlins, Anthony Giddens and William Sewell, have recently put forward eloquent defenses of the role of contingency in the historical process. Reacting against structuralist and poststructuralist theories which have difficulty theorizing qualitative social changes, William H. Sewell, for instance, has set out to improve the existing body of social theory by drawing attention to the contingent elements in structures and societies in order "to explain both social stability and social change within a unified framework and vocabulary,"[16] thus hoping to overcome sterile opposition between agency and structure, base and superstructure, or idealism versus materialism. "Contingent, unexpected and inherently unpredictable events, this view assumes, can undo or alter the most apparently durable trends of history."[17] At one point Sewell cautiously suggests that "global contingency means not that everything is constantly changing, but that nothing in social life is ultimately immune to change."[18] But in other moments in the exposition of his ideas, Sewell comes dangerously close to positing a universal and continuous role for contingency in the historical process, as, for instance, in his contention that he regards "the course of history as determined by a succession of largely contingent events."[19] Anthony Giddens likewise emphasizes on occasion that, in his view, "the reproduction of social systems is at every moment a contingent phenomenon which requires explanation,"[20] although Giddens, of course, like Sewell, is primarily concerned with the interplay of agency and structure and is generally careful to point out the limits of contingency in the historical process.

Other students of social change take a more nuanced view of the interplay of agency, structure and contingency. Michael S. Kimmel, in a recent survey of theories of revolution, draws attention "to the possibilities contained within any particular moment" of a revolution and suggests "that the process of revolution creates structural possibilities for transformation that were not present prior to the outbreak of a revolution," a powerful indicator of contingency, indeed. But Kimmel continuously stresses the unusual circumstances which have to coincide in order to engender such a sudden change: "[T]he capacity of individuals to act, to make strategic choices, and to influence one another are all especially salient *during revolutionary upheavals*."[21] And, indeed, it is my belief that the exceptionally prominent role of contingency throughout the 1930s, the sudden shifts in, and the rapid succession of, strategic choices, should be regarded as an unusual occurrence and not as the rule. The long-range history of social democracy is a history of stasis or gradual change, only infrequently interrupted by rapid evolution. The history of other political organizations parallels this characteristic pattern of punctuated equilibrium. Only at some crisis points is it possible for unexpected changes to become the norm. But such crisis points should indeed be regarded as extremely important, if rare, moments of opportunity.

My recognition of this specific and limited relevance of contingency is precisely where I differ from E. H. Carr, who, in his discussion of contingency in the historical process, does not deny the role of "accidents" in history but, in the end, dismisses them as elements over which any "rational interpretation of history" has no purchase.[22] While justifiably arguing against proponents of the universal validity of contingency as explanatory factors, Carr's ultimately fatalistic perspective leaves him as incapable of comprehending the conjunctural role of contingency as his more openly voluntaristic colleagues he critiques. A more constructive integration of contingency into an understanding of history is hinted at by some recent scholars who have drawn attention to varying levels of causality, related to different layers of abstraction, depending on which contingency may play a larger or smaller role. Ronald Aminzade, for instance, writes: "At a relatively high level of abstraction, contingent events do not loom very large. At a more fine-grained level of abstraction, outcomes become highly contingent."[23] And Charles Tilly suggests: "History's regularities appear not in repeated sequences, replicated structures and recurrent trends on the large scale but in the causal mechanisms that link contingent sets of circumstances."[24] Yet these observations, valid though they may be, shift the focus of attention away from the concrete role of contingency in particular moments of opportunity and crisis—the definite focus of my effort in this work.[25] Let me therefore bring the discussion back to the problems of how to conceptualize and analyze such choice points in history.

Social Movements and Contingency

Given the heightened importance of contingency in moments of radical flux, it is particularly expedient to limit severely the range of cases to which any generalizations may apply. Rather than finding the lowest common denominator to which an infinite number of cases may conform, I find it most useful to develop a detailed understanding of each particular historic situation. This is not meant to denote the absence of parallel trajectories of social and political evolution. Indeed, the basis for my comparative study is precisely the recognition of distinct common patterns beyond political frontiers where previous scholarship has tended to recognize ever so many peculiarities. There will never exist an unlimited range of choices, and, therefore, political responses will tend to conform to certain patterns. But the very notion of contingency cautions against undue generalizations, universal models of development and unwarranted comparisons.

What, then, triggered this particular moment of opportunity which I date from early 1933 to mid-1936? I believe that any view of this period which abstracts from the material consequences of the economic crisis is fundamentally flawed. For a societal crisis of confidence of this depth and duration to occur, a major social and/or economic cataclysm had to take place. The Great Depression was precisely such an event. Yet all this particular economic crisis was able to prepare were the material preconditions for the ensuing political turmoil. Which form the political crisis took in the different countries concerned was a matter left up to the concrete social and political actors operating in their respective terrains, although political traditions and other elements of continuity exerted important influences on the choices as well. Regarding the political choices for the Left, I have argued that the pattern of responses falls into two broad categories. Yet the reasons why social democracy chose one path over the other in any particular country have as much to do with the concrete circumstances of any given moment as with political traditions, social structure or cultural patterns of behavior.

The breakdown of long-established economic and social structures engenders political crisis. A political crisis, in turn, calls forth the contending forces of alternative political ideologies and concrete political strategies. And, within this battle for ensuing political hegemony, previously marginalized approaches may suddenly emerge in prominent positions of influence and may even emerge victorious. How did this work out in real life? This investigation is precisely an attempt to demonstrate the sequence of events traversed by one major political actor in five specific countries at one historical moment of opportunity. It is not meant to constitute a comprehensive survey of the response of Europe's Left, although, most definitely in this conclusion, I have on occasion ventured forth to draw more wide-ranging inferences. Within the five countries a number of radical alternatives emerged, briefly capturing the imagination of major segments of the respective populace. I argue, though, that by the end of this forty-month period the moment of opportunity had come to a close. What accounts for the eventual closure of such choice points in history? Again, I only wish to address the specific moment of the thirties, for I believe that what ultimately ended this period of experimentation was the ongoing experience of defeats for Europe's Left and the concomitant growth of the national, and especially international, menace of fascism. With each successive defeat of the Left, conservative opponents gained advantages. The cumulative effect of what initially triggered radicalization—massive working-class defeats—ultimately caused renewed moderation. No one was able foresee the precise moment when this change of direction occurred.

But there is more involved in the succession of events than the mere accumulation of defeats. No mobilization in defense of radical goals, no active social movement, can be indefinitely sustained without some tangible achievements. Thus, the radicalization in the five targeted countries had either to achieve its goal or suffer collapse. A good case in point is the trajectory of radical planism in Belgium. After raising hopes and expectations with an extensive multimedia campaign, the moment came when the qualitative break with the prevailing social order had to be attempted, or else the movement would lose its dynamic. In Belgium the POB leadership drew back. In other circumstances, in Austria and even more so in Spain, some social democrats engaged in open battle.

The explicit or implicit goal of the subjects of my study, I argue, was a democratic, noncapitalist, socialist society. This, most definitely, was never achieved. Twice, European social democracy resorted to arms, yet in both cases it suffered a serious defeat. These experiences were more than national defeats; they were interpreted as internationally significant lessons. The sobering of expectations followed on the heels of serious defeats just as much as the initial loss of Germany, and later Austria, triggered radicalization. It was a series of events which were unpredictable, though in hindsight they can be explained.

Notes

Chapter 1

1. The preceding, including the citations, is based on detailed reports in the SPD's daily newspaper *Vorwärts*, 30 January 1933, evening edition, pp. 1–3.

2. By "the Left" I generally refer to organizations—such as parties, trade unions or recreational associations—professing to represent and speak for the working class. In the Europe of the 1930s, this includes, above all, social democratic, communist and anarchist groups. I should add that on occasion I broaden the term to include the liberal, anticlerical Radical and Republican Parties of France and Spain. When this is the case, I will indicate this by appropriate qualifiers.

3. See the graph depicting electoral turnout in Peter Flora, *State, Economy, and Society in Western Europe, 1815–1975*, 2 vols. (Frankfurt: Campus, 1983), 1:92–93. While electoral turnout is never identical to the total number of the electorate, the graph underscores the drastic increase in electoral participation in the immediate postwar years. For the specific figures on the extension of the franchise, see Flora.

4. Geoff Eley, "Revolutionary Europe: Left-Wing Communism, 1917–1923" (manuscript in author's possession), p. 15. For a discussion of "reform as an enforced response to radical pressure, or a pre-emptive measure against future radicalisation" in the post–World War I conjuncture, see Eley, pp. 17–23.

5. See note 1 for the context and citation.

6. For the dating of the beginnings of authoritarian regimes, I have generally relied on information in Stanley Payne, *Fascism* (Madison: University of Wisconsin Press, 1980), citation on page 125. On politics in Albania, omitted in Payne's otherwise comprehensive discussion, see Stefanaq Pollo and Arben Puto, *Histoire de l'Albanie* (Roanne: Horvath, 1974).

7. For an empirical demonstration of the negative correlation of unemployment levels and the electoral strength of the Nazi Party in Germany, see Jürgen Falter et al., "Arbeitslosigkeit und Nationalsozialismus," *Kölner Zeitschrift für Soziologie und Sozialpsychologie* 35 (September 1983): 525–554.

8. The tale of Weimar Germany's demise has been captured in persuasive arguments, but from two different angles, by David Abraham, *The Collapse of the Weimar Republic* (New York: Holmes and Meier, 1986), and Larry Eugene Jones, *German Liberalism and the Dissolution of the Weimar Party System, 1918–1933* (Chapel Hill: University of North Carolina Press, 1988).

9. The standard reference work on the politics of the Spanish Radical Party is Octavio Ruiz Manjón, *El Partido Republicano Radical, 1880–1936* (Madrid: Tebas, 1976).

10. Julius Braunthal, *Geschichte der Internationale*, 2 vols. (Berlin: Dietz, 1978), 2:341.

11. Flora, *State*, 1:120.

12. See Flora, *State*, 1:115 (France) and 1:103 (Belgium); for Spain, I have taken the raw figures provided in Pedro Carasa Soto et al., *Historia de España* (Madrid: Gredos, 1991), 12:411, and made my own calculations.

13. See Flora, *State*, 1:99 (Austria), 1:103 (Belgium), 1:115 (France) and 1:120 (Germany); for the source of the Spanish figures, see previous note.

14. Peter Gourevitch, *Politics in Hard Times* (Ithaca, N.Y.: Cornell University Press, 1986), p. 240.

15. Gourevitch, *Politics in Hard Times*, p. 160.

16. Gourevitch, *Politics in Hard Times*, p. 240.

17. Gourevitch, *Politics in Hard Times*, p. 166.

18. On this neglected dimension of historical analysis, strewn with many false paths and obstacles as it may be, see Barrington Moore's chapter "'The Suppression of Historical Alternatives: Germany, 1918–1920," in his *Injustice: The Social Bases of Obedience and Revolt* (White Plains, N.Y.: Sharpe, 1978), pp. 376–397. On the role of contingency in the historical process, see my discussion in chapter 9.

19. The two short texts are Pierre Broué, "L'Année 1934," *Cahiers Léon Trotsky* 20 (December 1984): 3–11, and Broué, "Octubre del 34 en el contexto europeo," in *Octubre 1934*, ed. Gabriel Jackson et al. (Madrid: Siglo XXI, 1985), pp. 9–17.

20. See the works by Pierre Broué cited in the previous note for a detailed examination of the exceptional year 1934, an awareness which likewise underlies virtually all monographs on the Spanish Left in the Second Republic, although the latter works generally see the importance of 1934 as limited to Spain. Daniel R. Brower goes perhaps the furthest in the recognition of a distinct "united front" period prior to the era of popular fronts in *The New Jacobins* (Ithaca, N.Y.: Cornell University Press, 1968).

21. Paul Preston, *The Coming of the Spanish Civil War* (London: Macmillan, 1978), p. 2.

22. Marc Bloch, "A Contribution Towards a Comparative History of European Societies," in his *Land and Work in Medieval Europe* (New York: Harper and Row), pp. 70–71.

23. See Adolf Sturmthal, *The Tragedy of European Labor* (New York: Columbia University Press, 1943); G. D. H. Cole, *Socialism and Fascism, 1931–1939* (London: Macmillan, 1960); and Julius Braunthal, *Geschichte der Internationale*, vol. 2 (1963; reprint, Berlin: Dietz, 1978).

24. See the work by Cole cited in the previous note; see also the more recent survey by Jacques Droz, *Histoire de l'antifascisme en Europe, 1923–1939* (Paris: La Découverte, 1985), and Leo Michielsen, *Ekonomische krisis en fascistische agressie (1930–1939)*, vol. 3b of *Geschiedenis van de Europese arbeidersbeweging* (Gent: Frans Masereel Fonds, 1980).

25. See Larry Ceplair, *Under the Shadow of War: Fascism, Anti-Fascism and Marxists, 1918–1939* (New York: Columbia University Press, 1987). A useful anthology with identical limitations is David Beetham, *Marxists in the Face of Fascism* (Manchester: Manchester University Press, 1983).

26. See Ekkart Zimmermann and Thomas Saalfeld, "Economic and Political Reactions to the World Economic Crisis of the 1930s in Six European Countries," *International Studies Quarterly* 32 (1988): 305–334; Ekkart Zimmermann, "Interest Groups, Political Parties and Extremist Challenges in the Process of National Consensus Formation: On Assessing the Political Effect of the Great Depression in Eight Countries," manuscript, 1988; Gregory M. Luebbert, *Liberalism, Fascism, or Social Democracy* (New York: Oxford Uni-

versity Press, 1991); Mario Telò, *La socialdemocrazia europea nella crisi degli anni trenta* (Milan: Franco Angeli, 1985), translated, slightly abridged and amended as *Le New Deal Européenne* (Brussels: Éditions de l'Université de Bruxelles, 1988); and Margaret Weir and Theda Skocpol, "State Structures and the Possibilities for 'Keynesian' Responses to the Great Depression in Sweden, Britain, and the United States," in *Bringing the State Back In*, ed. Peter B. Evans, Dietrich Rueschemeyer and Theda Skocpol (Cambridge: Cambridge University Press, 1985), pp. 107–168.

27. For one recent example, see the discussion of Luebbert in chapter 9 of the present study.

28. Bloch, "Contribution," p. 56.

29. This turn of phrase is, of course, taken from the title of Charles Tilly's important work *Big Structures, Large Processes, Huge Comparisons* (New York: Russell Sage, 1985).

Chapter 2

1. On the radicalizing impact of the European revolutions of 1917–23 on social democracy, the best survey remains Albert S. Lindemann, *The "Red Years"* (Berkeley: University of California Press, 1974).

2. See Helmut Gruber, *Red Vienna* (New York: Oxford University Press, 1992), for a recent, comprehensive case study of the contradictions, the promises and the perils of interwar socialist engagement with practical politics in a bastion of the European labor movement, the capital city of Austria.

3. Peter Flora, *State, Economy, and Society in Western Europe, 1815–1975*, 2 vols. (Frankfurt: Campus, 1983), 1:156, 159, 173.

4. For the divergent attitudes of the various factions within the PSOE to Primo de Rivera's authoritarian government, see José Andrés Gallego, *El socialismo durante la dictadura, 1923–30* (Madrid: Tebas, 1977). This internal dispute is interesting insofar as Indalecio Prieto, the nemesis of the left-wing faction during the thirties, was actually the only consistent opponent of Primo de Rivera's dictatorship in the twenties. On this see also Alfonso Carlos Saiz Valdivielso, *Indalecio Prieto* (Barcelona: Planeta, 1984), pp. 82–104.

5. The most useful survey of these and other issues affecting the internal life of the SFIO remains Georges Lefranc, *Le Mouvement socialiste* (Paris: Payot, 1963), pp. 265–301. But see also the work by another participant in these events, Jules Moch, *Rencontres avec Léon Blum* (Paris: Plon, 1970), and the recent history of the SFIO, Alain Bergounioux and Gérard Grunberg, *Le Long Remords du pouvoir* (Paris: Fayard, 1992), particularly pp. 134–147.

6. Friedrich Adler, "The Task of the Emigration in the Persecuted Party," *International Information (II)*, 10 June 1933, pp. 269–270; emphasis in the original.

7. Gabriel Jackson's book *The Spanish Republic and the Civil War, 1931–1939* (Princeton, N.J.: Princeton University Press, 1965) remains the most convincing English-language study of this turbulent period in Spanish history. The early hours of the second republic are described on pages 25–55. But see also the more recent study by Stanley G. Payne, *Spain's First Democracy: The Second Republic, 1931–1936* (Madison: University of Wisconsin Press, 1993). The classic Spanish text on the second republic is Manuel Tuñon de Lara, *La II Republica* (Madrid: Siglo XXI, 1976).

8. The literature on PSOE factionalism under the second republic is, plainly speaking, enormous. One key work is Santos Juliá, *La izquierda del PSOE (1935–36)* (Madrid: Siglo XXI, 1977), which, however, focuses on the central years of the second republic. The study by Andrés de Blas Guerrero, *El socialismo radical en la II República* (Madrid: Tucar, 1978), likewise focuses on the emerging left faction around Largo Caballero but covers the entire period from 1931 to 1936. Marta Bizcarrondo furnishes, as usual, an insightful survey

of competing ideologies within the PSOE in her "La Segunda República: Ideologías socialistas," in *El socialismo en España*, ed. Santos Juliá (Madrid: Pablo Iglesias, 1986), pp. 255–274. The same volume contains Juliá's own important contribution, entitled "República, revolución y luchas internas," pp. 231–254. The superior English contribution on PSOE factionalism remains, however, Paul Preston's chapter "Social Democracy and Social Conflict: The PSOE in Power, 1931–3" in his *Coming of the Spanish Civil War* (London: Macmillan, 1978), pp. 51–91. For the most recent discussion in English, see Helen Graham, *Socialism and War: The Spanish Socialist Party in Power and Crisis, 1936–1939* (Cambridge: Cambridge University Press, 1991), pp. 15–50.

9. "Acta de la reunión celebrada por la Comisión Ejecutiva del Partido Socialista el día 11 de setiembre de 1933," p. 359. Fundación Pablo Iglesias (FPI) [Madrid], Archivo Histórico (AH)–I.

10. "Nuestra consigna: Un llamada al combate," *El Socialista*, 20 September 1933, p. 1. The PSOE national committee deliberations are summarized in "Acta de la reunión celebrada por el Comité Nacional del Partido Socialista el día 19 de setiembre de 1933." FPI, AH–III.

11. "Unas declaraciones de Largo Caballero," *El Socialista*, 24 September 1933, p. 1.

12. The series of immediate events which led up to the expulsion of the old UGT leadership, including the documents by Prieto, the PSOE executive and Besteiro, can be found in "Acta de la reunión celebrada por la Comisión Ejecutiva del Partido Socialista el día 18 de enero de 1934," pp. 11–15, with the quote on page 13. The relevant excerpts of the UGT national committee meeting minutes in the fall and winter of 1933–34 constitute the bulk of the second and third chapters of Amaro del Rosal, *1934: Movimiento revolucionario de octubre* (Madrid: Akal, 1983), pp. 25–204. Many of the most crucial documents of this period are also excerpted and summarized by Santos Juliá in Largo Caballero, *Escritos de la República* (Madrid: Pablo Iglesias, 1985), pp. 39–86.

13. See, for instance, the official May Day proclamation "El Partido Socialista y la Unión General de Trabajadores, al proletariado," *El Socialista*, 24 April 1934, p. 1, or the front-page headline two days later: THE SOLE AND INEVITABLE SOLUTION: ALL POWER TO THE SOCIALIST PARTY!

14. Many important documents regarding this affair are reprinted in Largo Caballero, *Escritos de la República*, pp. 85–158. A narrative account by a key organizer can be found, once again, in del Rosal, *1934*, pp. 207–256.

15. Amaro del Rosal is the best source of information on the inglorious behavior of the national leadership in this affair; see his *Historia de la UGT de España*, 2 vols. (Barcelona: Grijalbo, 1977), 1:401–408, and his *1934*, pp. 257–293. The most informative accounts of the rebellion itself are David Ruiz, *Insurrección defensiva y revolución obrera* (Barcelona: Labor, 1988); Bernardo Díaz Nosty, *La comuna asturiana* (Bilbao: Zero, 1974); and Paco Ignacio Taibo II, *Asturias 1934*, 2 vols. (Madrid: Júcar, 1980), the latter providing the most detailed description of the movement in Asturias, the center point of the uprising.

16. On the Schutzbund uprising, useful introductions are the anthologies by Erich Fröschl and Helge Zoitl, eds., *Februar 1934* (Vienna: Wiener Volksbuchhandlung, 1984), and Ludwig Jedlicka and Rudolf Neck, eds., *Das Jahr 1934: 12. Februar* (Munich: Oldenbourg, 1975). An informative account from a communist perspective is Arnold Reisberg, *Februar 1934* (Vienna: Globus, 1974). A leading activist in Austrian politics during these fateful years, Ilona Duczynska, married to Karl Polanyi, provides an additional background study in her *Workers in Arms* (New York: Monthly Review Press, 1978). Two further, important contemporaneous documents are Julius Deutsch, *Der Bürgerkrieg in Österreich* (Karlsbad: Graphia, 1934), and Otto Bauer, *Der Aufstand der österreichischen Arbeiter* (1934; reprint, Vienna: Löcker and Wögenstein, 1974).

17. The activist and, after the summer of 1935, national chairman of the American social democratic youth organization emphasized in a recent letter the activating stimulus provided by the events of Austria and Spain: "It is difficult for contemporary students to realize that in 1934 and 1935, mainly as a result of the armed stand against fascism by the Austrian socialists and the overthrow of the monarchy in Spain in 1931 and the armed uprising in 1934, socialists were regarded as revolutionaries who fought with guns in hand, while Communists talked revolution but did no fighting." Ernest Erber, letter to author, 23 June 1989, p. 2.

18. The most insightful attempts to analyze Austro-Marxism as a distinct ideological current are Peter Kulemann, *Am Beispiel des Austromarxismus* (Hamburg: Junius, 1982); Norbert Leser, *Zwischen Reformismus und Bolschewismus* (Vienna: Europa, 1968); Raimund Löw, Siegfried Mattl and Alfred Pfabigan, *Der Austromarxismus: Eine Autopsie* (Frankfurt: ISP, 1986); and the introduction to Giacomo Marramao, *Austromarxismo e socialismo di sinistra fra le due guerri* (Milan: La Pietra, 1977), pp. 9–135. On the political itinerary of the SPÖ up to February 1934, the most informative account remains Anson Rabinbach, *The Crisis of Austrian Socialism* (Chicago: University of Chicago Press, 1983).

19. For the initiative by the Upper Austrian executive around Richard Bernaschek, see his biography by Inez Kykal and Karl R. Stadler, *Richard Bernaschek: Odyssee eines Rebellen* (Vienna: Europa, 1976), pp. 78–97.

20. "Report on events in Austria," p. 31. Internationaal Instituut voor Sociale Geschiedenis (IISG) [Amsterdam], Sozialistische Arbeiter-Internationale (SAI), Mappe 2452.

21. On the vagaries of left-wing opposition to the party leadership see, most importantly, Rabinbach, *Crisis of Austrian Socialism*, pp. 32–154; Peter Pelinka, *Erbe und Neubeginn* (Vienna: Europa, 1981), pp. 5–31; Kulemann, *Am Beispiel des Austromarxismus*, pp. 380–394; Alfred Pfabigan, *Max Adler* (Frankfurt: Campus, 1982), pp. 253–272; and Ernst Fischer's autobiography, *Erinnerungen und Reflexionen* (Reinbek: Rowohlt, 1969), pp. 231–255. A series of programmatic documents by this left opposition can be found in Kykal and Stadler, *Richard Bernaschek*, pp. 229–263.

22. On the organizational realignment after February 1934, see Pelinka, *Erbe und Neubeginn*, pp. 52–81; Joseph Buttinger, *Das Ende der Massenpartei* (Frankfurt: Neue Kritik, 1972), pp. 7–201; Otto Leichter, *Zwischen zwei Diktaturen* (Vienna: Europa, 1968), pp. 107–188; and Everhard Holtmann, *Zwischen Unterdrückung und Befriedung* (Munich: Oldenbourg, 1978), pp. 155–221. Ernst Fischer's moving letter announcing his break with social democracy, addressed to his former mentor, Otto Bauer, is located in IISG, Otto Bauer, Mappe 7.

23. This so-called Hollandgutachten, the "Bericht über die Untersuchung des Zustandes in Österreich von E. Kupers und C. Woudenberg," dated June 1934, constitutes an interesting source on the mood of the Austrian underground in the spring of 1934, although some of its assessments reflect the difficulties of judging complex realignments in an emerging underground by observers unfamiliar with the terrain. IISG, SAI, Mappe 2451, p. 23.

24. This information is contained in a letter by Otto Bauer to Friedrich Adler, 4 July 1934. Verein für Geschichte der Arbeiterbewegung (VGA) [Vienna], Adler-Archiv, Mappe 84/69.

25. Otto Bauer, "Um die Demokratie," *Der Kampf* 26 (July 1933): 271–272, 270.

26. Otto Bauer, "Neue Wege zum alten Ziel," *Arbeiter-Zeitung* (AZ), 18 March 1934. All quotations are from pages 2–3; emphases in the original.

27. Central Committee of Revolutionary Socialists, "What We Expect from the International," *Documents and Discussions* (DD), 30 June 1934, p. 37; emphases in the original. *DD* was a regular supplement to the LSI's official publication, *International Information* (II).

28. Rudolf Breitscheid to Paul Hertz, 29 June 1933, p. 1. Archiv der sozialen Demokratie (AdsD) [Bonn], Paul Hertz, Film XLI, "53," "XVI." Five weeks earlier, Breitscheid actually predicted a split within the SPD over the lessons of the most recent past. See Rudolf Breitscheid to Paul Hertz, 25 May 1933, p. 1. AdsD, Paul Hertz, Film XLI, "53," "XVI."

29. Rudolf Breitscheid to Karl Kautsky, 23 February 1934, p. 2. IISG, Karl Kautsky papers, D VI 650.

30. Rudolf Breitscheid to Paul Hertz, 25 April 1935, p. 2. AdsD, Paul Hertz, Film XLI, "53," "XVI."

31. These regular reports contained the information for the monthly issues of the *Deutschland-Berichte* (Germany Reports), published from the spring of 1934 until April 1940 by the SPD party executive. They were usually divided into three separate portions, with the "C-Berichte" generally devoted to internal politics and the general state of the underground. Because of their particularly confidential nature, the "C-Berichte" were never included in the published version of the *Deutschland-Berichte*. For the recent multivolume reprint of the published reports, see *Deutschland-Berichte* (Frankfurt: Zweitausendeins, 1980). For background to these source materials, see Michael Voges, "Klassenkampf in der 'Betriebsgemeinschaft,'" *Archiv fuer Sozialgeschichte* 21 (1981), particularly pp. 329–343, and Hartmut Mehringer, *Waldemar von Knoeringen: Eine politische Biographie* (Munich: Saur, 1989), pp. 90–94.

32. Letter signed by "Eine Genossin aus Unterbaden," with handwritten notation: "übermittelt am 28. Sept. Reinbold." From the context it can be inferred that the year was 1933. AdsD, Sopade, Mappe 90.

33. Gustav Ferl to Sopade [the most common acronym for the SPD under Hitler], 17 August 1933, p. 2. AdsD, Sopade, Mappe 37.

34. Alfred Käseberg, "Bericht bis Januar 1935," p. 3. AdsD, Sopade, Mappe 59.

35. Hans Dill to Hans Vogel, 23 May 1934, p. 3. AdsD, Sopade, Mappe 31.

36. Franz Osterroth, "Spezielle Bemerkungen nach einer dreiwöchigen Deutschlandreise. Oktober 1934," p. 9. AdsD, Sopade, Mappe 86.

37. Ernst Schumacher, "Situationsbericht an Sopade für die Zeit vom 20. September bis 13. Oktober 1934," p. 3. AdsD, Sopade, Mappe 115.

38. Hans Dill, "Zweiter Bericht für August 1934," 17 August 1934, p. 18. AdsD, Sopade, Mappe 31.

39. Wilhelm Sander, "Bericht über eine Besprechung mit 15 ostsächsischen Genossen am 31.12.34 und 1.1.35," p. 3. AdsD, Sopade, Mappe 106. See also Hans Dill's conclusion: "The further we are moving away from March 1933, the more noticeable is the disappearance of all critical remarks about the politics and tactics of the party." See previous note for citation.

40. For a more detailed assessment of the nature and the sources of political conflict within the post-1933 SPD, see my "Pro-Unity Sentiments in Underground Social Democracy: 1933–1936," in *Between Reform and Revolution: Studies in the History of German Socialism and Communism from 1840 to 1990*, ed. David E. Barclay and Eric D. Weitz (Providence, R.I.: Berghahn, 1996).

41. The two key opposition groups within the Sopade were Neu Beginnen (NB) and the Revolutionary Socialists of Germany (RSD). On the former grouping, the most important works of analysis are Kurt Kliem, "Der sozialistische Widerstand gegen das Dritte Reich dargestellt an der Gruppe 'Neu Beginnen,'" (Ph.D. diss., Universität Marburg, 1957), and Hans J. Reichardt, "Neu Beginnen. Ein Beitrag zur Geschichte des Widerstandes der Arbeiterbewegung gegen den Nationalsozialismus," *Jahrbuch für die Geschichte Mittel- und Ostdeutschlands* 12 (1963): 150–188. The recent biography of Waldemar von Knoeringen by Hartmut Mehringer adds considerable substance to this picture. On the RSD, see, above all, Jutta von Freyberg, *Sozialdemokraten und Kommunisten* (Cologne: Pahl-Rugenstein,

1973), a work hampered by its openly procommunist bias. Both groups are included in the survey of splinter organizations by Jan Foitzik, *Zwischen den Fronten* (Bonn: Neue Gesellschaft, 1986).

42. In general, the best overview of SPD politics in these years remains Lewis Edinger, *German Exile Politics* (Berkeley: University of California Press, 1956). The article by Helmut Gruber, "The German Socialist Executive in Exile, 1933–1939," in *Chance und Illusion: Labour in Retreat,* ed. Wolfgang Maderthaner and Helmut Gruber (Vienna: Europa, 1988), pp. 185–245, furnishes additional important insights into the dynamics within the Prague headquarters.

43. I choose merely to highlight French developments in socialist depression politics since an abundance of pertinent literature already exists and makes detailed explanations superfluous. The most important works on this period in France are John T. Marcus, *French Socialism in the Crisis Years (1933–1936)* (New York: Praeger, 1958); Nathanael Greene, *Crisis and Decline* (Ithaca, N.Y.: Cornell University Press, 1969); Karl G. Harr Jr., *The Genesis and Effect of the Popular Front in France* (Lanham, Md.: University Press of America, 1987); Jean-Paul Joubert, *Révolutionnaires de la SFIO* (Paris: FNSP, 1977); and Frank Georgi, "La première 'Bataille Socialiste,'" (Thèse d'Etat, University of Paris, 1983).

44. I will more fully address Belgian socialist experiments in chapter 5.

45. The most detailed analysis and discussion of "Third Period communism," the label frequently attached to this period of communist politics, remains Peer H. Lange, *Stalinismus versus "Sozialfaschismus" und "Nationalfaschismus,"* (Göppingen: Alfred Kuemmerle, 1969). On the genesis of the term "social fascism," see Lange, pp. 185–195, and Siegfried Bahne, "'Sozialfaschismus' in Deutschland: Zur Geschichte eines politischen Begriffs," *International Review of Social History* 10 (1965): 211–245.

46. For a full exposition of the differences between united and popular front strategies, see chapters 4 and 6.

47. Most observers are well aware of the fluid nature of Comintern strategic and tactical changes between 1934 and 1936, and few would dispute E. H. Carr's cautious statement that "the advance to the popular front was slow and faltering" (see E. H. Carr, *The Twilight of the Comintern, 1930–1935* [London: Macmillan, 1982], p. 148). But virtually all historians of this period in communist politics are content to stress the unstable nature of this moment. And thus far, no one has recognized the specific character of this crucial year between May 1934 and May 1935, particularly in contradistinction to the subsequent period of popular fronts.

48. This citation from the 15 August 1934 *Cahiers du Bolshévisme* is taken from Duclos's excerpts from this article in Jacques Duclos, *Mémoires 1896–1934* (Paris: Fayard, 1968), p. 417. The left bourgeois Radical-Socialist Party was usually referred to as the Radical Party.

49. Daniel P. Brower, *The New Jacobins: The French Communist Party and the Popular Front* (Ithaca, N.Y.: Cornell University Press, 1968), p. 73.

50. Carr, *Twilight of the Comintern,* citations on pages 197, 199–200. The Radical-Socialist Party was the full name of the organization usually referred to by "Radical Party" (Parti Radical).

51. For a brief discussion and refutation of such claims, see Denis Peschanski, *Et pourtant ils tournent* (Paris: Kliencksieck, 1988), particularly pp. 48–49. Peschanski is associated with the PCF research institute.

52. Brower, *The New Jacobins,* p. 75.

53. Jacques Kergoat, *La France du front populaire* (Paris: La Découverte, 1986), pp. 51–52.

54. Duclos, *Mémoires,* p. 422.

55. Maurice Thorez, "Les Communistes et le front populaire," in his *Oeuvres,* 23 vols. (Paris: Éditions Sociales, 1952), II/7:81.

56. Thorez, "Les Communistes," p. 77.

57. Thorez, "Les Communistes," p. 81.

58. Brower, *The New Jacobins*, p. 76.

59. Maurice Thorez, "Le Front unique c'est l'action," in *Oeuvres*, II/7:183, where he states that the PCF has appealed for common action "*even* to the local sections of the Radical Party and of the League of the Rights of Man which oppose the so-called policy of National Union and the evil deeds of the fascist gangs"; emphasis added.

60. Julian Jackson, *The Popular Front in France* (Cambridge: Cambridge University Press, 1988), p. 38.

61. On these Comintern discussions, see Branko Lazitch, "Le Komintern et le front populaire," *Contrepoint* 3 (1971): 91, and Peschanski, *Et pourtant ils tournent*, p. 178 n. 57.

62. This intervention is reprinted as "La Tactique unitaire des communistes," in Thorez, *Oeuvres*, II/8:71–74.

63. Cited in Brower, *The New Jacobins*, p. 86.

64. Brower's analysis of the May 1935 elections are in *The New Jacobins*, pp. 85–88; but see also Jackson, *Popular Front in France*, p. 39, and Georges Lefranc, *Histoire du front populaire* (Paris: Payot, 1965), pp. 71–72. The description of Paul Rivet can be found in Lefranc, p. 72.

65. Excerpts of this speech are reprinted as "Les Succès du Parti communiste aux élections municipales et l'avenir du front populaire," in *Oeuvres*, II/8:197–207, citation on page 201.

66. Brower, *The New Jacobins*, p. 85, relies on an unpublished manuscript by Vassart. In a recent interview Claude Harmel, who together with Branko Lazitch held extensive talks with Vassart during the 1950s, confirmed this remarkable episode in vivid terms. My conversation with Harmel took place in Paris on 7 June 1990.

67. For the original pathbreaking work which launched the recent trend in French historiography, see Régine Robin, *Histoire et linguistique* (Paris: Armand Colin, 1973). For a useful, if too uncritical, survey of lexicometric discourse analysis in France and related developments in the historical profession elsewhere, see Peter Schöttler, "Historians and Discourse Analysis," *History Workshop Journal* 27 (spring 1989): 37–65.

68. Annie Kriegel's presentation "Pro-unity Vocabulary and the Periodisation of Communist Politics: The Example of the Popular Front" is reprinted as "Langage et stratégie," in her *Communismes au miroir français* (Paris: Gallimard, 1974), pp. 95–114. Advocacy of united fronts "from below" was the euphemistic description of Communist "Third Period" politics toward other organizations of the working-class Left. United fronts "from above" refers to officially sanctioned unity agreements between working-class organizations.

69. Kriegel, "Langage et stratégie," p. 108; emphasis in the original.

70. These quotes from Thorez are likewise cited in Kriegel, "Langage et stratégie," p. 109.

71. Kriegel, "Langage et stratégie," p. 114.

72. Peschanski, *Et pourtant ils tournent*, p. 65; emphasis in the original.

73. Peschanski, *Et pourtant ils tournent*, p. 66.

74. Peschanski, *Et pourtant ils tournent*, p. 91.

75. Peschanski, *Et pourtant ils tournent*, p. 66. See also the changing frequency of references to "workers" and "the people" displayed in Table 39a on page 131 of his work.

76. Peschanski, *Et pourtant ils tournent*, pp. 85–88.

77. Peschanski, *Et pourtant ils tournent*, pp. 91–92.

78. Peschanski, *Et pourtant ils tournent*, p. 142.

79. Peschanski, *Et pourtant ils tournent*, pp. 102–112.

80. Peschanski, *Et pourtant ils tournent*, p. 91.

81. Peschanski, *Et pourtant ils tournent*, p. 95.

82. Peschanski, *Et pourtant ils tournent*, p. 169.

83. See note 71.

84. Bernhard Bayerlein, "El significado internacional de Octubre de 1934 en Asturias, la Comuna Asturiana y el Komintern," in *Octubre 1934*, ed. Gabriel Jackson et al. (Madrid: Siglo XXI, 1985), p. 24.

85. Rafael Cruz, *El Partido Comunista de España en la II República* (Madrid: Alianza, 1987), p. 230. Cruz's monograph should now be considered the best overview of Spanish communism under the second republic.

86. Cited in Cruz, *El Partido Communista*, p. 230.

87. Cruz, *El Partido Communista*, p. 230; emphasis added.

88. Cruz, *El Partido Communista*, p. 231.

89. Cruz, *El Partido Communista*, pp. 231–232.

90. Manuel Tuñón de Lara, "Frentes populares / Unidad popular," in his *Tres claves de la Segunda República* (Madrid: Alianza, 1985), p. 334. For other concrete examples of PCE advocacy of popular fronts "from below" between October 1934 and May 1935, see pp. 333–335.

91. Another useful listing of the PCE's hesitations between the fall of 1934 and May 1935 can be found in Bernhard Bayerlein, "Die Genese der Volksfront in Spanien," in *Internationale Tagung der Historiker der Arbeiterbewegung. 22.Linzer Konferenz 1986*, ed. Gabriella Hauch (Vienna: Europa, 1987), pp. 379–380, although he tends to read into this evolution a progressive development toward full-fledged popular fronts which the evidence does not uphold. Marta Bizcarrondo is likewise well aware of "the blurred nature and the vacillation of the politics of 'popular blocs' and 'popular antifascist concentrations' up to May/June 1935"; see her "Le VII Congrès de l'Internationale communiste et la classe ouvrière en Espagne," *Cahiers d'Histoire de l'Institut de Recherches Marxistes* 27 (1987): 86.

92. PCE central committee, "A todos los Comités del Partido," p. 2. Archivo Histórico del Partido Communista de España [Madrid] (AHPCE), Rollo X, 137; emphases in the original.

93. Tuñon de Lara, "Frentes populares," pp. 334–335.

94. "¡Contra el nuevo gobierno de la reacción y del fascismo! ¡Por los Soviets, por el Gobierno Obrero y Campesino!", p. 2. AHPCE, legajo 16; emphasis in the original.

95. Note also Santos Juliá's assessment that the PCE, when it first hinted at the broadening of fronts in the fall of 1934, decided to ascribe only secondary importance to such novel alliances; see Santos Juliá, "República, revolución y luchas internas," in *El socialismo en España*, ed. Santos Juliá (Madrid: Pablo Iglesias, 1986), p. 246.

96. "Boletín de orientación para el trabajo del Partido. Guión para las oradores del Partido en los mítines," p. 3. AHPCE, legajo 16. The precise date of this highly suggestive document can be ascertained from the copy in AHPCE, Rollo X, 137.

97. On the Catalan party system, see Alberto Balcells, "El sistema de partidos políticos en Cataluña entre 1934 y 1936," in *La II República Española*, ed. José Luis García Delgado (Madrid: Siglo XXI, 1988), pp. 83–104.

98. See note 68 in Cruz, *El Partido Communista*, p. 235, where he mentions 20 May 1935 as the date when the statutes of the "Popular Antifascist Concentration" were published.

Chapter 3

1. The appeal is reprinted in *II*, 20 February 1933, pp. 76–78.

2. Jonathan Haslam, "The Comintern and the Origins of the Popular Front 1934–1935," *Historical Journal* 22 (1979): 675.

3. The Comintern appeal is reprinted in *Rundschau*, 11 March 1933, pp. 91–92. Fridrich Firsov suggests that an earlier draft of the Comintern's official response, while also less than diplomatic, did not outright reject the possibility of a top-level meeting between the two Internationals. Only in the final draft, personally revised by Joseph Stalin, did this option disappear from the text; see Fridrich Firsov, "Stalin und Fragen der Einheitsfrontpolitik," in *Tödliche Umarmung: Einheitsfront: Ein stalinistisches Manöver?* ed. Viola Godemann (Berlin: Dietz, 1991), pp. 38–39, and Firsov, "Stalin und die Komintern," in *Die Komintern und Stalin*, ed. Helmut Heinz et al. (Berlin: Dietz, 1990), p. 108.

4. Resolution on "The Unity of the Labour Movement," reprinted in *II*, 27 March 1933, p. 139

5. The watershed appears to have been the Comintern executive (EKKI) resolution on the German situation of 1 April 1933, reprinted in Aldo Agosti, *La Terza Internazionale* (Roma: Riuniti, 1979), III/2:475–481. Agosti's commentary to this effect is on pages 442–443.

6. Agosti, *Terza Internazionale*, III/1:440.

7. Jocelyne Prézeau, "Le Mouvement Amsterdam-Pleyel (1932–1934): Un camp d'essai du Front unique," *Cahiers d'Histoire de l'Institut de Recherches Marxistes* 18 (July–September 1984): 90.

8. Only the letter to Adler survives, but a postscript by Barbusse to this very letter indicates that his communications to Bauer and Vandervelde were identical in content. See Henri Barbusse to Friedrich Adler, 20 March 1933. IISG, SAI, Mappe 3039.

9. Émile Vandervelde to Friedrich Adler, 3 April 1933. IISG, SAI, Mappen 1302, 3039 (two copies).

10. This can be gauged from Barbusse's response to Bauer in Henri Barbusse to Otto Bauer, 4 April 1933. IISG, SAI, Mappe 3039.

11. The quote stems from Henri Barbusse to Émile Vandervelde, 4 April 1933, of which two copies exist in IISG, SAI, Mappen 1302 and 3039. The briefer response to Bauer is in Mappe 3039.

12. See Henri Barbusse to "Herr Walter," 10 April 1933. IISG, SAI, Mappe 3039.

13. Émile Vandervelde to Friedrich Adler, 3 April 1933. IISG, SAI, Mappen 1302 and 3039.

14. Émile Vandervelde to Friedrich Adler, 2 May 1933. IISG, SAI, Mappe 3039.

15. Jacques Rupnik, *Histoire du Parti Communiste Tchécoslovaque* (Paris: FNSP, 1981), pp. 98–102.

16. Siegfried Bahne, *Die KPD und das Ende von Weimar* (Frankfurt: Campus, 1976), pp. 44–45.

17. Jules Humbert-Droz, *Dix ans de lutte antifasciste* (Neuchâtel: La Baconnière, 1972), pp. 88–90.

18. "Erde" [= Karl Retzlaw] to "L.G.T.," 15 June 1933. IISG, Leon Trotsky papers, Mappe 1510 (old number).

19. The most useful accounts of the 1934–35 attempts to break down the barriers between social democracy and communism are Giuliano Procacci, *Il socialismo internazionale e la guerra di Etiopia* (Rome: Riuniti, 1978); Agosti, *Terza Internazionale*, III/2:711–763, 903–910; Marta Dassú, "Fronte unico e fronte popolare: Il VII Congresso del Comintern," in *Storia del marxismo* (Torino: Einaudi, 1981), III/2:589–626; Herbert Mayer, "Die SAI und die antifaschistische Einheitsfront im Herbst 1934," *Beiträge zur Geschichte der Arbeiterbewegung* 24 (1982): 92–102; Werner Kowalski, ed., *Geschichte der Sozialistischen Arbeiter-Internationale (1923–1940)* (Berlin: Verlag der Wissenschaften, 1985), pp. 178–249; Mario Mancini, "L'IOS e la questione del fronte unico negli anni Trenta," in *L'Internazionale Operaia e Socialista tra le due guerre*, ed. Enzo Collotti (Milan: Feltrinelli, 1985), pp. 177–198; and Enzo Collotti, "Il dibattito sull'unità d'azione e sul fronte popolare nell'

Internazionale Operaia e Socialista," in *La stagione dei fronti popolari*, ed. Aldo Agosti (Bologna: Cappelli, 1989), pp. 33–64.

20. For a suggestive description and justification of a similar periodization of Comintern policy, see Phillippe Burrin, "Diplomatie soviétique, Internationale communiste et PCF au tournant du front populaire (1934–1935)," *Relations Internationales* 45 (spring 1986): 19–34.

21. The most informative account of the pre-1932 LSI-Left can be found in Willy Buschak, *Das Londoner Büro* (Amsterdam: IISG, 1985), pp. 1–60.

22. *II*, 20 February 1933, p. 76.

23. See *II*, 27 March 1933, p. 137.

24. See the Belgian Workers' Party's reference to this "fact" in their letter refusing the Belgian Communist Party's offer of a Belgian united front in *Le Peuple*, 1 April 1933, p. 2.

25. Henryk Ehrlich to Friedrich Adler, 6 April 1933. IISG, SAI, Mappe 2536.

26. "Pour la séance du Comité exécutif de l'IOS, Zurich, le 19 mars 1933. Projet de la Commission. L'unité du mouvement ouvrier." Institut für Geschichte der Arbeiterbewegung (IGA) [Berlin]. Zentrales Partei Archiv (ZPA), I 6/2/47 Blatt 9.

27. "Meetings of the Labour and Socialist International," *II*, 27 March 1933, p. 137.

28. For the majority and minority resolutions, as well as the vote distribution by countries, see the unpaginated annexes A, B and C of the mimeographed "Protokoll: Internationale Konferenz der Sozialistischen Arbeiter-Internationale," Paris, Maison de la Mutualité, 21–25 August 1933. Paul-Henri Spaak, the Belgian leader of a significant radical tendency within the BWP/POB, and an Estonian representative likewise signed the minority resolutions.

29. Quoted from the English-language version published in *II*, 26 August 1933, p. 471.

30. On this point, see also Kowalski, *Geschichte der Sozialistischen*, p. 193.

31. "Protokoll," p. 202.

32. A straightforward assessment of the situation within the LSI, from a conservative point of view, is provided in a confidential report by the Dutch J. W. Albarda to the political bureau of his party. "Verslag aan het P.B. over de vergadering van het Bureau der SAI, gehouden te Parijs, op 24 en 25 Maart 1934." IGA, ZPA, I 6/2/52, Blätter 42–43.

33. These are the words of one of their leading individuals, the SFIO leader Marceau Pivert, in "Et maintenant, rassemblement sur le front international," *Bataille Socialiste* 80 (July–August 1934): 5.

34. The document is entitled "Déclaration de la gauche Socialiste Internationale," *Bataille Socialiste* 80 (July–August 1934): 5–8, and "Manifeste de la gauche Socialiste Internationale," in the Belgian *Action Socialiste*, 11 August 1934, p. 4.

35. See "Eine Erklärung von sieben sozialdemokratischen Parteien," in the annex to *Protokoll der Verhandlungen zwischen der II. und III. Internationale über die Unterstützung des heldenhaften Kampfes der Werktätigen Spaniens, und ihre Ergebnisse* (Strasbourg: Prometheus, 1935), pp. 34–35.

36. "Letter from Austria: What We Expect from the International," *DD*, 30 June 1934, p. 36; emphases in the original. Richard Bernaschek, the undisputed leader of the Linz Schutzbund uprising, the conflict which triggered the Austrian revolt of February 1934, even took it upon himself to personally travel to Moscow to plead for unity. In August he met Knorin, Bela Kun and Manuilski, but he returned to the West when he was told by the latter that such ventures would be premature. Richard Bernaschek to Friedrich Adler, 17 October 1934. VGA, Adler-Archiv, Mappe 85. See also Inez Kykal and Karl Stadler, *Richard Bernaschek: Odyssey eines Rebellen* (Wien: Europaverlag, 1976), pp. 171–193.

37. Otto Bauer to Friedrich Adler, 11 July 1934, p. 1. VGA, Adler-Archiv, Mappe 84/70. The expression Pfundblock was used by the LSI-Left to describe the conservative wing of the LSI, particularly the Scandinavians and the British. It became synonymous with the term Rechtsblock.

38. See Kowalski, *Geschichte der Sozialistischen*, p. 208.

39. "The Events in Spain," *II*, 13 October 1934, pp. 497–498; and the introduction to the document collection on "The Negotiations in Brussels on Joint Action Between Communist International and LSI," *II*, 20 October 1934, p. 499.

40. For the immediate reaction in Prague, see the memorandum by the LSI secretariat, dated 11 October 1934, "An die Mitglieder des Bureaus der SAI." IISG, SAI, Mappe 3041. On Albarda's subsequent claim to such an immediate principled opposition, see his letter to Friedrich Adler, 15 October 1934, reprinted on pages 2–3 of the appendix to the LSI secretariat's memorandum "An die Mitglieder des Bureaus der SAI," dated 17 October 1934. AdsD, Sopade, Mappe 210.

41. On the flurry of activities within the LSI between 11 and 15 October 1934, see the last of the two memoranda cited in the previous note.

42. See the *Protokoll der Verhandlungen*, which also includes the text of the original Comintern offer.

43. The most informative account of this executive meeting is a firsthand report by Alvarez del Vayo, one of the Spanish socialists present, dated 23 November 1934, "A la Comisión Ejecutiva del Partido Socialista." FPI, AH-22–22. A less detailed summary of the proceedings is given in "Labour Party, International Department. Executive of the Labour and Socialist International. Paris, November 12–16, 1934." IGA, ZPA, I 6/2/45, Blätter 87–92.

44. Reprinted in *II*, 17 November 1934, pp. 568–569.

45. Otto Bauer to Friedrich Adler, 19 October 1934. IISG, Otto Bauer papers, Mappe 1 "Friedrich Adler." The quotations are from pages 2 and 3 of this highly suggestive document.

46. Friedrich Adler to Otto Bauer, 2 November 1934. IISG, Otto Bauer, Mappe 1 "Friedrich Adler." All citations can be found on page 1 of this letter; emphasis in the original. Another copy of this document exists in VGA, Adler-Archiv, Mappe 84/79.

47. "For the Commission on Item 2 of the Agenda. Draft Resolution submitted by Albarda." IISG, SAI, Mappe 439.

48. Jacques Duclos, *Mémoires 1935–1939* (Paris: Fayard, 1969), pp. 17–18.

49. "Paul" [= Henry Ehrmann] to "Lieber Freund," 19 November 1934. IISG, Otto Bauer, Mappe 2 "Paul Bernhard."

50. Otto Bauer to Theodore Dan, 13 September 1935, p. 1. IISG, Otto Bauer, Mappe 5 "Theodore Dan."

51. His identity is obvious from the description by Bauer quoted previously and from a brief notation by Bauer, according to which the conversation with Fischer took place in Prague on 11–12 September 1935; "Besprechung in Prag am 11. und 12.9.1935." IISG, Otto Bauer, Mappe 37 "Bechyne."

52. See note 50.

53. Theodore Dan to Otto Bauer, 17 September 1935, p. 2. IISG, Otto Bauer, Mappe 5 "Theodore Dan."

54. Theodore Dan to Otto Bauer, 25 September 1935. IISG, Otto Bauer, Mappe 5 "Theodore Dan"; this letter can also be found in Boris Sapir, ed., *Theodore Dan: Letters (1899–1946)* (Amsterdam: IISG, 1985); the citations are on pages 462–463 of the published version. This is the sole letter regarding this secretive enterprise included in this volume. According to the notes supplied by Boris Sapir, the Comintern functionary was most likely Willi Münzenberg, who at that time "had political conversations" with two former Mensheviks, Georg Decker and Alexander Schiffrin, who were then closely associated with the German exile Left. (I thank Padraic Kenney for translating the Russian notes to this German-language document.)

55. Otto Bauer to Theodore Dan, 27 September 1935, p. 1. IISG, Otto Bauer, Mappe 5 "Theodore Dan." The interlocutor was to be the Czech Communist Party leader Smeral; see Bauer's memory protocol, "15.9.1935. Hans Fischer berichtet." IISG, Otto Bauer, Mappe 37.

56. Theodore Dan to Otto Bauer, 30 September 1935, p. 4. IISG, Otto Bauer, Mappe 5 "Theodore Dan."

57. "Translation of Telegram from Executive of Communist International, dated Moscow, September 25th, 1935," in DD, 21 October 1935, pp. 53–54.

58. "Translation of Telegram from Secretary of LSI, dated Brussels, September 25th, 1935," in DD, 21 October 1935, p. 54.

59. Georges Vereeken to Leon Trotsky, 27 September 1935. IISG, Vereeken papers, Classeur 3, Nr.73. "3/73." In this letter Vereeken conveys information received from someone with close ties to the LSI secretariat. On the day of the telegram's arrival, Trotsky had already been notified of this development; see Georges Vereeken to Leon Trotsky, 25 September 1935. IISG, Vereeken papers, Classeur 3, Nr.73. "3/73." Vereeken sent the second letter in part to correct false information included in the first communication.

60. Oskar Pollak to Otto Bauer, 28 September 1935, p. 1. IISG, Otto Bauer, Mappe 13 "Oskar Pollak."

61. Memorandum of the LSI secretariat, "To the Members of the Bureau of the LSI," 29 September 1935. IISG, SAI, Mappe 667.

62. See note 60.

63. The resolution is reprinted in II, 14 October 1935, p. 360. An official statement by the Rechtsblock, including the signature of the SPD's Otto Wels but, significantly, not that of the second German delegate, Rudolf Hilferding, can be found in IISG, SAI, Mappe 458: "Zur Sitzung der Exekutive der SAI, Brüssel, 12. Oktober 1935. Zu Punkt 3 der Tagesordnung." It suggested that their decision to vote in favor of the official resolution, proposed by Bauer, was merely a compromise gesture, and the signatories underscored their firm resolve to abstain from any contact with the Comintern.

The East German contention that the unity advocates actually had a majority in Brussels and that the leadership "waived its statutory right to reach decisions by majority vote" by acceding to the preferences of the more conservative "minority," is, at best, based on wishful thinking. A simple comparison of the voting strength of the representatives present at Brussels shows that the pro–united front forces remained a minority, essentially similar in size to the relationship of forces at the November 1934 executive. For the contention, see Kowalski, Geschichte der Sozialistischen, pp. 218–219 (citation on page 219). A list of the delegates is found in II, 14 October 1935, p. 359, and the pertinent LSI congressional vote distribution table in the unpaginated appendix to Kowalski, "Tabelle zu 6.2.: Die Verteilung der Kongresstimmen." A direct comparison to 1934 can be made on the basis of the data furnished on page 89 in "Labour Party, International Department."

64. For his article, see Otto Bauer, "Einheitsfront in der Weltpolitik," originally published in Der Kampf 2 (October 1935); reprinted in Otto Bauer, Werkausgabe, (Wien: Europaverlag, 1980), 9:544–567. In a series of internal documents for discussion within the LSI-Left, he advocated an identical strategy. Two surviving versions of Bauer's proposals drawn up on the occasion of the Brussels executive can be found in IISG, SAI, Mappen 458 and 3043, IISG, Rafael Abramowitsch papers, Mappe 24 (three copies of the same lengthy document) and IISG, Rafael Abramowitsch, Mappe 24, the latter document being a one-page statement, untitled but with the Russian-language handwritten remark "Zhenia Zyromsky," in the upper left-hand corner. This short form was perhaps the version which Zyromski was prepared to proclaim at Brussels, in case the assembly had found itself completely deadlocked; on this see later discussion. (I thank Ronald Suny for translating the remark.)

65. Otto Bauer to Theodore Dan, 22 October 1935, p. 1. IISG, Otto Bauer, Mappe 5 "Theodore Dan."

66. Otto Bauer to Karl Böchel, 22 October 1935, p. 1. IISG, Otto Bauer, Mappe 3 "Karl Böchel."

67. For a brief survey of these post-1935 interactions, see Kowalski, *Geschichte der Sozialistischen*, pp. 219–249.

68. Handwritten note by Abramovich, in German, undated. IISG, SAI, Mappe 458.

69. Theodore Dan to Otto Bauer, 10 October 1935, p. 1. IISG, Otto Bauer, Mappe 5 "Theodore Dan."

70. Dan to Bauer, 10 October 1935, p. 1.

71. On this, see Otto Bauer, "Einheitsfront in der Weltpolitik," p. 557.

72. Otto Bauer addressed a long letter to Adler spelling out the dangers of this move. Bauer also contacted to this effect Léon Blum, Auguste Bracke, Jean-Baptiste Séverac and Jean Zyromski. See Otto Bauer to Friedrich Adler, 30 November 1935. IISG, Otto Bauer, Mappe 1 "Friedrich Adler." See also Otto Bauer to Léon Blum, 5 December 1935. IISG, Otto Bauer, Mappe 2 "Léon Blum." The major turnaround in the SFIO's slow drift toward the PCF may have been a dramatic confrontation between the consistently more critical general secretary of the SFIO, Paul Faure, and Léon Blum in late January 1936. On this telling episode, see Theodore Dan to Otto Bauer, 28 January 1936. IISG, Otto Bauer, Mappe 5 "Theodore Dan."

73. Theodore Dan to Otto Bauer, 20 December 1935. IISG, Otto Bauer, Mappe 5 "Theodore Dan."

74. Bauer pressed for the elimination of Harry Pollitt from the negotiating team. The nomination of Pollitt was a red herring for the members of the Pfundblock, as, in their eyes, Pollitt represented no one but himself and the few members of his tiny British Communist Party. Pollitt was promptly dropped from the team at Brussels. The memory protocol of Bauer's talk with Smeral, "Gespräch mit Smeral am 15. X. 1935," can be consulted in IISG, Otto Bauer, Mappe 37.

75. "Gespräch mit Ernst Fischer am 19. X. 1935 in Böhmisch-Trübau." IISG, Otto Bauer, Mappe 37. This may have been the one meeting with Bauer that Ernst Fischer claims to remember, although he gives a different location for this encounter. Fischer distorts the content of his exchange with Bauer and depicts it as a last nostalgic meeting with his former mentor. Ernst Fischer, *Erinnerungen und Reflexionen* (Reinbek: Rowohlt, 1969), pp. 340–349. Interestingly, the English translation of this book (Ernst Fischer, *An Opposing Man* [London: Allen Lane, 1974]) simply omits this chapter without any information to this effect.

76. "Bericht Fritz Brügels über ein Gespräch mit Manuilski in Moskau. (Gespräch mit Br. am 20. XII. 1935.)" IISG, Otto Bauer, Mappe 37.

77. "Vaclav" [= Fritz Brügel] to Otto Bauer, 3 January 1936, p. 1. IISG, Otto Bauer, Mappe 3 "Fritz Brügel." The last two sentences are worded as follows in the German original: "Ich glaube dass der Faden, der sich da zu Ihnen spinnt, zu einer wirklichen Brücke werden könnte. Ich glaube, dass unsere ganze Sache davon abhängt, ob es gelingt, die Brücke zu schlagen."

78. "Gespräch in Prag am 5. und 6. Jänner 1936. Gespräch mit Ernst Fischer." IISG, Otto Bauer, Mappe 37. The quote is on page 2.

79. See "Gespräch mit Ernst Fischer in Brünn am 17. Juni 1936" and "Gespräch mit Johann Koplenig in Brünn am 7. Juli 1936." The "Gespräch mit Bucharin in Prag am 2.3.1936" in Fritz Brügel's Prague apartment took place on the occasion of Bukharin's last journey to the West in the course of Moscow's plan to purchase the Marx-Engels Archiv in the possession of the SPD. All memory protocols in IISG, Otto Bauer, Mappe 37.

80. Originally published in *Der Kampf* 3 (October 1936), it is reprinted in Bauer, *Werkausgabe*, 9:671–680.

81. "Gespräch mit Fritz Brügel in Prag am 1. Oktober 1936." IISG, Otto Bauer, Mappe 37. Brügel himself soon moved to the Soviet Union, drifted out of the orbit of the LSI and, in a letter to Bauer in the second half of 1937, showed himself in agreement with the Moscow "line." Undated "Brief aus der Sowjetunion." IISG, Otto Bauer, Mappe 3 "Fritz Brügel."

82. See my brief allusion to this split in European socialist responses to the crisis of the 1930s in chapter 9.

83. Agosti, *Terza Internazionale*, III/2:723.

84. Geoff Eley, "Some Unfinished Thoughts on the Comintern" (manuscript in author's possession, 1985), p. 33.

85. See the works by Roy Medvedev, *Let History Judge* (New York: Alfred A. Knopf, 1972), pp. 152–157, and Pierre Broué, "Trotsky et le bloc des oppositions en 1932," *Cahiers Léon Trotsky* 5 (January–March 1980): 5–33, for the existence of organized factions. J. Arch Getty, *Origins of the Great Purges* (Cambridge: Cambridge University Press, 1985), goes perhaps too far but certainly makes explicit the general sense of fragmentation pervading Soviet society and politics at that time. Finally, reading Moshe Lewin, *The Making of the Soviet System* (New York: Pantheon, 1985), one gets a good sense of a society in flux precisely in the years around 1934.

86. Otto Bauer, for one, was well aware of this connection. In one of his many letters to Dan he ruminated about the motives behind the sudden end of Comintern openness. After consideration of several conjunctural factors he wrote: "But perhaps our attitude is also a reason. The LSI had neglected to use the opportunity offered by the VII [Comintern] Congress. Also the surrogate, to establish contact via the President and Chairman [of the LSI], has not accomplished what was within the range of possibilities. I believe we made a major mistake. *Was Du vor der Minute ausgeschlagen, bringt keine Ewigkeit zurück. . . .*" Otto Bauer to Theodore Dan, 8 February 1936, p. 1. IISG, Otto Bauer, Mappe 5 "Theodore Dan." Ellipses in the original; emphasis added.

87. Theodore Dan to Otto Bauer, 10 February 1936, pp. 1–2. IISG, Otto Bauer, Mappe 5 "Theodore Dan."

88. Theodore Dan to Otto Bauer, 28 January 1936, p. 2. IISG, Otto Bauer, Mappe 5 "Theodore Dan."

89. Dan to Bauer, 28 January 1936, p. 9.

Chapter 4

1. See B. R. Mitchell, *European Historical Statistics, 1750–1970* (London: Macmillan, 1975), p. 161, for the exact figure, which includes the categories of forestry and fishing.

2. Gabriel Jackson furnishes a superb analysis of the promise and structural limitations of Spanish society and economy in the years of the second republic on pp. 78–97 of his classic *The Spanish Republic and the Civil War* (Princeton, N.J.: Princeton University Press, 1967), citation on page 80. An additional insightful assessment of the socioeconomic background to Spanish politics in these years is Manuel Tuñon de Lara, *El movimiento obrero en la historia de España* (Madrid: Taurus, 1972), pp. 805–840.

3. James Joll, *The Anarchists* (London: Methuen, 1979), p. 259.

4. George Woodcock, *Anarchism* (Cleveland: Meridian, 1962), p. 25.

5. E. J. Hobsbawm, *Primitive Rebels*, (New York: Norton, 1965), p. 92; the study is characteristically subtitled *Studies in Archaic Forms of Social Movements in the 19th and*

20th Centuries. In his section on anarchism, Hobsbawm focuses almost exclusively on Andalusian agrarian anarchism of the nineteenth century. That his overall assessment of Catalan anarchism in the 1930s is virtually identical to his treatment of the Andalusian "millenarians" can be gauged from his "Was kann man noch vom Anarchismus lernen?" *Kursbuch* 19 (December 1969): 47–57.

6. Michael Seidman, *Workers Against Work* (Berkeley: University of California Press, 1991), p. 38.

7. Seidman, *Workers Against Work*, p. 42.

8. Seidman's second chapter, entitled "Anarchosyndicalist Ideology," is in general a cogent counterpart to traditional Anglo-Saxon explanations of anarchist successes.

9. On the radicalization of the Spanish social democrats, organized in the PSOE, see chapter 2. The impact of class tensions throughout the Spanish state is masterfully depicted in the model social history of an important European city during these years; see Santos Julià Díaz, *Madrid, 1931–1934: De la fiesta popular a la lucha de clases* (Madrid: Siglo XXI, 1984). Paying equal attention to bourgeois and working-class learning processes, integrating statistical evidence with painstaking attention to the changing dimension of everyday life, Julià convincingly describes the rising cycle of class antagonisms up to their apex in the summer and fall of 1934.

10. For a brief but pithy survey of Catalan bourgeois and petit-bourgeois politics in the second half of the short life of the second Spanish republic, see Albert Balcells, "El sistema de partidos políticos en Cataluña entre 1934 y 1936," in *La II República Española: Bienio rectificador y frente popular, 1934–1936*, ed. José Luis García Delgado (Madrid: Siglo XXI, 1988), pp. 83–104.

11. The best survey of this spectrum of Marxist organizations remains Josep Lluís Martín i Ramos, *Els orígens del Partit Socialista Unificat de Catalunya (1930–1936)* (Barcelona: Curial, 1977), pp. 42–139. The political itinerary of the important USC can also be accessed through the biography of its leading spokesperson; see Miquel Caminal, *Joan Comorera*, 2 vols. (Barcelona: Empúries, 1984), 1:67–238.

12. On the role of Andreu Nin in Spanish politics during the thirties, see Francesc Bonamusa, *Andreu Nin y el movimiento comunista en España (1930–1937)* (Barcelona: Anagrama, 1977), and Pelai Pagès, *Andreu Nin* (Bilbao: Zero, 1975), pp. 131–270. Nin began his activist career in the CNT; he was a CNT delegate to the 1921 founding congress of the Red Trade Union International in Moscow, and he became the secretary general of this International until 1930.

13. The following are key works on the trajectory of the current around Angel Pestaña: Eulàlia Vega, *El trentisme a Catalunya* (Barcelona: Curial, 1980); Angel Maria de Lera, *Angel Pestaña* (Barcelona: Argos, 1978), pp. 263–325; the introductory essay by Antonio Elorza, "El sindicalismo de Angel Pestaña," in Angel Pestaña, *Trayectoria Sindicalista* (Madrid: Tebas, 1974), pp. 5–77; José Peirats, *La CNT en la revolución española*, 2 vols. (Paris: Ruedo Ibérico, 1971), 1:51–73; Angeles Barrio Alonso, *Anarquismo y anarcosindicalismo en Asturias (1890–1936)* (Madrid: Siglo XXI, 1988), pp. 289–359; and John Brademas, *Anarcosindicalismo y revolución en España (1930–1937)* (Esplugues de Llobregat: Ariel, 1974), pp. 70–140. Brademas's slightly reworked 1953 dissertation is perhaps the most solid overall survey of Spanish anarcho-syndicalism in this turbulent decade. Albert Balcells's study of the Pestañist Catalan stronghold, Sabadell, is particularly successful in the depiction of this current's evolution toward political interventionism and the role of united front politics as a crucial element reinforcing this trend away from apoliticism, see Albert Balcells, "La crisis del anarcosindicalismo y el movimiento obrero en Sabadell entre 1930 y 1936," in his *Trabajo industrial y organización obrera en la Cataluña contemporanea (1900–1939)* (Barcelona: Laia, 1974), pp. 181–320. I

also thank Andrew Durgan for pointing out several crucial details in the political evolution of the Pestañist current; see Andrew Durgan to author, 8 December 1994, p. 3.

14. On the BOC's response to fascism in Europe, see Andrew Durgan, "Dissident Communism in Catalonia 1930–1936" (Ph.D. diss., Queen Mary College, University of London, 1988), pp. 136–137, and Victor Alba and Stephen Schwartz, *Spanish Marxism Versus Soviet Communism* (New Brunswick, N.J.: Transaction, 1988), pp. 58–59. For the attention to questions of united front politics on the part of the Spanish Trotskyists, see, for instance, the 1931 article by Andreu Nin, "La situación política, el peligro fascista y la necesidad del frente único del proletariado," reprinted in *Revista "Comunismo" (1931–1934)*, ed. Jesús Pérez (Barcelona: Fontamara, 1978), pp. 295–299. For Pestaña's early interest in the fascist danger, see Lera, *Angel Pestaña*, pp. 295–304.

15. Durgan, "Dissident Communism in Catalonia," pp. 134–136.

16. See Victor Alba, *La alianza obrera* (Madrid: Júcar, 1978), pp. 89–90; Durgan, "Dissident Communism in Catalonia," p. 138; and the minutes of the April meeting, "Informe del delegado del Comité Antifascista Estudiantil a la reunión de la 'Alianza Obrera Contra El Fascismo' celebrada el día 22 de abril en el Ateneo Enciclopedico." IISG, Leon Trotsky papers, Mappe 1153. Alba refers to the presence of the social democratic PSOE and its trade union federation, the UGT, at the first general meeting in the Ateneu, an assertion not corroborated by any other source. The communist presence at the April meeting was a short-lived aftereffect of the brief thaw in Third International politics in the first quarter of 1933 I briefly alluded to in chapter 2.

17. "Ocho mil trabajadores acuden al mitin de Frente Unico," *La Batalla*, 3 August 1933, p. 1; "Alianza Obrera contra el fascismo," *La Batalla*, 10 August 1933, p. 1.

18. Alba, *La alianza obrera*, pp. 76–82; Durgan, "Dissident Communism in Catalonia," pp. 139–145.

19. The founding statement of this unprecedented coalition is reprinted in *La Batalla*, 2 November 1933, p. 1.

20. "¡A todos los trabajadores!" *Adelante*, 10 December 1933, p. 1; reprinted in Alba, *La alianza obrera*, pp. 189–190.

21. Alba, *La alianza obrera*, pp. 98–99.

22. Alba, *La alianza obrera*, pp. 96–98; Marta Bizcarrondo, "Introducción," in *Octubre del 34*, ed. Marta Bizcarrondo (Madrid: Ayuso, 1977), p. 28.

23. *La Lucha*, 20 January 1934, pp. 1–2. This important document can also be consulted in the PCE archive in Madrid under the heading "Una proposición importante del Comité Central del Partido Comunista." AHPCE, legajo 15.

24. "Las Juventudes Comunistas de España proponen a las demás organizaciones juveniles el frente único," *La Lucha*, 24 January 1934, p. 3.

25. See *Adelante*, 3 February 1934, p. 1; 8 February 1934, p. 4; 16 February 1934, p. 4; 18 February 1934, p. 4; *Sindicalismo*, 7 March 1934, p. 3; and *Avance*, 6 February 1934, p. 4, for some instances of communist collaboration in genuine united front ventures.

26. See "Comunicación del Comité Central del Partido Comunista de España" published in *La Lucha*, 6 March 1934. AHPCE, legajo 15; Balbontín's open letter of 5 March, published in *El Socialista*, 6 March 1934, p. 3; and Balbontín's later reminiscence of this incident in his autobiography, *La España de mi experiencia* (Mexico: n.p., 1952), pp. 262–281.

27. See, for instance, "El Partido Comunista Oficial ha sido expulsado, por unanimidad, de la Alianza Obrera de Valencia," *Adelante*, 18 February 1934, p. 1.

28. "Largo Caballero recuerda, con textos de Pablo Iglesias, cuál es la línea tradicional del Partido Socialista, a la que rinde máximo acatamiento," *El Socialista*, 23 January 1991, p. 4.

29. "Acta de la reunión de la Comisión Ejecutiva del Partido Socialista celebrada el día 25 de noviembre de 1933." FPI, AH-I, p. 407.

30. "Acta de la réunion de la Comisión Ejecutiva del Partido Socialista celebrada el día 3 de enero de 1934." FPI, AH-II-1, p. 1.

31. "Acta de la réunion de la Comisión Ejecutiva del Partido Socialista celebrada el día 13 de junio de 1934." FPI, AH-II-1, p. 40.

32. On the post–World War I history of the CNT federation representing the regions of Asturias, León and Palencia, see Barrio Alonso, *Anarquismo y anarcosindicalismo*, pp. 345–402; Ramón Alvarez, *Eleuterio Quintanilla* (Mexico City: Mexicanos Unidos, 1973), pp. 207–342; Peirats, *La CNT en la revolución española*, pp. 82–91; and Alba, *La alianza obrera*, pp. 117–131.

33. The text can be consulted in Paco Ignacio Taibo II, *Asturias 1934*, 2 vols. (Madrid: Júcar, 1980), 1:20–21; Alba, *La alianza obrera*, pp. 205–206; and Peirats, *La CNT en la revolución española*, pp. 90–91. A facsimile of the handwritten text is reproduced in Taibo, *Asturias 1934*, p. 20, which furnishes a detailed narrative of the decisive exchanges leading up to this historic pact. Alba and Peirats reproduce a slightly different version of the pact and date the text to 28 March 1934.

34. For background material on Asturian class relations, see David Ruiz, *Insurrección defensiva y revolución obrera* (Barcelona: Labor, 1988), pp. 70–72, and, above all, Adrian Shubert, *The Road to Revolution in Spain* (Urbana: University of Illinois Press, 1987), pp. 141–162.

35. Taibo, *Asturias 1934*, 1:24–48, vividly depicts the concentrated efforts of the Asturian Left to overcome all odds in their successful attempt to win the population to their side. Another insightful brief analysis of the Asturian Workers' Alliance and its leading individuals can be consulted in Georges Garnier, "Presentación," in *La insurrección de Asturias*, ed. Manuel Grossi Mier (Madrid: Júcar, 1978), pp. i–x. See also Bernardo Díaz Nosty, *La Comuna Asturiana* (Bilbao: Zero, 1975), pp. 84–102.

36. My description of Asturian politics and social conflicts between March and September 1934 relies on the detailed narrative in the first volume of Paco Ignacio Taibo's thoughtfully illustrated two-volume history of the Asturian Commune which must now be regarded as the standard work for years to come.

37. On the PCE's about-face in September, see Rafael Cruz, *El Partido Comunista de España en la II República* (Madrid: Alianza, 1987), pp. 188–195; and the "Resolución del C.C. extraordinario del P.C. de España (Sección de la I.C.) sobre la participación en las Alianzas Obreras." AHPCE, legajo 15. Ever since June, the PCE had approved of the Comintern turn in favor of united fronts "from above," but refused to join existing alliance structures because of their alleged shortcomings.

38. The most insightful works on the post-October history of the Alianzas are Alba, *La alianza obrera*, pp. 164–181, and Marta Bizcarrondo, "Socialistas y comunistas ante la unidad: Las Alianzas Obreras en 1935," in *Estudios de historia de España*, ed. Santiago Castillo, 3 vols. (Madrid: Universidad Internacional "M. Pelayo," 1981), 2:95–111. But see also Emilio Ruiz [= Juan Andrade], "Las Alianzas Obreras y el Partido Socialista," in Bizcarrondo, *Octubre*, pp. 273–288, and the brief but moving report on the last gasp of the movement in favor of united fronts, a meeting of forty thousand supporters in Valencia: Julián Gorkín, "Importancia del mitin de la A.O. de Valencia," *La Batalla*, 13 September 1935, p. 1.

39. Note Hans Hautmann's comment on the growth of the KPÖ after February 1934. According to Hautmann, the KPÖ "constitutes the extremely rare example of a workers' party, which was able to become a mass party under conditions of illegality." Hans Hautmann, "Die Kommunisten," in *Widerstand und Verfolgung in Wien 1934–1945*, ed. Wolfgang Neugebauer (Vienna: Österreichischer Bundesverlag, 1984), p. 213. On this phenomenon,

widely commented on at the time, see also Peter Pelinka, *Erbe und Neubeginn* (Vienna: Europa, 1981), pp. 56–58; Everhard Holtmann, *Zwischen Unterdrückung und Befreiung* (Munich: Oldenbourg, 1978), pp. 177–178; and Franz West, *Die Linke im Ständestaat* (Vienna: Europa, 1978), pp. 63–67.

40. West, *Die Linke im Ständestaat*, pp. 65–67.

41. Joseph Buttinger, *Das Ende der Massenpartei* (Frankfurt: Neue Kritik, 1972), p. 160.

42. See, above all, Margrit Frischauer, "Auseinandersetzungen und Kontakte zwischen Sozialdemokraten und Kommunisten vom 15. Juli 1927 bis zum 12. Februar 1934" (Ph.D. diss., University of Vienna, 1976), pp. 198–208.

43. The trilateral agreement is discussed in West, *Die Linke im Ständestaat*, pp. 71–72, and Pelinka, *Erbe und Neubeginn*, p. 101. The RSÖ was the new name of the SPÖ underground.

44. West, *Die Linke im Ständestaat*, pp. 93–96.

45. "Richtlinien zu unserer Einheitsfrontpolitik," *Die Revolution*, "Mitte April 1935," pp. 5–8, citation on page 7. Already in March 1935 the social democratic youth group sent a similar message to their communist allies; see "Communication from the Revolutionary Socialist Youth of Austria to the Communist Youth Federation of Austria." IISG, Sozialistische Jugend-Internationale, Mappe 257.

46. Letter by Karl Hans Sailer to Otto Bauer, September 1936, p. 13. IISG, Otto Bauer Papers, Mappe 14 "Karl Hans Sailer."

47. Otto Leichter, *Zwischen zwei Diktaturen* (Vienna: Europa, 1968), p. 179.

48. "Übereinkommen zwischen den Revolutionären Sozialisten und der Kommunistischen Partei Österreichs," *Die Revolution*, April 1936, pp. 3–5.

49. For the general context of last-minute overtures of either side, see the contributions by Erich Matthias, "Die Sozialdemokratische Partei Deutschlands," and Siegfried Bahne, "Die Kommunistische Partei Deutschlands," in *Das Ende der Parteien*, ed. Erich Matthias and Rudolf Morsey (Düsseldorf: Droste, 1960), particularly pp. 154–158 and 684–692. But note also the recent study by Donna Harsch, *German Social Democracy and the Rise of Nazism* (Chapel Hill: University of North Carolina Press, 1993).

50. The best surveys of this painful period of transition for the German communists remains Horst Duhnke, *Die KPD von 1933 bis 1945* (Cologne: Kiepenheuer and Witsch, 1972), pp. 137–150, and, from a communist perspective, Siegfried Vietzke, *Die KPD auf dem Wege zur Brüsseler Konferenz* (Berlin: Dietz, 1966), pp. 119–176. On the exceptional flexibility of the Saar KPD, see later discussion.

51. The KPD communication to the SPD asking for this meeting and a SPD protocol of the negotiations are reprinted on pages 238–250 of Erich Matthias, ed., *Mit dem Gesicht nach Deutschland* (Düsseldorf: Droste, 1968).

52. "Rundschreiben des Parteivorstandes der Sopade," "An die Grenzsekretäre und Vertrauensleute," 24 January 1936, citation on page 2. AdsD, Sopade, Mappe 8. The most informative description of the failed attempts to establish a top-level German united front remains Lewis J. Edinger, *German Exile Politics* (Berkeley: University of California Press, 1956), pp. 145–178.

53. Duhnke, *Die KPD von 1933 bis 1945*, p. 142; Vietzke, *Die KPD auf dem Wege zur Brüsseler Konferenz*, p. 189; Detlev Peukert, *Die KPD im Widerstand* (Wuppertal: Peter Hammer, 1980), p. 244. For united front agreements among youth organizations in the underground, see Karl Heinz Jahnke, *Jungkommunisten im Widerstandskampf gegen den Hitlerfaschismus* (Dortmund: Weltkreis, 1977), pp. 132–136.

54. See the text of the agreement and "Material über das Abkommen zwischen den Bezirksleitungen der SPD und der 'Roten Hilfe' in Berlin-Brandenburg" in AdsD, Paul Hertz,

Film XXIII, "33"d. Frank Moraw, in his brief description of this affair, underscores the Prague executive's contention that it was not the "real" Berlin SPD leadership which was behind this venture but only a few individuals. Moraw suggests that these charges cannot be adequately answered, given the lack of documentation. Yet some facts in the SPD materials collection on this case clearly show that even the officially sanctioned Berlin SPD leadership was not at all uninterested in negotiations for a pact. Moraw's summary is on pages 38–40 of his *Die Parole der "Einheit" und die Sozialdemokratie* (Bonn: J. H. W. Dietz Nachf., 1990).

55. See my "Pro-Unity Sentiments in Underground Social Democracy: 1933–1936," in *Between Reform and Revolution: Studies in the History of German Socialism and Communism from 1840 to 1990*, ed. David E. Barclay and Eric D. Weitz (Providence, R.I.: Berghahn, 1996).

56. The best surveys of this episode are contained in Patrik von zur Mühlen, "*Schlagt Hitler an der Saar!*" (Bonn: Neue Gesellschaft, 1979), and Gerhard Paul, "*Deutsche Mutter: heim zu Dir!*" (Cologne: Bund, 1984). The international echo of the Saar united front can be gauged from the fact that the second day's entire afternoon session of the all-important LSI executive committee meeting in November 1934 was devoted to the analysis of the Asturian defeat and the Saar plebiscite. See Julio Alvarez del Vayo's report, "A la Comisión Ejecutiva del Partido Socialista [de España]," p. 6. FPI, AH-22-22.

57. zur Mühlen, "*Schlagt Hitler an der Saar!*" pp. 81–96, gives a succinct overview of the Saar SPD's evolution on this question.

58. zur Mühlen, "*Schlagt Hitler an der Saar!*" pp. 104–116.

59. zur Mühlen, "*Schlagt Hitler an der Saar!*" p. 112.

60. Duhnke, *Die KPD von 1933 bis 1945*, p. 160.

61. Letter by "Max" [= Hermann Schubert] to the KPD politburo, 4 June 1934. IGA, ZPA I 2/3/250 Blatt 108. In this highly suggestive letter Schubert proposed, as one possible response, the offer of a united front "from above."

62. For Wilhelm Pieck's cautious first reply to Schubert, recommending, after consultations with the politburo, an intensification of united fronts "from below," saving a possible top-level approach for a later state, see the letter by "Rich." [= Wilhelm Pieck] to "Max" [= Hermann Schubert], 6 June 1934. IGA, ZPA I 2/3/250, Blatt 109. The 8 June 1934 answer by Schubert is in IGA, ZPA I 2/3/250, Blatt 111. For the 29 June 1934 KPD united front proposal, see *Deutsche Freiheit*, 1/2 July 1934. The agreement itself is reprinted in facsimile in Paul, *Deutsche Mutter*, p. 277.

63. zur Mühlen, "*Schlagt Hitler an der Saar!*" pp. 81–86, and Gerhard Paul, *Max Braun* (St. Ingbert: Werner J. Röhrig, 1987), pp. 64–67.

64. *Deutsche Freiheit*, 18/19 February 1934.

65. Letter by Karl Böchel to Siegmund Crummenerl, 19 August 1934, p. 4. AdsD, Sopade, Mappe 19.

66. The pact is reprinted in facsimile in Rudy Velghe, "De Socialistische Jonge Wacht (1930–1940)" (Ph.D. diss., Rijksuniversiteit Gent, 1981–82), p. 266; major excerpts in English appear in *International Socialist Youth Correspondence* 11 (September 1934): 2–3, emphasis added.

67. Flora, *State, Economy and Society in Western Europe, 1815–1975*, 2 vols. (Frankfurt: Campus, 1983), 1:115.

68. The most detailed accounts of the 6 February 1934 émeute in Paris and the subsequent unity maneuvers of the French Left are Serge Berstein, *Le 6 février 1934* (Paris: Gallimard/Julliard, 1975), and Laurent Bonnevay, *Les Journées sanglantes de février 1934* (Paris: Flammarion, 1935). There are no in-depth studies of 12 February 1934 in Paris. The provincial dimensions of 12 February in France, by contrast, are adequately presented in Antoine Prost, "Les Manifestations du 12 février 1934 en province," in *La France en mouvement*, ed. Jean-Charles Asselaine et al. (Seyssel: Champs Vallon, 1986), pp. 12–30.

69. On the origins of the Comintern's turn toward the united front, see, for instance, Aldo Agosti, *La Terza Internazionale*, 3 vols. in 6 (Rome: Riuniti, 1979) III/2:711–761. Perhaps the most detailed secondary source on the French turn with an eye on internal communist moves is Philippe Robrieux, "1934: On tourne à Moscou," *Cahiers Léon Trotsky* 27 (September 1986): 7–26, and *Cahiers Léon Trotsky* 31 (September 1987): 4–61. Interesting published document collections regarding negotiations in France are (1) *DD*, a supplement to the LSI's official publication *II*, 30 June 1934, pp. 45–56; *DD*, 14 July 1934, pp. 57–68; and, finally, the text of the agreement itself in *DD*, 4 August 1934, pp. 69–70; (2) Marceau Pivert and E. Descourtieux, "La Marche à l'unité d'action antifasciste," *Bataille Socialiste*, 15 November 1934, pp. 6–12, and *Bataille Socialiste*, 15 December 1934, pp. 3–11; (3) Jacques Doriot's open letter to the Communist International, *Pour l'unité d'action* (n.p., [1934]), with a densely packed four-page listing of local united fronts throughout France, including their respective composition, on pages 27–30; and (4) "Archives communistes: Février 1934–juin 1934," *Cahiers d'Histoire de l'Institut de Recherches Marxistes* 18 (1984): 25–83.

70. Pietro Nenni, "The Reclassification of Italian Anti-Fascism," *II*, August 1934, p. 436. For the general context of the Italian agreement, see Alexander De Grand, *The Italian Left in the Twentieth Century* (Bloomington: Indiana University Press, 1989), pp. 68–72. The Italian "Pact for United Action" itself is documented in *DD*, 1 September 1934, pp. 75–76.

71. Nenni, "Reclassification of Italian Anti-Fascism," p. 435; emphasis added.

72. "Manifiesto de presentación de la Alianza Obrera de Cataluña," in Alba, *La alianza obrera*, p. 190.

73. "Übereinkommen," p. 4.

74. "A United Front Agreement in Belgium," *International Socialist Youth Correspondence*, September 1934, p. 2.

75. Here it is worth noting that the lack of a representative sample of *local* united front agreements is a potential handicap for my analysis of united front agreements. Yet the few examples gathered in the course of my research suggest that the major difference merely lies in the greater attention to concrete detail rather than a qualitatively different conception. For one important detail, the occasional inclusion of nonproletarian forces in local alliances, see chapter 8.

76. "Arbeiter, Arbeiterinnen, Schutzbündler, Jungarbeiter!" *Die Revolution*, "Ende Juli" [1934], p. 1: "Für die Befreiung der gefangenen Klassenkämpfer!"

77. "Manifiesto de presentación," pp. 189–190.

78. *DD*, 4 August 1934, p. 69.

79. I have been unable to locate the text of the July 1934 Austrian agreement, if indeed such a text was ever formulated. See note 43 for the initial joint communiqué of the RSÖ and the KPÖ. The first public statement of the Asturian Alianza Obrera was published as "La unión proletaria: Una Alianza entre las fuerzas sindicales de la UGT y CNT y la Federación Socialista Asturiana" in *Avance*, 1 April 1934, p. 1.

80. *DD*, 4 August 1934, p. 69.

81. "La unión proletaria," p. 1.

82. Otto Bauer, "Zwischen zwei Weltkriegen," in his *Werkausgabe*, 9 vols. (Vienna: Europa, 1976), 4:285, 287.

83. "Übereinkommen zwischen RS and KP Floridsdorf," undated, p. 1. VGA, Partei-Archiv, Mappe 137/C; emphasis added.

84. Taibo, *Asturias 1934*, p. 20.

85. Cited in Alvarez del Vayo, "A la Comisión Ejecutiva," p. 7.

86. Alvarez del Vayo, "A la Comisión Ejecutiva," p. 5.

87. Theodore Dan, "Auf dem Wege zur Einheit," *Kampf* (November 1934): 249.

88. Arbeitskreis revolutionärer Sozialisten, "Der Weg zum sozialistischen Deutschland. Eine Plattform für eine Einheitsfront," *Zeitschrift für Sozialismus* 12/13 (September/October 1934): 377–378.

89. Jean Zyromski, "L'Unité d'action en France," undated, p. 5. Centre de Recherches sur l'Histoire des Mouvements Sociaux et du Syndicalisme (CRHMSS) [Paris], Fonds Zyromski, D IV 35; emphasis in the original.

90. Starting in the summer of 1934, parallel to the moves to consolidate united fronts, the forces of radicalized social democracy and sobered Third International communism undertook major initiatives with the ultimate goal of reunifying their forces in one organization. These efforts to overcome the post–World War I division of the working-class Left have thus far received scant attention in the literature on proletarian politics in the thirties. For a first assessment of these efforts from an international perspective, see Reiner Tosstorff, "Die Kommunistische Internationale und die Frage der Einheitspartei während der Volksfront," in *Actes du Colloque sur l'Internationale Communiste: Centenaire Jules Humbert-Droz* (La Chaux-de-Fonds: Fondation Jules Humbert-Droz, 1992), pp. 361–396.

Chapter 5

1. H. S. Person, "Scientific Management as a Philosophy and Technique of Progressive Industrial Stabilization," in *World Social Economic Planning*, ed. M. L. Fleddérus (The Hague: International Industrial Relations Institute, [1932]), p. 153, emphasis in the original.

2. "Diskussion von Dr. F. Meyer zu Schwabedissen," in Fleddérus, *World Social Economic Planning*, p. 281.

3. Alfredo Salsano, "Gli ingegneri e il socialismo: Taylorismo e planismo di fronte alla grande crisi," in *L'Internazionale Oparaia e Socialista tra le due guerre*, ed. Enzo Colloti (Milan: Feltrinelli, 1985), pp. 1181–1216. Salsano is the only scholar to have drawn attention to this 1931 World Social Economic Planning Congress. To the best of my knowledge, this crucial meeting has otherwise been completely ignored by subsequent historiography. Salsano's key contribution, I believe, is his attempt to stress the existence of "a democratic and socialist version of state-centered thinking [*statalismo*]" (p. 1184) away from orthodox liberalism, a flirtation with socialist ideals located in the brief space between the onset of the Great Depression and the rise of Nazism and the horrors of Stalinism, the latter developments facilitating subsequent denunciations of planist approaches as illiberal. This democratic socialist dimension of technocratic thinking in the interwar years is sorely lacking in Charles Maier's seminal piece, "From Taylorism to Technocracy," *Journal of Contemporary History* 5 (1970): 27–61, as well as in Mary Nolan, "The Infatuation with Fordism: Social Democracy and Economic Rationalisation in Weimar Germany," in *Chance und Illusion: Labor in Retreat*, ed. Wolfgang Maderthaner and Helmut Gruber (Vienna: Europa, 1988), pp. 151–184, and Nolan's book-length study, *Visions of Modernity* (New York: Oxford University Press, 1994). Both Nolan and Meier neglect debates in the early years of the Great Depression. Still, their contributions are useful reminders that not everybody in the Amsterdam Koloniaal Instituut subscribed to identical emancipatory ideals.

4. The preceding is based on information from a number of sources, including three different autobiographies written by de Man later in his life: Henri de Man, *Après coup* (Brussels: Toison d'Or, 1941); Henri de Man, *Cavalier Seul* (Geneva: Cheval Ainé, 1948); and Hendrik de Man, *Gegen den Strom* (Stuttgart: Deutsche Verlags-Anstalt, 1953). The most informative biographies are, in chronological order, Peter Dodge, *Beyond Marxism: The Faith and Works of Hendrik de Man* (The Hague: Nijhoff, 1966); Mieke Claeys–Van Haegendoren, *Hendrik de Man* (Antwerp: De Nederlandsche Boekhandel, 1972); and Michel Brélaz, *Henri de Man* (Geneva: Antipodes, 1985).

My stress on the formative experience of World War I should not be interpreted as a tacit agreement with all aspects of Dan S. White's somewhat artificial creation of an analytical category—"socialists of the front generation"—that may very well cover up more than it can possibly reveal; for White's model see his *Lost Comrades: Socialists of the Front Generation 1918–1945* (Cambridge, Mass.: Harvard University Press, 1992).

5. Henry de Man, *The Psychology of Marxian Socialism* (New Brunswick, N.J.: Transaction, 1985), pp. 468–469.

6. De Man, *Gegen den Strom*, p. 197.

7. See Dodge, *Beyond Marxism*, pp. 65–89; Claeys-Van Haegendoren, *Hendrik de Man*, pp. 131–146; and Brélaz, *Henri de Man*, pp. 189–404. An all-too-brief but useful assessment of *Zur Psychologie des Sozialismus* is Peter J. Steinberger's introduction to the 1985 reprint of the English edition, *The Psychology of Marxian Socialism*, (New Brunswick, N.J.: Transaction), pp. v–xiv.

8. This work has been reprinted; see Hendrik de Man, *Joy in Work* (New York: Arno Press, 1977).

9. The exchange of letters between Horkheimer and Friedrich Pollock is recorded in IISG, Nachlass Hendrik de Man, Mappe 336. The text of his speech was published in two parts as "Der neuentdeckte Marx" in the Austro-Marxist journal *Der Kampf* 25 (May 1932): 224–239 and in *Der Kampf* 25 (June 1932): 267–277. This episode may serve as a useful reminder of the intellectual affinities between iconoclasts such as de Man, the Frankfurt School and Austro-Marxism.

10. Archival material regarding the creation and performance of *Wir* can be found in IISG, Hendrik de Man, Mappen 111, 112, 117, 118, 173, 215 and others. To my knowledge, the sole substantive reference to *Wir* in secondary sources is Brélaz, *Henri de Man*, pp. 583–596.

11. This episode can be reconstructed on the basis of material collected in IISG, Hendrik de Man, Mappen 215 and 609. Masereel was just then finishing a similar film with music by the noted composer Arthur Honegger. De Man expected his coproduction with Masereel to have a major impact on socialist cultural productions. "Terribly much has been neglected in this field up to now. If one, for instance, keeps track of what social democracy has been able to come up with in the area of film, one cannot be surprised that, for so many intellectuals, the concept 'social democracy' is linked with the concepts 'mindlessness' and 'artistic backwardness'"; Hendrik de Man to Leo Kerstenberg, late June 1932, p. 3. Mappe 609.

12. Henry de Man, *L'Idée socialiste* (Paris: Grasset, 1935); I have been unable to consult the German original.

13. See his "Vorwort des Verfassers," to Hendrik de Man, *Wende des Sozialismus* (Zurich: VPDD, 1934), p. 6.

14. De Man, *L'Idée socialiste*, p. 504.

15. De Man, *L'Idée socialiste*, pp. 506–507.

16. De Man, *L'Idée socialiste*, p. 523; emphases in the original. On de Man's consistent advocacy of some form of united front politics up to the midthirties, the most instructive evidence dates from the summer of 1927, when he was invited to give the keynote address at the twentieth anniversary festivities of the SYI in Stuttgart. De Man regretted that he could not fit it into his schedule and went on to say, in a letter to Erich Ollenhauer, that if he could have delivered his speech he would have focused on the need to establish a united front between young socialists and young communists as the task of the day. On this, and Ollenhauer's rather hostile response, see the exchange of letters in IISG, Sozialistische Jugend-Internationale, Mappe 520.

17. Henri de Man, *Refléxions sur l'économie dirigée* (Paris: L'Églantine, 1932), pp. 39–40.

18. On the origins of the BES, see Brélaz, *Henri de Man*, pp. 631–639. The letter from de Man to Émile Vandervelde, dated 29 October 1932, is reprinted in Robert Abs, *Catalogue [du fonds Émile Vandervelde]*, 2 vols., 2:33–34, citation on page 33.

19. See "Vorwort des Verfassers," in his *Wende des Sozialismus*, p. 6.

20. The articles in the *Hamburger Echo* were eventually republished in a brochure by the Swiss union of public employees in early 1934 as *Wende des Sozialismus*.

21. De Man, *Wende des Sozialismus*, p. 21; emphasis in the original.

22. De Man, *Wende des Sozialismus*, p. 21; emphases in the original. It is unlikely that de Man knew of Gramsci's work at this time, although Gramsci knew the work of de Man. On ideological affinities between Gramsci and de Man, see Brélaz, *Henri de Man*, pp. 309–346.

23. De Man, *Wende des Sozialismus*, p. 21; emphases in the original.

24. See the schematic outline, entitled "Bureau (ou Institut) d'Études et de Documentation Pour l'Économie Planée." IISG, Hendrik de Man, Mappe 421; the date is given in the index to the de Man papers in the Amsterdam IISG.

25. On the work of the BES, see Brélaz, *Henri de Man*, pp. 687–695; the abridged minutes of the Séminaire d'Études Économiques et Financières du Groupement Universitaire d'Études Sociales can be consulted in IISG, Hendrik de Man, Mappe 396. Autobiographical fragments of one of the members of the BES brain trust can be consulted in Jef Rens, *Rencontres avec le siècle* (Paris: Duculot, 1987). A lengthy interview with Jef Rens, "Jef Rens and Belgian Socialism," is included in Steven Philip Kramer, *Socialism in Western Europe* (Boulder, Colo.: Westview, 1984), pp. 91–130.

26. The most detailed description of the mechanism of adoption of the plan in the second half of 1933 is provided in Monique Biart-Gosset, "Le POB et l'adoption du Plan du Travail" (Mémoire de licence, Université Catholique de Louvain, 1974), pp. 93–121. Two copies of one crucial document, the "Note soumise par H. de Man au Bureau du C.G. du P.O.B. en vue de sa séance du 27 octobre 1933," can be consulted either in IISG, Hendrik de Man, Mappe 422, or in the Archief en Museum van het Vlaamse Cultuurleven (AMVC) [Antwerp], Verzameling Hendrik de Man, Mappe F304.

27. Henri de Man, *Pour un plan d'action* (Brussels: L'Églantine, 1933).

28. De Man, *Pour un plan*, p. 5; emphasis in the original.

29. De Man, *Pour un plan*, p. 6.

30. De Man, *Pour un plan*, p. 9.

31. De Man, *Pour un plan*, p. 14.

32. De Man, *Pour un plan*, p. 15; emphasis in the original.

33. De Man, *Pour un plan*, p. 21. This theme was enhanced upon in later writings by de Man. In September 1934, for instance, he postulated that "[t]he essence of nationalisation is less the transfer of ownership than the transfer of authority; or, more exactly, the problem of administration takes precedence over that of possession, and changes in the property system are functions of changes in the system of authority required by the managed economy." "Thesis of Pontigny," in *A Documentary Study of Hendrik de Man, Socialist Critic of Marxism*, ed. Peter Dodge (Princeton, N.J.: Princeton University Press, 1979), p. 303.

34. De Man, *Pour un plan*, pp. 21–22.

35. De Man, *Pour un plan*, p. 28.

36. The English-language text of the Plan of Labor can be consulted in Dodge, *Documentary Study of Hendrik de Man*, pp. 290–299.

37. José Gotovitch, "Du collectivisme au Plan du Travail," in *1885/1985: Du Parti Ouvrier Belge au Parti Socialiste*, ed. Claude Desama (Brussels: Labor, 1985), pp. 123–143, citation on page 133.

38. See, for instance, Isi Delvigne, *Tuons la crise: Le Plan du Travail* (Brussels: Éditions de la Presse Socialiste, n.d.), an approximately eighty-page brochure with photos, art reproductions, cartoons and statistics; Herman Vos, *Le Plan du Travail et l'Encyclique Papale Quadragesimo Anno* (Brussels: L'Églantine, 1934), a thirty-page pamphlet geared toward the Catholic sector; or Oscar de Swaef, *Plan van den Arbeid* (Brussels: Actiebureau voor het Plan, n.d.), a twenty-five-page pamphlet directed specifically at Christian workers.

39. The preceding draws on information in Gotovitch, "Du collectivisme"; Freddy Verbruggen, "Terug naar het Plan van den Arbeid (1933)," *Bulletin de l'Association pour l'Étude de l'Oeuvre d'Henri de Man* 12 (December 1984): 3–28; and Wouter Steenhaut, "De propaganda voor het Plan van de Arbeid," *Bulletin de l'Association pour l'Étude de l'Oeuvre d'Henri de Man* 16 (November 1989): 13–15. Unfortunately, I have been unable to procure a copy of the thesis by Frank Eelens, "De propaganda voor en de reakties op het Plan van den Arbeid" (Licentiaatsverhandeling, Rijksuniversiteit Gent, 1976).

40. Henri de Man, "Le Socialisme devant la crise," *La Vie Socialiste*, 22 December 1934, p. 9.

41. On the history of Action Socialiste see, above all, Michel Staszewski, "L'Action Socialiste" (Mémoire de licence, Université Libre de Bruxelles, 1974–75).

42. See Rudy Velghe, "De Socialistische Jonge Wacht (1930–40)" (Licentiaatsverhandeling, Rijksuniversiteit Gent, 1981–82), on the impact of the JGS on Belgian politics. The international dimension is touched upon in Erich Wittmann, *Zwischen Faschismus und Krieg: Die Sozialistische Jugendinternationale 1932–1940* (Vienna: Europa, 1982).

43. See the English translation of the text in Dodge, *Documentary Study of Hendrik de Man*, p. 291; emphasis added.

44. Speech by Hendrik de Man in *Compte rendu sténographique du XXXXVIII Congrès* (Brussels: L'Églantine, 1934), p. 33.

45. De Man, "Socialisme devant la crise," p. 8.

46. Speech by Paul-Henri Spaak, *Compte rendu stenographique du XXXXVIII Congrès*, pp. 105–106.

47. See the table on page 143 of the *Compte rendu Stenographique du XXXXVIII Congrès*, which reports the complete results of the congress vote.

48. Paul-Henri Spaak, "Le Plan du Travail: III. Ses mérites," *L'Action Socialiste*, 16 December 1933, p. 1.

49. Paul-Henri Spaak, "Le Plan du Travail: II. Ses mérites," *L'Action Socialiste*, 9 December 1933, p. 1; emphasis in the original.

50. Fernand Godefroid, "Rapport Moral 1934," in *Congrès National: 10–11 Novembre 1934* (Brussels: FNJGS, n.d.), p. 12.

51. Walter Dauge, "Réponse à de Man," *L'Action Socialiste*, 9 June 1934, p. 2.

52. Hendrik de Man to Paul-Henri Spaak, 4 June 1934, reprinted in *L'Action Socialiste*, 9 June 1934, p. 2.

53. Léo Moulin to author, cassette, 14 January 1991.

54. Michael Schneider, letter to author, 21 January 1991.

55. See, for instance, the document in the annex to Fritz Weber, "Zwischen Marx und Keynes," in Maderthaner and Gruber, *Chance und Illusion*, pp. 106–109. On the pre-1933 German trade union's elaboration of a work creation program, see, above all, Michael Schneider, *Das Arbeitsbeschaffungsprogramm des ADGB* (Bonn: Neue Gesellschaft, 1975).

56. Although Jakob Marschak was at least once, on 6 October 1933, invited to give a lecture in Brussels on "Money, Credit and the Conjuncture" to the group of experts deliberating the contours of the Plan de Man. Alfred Braunthal, a native Austrian who for many years worked at the Berlin economic research institute of the German trade union federa-

tion, for a while actively participated in the deliberations of the Belgian planist brain trust as well. See "Compte rendu(s) abrégé(s) des interventions du Séminaire d'Études Économiques . . ." in IISG, Hendrik de Man, Mappe 396.

57. Wilhelm Hoegner to "Michel" [= Waldemar von Knoeringen], 1 March 1935, p. 2. Institut für Zeitgeschichte (IfZ) [Munich], Nachlass Wilhelm Hoegner, Band 6.

58. Alexander Schifrin, "Revolutionäre Sozialdemokratie," *Zeitschrift für Sozialismus* (*ZfS*) (December 1933): 87.

59. Max Klinger [= Curt Geyer], "Sozialistische Erneuerung," *Neuer Vorwärts*, 7 January 1934, p. 1.

60. See, for instance, Richard Kern [= Rudolf Hilferding], "Das planwirtschaftliche Experiment Nordamerikas," subtitled "Die Unmöglichkeit der kapitalistischen Versuche zur Lösung der Weltkrise," *Deutsche Freiheit*, 3 August 1933.

61. See the report on the national conference of Austrian socialist trade unions "Arbeit für zweihunderttausend Arbeitslose!", *AZ*, 16 July 1933.

62. O[skar] P[ollak], "Das Ende des Reformismus," *AZ*, 30 July 1933, p. 4.

63. "Acta de la Reunión Celebrada por la Comisión Ejecutiva del Partido Socialista el día 9 de diciembre de 1933," p. 416 (de los Ríos) and p. 417 (Largo Caballero). FPI, AH-I.

64. Besteiro's penchant for the thought of Hendrik de Man, though perhaps more for the de Man of *Zur Psychologie des Sozialismus* than the de Man of *Wende des Sozialismus*, and for planist ideology in general can be gauged, for instance, from a parliamentary intervention in March 1934, where Besteiro called de Man "more Marxist than Marx"; see "El Parlamento en funciones: Brillante disertación del compañero Besteiro sobre Economía política, en busca de soluciones efectivas y permanentes al problema del paro," *El Socialista*, 16 March 1934, p. 4. See also his "El marxismo y la actualidad política"; "Prólogo a Sir Stafford Cripps, 'Problemas de gobierno socialista'"; and "La nueva política: Roosevelt" in *Obras Completas*, 3 vols. (Madrid: Centro de Estudios Constitucionales, 1983), 3:15–42, 117–125, 139–148.

65. On this episode see Achille Dauphin-Meunier, "Lucien Laurat, l'Espagne et le plan," *Est & Ouest* 515 (16–30 September 1973): 8–9. Laurat was actually an Austrian by the name of Otto Maschl.

A first assessment of the impact of radical planism on Italian antifascist circles is Leonardo Rapone, "Il planismo nei dibattiti dell'antifascismo italiano," in *Crisi e piano*, ed. Mario Telò (Bari: De Donato, 1979), pp. 269–288. On the important Swiss campaign for planism, strongest among public employees, see Michel Brélaz, "Le Plan du travail suisse," *Bulletin de l'Association pour l'Étude de l'Oeuvre d'Henri de Man* 12 (December 1984): 45–66.

66. Amédée Dunois, "Refléxions sur le 'Plan,'" *Bataille Socialiste* 78 (15 April 1934), p. 8. I adopt the term "planomania" from one of the subchapter headings of Julian Jackson, *The Politics of Depression in France, 1932–1936* (Cambridge: Cambridge University Press, 1985).

67. Lucien Laurat, "Mémoires d'un planiste (1932–1939)," *Études Sociales et Syndicales* 120 (September 1965): 19–24.

68. On the history of Révolution Constructive, see Georges Lefranc, "Histoire d'un groupe du Parti Socialiste SFIO: Révolution Constructive (1930–1938)," in his *Essais sur les problèmes socialistes et syndicaux* (Paris: Payot, 1970), pp. 169–196; but especially the recent work by Stéphane Clouet, *De la rénovation á l'utopie socialistes* (Nancy: Presses Universitaires de Nancy, 1991). The original book which gave the group its name is Georges Lefranc et al., *Révolution Constructive* (Paris: Valois, 1932).

69. Georges Lefranc, *Le Mouvement socialiste* (Paris: Payot, 1963), p. 309; but see also Lefranc, "Le Courant planiste dans le mouvement ouvrier français de 1933 à 1936," in *Essais*, pp. 197–220; Richard Kuisel, *Capitalism and the State in Modern France* (Cambridge:

Cambridge University Press), pp. 108–119; Jackson, *Politics of Depression in France*, pp. 137–155; and especially Jean-François Biard, *Le Socialisme devant ses choix* (Paris: Publications de la Sorbonne, 1985), pp. 109–246. The resolution is reprinted as "Pour l'offensive socialiste," in *Le Combat Marxiste*, 15 February 1934, p. 4.

70. Lefranc, *Le Mouvement socialiste*, p. 309.

71. "Manifeste," *Bataille Socialiste*, 15 January 1935, p. 1. Some of the more prominent plans were Groupe de Révolution Constructive, *Éléments d'un plan français* (Asnières: Cahier de Révolution Constructive, 1934); the *Plan du 9 juillet* (Paris: Gallimard, 1934), with a preface by the novelist Jules Romains; and the "Exposé sur le plan de rénovation économique de la C.G.T.," *La Voix du Peuple* 167 (September 1934); followed by the publication of the final version of the CGT's plan, Léon Jouhaux, *Le Plan de rénovation économique et sociale* (Paris: Confédération Générale du Travail, 1935). Perhaps the most succinct description of the various planist alternatives, socialist and nonsocialist alike, can be found in Jackson, *Politics of Depression in France*, pp. 137–166. But see also the "Revue des plans français," in the Belgian weekly devoted to planist propaganda *Plan*, 8 July 1934, p. 6, and 15 July 1934, p. 6.

72. The final occlusion of radical planism is brilliantly analyzed in Biard, *Le Socialisme*, pp. 249–288. But see also Claude Harmel, "Le Front populaire contre le planisme," *Études Sociales et Syndicales* 120 (September 1965): 2–18. Harmel calls the popular front "the tomb of planism" (p. 2).

73. "La Troisième Vague," *Plan*, 16 December 1934, p. 1.

74. "Vive le front du travail! Les Commerçants de Liège y adhèrent," *Plan*, 10 February 1935, p. 2. The degree of success in attracting nonsocialist population groups to the banner of the plan needs further research. For some cautionary remarks on the limited impact of planist propaganda among Catholics, see Claeys–Van Haegendoren, *Hendrik de Man*, pp. 201–206.

75. Léo Moulin, cassette to author, 16 March 1991. Commenting on this passage, a biographer of Hendrik de Man, A. M. Peski, in a recent communication, voiced his qualified dissent: "That de Man was only a man of books and open air is not true; he had political experience." His shortcomings in relation to his role in government administration and the shaping of party tactics were rather "a certain straightforwardness and inflexibility." See A. M. van Peski, letter to author, 24 August 1992, p. 2. For van Peski's biography of de Man, see A. M. van Peski, *Hendrik de Man* (Bruges: Desclée de Brouwer, 1969).

76. De Man, *Après coup*, p. 231; I have taken over the translation of this passage in Dick Pels, "Hendrik de Man and the Ideology of Planism," *International Review of Social History* 32 (1987): 207.

77. De Man, *Après coup*, p. 237.

78. Henri de Man, "Impressions du Borinage: Il est moins cinq," *Le Peuple*, 20 January 1934, p. 1.

79. Léo Moulin, cassette to author, 16 March 1991.

80. Jan de Man, letter to author, 24 March 1991, p. 2.

81. De Man, "Impressions du Borinage," p. 2.

82. Henri de Man, "L'Heure du plan doit venir avant l'heure de la grève générale," *Le Peuple*, 23 January 1935.

83. *Congrès extraordinaire du P.O.B. et de la C.S.B.* (n.p.: [1935]), p. 28.

84. De Man, *Après coup*, p. 242.

85. *Congrès extraordinaire* (n.p.: [1935]), p. 172.

86. *Congrès extraordinaire*, p. 170.

87. De Man, "Le Socialisme devant la crise," p. 9.

88. De Man, *Die Sozialistische Idee*, p. 499.

89. Max Buset, "Aux J.G.S.," *Plan*, 24 November 1935, p. 1.

90. Blum's ten articles all appeared in January 1934. They are reprinted in Biard, *Le Socialisme*, pp. 293–309.

91. Jean Zyromski, "Pour le Congrès national," *Bataille Socialiste*, 15 April 1934, pp. 1–2. See also his "Précisions pour le Congrès de Toulouse," 7 May 1934. Office Universitaire de Recherche Socialiste (OURS) [Paris], Papiers Maurice Deixonne, 1 APO 5, Dossier 5.

92. Pierre Boivin, "Le Plan et l'unité," originally published in February 1935, reprinted in his *Choix d'écrits* (Paris: Centre Confédérale d'Éducation Ouvrière, 1938), citation on page 239.

93. Robert Marjolin, "Pour une conception révolutionnaire du plan," *Révolution Constructive*, December 1934, p. 2.

94. Étienne [= Claude] Beaurepaire, "Plan et insurrection," *Révolution Constructive*, 31 May 1935, pp. 2–3. An insightful discussion of the appropriation of planism by the SFIO-Left can be studied in Biard, *Le Socialisme*, pp. 197–207.

95. The best overview of moderate experiments at social Keynesianism by European social democrats in the mid-1930s is Mario Telò, *Le New Deal Européen*. Telò portrays Swedish and British social democratic variations of planist theory and practice, on top of the Belgian case, which he includes in the same category of essentially reformist enterprises. While the lineage and filiation of British and Swedish planisms are subject to debate, one clear case of a moderate adaptation of the Belgian model is the Dutch Plan, which is best depicted in John Jansen van Galen et al., *Het moet, het kan! Op voor het Plan!* (Amsterdam: Bert Bakker, 1985).

96. Witness the absence of references to Belgian or French radical planist thought in Robin Blackburn's otherwise lucid discussion of the antecedents of contemporary market socialist ideas in his "Fin de Siècle: Socialism After the Crash," *New Left Review* 185 (January–February 1991): 5–66. But note, for instance, the revival of interest in the legacy of radical planism in Belgium starting in the 1960s, strongly suggested by Denise De Weerdt; see Denise De Weerdt to author, 24 August 1995.

97. Goetz Briefs, "Diskussion," in Fleddérus, pp. 252–253.

98. Charles Maier, "From Taylorism to Technocracy," *Journal of Contemporary History* 5 (1970):60.

Chapter 6

1. *Compte rendu sténographique du XXXXVIII Congrès* (Brussels: L'Églantine, 1934), p. 25.

2. *Compte rendu sténographique du XXXXVIII Congrès*, p. 20.

3. "Informe del delegado del Comité Antifascista Estudiantil a la reunión de la 'Alianza Obrera Contra el Fascismo' celebrada el día 22 de abril en el Ateneo Enciclopedico," pp. 1–2. IISG, Leon Trotsky papers, Mappe 1153.

4. Robert O. Paxton, *Europe in the Twentieth Century* (New York: Harcourt Brace Jovanovich, 1975), p. 379.

5. On the difficulties of judging the social basis of Radical parties, see Jacques Kergoat, *La France du front populaire* (Paris: La Découverte, 1986), pp. 14–16, and Juan Avilés Farré, *La izquierda burguesa en la II República* (Madrid: Espasa-Calpe, 1985), p. 340.

6. Quoted in Jean-Thomas Nordmann, *Histoire des Radicaux* (Paris: La Table Ronde, 1974), p. 323.

7. Leon Trotsky, *Whither France?* (New York: Merit, 1968), p. 57.

8. Louis-Olivier Frossard, "Contre le fascisme: Le Front de la République," *Le Populaire*, 24 October 1934, p. 6.

9. Jean Zyromski, "L'Unité d'action et les 'classes moyennes,'" *Le Populaire*, 24 October 1934, p. 6.

10. Jean-Baptiste Lebas, "La Marche à l'unité organique," *Le Populaire*, 29 October 1934, p. 6.

11. Louis-Olivier Frossard, "La Défense de la République," *Le Populaire*, 1 November 1934, p. 6.

12. "Histoire du Parti Socialiste SFIO," vol. 10, *Cahiers & Revue de l'Ours* 63 (October 1975): 70–71.

13. John T. Marcus, *French Socialism in the Crisis Years 1933–1936* (New York: Praeger, 1958), p. 150.

14. Karl G. Harr Jr., *The Genesis and Effect of the Popular Front in France* (Lanham, Md.: University Press of America, 1987), p. 199.

15. See chapter 10, "Mulhouse, June 1935," in Harr, *Genesis and Effect*, pp. 198–229, citations on pages 213, 217.

16. The literature on the French popular front is enormous, and I will therefore highlight only some of the standard works which I found most useful in my analysis of this phenomenon. The course of social democracy toward the embrace of a popular front orientation can be best followed in the aforementioned chapter 10 of Harr's dissertation and in Marcus, *French Socialism in the Crisis Years*, pp. 119–174. Daniel P. Brower, *The New Jacobins* (Ithaca, N.Y.: Cornell University Press, 1968), pp. 85–122, adequately covers the PCF turn. The Radical Party's decision to abandon participation in a series of National Union governments and to throw in its lot with the working-class Left is best described in Serge Berstein, *Histoire du Parti Radical*, 2 vols. (Paris: FNSP, 1982), 2:354–418. The best general surveys are Kergoat, *La France du front populaire*; Georges Lefranc, *Histoire du front populaire* (Paris: Payot, 1965); Jacques Delperrié de Bayac, *Histoire du front populaire* (Paris: Fayard, 1972); Julian Jackson, *The Popular Front in France Defending Democracy, 1934–1938* (Cambridge: Cambridge University Press, 1988); and Jean-Paul Brunet, *Histoire du front populaire (1934–1938)* (Paris: PUF, 1991).

17. George Lefranc (*Histoire du front populaire*) on pages 66–67, reports a socialist gain of 14 seats, a communist advance of 18 seats, and a Radical loss of 21; the author of the "Histoire du Parti Socialiste SFIO," 10:67, reports an SFIO gain of 16 and 20 additional communist representatives; according to Berstein (*Histoire du Parti Radical*, 2:336), the Radicals lost 17 seats, and Berstein calls it "an incontestable defeat"; Brower (*The New Jacobins*), on pages 73–74, reports a net gain of only 3 more SFIO councillors, 17 more communists and, lumping together the Radicals with other left-center groups and individuals, reports their loss of 49 seats.

18. The quote is from Berstein, *Histoire du Parti Radical*, 2:349. On socialist gains, see "Histoire du Parti Socialiste SFIO," 10:8, and Lefranc, *Histoire du front populaire*, pp. 71–72; these two analyses also refer to the doubling of the PCF's municipal councillors.

19. Berstein, *Histoire du Parti Radical*, 2:349.

20. Berstein, *Histoire du Parti Radical*, 2:436–445, Lefranc, *Histoire du front populaire*, pp. 125–129, and Delperrié de Bayac, *Histoire du front populaire*, pp. 193–197, are the most informative sources on electoral results. Again, depending on the count, reports differ on the specific impact. Kergoat, for instance, reports a communist gain of 61, a socialist gain of only 16, but a Radical decline of 51 seats; see *La France du front populaire*, p. 94.

21. Berstein, *Histoire du Parti Radical*, 2:437.

22. Daniel Guérin, *Front populaire, révolution manquée* (Paris: René Julliard, 1963), p. 79.

23. Ricard Vinyes i Ribes, *La Catalunya internacional: El frontpopulisme en l'exemple Català* (Barcelona: Curial, 1983).

24. Manuel Tuñon de Lara, "Frentes populares / Unidad popular," in *Tres Claves de la Segunda República* (Madrid: Alianza, 1985), p. 327. See also Victor Alba, "La obsesión por la amnistía," in his *La Alianza Obrera* (Madrid: Júcar, 1978), pp. 174–177, and Alba, "¿Elecciones para la amnistía?" in *El Frente Popular* (Barcelona: Planeta, 1976), pp. 273–277.

25. On this see, above all, Santos Juliá, *Orígenes del Frente Popular en España (1934–1936)* (Madrid: Siglo XXI, 1979); Santos Juliá, *Manuel Azaña, una biografía política* (Madrid: Alianza, 1990), pp. 387–439; Alfonso Carlos Saíz Valdivielso, *Indalecio Prieto* (Barcelona: Planeta, 1984), pp. 175–185; Juan Avilés Farré, *La izquierda burguesa en la II República* (Madrid: Espasa-Culpe, 1985), pp. 253–274; Marta Bizcarrondo, "Democracia y revolución en la estrategía socialista de la II República," *Estudos de Historia Social* 16–17 (January–June 1981): 312–458; and the two contemporary document collections advertising Prieto's point of view: Indalecio Prieto et al., *Documentos socialistas* (Madrid: Indice, [1935]), and Prieto, *Posiciones socialistas* (Madrid: Indice, 1935).

26. The outstanding reference work on the evolution of the PSOE-Left remains Santos Juliá, *La izquierda del PSOE (1935–1936)* (Madrid: Siglo XXI, 1977). But see also Francisco Largo Caballero, *Escritos de la República* (Madrid: Pablo Iglesias, 1985), pp. 159–298, and the two contributions by Santos Juliá, "República, revolución y luchas internas," and Marta Bizcarrondo, "La Segunda República: Ideologías socialistas," in *El socialismo en España*, ed. Santos Julià (Madrid: Pablo Iglesias, 1986), pp. 231–254, 255–274. Imprisoned PSOE members by no means solely included supporters of Largo Caballero's team. The Asturian leadership, for instance, was likewise incarcerated, although they fully supported the more moderate orientation advocated by Prieto almost immediately after the Asturian defeat.

27. See Paco Ignacio Taibo II, *Asturias 1934*, 2 vols. (Madrid: Júcar, 1980) 1:15.

28. An insightful, brief analysis of the changes affecting the outlook of the Asturian Left is Adrian Shubert, "A Reinterpretation of the Spanish Popular Front: The Case of Asturias," in *The French and Spanish Popular Fronts*, ed. Martin S. Alexander and Helen Graham (Cambridge: Cambridge University Press, 1989), pp. 213–225. The citation is from a letter by Adrian Shubert to the author, 11 May 1992, p. 1.

29. The most detailed reconstruction of this period of initial preparation of the pact is the collection of Largo Caballero's writings, annotated by Santos Juliá, *Escritos de la República*, pp. 254–287.

30. Juliá, *Orígenes*, pp. 137–138.

31. "Frente Popular: Documentación sobre el pacto electoral de febrero de 1936," p. 3. FPI, AH-25–29.

32. "Frente Popular: Documentación," p. 4.

33. "Frente Popular: Documentación," pp. 4–5.

34. "Frente Popular: Documentación," p. 5.

35. "Manifiesto electoral de Izquierda (Pacto del Frente Popular)," in Juliá, *Orígenes*, pp. 216–217.

36. "Frente Popular: Documentación," pp. 6–7; Juliá, *Orígenes*, pp. 140–141; "Manifiesto electoral," pp. 218–221.

37. Juliá's description of these events is unsurpassed; see his *Orígenes*, pp. 138–145, citation on page 144.

38. On these behind-the-scenes maneuvers see, above all, Juliá, *Orígenes*, pp. 145–146; Juliá, *Manuel Azaña*, pp. 447–449; and Javier Tusell, *Las elecciones del frente popular en España*, 2 vols. (Madrid: Cuadernos para el Diálogo, 1971), 1:66–68. Alba, *Frente popular,*

pp. 372–382, is an additional source of information and furnishes a useful brief introduction to the mechanics of the Spanish electoral system in 1936.

39. Ricardo Miralles Palencia, *El socialismo vasco durante la II República* (Bilbao: Servicio, 1988), p. 290.

40. Juan-Simeón Vidarte, *Todos fuimos culpables* (Barcelona: Grijalbo, 1978), p. 38.

41. Maria Concepción Marcos del Olmo, *Las elecciones del frente popular en Valladolid* (Valladolid: Diputación Provincial de Valladolid, 1986), p. 93.

42. Juliá, *Manuel Azaña*, pp. 449-450.

4343. One-page memorandum from the PSOE headquarters to its federations in FPI, AH-19-15, 9. The extant document is undated, but the response by the federations uniformly refers to it as written on 27 December 1935.

44. Federación Provincial Socialista de Madrid to the PSOE executive, 31 December 1935. FPI, AH-17-42, 1.

45. Federación Provincial Socialista de Madrid to the national PSOE executive, 21 January 1936. FPI, AH-17-42, 3–5; citation on page 4.

46. Federación Provincial Socialista de Madrid to the PSOE executive, 29 February 1936. FPI, AH-17-12, 20.

47. Federación Socialista Murciana to the PSOE national executive, 31 December 1935. FPI, AH-6-15, 32.

48. Minutes of a meeting by the Murcia popular front, 20 January 1936. FPI, AH-6-15, 37.

49. Minutes, 20 January 1936. FPI, AH-6-15, 37 y reverso.

50. Agrupación Socialista de Murcia to the PSOE executive, undated. FPI, AH-6-15, 59.

51. Comisión Ejecutiva de la Federación Provincial de Alicante to the PSOE national executive, 31 December 1935. FPI, AH-4-26, 2 y reverso.

52. Comisión Ejecutiva de la Federación Provincial de Alicante to the PSOE national executive, 21 January 1936. FPI, AH-4-26, 8 y reverso.

53. Comisión Ejecutiva de la Federación Provincial de Alicante to the PSOE national executive, 23 January 1936. FPI, AH-4-26, 10. See also the joint letter of protest by the Alicante PSOE, PCE and their respective youth organizations sent to the national arbitration committee in FPI, AH-4-26, 12.

54. Comisión Ejecutiva de la Federación Provincial de Alicante to the PSOE national executive, 30 January 1936. FPI, AH-4-26, 13.

55. Juliá, *Orígenes*, pp. 145–146.

56. Tusell, *Las elecciones del frente popular*, 2:13.

57. Tusell, *Las elecciones del frente popular*, 2:82-83.

58. Estimates by *Le Temps*, reported in Kergoat, *La France du front populaire*, p. 90 n. 53.

59. Kergoat, *La France du front populaire*, p. 96; eight representatives were independent.

60. Kergoat, *La France du front populaire*, p. 96, for the French figures; Tusell, *Las elecciones del frente popular*, 2:83, for the Spanish case.

61. Federación Socialista Murciana to the PSOE national executive, 6 June 1936. FPI, AH-6-16, 37.

62. Agrupación Socialista de Alhama de Murcia to the Agrupación Socialista de Madrid, 13 April 1936. FPI, AH-5-7, 1.

63. Agrupación Socialista de La Roda (Albacete) to the PSOE national executive, 28 March 1936. FPI, AH-11-35, 1.

64. Agrupación Socialista de La Roda (Albacete) to the PSOE national executive, 14 May 1936. FPI, AH-11-35, 3.

65. Letter by the PSOE to the IR, 21 June 1936. FPI, AH-11-35, 4. The IR response, dated 26 May 1936, is in FPI, AH-11-35, 7.

66. Agrupación Socialista de La Roda (Albacete) to the PSOE national committee, 16 June 1936. FPI, AH-11-35, 9.

67. For the Ciudad Real case, see Comisión Ejecutiva de la Federación Socialista Provincial, Ciudad Real to the PSOE national executive, 31 May 1936. FPI, AH-5-1. The Agrupación Socialista de Sayatón (Guadalajara) informed the PSOE executive on 18 June 1936 of the preponderance of known reactionaries ("caciques sempiternos o esbirros de ellos, romanonistas y clericales siempre, que se han distinguido por su boicoteo a las leyes sociales y laicas de la República") in the local branch of the IR. FPI, AH-4-37, 8.

68. "Reseña de la fiesta que para commemorar el 5 anniversario de la República se ha celebrada en El Provencio." FPI, AH-12-12, 2.

69. To grasp the magnitude of this dimension of the problem, consider the following plea by the Pontevedra local of the PCE to its parliamentary faction in Madrid. The Galician communists enjoined their representatives "to defend the possibility that the Isla de Ons [an island off the Galician coast] may partake of the agrarian reform, as the workers of this island still live in conditions of slavery." And a host of similar complaints from all parts of Spain suggest that the choice of words by the Pontevedra communists was hardly an exaggeration. See PCE, Radio de Pontevedra to Minoría Parlamentaria Comunista, 15 June 1936. Archivo Histórico Nacional de Salamanca (AHNS) [Salamanca], sección Madrid, carpeta 34, legajo 688, 500.

70. Pierre Broué and Émile Témime, *The Revolution and the Civil War in Spain* (Cambridge, Mass.: MIT Press, 1972), p. 80.

71. Broué and Témime, *Revolution and Civil War in Spain*, p. 90.

72. Kergoat, *La France du front populaire*, p. 160; on this see also Guérin, *Front populaire*, pp. 63–131, and Jacques Danos and Marcel Gibelin, *June '36* (London: Bookmarks, 1986).

73. Jules Moch, *Le Front populaire* (Paris: Académique Perrin, 1971), p. 89.

Chapter 7

1. Adolf Sturmthal, *Zwei Leben* (Vienna: Böhlau, 1989); see particularly pp. 73–183. This autobiography contains countless colorful vignettes of high-profile personalities of interwar European socialism, thus providing interesting insights into the personalities determining the outlook of the LSI in this most crucial conjuncture. Unfortunately, not all details related by Sturmthal conform to historical reality.

2. For a brief biographical sketch, see Walter Euchner, "Rudolf Hilferding (1877–1941)," in *Vor dem Vergessen bewahren*, ed. Peter Lösche, Michael Scholing and Franz Walter (Berlin: Colloquium, 1988), pp. 170–192. For an in-depth view of the Austro-Marxist social democrat, see William Smaldone, "Rudolf Hilferding: The Tragedy of a German Social Democrat" (Ph.D. diss.: State University of New York at Binghamton, 1989).

3. An all-too-brief commentary on the trajectory of the *ZfS* can be found in Lieselotte Maas, *Handbuch der deutschen Exilpresse 1933–1945*, 4 vols. (Munich: Hanser, 1990), 4:334–336.

4. Marta Bizcarrondo, *Araquistain y la crisis socialista en la II República* (Madrid: Siglo XXI, 1975), pp. 121–134, citation on page 125. Araquistain's state of mind in 1933 can best be gauged in the reprint of a speech he delivered in Madrid's *casa del pueblo* on the topic of German socialism, *El derrumbamiento del socialismo alemán* (Madrid: Gráfica Socialista, [1933]).

5. Much useful information on the trajectory of NZ can be found in Gary P. Steenson, *Karl Kautsky, 1854–1938* (Pittsburgh: University of Pittsburgh Press, 1978).

6. Frans Liebaers, *Critique de la politique et de la tactique du mouvement syndical national et international* (Brussels: Le Réveil, 1933), pp. 18–19.

7. Alexander Schifrin, "Revolutionäre Sozialdemokratie," *ZfS* 1 (December 1933): 82.

8. Rudolf Hilferding to Karl Kautsky, 13 April 1933, pp. 1–2. IISG, Karl Kautsky papers, D XII 660.

9. The sole substantive work focusing on Menshevik fortunes in the 1930s remains André Liebich, *Les Mencheviks en exil face á l'Union Soviétique* (Montréal: Centre Interuniversitaire d'Études Européennes, 1982).

10. Peter Garwy to Karl Kautsky, 25 April 1933, citations on pages 11–14, except for his concluding sentence on page 20. IISG, Karl Kautsky, D XI 49.

11. "A todos los trabajadores," *La Batalla*, 2 November 1933, p. 1. The 10 December 1933 manifesto announcing the formation of the Catalan united front referred to the lessons of Germany and Italy in the second sentence of the document; see "Manifiesto de presentación de la Alianza Obrera de Cataluña," in Victor Alba, *La Alianza Obrera* (Madrid: Júcar, 1977), p. 189.

12. Speech by Ramón Rodriguez, paraphrased in "El domingo se celebraran importantes actos en Mieres y Sama, a los que acudieron millares de obreros de todas las organizaciones sindicales," *Avance*, 6 February 1934, p. 8.

13. "Han fracasado los hombres," *El Socialista*, 29 September 1933, p. 1.

14. "El frente único obrero," *El Socialista*, 29 December 1933, p. 1.

15. Letter by four members of the JJSS to the Comité de la Juventud Socialista [de Bilbao], 19 October 1933. AHNS, sección Bilbao, legajo 174, exp. 3, p. 19.

16. Agrupación Socialista de Nerva (Huelva) to the PSOE executive, 24 January 1934. FPI, AH-22-18, 21; emphasis in the original.

17. This speech is reproduced as "Le Malaise du Parti Socialiste," in Pierre Boivin, *Choix d'écrits* (Paris: Centre Confédérale d'Education Ouvrière, 1938), citation on page 223.

18. *Compte rendu sténographique du XXXe Congrès National* (Paris: Librairie Populaire, 1933), p. 414.

19. "Mémorandum du Parti Socialiste de France—Union Jean Jaurès," 25 January 1934, p. 17. IISG, Sozialistische Arbeiter Internationale, Mappe 830.

20. "Mémorandum," p. 50.

21. Frans Liebaers, "'Plan' ou ligne?" *L'Action Socialiste*, 11 May 1935, p. 4.

22. Intervention by Émile Vandervelde in *Protokoll*. Internationale Konferenz der Sozialistischen Arbeiter-Internationale, Paris, Maison de la Mutualité, 21–25 August 1933, p. 16. The most thorough analysis and critique of this conference on "The Strategy and Tactics of the International Labour Movement During the Period of Fascist Reaction" is found in Gilles Vergnon, "Catastrophe et renouveau: Socialistes, communistes et oppositionnels d'Europe et d'Amérique du nord sous l'impact de la victoire nazie: Crises et reclassements (1933–1934)" (Thèse: Université de Grenoble-II, 1993), part 4, chapter 1.

23. To my knowledge, only two historians have ever studied the impact of the Nazi victory on the workers' movement abroad: Claude Willard, "Les Réactions du PC et de la SFIO à l'arrivée de Hitler au pouvoir," in *Mélanges d'histoire sociale offerts à Jean Maitron* (Paris: Éditions Ouvrières, 1976), pp. 265–274, and, most recently and with a distinctly transnational focus, Vergnon, "Catastrophe et renouveau," pp. 193–268. Yet Willard's short article focuses on concrete forms of solidarity and neglects to address the issues that I am most concerned with in this chapter: the impact on policy reorientation. However, with Friedrich Taubert's *Französische Linke und Hitlerdeutschland: Deutschlandbilder und*

Strategieentwürfe (Bern: Peter Lang, 1991) there now exists a solid book-length study of the reaction of the Left in a "foreign" country to the presence of a fascist neighboring state. Yet Taubert deals with the concrete effect of January 1933 only in passing and focuses instead on later stages of Hitler's regime and the corresponding lessons for the French Left.

24. "Die Ursache der Niederlage," *Sozialistische Aktion*, 18 March 1934; emphasis in the original.

25. René Dumon to Erich Ollenhauer, 20 June 1934, p. 1. IISG, Sozialistische Jugend Internationale, Mappe 725.

26. Alexander Schifrin, "Österreichischer Aufstand und deutscher Sozialismus," *ZfS* (May 1934): 248, 254.

27. "Freiheitsschlacht der Sozialdemokratie: Österreichs bewaffnete Arbeiter retten die Ehre und zeigen den Zukunftsweg," *Deutsche Freiheit*, 14 February 1934, p. 1.

28. "Ruhmvolle Niederlage," *Deutsche Freiheit*, 15 February 1934, p. 1.

29. "Die Februarschlacht in Wien," *Neuer Vorwärts*, 18 February 1934, p. 1.

30. Léon Blum, "Le Prolétariat héroïque de l'Autriche a succombé dans la lutte inégale," *Le Populaire*, 16 February 1934, p. 1.

31. Paul-Henri Spaak to Hendrik de Man, 6 June 1934; published in *L'Action Socialiste*, 9 June 1934.

32. "Weenen—Parijs: Twee lessen," *Het Liga Sinjaal*, 2 June 1934, p. 1.

33. Herman van der Goes, "Geweld—Macht—Overwinning," *Het Liga Sinjaal*, 21 July 1934, p. 7.

34. "Trágica advertencia," *El Socialista*, 14 February 1934, p. 6.

35. "Una nueva lección: La de los socialistas austríacos," *El Socialista*, 16 February 1934, p. 1. On 16 February 1934 the Workers' Alliance of Catalonia drafted a manifesto which paralleled *El Socialista*'s stance: "The lesson of Austria is tragic and we need to make use of it. Our position must not be defensive, but a position of attack." This call to action was published in *Adelante*, 17 February 1934, p. 1.

36. "El caso de Austria: Una derrota que no lo es," *El Socialista*, 17 February 1934, p. 1.

37. "La ejemplaridad de la revolución austríaca," *El Socialista*, 18 February 1934, p. 1.

38. Fedor [= Federico Melchor?], "Austria y la Internacional," *Renovación*, 24 February 1934, p. 4.

39. This paradigmatic statement by his Spanish comrades was prominently underscored in an article by Léo Moulin in the Belgian *Action Socialiste*, 17 March 1934, p. 3, entitled "La Lutte finale," reporting on the situation in Spain.

40. "El espíritu proletario en Austria: La única revolución desastrosa será la que no se intente," *Avance*, 4 September 1934, p. 1.

41. "España ni es ni será Austria," *El Socialista*, 4 October 1934, p. 6.

42. Intervention by Marx Dormoy, reported in "National Council of French Party and the United Front," *II*, July 1934, p. 368.

43. The prescient, eleven-page document by Alfred Braunthal, "Neue Grundlagen der Bewegung," was written in mid-May 1934. It is included in AdsD, Nachlass Paul Hertz, Film XXX, "Ba" j; citations on page 1.

44. [Karl Kautsky], *Grenzen der Gewalt: Aussichten und Wirkungen bewaffneter Erhebungen des Proletariats* (Karlsbad: Graphia, 1934), p. 42.

45. Émile Vandervelde, "La Défaite glorieuse des socialistes autrichiens," *Le Peuple*, 17 February 1934, p. 1.

46. The Austrian social democrat Oskar Pollak, a left critic of Austro-Marxism himself, was keenly aware of the contradictory dynamics of the lesson of Vienna: "The events in Austria, just like Hitler's victory in Germany, have had the effect to push most socialist parties in the remaining democratic countries far to the right. . . ." "Austriacus" [= Oskar Pollak],

"Massenpartei und Kampforganisation," *Der Kampf* 1 (May 1934): 18. Pollak's assertion of the moderation of "most socialist parties in the remaining democracies," however, only applies to those countries outside the framework of this study.

47. "Lehren der spanischen Revolution," AZ, 18 November 1934, p. 3; emphasis in the original.

48. Louis Piérard to Paul-Henri Spaak, *L'Action Socialiste*, 17 November 1934, p. 3.

49. Eugène [= Claude] Beaurepaire, "Plan et insurrection," *Révolution Constructive*, 31 January 1935, p. 2.

50. Marcelle Pommera, "Le Prolétariat et la prochaine guerre," *Le Combat Marxiste* 30 (April 1936): 5.

51. "Lehren der spanischen Revolution," p. 3.

52. "Fragen der Revolution," *Rote Jugend* 8 [1936]: 8.

53. Raymond Renaud [= Raymond Bottelberghs], "Problèmes et perspectives de l'expérience belge," *Le Combat Marxiste* 20 (June 1935): 12. Bottelberghs essentially repeated an argument first advanced by Émile Vandervelde during the crucial debate at the March 1935 BWP/POB congress over the decision to enter the Van Zeeland government, where Vandervelde admonished his audience: "[Y]ou may chose between a dictatorship and a government which you form part of." *Congrès extraordinaire des 30 et 31 mars 1935* (Brussels: Conseil Général du POB, 1935), p. 35.

54. Julio Alvarez del Vayo, "A la Comisión ejecutiva del Partido Socialista," 23 November 1934, pp. 3, 11. FPI, AH-22-22. In February 1936 Marceau Pivert vented his frustration over the conservative reinterpretation of the Asturian Commune in the following rhetorical question: "How many pages have been written against the heroic movement of October inscribed in working-class history with the blood of the Asturian miners?" in an article entitled "Lumière d'Espagne," *Le Populaire*, 26 February 1936, p. 6.

55. Vo. Sch. [= Viktor Schiff], "Die spanische Kommune," *Neuer Vorwärts*, 28 October 1934.

56. Karl Böchel, "Die Lehren der Niederlagen. Revolutionärer Aufstand oder kampflose Kapitulation," *Neuer Vorwärts*, 4 November 1934.

57. Some examples are R. Piron, "Pour une politique nouvelle," *L'Action Socialiste*, 5 January 1935, p. 4; Pivert, "Lumière d'Espagne," p. 6; René Modiano and Hélène Modiano, "Par le Plan, vers la Révolution," *Bataille Socialiste*, 15 January 1935, pp. 3–4; and Paul Sering [= Richard Löwenthal], "Die internationale Einheitsbewegung und die Aufgaben der sozialistischen Linken," *Nachrichten des Auslandsbüros "Neu Beginnen"* 3 ("Ende Dezember 1935"), pp. 3–5.

58. "Unsere Aufgabe in der Internationale," *Die Revolution* 7 ("Mitte Dezember 1934"), p. 4; emphasis added.

59. Wilhelm Sander, "Bericht über eine Besprechung mit 15 ostsächsischen Genossen am 31.12.34 und 1.1.35," p. 4. AdsD, Sopade, Mappe 106.

60. Louis-Olivier Frossard, "La Défense de la République," *Le Populaire*, 1 November 1934, p. 6.

61. "Victory in Spain," II, 20 February 1936, p. 54; emphasis in the original.

62. Auguste Bracke, "Rapport de la délégation à l'Internationale," in *Compte rendu sténographique du XXXIIIe congrès national* (Paris: Librairie Populaire, 1936), p. 50.

63. On the issue of the LSI's stance on popular fronts, see Gábor Skékely, "Le Komintern, l'Internationale Ouvrière Socialiste et le Front populaire français," *Cahiers d'Histoire de l'Institut de Recherches Marxistes* 27 (1987): 123–136.

64. Paul Faure, "Vers la victoire et ses lendemains," *Le Populaire*, 19 February 1936, p. 1.

65. Pivert, "Lumière d'Espagne," p. 6.

66. "El alcance internacional de las elecciones francesas," *El Socialista*, 24 April 1936, p. 6; emphases added.

67. "Las elecciones francesas son la derrota del fascismo," *El Socialista*, 28 April 1936, p. 6.

68. "¡Hosanna a nuestros hermanos de Francia!" *El Socialista*, 5 May 1936, p. 6.

69. See the letter of congratulation sent by the exiled leadership in Brünn to the PSOE in Madrid, 25 February 1936. FPI, AH-73-3, 4. A letter from the jailed socialist and communist prisoners in the Viennese jail to their Spanish cohorts, dated 19 February 1936, was reprinted in the *AZ*, 1 March 1936, p. 2. A useful survey of the impasse of popular front politics in Austria is provided in Martin Kitchen, "The Austrian Left and the Popular Front," in *The Popular Front in Europe*, ed. Helen Graham and Paul Preston (London: Macmillan, 1987), pp. 35–57.

70. "Wir wollen spanisch reden!" *AZ*, 1 March 1936, p. 2; emphasis in the original.

71. "Sieg in Frankreich," *AZ*, 10 May 1936, p. 1; emphasis in the original.

72. "Helmut" [Hertel] [= Franz Bögler], "Bericht aus Schlesien. März–April 1936." AdsD, Sopade, Mappe 20.

73. Gustav Ferl, "[Lagebericht] Rheinland-Westfalen," May 1936, p. 15. AdsD, Sopade, Mappe 38, Korrespondenz F.

74. Gustav Ferl, "[Lagebericht] Rheinland-Westfalen," May 1936, p. 15. AdsD, Sopade, Mappe 38.

75. Alexander Schifrin, "Vierte Republik in Frankreich?" *ZfS*, 22/23 (July–August 1935): 740.

76. Fritz Alsen [= Heinrich Ehrmann], "Volksfrontwahlen in Frankreich," *ZfS* 32 (May 1936): 1009. Note also Rudolf Breitscheid's remark: "A comparison between this [French] popular front politics and that of our coalition governments [in the Weimar Republic] will make us blush with shame even retroactively." Rudolf Breitscheid to Wilhelm Hoegner, 17 August 1936, p. 5. IfZ, Nachlass Wilhelm Hoegner, Band 2.

77. See, for instance, the contributions to a conference on the international echo of February 1934, including articles on reactions in Hungary, Poland, the Soviet Union, Yugoslavia, China, Bulgaria and Denmark, in Hans Hautmann, ed., *Internationale Tagung der Historiker der Arbeiterbewegung. 20. Linzer Konferenz 1984* (Vienna: Europa, 1989). Three exceptions in this volume are Gábor Székely, "Der Wiener Aufstand und die Komintern," pp. 530–538; Péter Sipos, "Die internationale Gewerkschaftsbewegung und der Wiener Arbeiteraufstand," pp. 539–544; and Karl Christian Lammers et al., "Die 'Demokratie-Diktatur': Problematik in dem zentraleuropäischen Sozialismus 1925–35 mit besonderem Hinblick auf die politische Theorie-Entwicklung," pp. 626–633. Székely's analysis, in particular, supports my argument of the radicalizing momentum emanating from the Schutzbund revolt.

For an insightful survey of comparativist work in the social sciences, highlighting similar shortcomings, see Peter Gourevitch, "The Second Image Reversed: The International Sources of Domestic Politics," *International Organization* 32 (autumn 1978): 881–912. Gourevitch complains rightfully "that students of comparative politics treat domestic structure too much as an independent variable, underplaying the extent to which it and the international system are parts of an interactive system" and concludes that, contrary to accepted tradition, "international relations and domestic politics . . . should be analyzed simultaneously, as wholes" (pp. 900, 911).

Chapter 8

1. On this, see chapter 8, "Between Communism and Social Democracy," in my "European Socialists Respond to Fascism: The Drive Towards Unity, Radicalisation and Strategic Innovation in Austria, Belgium, France, Germany and Spain, 1933–1936" (Ph.D. diss.: University of Michigan, 1992), pp. 363–420.

2. Michel Brot, *Le Front populaire dans les Alpes-Maritimes 1934–1937* (Nice: Serre, 1988), p. 20.

3. Michel Cadé, *Le Parti des campagnes rouges* (Vinça: Chiendent, 1988), p. 167; see page 158 for the voting results of the 1932 elections.

4. Speech by Floirac (Lot), *Compte rendu sténographique du XXXe Congrès National* (Paris: Librairie Populaire, 1933), p. 380.

5. See Cadé's section on "The Fall of the 'Red Fortress,'" i.e., Rivesaltes, *Le Parti des campagnes rouges*, pp. 141–147.

6. Brot, *Le Front populaire*, p. 16.

7. On the Lot federation's support to the motion of Révolution Constructive, see note 4; the joint letter of 25 May 1933 is extant as an unidentified newspaper clipping, probably from *Le Populaire*, in CRHMSS, Fonds Jean Zyromski, D IV 14.

8. Henri Heldman, *Les Fils du peuple* ([Paris]: Heldman, 1989), pp. 195–198.

9. On the Alsatian Communist Opposition, see Robert Alexander, *The Right Opposition* (Westport, Conn.: Greenwood, 1981), pp. 264–268.

10. Antoine Prost, "Les Manifestations du 12 février 1934 en province," in *La France en mouvement*, ed. Jean-Charles Asselaine et al. (Seyssel: Champs Vallon, 1986), p. 27.

11. Heldman, *Les Fils du peuple*, p. 203.

12. For the total figure of 346, see Prost, "Les Manifestations," p. 20; on the breakdown of that figure, see page 28.

13. Prost, "Les Manifestations," pp. 27–28; citation on page 28.

14. Prost, "Les Manifestations," p. 21.

15. Heldman, *Les Fils du peuple*, p. 211. Heldman tends to regard such actions as some form of communist manipulation of the socialist ranks. Reports of concrete experiences belie such wholesale judgments; see, for instance, the detailed chronicle of the attempts by the SFIO federations of Greater Paris to establish unity in action with the PCF, contained in the series of articles in *Bataille Socialiste*, referred to in note 69 of chapter 4, or the experience in the *départements* of Alpes-Maritimes and Pyrénées-Orientales; see Brot, *Le Front populaire*, pp. 24–31, and Cadé, *Le Parti des campagnes rouges*, pp. 177–182. For a recent local study strongly suggesting the vitality of unity at the provincial base before and after 12 February, see Gilles Vergnon, "Les Mobilisations républicaines de février 1934 dans l'Ardèche et dans la Drôme," *Revue du Vivarais* (October–December): 273–284.

16. "Réunion d'information des secrétaires fédéraux du 15 avril 1934," p. 1. CRHMSS, Jean Zyromski, unmarked box. This document offers a rare glimpse into the inner life of the SFIO at a crucial conjuncture.

17. I slightly amended the translation of this article by Léon Blum in *Le Populaire* of 7 July 1934, furnished in *DD*, 14 July 1934, p. 67.

18. Joseph Buttinger, *Das Ende der Massenpartei* (Frankfurt: Neue Kritik, 1972), pp. 160–167.

19. "Signale der sozialistischen Erhebung," *Deutsche Freiheit*, 6 July 1934. On the political outlook of Saar organizations on the working-class Left, see chapter 4.

20. Wilhelm Sollmann to Paul Hertz, 26 December 1934, pp. 2–3. AdsD, Nachlass Paul Hertz, Film XXXVI, "48 I."

21. Cited in Victor Alba, *La Alianza Obrera* (Madrid: Júcar, 1978), p. 97.

22. "Acta de la reunión celebrada por la comisión ejecutiva del Partido Socialista el día 7 de febrero de 1934," p. 19. FPI, AH-II-1.

23. Paco Ignacio Taibo II, *Asturias 1934*, 2 vols. (Madrid: Júcar, 1984) 1:26.

24. Alba, *Alianza Obrera* p. 97.

25. Salvador Forner Muñoz, *Industrialización y movimiento obrera. Alicante 1923–1936* (Valencia: Institución Alfonso Magnánimo, 1982), p. 365.

26. The letters by the Federación de Tabaqueros and ICE, the Bilbao JJSS and the Vizcaya federation of the JJSS are all in the AHNS, sección Bilbao, legajo 174, exp. 6, 46–8; Carrillo's response can be found in AHNS, sección Bilbao, legajo 174, exp. 7, 27.

27. Ricardo Miralles Palencia, *El socialismo vasco durante la II República* (Bilbao: Universidad del País Vasco, 1988), p. 231.

28. Paul Preston, *The Coming of the Spanish Civil War* (London: Macmillan, 1978), p. 78.

29. Preston, *Coming of the Spanish Civil War*, pp. 127–128. The same phenomenon of outlying areas triggering a revolt was, of course, a prominent feature of the February 1934 Austrian Schutzbund rising.

30. Sociedad Obrera La Unión, Gabia Chica to *El Socialista*, undated. FPI, AH-22-18, 42. This document is one of sixty-five similar letters, all written in January and February 1934 by party locals and workers' associations throughout Spain, contained in the same folder.

31. Federación Socialista Provincial de Sevilla to Ramón Lamoneda, 17 August 1935. FPI, AH-2–27, 1.

32. Contained in a document collection regarding the *casa del pueblo de Madrid*, p. 49. FPI, AH-23-7.

33. "Acta de la reunión celebrada por la comisión ejecutiva del Partido Socialista el día 13 de marzo de 1935," p. 68. FPI, AH-II-1.

34. "Acta de la reunión celebrada por la comisión ejecutiva del Partido Socialista el día 9 de abril de 1935," p. 71. FPI, AH-II-1.

35. Taibo, *Asturias 1934*, 2:214.

36. For the Catalan experience, see Ricard Vinyes i Ribes, *La Catalunya internacional* (Barcelona: Curial, 1983). Victor Alba, "¿Elecciones para la amnestía?" in his *El frente popular* (Barcelona: Planeta, 1976), pp. 273–277, points out the truly national dimension of this phenomenon.

37. All foregoing citations are from Adrian Shubert, "A Reinterpretation of the Spanish Popular Front: The Case of Asturias," in *The French and Spanish Popular Fronts*, ed. Martin S. Alexander and Helen Graham (Cambridge: Cambridge University Press, 1989), pp. 223–224.

38. Shubert, "Reinterpretation of the Spanish Popular Front," pp. 224–225.

39. Manuel Tuñon de Lara, "Frente popular / Unidad popular," in his *Tres claves de la Segunda República* (Madrid: Alianza, 1985), p. 364.

40. Jacques Doriot, *Pour l'unité d'action!* (Paris: n.p., 1934), pp. 27–30.

41. Jacques Varin, *Jeunes comme JC* (Paris: Éditions Sociales, 1975), pp. 189–196. On the strong presence of Radical politicians in various local united fronts, see also Vergnon, "Les Mobilisations républicaines."

42. On these two faces of the PCF, see Michel Margairaz, "Le Parti communiste, l'économie, les finances el la monnaie en 1935–1936: Le 'chaud' et le 'froid,'" *Cahiers d'Histoire de l'Institut de Recherche Marxiste* 24 (1986): 6–23. On the PCF's contradictory attitude toward this "ministry of the masses" after the victory of the popular front, see Danielle Tartakowsky, "Des grèves de juin à la pause, 'Le ministère des masses' au coeur des contradictions," *Cahiers d'Histoire de l'Institute de Recherche Marxiste* 24 (1986) 36–53.

43. Speech by André Philip, *Compte rendu sténographique du XXXIIIe Congrès National* (Paris: Librairie Populaire, 1936), pp. 130–131.

44. Speech by Durel, *Compte rendu sténographique du XXXIIIe Congrès*, p. 146.

45. Speech by Durel, p. 148.

46. Speech by Durel, p. 149.

47. Speech by Jean Zyromski, *Compte rendu sténographique du XXXIIe Congrès National* (Paris: Librairie Populaire, 1935), p. 563.

48. Speech by Léon Blum, *Compte rendu sténographique du XXXIIIe Congrès*; citations on pages 191–192.

49. See Tartakowsky, "Des grèves de juin," Daniel Guérin, *Front populaire, révolution manquée* (Paris: Julliard, 1963), passim; Jacques Danos and Marcel Gibelin, *June '36* (London: Bookmarks, 1986), pp. 147–154; Heldman, *Les Fils du peuple*, pp. 262–286; and Daniel R. Brower, *The New Jacobins* (Ithaca, N.Y.: Cornell University Press, 1968), pp. 140–156.

50. A recent defender of this thesis is Jacques Kergoat, *La France du front populaire* (Paris: La Découverte, 1986), p. 150.

51. Kergoat, *La France du front populaire*, p. 99.

52. Here, the following two studies are key examples of this point of view: Bertrand Badie, "Les Grèves de 1936 aux usines Renault," and Raymond Hainsworth, "Les Grèves de mai-juin 1936 chez les mineurs du Nord et du Pas-de-Calais," in Asselain et al., *La France en mouvement*, pp. 68–85, 86–112.

53. Hainsworth, "Les Grèves de mai-juin 1936," p. 110.

54. Denis Peschanski, in his lexicographic study of PCF language in the midthirties referred to in chapter 2, makes an interesting statement toward the end of his study. One may recall that Peschanski's point was the sudden switch from a language of "class" and "struggle" to a language of "people" and attention to the system of parliamentary rule precisely at the time when, according to my thesis, the PCF carried out its move from united to popular fronts, i.e., in May–June 1935. Peschanski relied on the PCF daily *L'Humanité*. When carrying out a similar analysis of a PCF local paper "on an experimental basis" to find out how widespread this change was adhered to, Peschanski found little correlation between the language of *L'Humanité* and the vocabulary employed by the *Prolétaire Drancéen*, a communist monthly paper in a working-class suburb of Paris. Undaunted by the new vocabulary of the summit, the local journalists and writers continued to employ a vocabulary of "combat" characteristic of the pre–popular front era. See, Denis Peschanski, *Et pourtant ils tournent* (Paris: Kliencksieck, 1988), p. 171.

55. Sociedad de Trabajadores de la Tierra, Torrubia del Campo (Cuenca) to the PSOE executive, 12 February 1936. FPI, AH-12-31, 1.

56. Although, judging from the initial reference to the speakers as "Comrade Almagro and Don Lopez Malo," it is probable that the second individual was a member of the Republican Left. This, of course, would not change the meaning of this incident.

57. Leon Trotsky, *The History of the Russian Revolution*, trans. Max Eastman (New York: Pathfinder, 1980), p. xix.

Chapter 9

1. Andre Gunder Frank and Marta Fuentes, "Civil Democracy: Social Movements in Recent World History," in *Transforming the Revolution: Social Movements and the World System*, ed. Samir Amin et al. (New York: Monthly Review, 1990), particularly pp. 142–153.

2. Sidney Tarrow, *Struggling to Reform: Social Movements and Policy Change During Cycles of Protest* (Ithaca, N.Y.: Cornell University Press, 1983), p. 3. See also Tarrow's more recent discussion of political opportunity structures in his *Struggle, Politics and Reform* (Ithaca, N.Y.: Cornell University Press, 1991), pp. 32–40.

3. Karl-Werner Brand, "Cyclical Aspects of New Social Movements: Waves of Cultural Criticism and Mobilization Cycles of New Middle-Class Radicalism," in *Challenging the Political Order*, ed. Russell J. Dalton and Manfred Kuechler (Cambridge: Polity, 1990), pp. 23–42; citations on pages 25 and 33. See also Brand's unpublished "Zyklen des 'middle-class radicalism:' Eine international und historisch vergleichende Untersuchung der 'neuen sozialen Bewegungen'" (Habilitationsschrift: Technische Universität München, 1989).

4. See Brand's chart in "Cyclical Aspects," p. 34, and Frank and Fuentes's chart in "Civil Democracy," p. 146. On the phenomena called Kondratieff cycles see, for instance, Ernest Mandel, *Long Waves of Capitalist Development* (Cambridge: Cambridge University Press, 1980).

5. Tarrow, *Struggling to Reform*, p. 4.

6. Zimmermann's views on this are most clearly developed in Ekkart Zimmermann and Thomas Saalfeld, "Economic and Political Reactions to the World Economic Crisis of the 1930s in Six European Countries," *International Studies Quarterly* 32 (1988): 305–334, and Zimmermann, "Interest Groups, Political Parties and Extremist Challenges in the Process of National Consensus Formation: On Assessing the Political Effects of the Depression in Eight Countries" (manuscript in author's possession, 1988).

7. On Gerschenkron's and Moore's views, see Alexander Gerschenkron, *Bread and Democracy in Germany* (Berkeley: University of California Press, 1943), and Barrington Moore Jr., *Social Origins of Democracy and Dictatorship* (Boston: Beacon: 1966). For a recent restatement of this position, see Dietrich Rueschemeyer, Evelyn Huber Stephens, and John D. Stephens, *Capitalist Development and Democracy* (Cambridge: Polity, 1992), pp. 79–154. For Gregory Luebbert's explicit discussion of the Gerschenkron-Moore thesis, see Gregory M. Luebbert, *Liberalism, Fascism, or Social Democracy* (New York: Oxford University Press, 1991), pp. 308–309.

8. Luebbert, *Liberalism, Facism, or Social Democracy*, p. 192.

9. Luebbert, *Liberalism, Facism, or Social Democracy*, pp. 248–249 and passim.

10. Luebbert, *Liberalism, Facism, or Social Democracy*, p. 306.

11. Luebbert, *Liberalism, Facism, or Social Democracy*, p. 309.

12. See Peter Jan Knegtmans, *Socialisme en democratie* (Amsterdam: IISG, 1989), pp. 77–81, 125–127, for a discussion of these incidents and social democratic reactions.

13. See Oskar Scheiben, *Krise und Integration* (Zurich: Chronos, 1987), pp. 126–130, for social democratic involvement in, and reactions to, the "blood night of Geneva."

14. Scheiben, *Krise und Integration*, pp. 130–141 and passim.

15. See Knegtmans, *Socialisme en democratie*, particularly chapters 2 and 3, pp. 76–144.

16. William H. Sewell Jr., "Towards a Theory of Structure: Duality, Agency and Transformation," CSST working paper no. 29, University of Michigan, Ann Arbor, 1989, p. 31.

17. William H. Sewell Jr., "Three Temporalities: Towards a Sociology of the Event" (manuscript in author's possession, 1990), p. 17.

18. Sewell, "Three Temporalities," pp. 17–18.

19. Sewell, "Three Temporalities," p. 2.

20. Anthony Giddens, *A Contemporary Critique of Historical Materialism* (Berkeley: University of California Press, 1981), p. 64. The same indeterminate range of applicability of contingency in the historical process permeates two works by Marshall Sahlins, *Historical Metaphors and Mythical Realities* (Ann Arbor: University of Michigan Press, 1981), and *Islands of History* (Chicago: University of Chicago Press, 1985).

21. Michael S. Kimmel, *Revolution: A Sociological Interpretation* (Cambridge: Polity, 1990), citations on pages 190–191; emphasis added.

22. E. H. Carr, *What Is History?* (New York: Vintage, 1961), p. 135.

23. Ronald Aminzade, *Ballots and Barricades: Class Formation and Republican Politics in France, 1830–1871* (Princeton, N.J.: Princeton University Press, 1993), p. 10. Similar mechanism have been suggested by Fritz Ringer in a series of conversations with the author in February 1993.

24. Charles Tilly, *European Revolutions, 1492–1992* (Oxford: Blackwell, 1993), p. 16.

25. I aim to present a more fully developed analysis of the interplay of agency and structure in a future publication.

Index